EAR TRAINING: LITERARY ESSAYS

Ear Training: Literary Essays

William H. Pritchard

PAUL DRY BOOKS
Philadelphia 2023

First Paul Dry Books Edition, 2023

Paul Dry Books, Inc.
Philadelphia, Pennsylvania
www.pauldrybooks.com

Designed and typeset by Gopa & Ted2, Inc.

Printed in the United States of America

Library of Congress Control Number: 2023941938
ISBN 978-1-58988-182-2

Table of Contents

˙Preface

WHEN OUR YOUNGEST son went off to graduate school, I made him an audio tape, reading aloud some of my favorite poems. He listened to them while out walking and claimed that it had been a good experience, helpful, even, as he studied for his Ph.D. orals. When I turned sixty, he returned the favor by making me a birthday tape with a song he'd composed titled "Ear Training." Sung to an acoustic guitar, he performed it with a bit of a Texas twang, like a traditional Country Western tune. It opens: "People always ask me 'bout my daddy. / Saying, 'What's the secret of his great success?'" And it continues: "Ear training, he's got ear training / He trains his ears on everything he hears."

And it was true. Not only had I long advocated for better listening to poetry, but to prose as well. Blame it all on my mother, who, when I was two or three years old, sang to me a Stephen Foster song that began with the words "Way Down Upon the Swanee River." She was music supervisor in the public schools of Johnson City, New York, an "incorporated village" close to the Pennsylvania border. Other songs followed and took root, and by easy stages just before I turned five, I began piano lessons. Hesitantly, but faithfully, I practiced on the formidable Steinway grand in our living room that the music supervisor had purchased with fifteen hundred dollars of her hard-earned money. I never took official lessons from my mother, but, supervising from the kitchen, she made frequent and telling commentary on my progress: the oft-repeated instruction being: "Hands Alone." As I progressed in skill and learned this or that piece, a crucial article of practice held that no piece was fully explored until it was memorized. I had already been praised for my skill at memorizing bits from children's books, and the connection between the sound of musical notes and that of words grew strong. Even before proper elementary schooling began, I had put in an appearance or two as vocalist in "adult" productions on stage and radio, and as my piano skills developed, I was able to add them to the vocal ones.

There was undeniably a deep connection between those memorizings and the discovery some years later that I was good at keeping in my head and ears poems that caught my fancy. I felt surprise and pleasure at being able to play a favorite song from 1939 ("Careless") and to recite a Donne poem ("The Canonization") memorized in Riverside Park in 1953. Lyric poetry and the lyrics of a Broadway songwriter joined hands (instead of Hands Alone). By the time I became a graduate student, then an English instructor, I discovered that there were lots of academics who could write convincing analyses of poems, but not so many able to recite the lines. Harold Bloom, the great exaggerator, was famed for being able to declaim *Paradise Lost* from memory, but I was no mean competitor in the reciter-sweepstakes.

Readers of one or more of these selections should be warned that, invariably, they will run up against something quoted from Robert Frost. Even though I haven't included essays that take on the poet directly, the abundance of Frost allusions testifies to his centrality in my imaginative life since I was a college sophomore. His insistence early in his career that "The ear does it—the ear is the only true writer and the only true reader—" is well known, but not so much the following passage from his *Notebooks* under the rubric "Pushing things around," which gives advice in no uncertain terms: "Pushing things around—things & people. It may be affectionately or hatefully. It may be affectionately and still roughly and the more roughly the better. But whether affectionately or hatefully it is always playfully." The final stanza of his poem "Two Tramps in Mud Time" draws out the thought:

Only where love and need are one
And the work is play for mortal stakes,
Is the deed ever really done
For Heaven and the future's sakes.

Another directive from *Notebooks* has it, "Play no matter how deep has got to be so playful that the audience are left in doubt whether it be deep or shallow." And he ends his tribute to Edwin Arlington Robinson by enlisting Shakespeare on his side: "The play's the thing. Play's the thing. All virtue in 'as if.'"

To push a thing around so roughly and playfully that the reader is in doubt about its depth is Frost's deep insistence. Whether or what sort of relation this doubt bears to a reader who presumes to speak back to the utterance Frost has made is a question not to be settled too quickly. In one of his early letters home from England, he declared that every line he wrote that was worth anything must carry its own "special posture." At the same time, he wanted to make it virtually impossible for the work of poetry as "play for mortal stakes" to issue in something stabilized, fixed in our apprehension. It's likely that the ideal of "playing it by ear," my title for an earlier collection of essays, many of which appear here, is similarly motivated by an impulse that can't be encompassed in paragraphs, sentences, or lines. If play is really the thing, wouldn't it be a mistake to stop short, assuming that something has been put to rest?

This attempt to make an analogy between Frost's invocation of the "special posture" of poetry and my own dedication to playing it by ear may be pretentious if not just plain erroneous. It's also the case that insistence that the ear does it risks overlooking (overhearing?) the part played by visually apprehending words on the page. (Gordon Teskey's fine book on Milton has some convincing passages on how important it is to "see" the lines of *Paradise Lost* as they unfold.) So playing it by eye gets into the mix.

One of my books is titled rather cheekily or playfully *Talking Back to Emily Dickinson*, the title picking up from my aggressive attempt to push around some claims made about her poems by other critics. But I should hope that in all these essays there is an implicit invitation to talk back to the formulations contained in them. To invoke Frost yet once more, he was interested in, as he put it, "formulations that don't quite formulate." If readers are moved to play around with my formulations in the interest of showing how they don't quite formulate, I shall be satisfied.

Introduction: Ear Training

THE CRITIC WILLIAM EMPSON once said that he did not know how much of his mind T. S. Eliot had invented. In setting out to write about myself as a teacher in Amherst classrooms, the only proper place to begin is with an earlier self in those same classrooms, forty or so years ago, when my mind—such as it is—was invented. The inventors were essentially three in number—Theodore Baird and G. Armour Craig, both professors of English at the college, and their colleague Reuben Brower, who had an effect on me at Amherst but even more when he became a teacher and I a graduate student at Harvard. I encountered Armour Craig in the fall of freshman year when I took the required Composition course, conceived by Theodore Baird some years previously and—by 1949—having come fully into its own as a brilliantly original approach to writing as an activity. That activity, performed by us three times each week—in short responses to difficult, sometimes impossible questions about thinking, meaning, knowing, and other essential human pastimes—was my introduction to serious intellectual inquiry. Having graduated from high school, I had already become an expert in solemnity, but the Amherst English inquiry, as it was conducted in the questions asked us and in the professor's response to our papers, was invariably playful, therefore puzzling to us. By the end of the term if not earlier, we began to suspect that language was something other than the mirror of reality; that—in a phrase of Joseph Conrad's I would come to later on—words are, among other things, "the great foes of reality"; and that the way we went about marshaling our words into sentences, "composing" reality, could be a matter both for despair and for hopefulness, but was nothing less than central to what we did every day.

Freshman Composition was valuable to me partly as a deterrent to flatulence. Since among other things the course was an elementary education in irony, it was salutary for a young achiever whose high school valedictory address three months previously was titled "Health" and stressed the importance of all of us staying healthy. In the extended activity of writing as practiced in English I (thirty-three times the first term) we—teacher and students—looked at what we had written, at what could or couldn't be said in a sentence. The course took no notice of literature; that noticing occurred the following year in the sophomore "Introduction to Literature," another staff course, this one mainly the creation of Reuben Brower. English 21-22 had the effect, whether intended or not, of helping us regain some of the confidence we might have lost the previous year, since Brower and his staffmates had what looked to be a useful vocabulary for talking about what went on in poems and stories and novels. That vocabulary, which featured such terms as tone, attitude, dramatic situation, was derived from Brower's study with I. A. Richards, author of the extraordinarily influential *Practical Criticism.* In Sophomore English, and in the Humanities 6 course Brower subsequently introduced at Harvard (in which I did my first teaching), we engaged in collaborative reading carried on in both a leisurely and a sharply focused manner. Just as Freshman Composition consisted in examining the particular essays, paragraphs, and sentences we students had produced, so the literature course never wandered for long from its intent consideration of the words on the page—of the individual poem or stanza or line or word that momentarily engaged us.

The words on the page—well, yes; but what I remember most about my Amherst English teachers is the way they took words off the page and brought them to life through the speaking voice. Baird reading aloud a soliloquy from *Hamlet* in a rather self-consciously loud, deliberately unactorish way, yet one that was scrupulously observant of the syntax and sense of the lines; Craig beginning his consideration of Milton's poetry with an extended reading out of "Lycidas" ("Yet once more, O ye laurels, and once more / Ye myrtles brown, with ivy never sere"); Brower imitating the finicky, weary cadences of the lady in T. S. Eliot's "Portrait of a Lady":

> So intimate, this Chopin, that I think his soul
> Should be resurrected only among friends
> Some two or three, who will not touch the bloom
> That is rubbed and questioned in the concert room.

Behind such performances—the insistence that in the beginning, first of all, the poem needed to be *heard,* realized in the manner through which it was read aloud—was the example of Frost ("Now I'm gonna *say* a few poems for ya"). It was the same Frost who remembered hearing Brower, when he was a student at Amherst, read aloud in class a sixteenth-century poem by an otherwise forgotten poet, Richard Edwards, which began "In going to my naked bed as one that would have slept." "Goodness sake, the way his voice fell into those lines, the natural way he did that very difficult poem," said Frost years after the event.

This primacy of the speaking voice, this insistence on getting the tone right—of (in Frost's own words) seizing the special "posture" needed to deliver it correctly—informed, in ways I surely wasn't conscious of at the time, my "approach" to literature and eventually my dealings with it in the classroom. Nor was I conscious that Frost's discovery, so he truly thought it, of the primacy of voice in poetry was the cornerstone of what theorizing he did about the act and the art of reading. He put these thoughts power-fully and succinctly in a letter written home from England in February of 1914:

> *The ear does it.* The ear is the only true writer and the only true reader. I have known people who could read without hearing the sentence sounds and they were the fastest readers. Eye read-ers we call them. They can get the meaning by glances. But they are bad readers because they miss the best part of what a good writer puts into his work.

My education at Amherst—that part of it conducted within the English department, both in the composition and the literature course, and in their successors—was essentially a training in ear reading, whether the bit of writing under scrutiny was (as it often was) a lyric of Frost's, or the opening of Henry James's *Portrait of a Lady* ("Under certain circumstances there are few hours in life more agreeable than the hour dedicated to the ceremony known as afternoon tea"), or one of the unwittingly fatuous sentences I turned out in my papers. Do you want to sound like *that?* was the direct or implied question we were invited to put to our own prose, while practice in listening to Frost and James brought the awareness that other designs, other ways of sounding, were possible, at least within reach of our ears.

Despite my introduction to ear-reading, I graduated from Amherst a philosophy major, with the intention of becoming a teacher of that discipline. Accordingly, I spent a year listening to some very good eye-readers in the Columbia University department of philosophy. Unlike Frost's eye-readers, who speedily picked up the meaning by glances, these professors were hard-nosed teasers-out of the sense of passages in Locke or Kant or Whitehead. But outside of class I was reading Kenneth Burke's *A Grammar of Motives,* in which Burke performed "dramatistic" readings of and listenings to the philosophers, showing how their sentences talked to each other and made for a "life" in their words analogous to that found in poetry or fiction. Burke's subversive demonstrations of how philosophic meaning was as much a creation of language, of voice even, as was "literary" meaning, pushed me out of the formal study of philosophy and into literature. Subsequent work quickly showed me, however, that the academic study of literature could be every bit as "eye"-oriented as traditional academic philosophy. With the important exception of Brower, by then teaching at Harvard (the institution to which I transferred), professors of literature were either scholars or historians of ideas, English literature being conceived of as a matter of sources and influences, traditions and literary movements. Reading, it was assumed, was something people did on their own time and presumably were perfectly capable of doing. Were we not, after all, in graduate school and at Fair Harvard to boot?

Whether Harvard English was right or wrong in its procedures and assumptions, "we"—the Amherst people studying literature there, a substantial number—were up to something rather different. Insofar as we conceived of our purpose in criticizing and teaching literature, it was something dearly distinct from the way Harvard laid out the map of literature and placed individual figures and groups on that map. Most of us in the "Amherst contingent" (we were sometimes referred to as such) didn't think of ourselves as scholars, or even as potential writers of books. There was rather—and I think in contrast to many of our peers from other institutions—an eagerness to get into the classroom and instruct others about the kinds of literary discoveries we were making. While our peers were busily contriving to get a first article published (so it seemed to us, perhaps paranoically), we contrived to ignore the whole matter of publication, even though it might be necessary to move our professional careers into orbit.

If my own career didn't exactly get into orbit, it began to assume a direction when, suddenly and unforgettably, a call came in December of 1957 from the then chairman of the Amherst English department, Benjamin DeMott, asking me how I'd like to come down for an interview with the president and the department, with the likely outcome of an appointment at the college. For someone who had carried around with him since undergraduate days the notion of teaching at a small college like Amherst, this was a heady and risky invitation—for now it was to be not just "like" Amherst but the very thing itself. How fitting it was that, in preparation for my interview with President Charles W. Cole, the only piece of advice I received was a simple, memorable injunction from Theodore Baird: "Speak up!" I was, in other words, to announce myself at the outset as a young man with a voice, someone who was going to be heard. I must have spoken up at least enough to convince the department and president of my adequacy; later, when it came time for the tenure decision to be made, I was smiled upon and became—in one colleague's word—a "keeper." Except for terms spent on sabbatical leave I've been teaching at this college since the fall of 1958.

So much, then, for autobiography: there follows an attempt to say what I've been doing in the classroom during the past three decades. Along with describing one or two pedagogical clarities or discoveries, I need also to name what I'm "against"—approaches to teaching, to literature, to students, that seem to me markedly unhelpful toward, sometimes destructive of, good reading and writing. My examples are taken from courses I've taught over the past few years: ones in Romantic and Modern British poetry; seminars in literary criticism and in seventeenth-century poetry; larger lecture courses in Reading Fiction and Modern Satiric Fiction; and the introductory course, Writing About Reading, which I teach every fall.

Recently a secondary school teacher of English asked me what I expected or hoped my students would "know" about poetry, about literature, when they came to college as first-year students. My response was, after thinking about it for a while, that students need not know anything in particular— need own nothing except, in Yeats's phrase, their blind stupefied hearts. Less melodramatically, let them own an ear open to the soundings of words; let them also own feelings not wholly dedicated to immediate suppression in favor of preparing for law or medical school exams. What then do they need, to read with some success the following lines from Shakespeare's *Antony and Cleopatra* in which Cleopatra eulogizes her dead lover:

> For his bounty,
> There was no winter in't: an autumn 'twas
> That grew the more by reaping: his delights
> Were dolphin-like, they show'd his back above
> The elements they lived in: in his livery
> Walk'd crown and crownets: realms and islands were
> As plates dropp'd from his pockets.

In asking a class of students what's going on in this sequence I don't expect they will immediately begin talking about the difference it makes that the lines are enjambed; that the sentence units run over the lines and create an impassioned—and vividly metaphorical—utterance quite different from, say, a speech in *Romeo and Juliet.* My main concern has to do rather with the quality of feeling these lines about Antony project or express through the extraordinary language Shakespeare gives Cleopatra. But of course that quality of feeling can be approached only by readers who listen to the pace and cadence of the verse instead of merely moving their eyes across the lines.

For a moment, suppose we forget that poetry is written in feet and lines, thereby presenting special challenges to the reader who is attempting to tune in. One of the hoariest prejudices or assumptions among my students is that it takes a special talent or faculty to read poetry well, whereas everybody is pretty much equal before prose. (My fiction courses are much more heavily enrolled in than the poetry ones.) In fact, as I try to show them, such is not the case. Consider the ending of one of Hemingway's early stories, "Indian Camp," in which the young Nick Adams witnesses his father-doctor's makeshift Caesarean operation on an Indian woman, the operation undertaken with "a jackknife and nine-foot, tapered gut leaders." During this operation the woman's husband slits his throat, and as Nick and his father return home in their boat the following dialogue between them concludes the story:

> "Why did he kill himself, Daddy?"
> "I don't know, Nick. He couldn't stand things, I guess."
> "Do many men kill themselves, Daddy?"
> "Not very many, Nick."
> "Is dying hard, Daddy?"
> "No, I think it's pretty easy, Nick. It all depends."

> They were seated in the boat, Nick in the stern, his father row-
> ing. The sun was coming up over the hills. A bass jumped, mak-
> ing a circle in the water. Nick trailed his hand in the water. It felt
> warm in the sharp chill of the morning.
>
> In the early morning on the lake sitting in the stern of the boat
> with his father rowing he felt quite sure that he would never die.

This lovely moment in Hemingway's work is especially vulnerable, in its
delicate poise, to unlovely attempts by interpreters of the story concerned
to tell us what it Really Means: one of them has called "Indian Camp" "the
story of a boy coming into contact with violence and evil," while another
has informed us that, at the story's end, Nick has "rejected his father and
retreated from reality."

With Shakespeare's figurative and tonal richness everywhere evident
("For his bounty, / There was no winter in't"), it would be a travesty to say
that in praising Antony lavishly Cleopatra has "retreated from reality" or
has exaggerated his virtues through the enlargements of metaphor. These
would be unfortunate attempts to "understand" Shakespeare's language by
reducing it to formula and pretending that the characters made up their
own speeches. With Hemingway, who—unlike Shakespeare—leaves out
rather than puts in, aggressive and all-too-confident ways of understanding (such as are offered by the critics above) get in the way of good reading. They do so by providing crude and hasty way for us to avoid what we
should be engaged in; namely, with *listening* to the rhythms and manner of
presentation, the "feel" of the scene. "A bass jumped, making a circle in the
water. . . . It felt warm in the sharp chill of the morning": how could anyone
who really listens to those sentences want to go on and talk about rejection
of the father or retreating from reality? Why would they not want instead
to talk about the beautiful sequence Hemingway has created here, from the
father rowing, to the sun coming up over the hills, to the jumping bass, to
Nick trailing his hand in the water and feeling it "warm in the sharp chill
of the morning." Why would they not want to engage with what Frost says
all poetry is about—"Performance and prowess and feats of association."
"Why don't critics talk about those things?" Frost went on to ask. "What a
feat it was to turn that that way, and what a feat it was to remember that, to
be reminded of that by this. Why don't they talk about that?"

"They" don't—and here I mean by "they" many secondary school and
college teachers of literature, as well as professional critics—because they

are looking for literature to provide kinds of stabilities, the moral and psychological certainties writers like Shakespeare and Hemingway are concerned to undermine, or at least to ignore. When students of mine begin sentences telling me that in such a poem Keats or Emily Dickinson says that. . ., or how, in "Sunday Morning," Wallace Stevens believes that. . . , or how Shakespeare thinks that. . . —such sentences are tip-offs to a conception of literature as the repository of messages, opinions, and beliefs about life held by the writer and conveyed (doubtless in excellent language) to readers ready to be instructed. And if the teacher or critic has a strong agenda, the poem or story may be enlisted as an ally in furthering the cause. Or perhaps it is simply that teachers confronting a class and critics trying to get their essay written are reluctant to live with the instabilities and fluidities that imaginative writing like Shakespeare's or Hemingway's presents us with. "Did Shakespeare think anything at all?" T. S. Eliot once asked somewhat mischievously. "He was preoccupied with turning human actions into poetry," added Eliot. And it was Eliot also who remarked that Henry James had a mind so fine "no idea could violate it." Such challenges were aimed at disconcerting readers eager to extract ideas or beliefs from the work of notable artists; Eliot reminds us that these artists will not be reduced to the pedagogical or analytical needs of those who talk and write about their art.

One of our best critics and teachers of poetry, Helen Vendler, wrote recently of her teacher at Harvard, I. A. Richards (who years previously had been Brower's teacher at Cambridge), that he was the only professor she encountered there who—as she put it to herself at the time—"taught poetry":

> My other teachers rarely talked in detail about poems they had
> assigned: they talked about history, or politics, or theology, or
> literary movements, or archetypes but not about those radiant
> and annihilating complexes of words that seemed to me to be
> crying out for attention, so inexplicable was their power and so
> compelling their effect.

My experience at Harvard tallies with Vendler's, though with Brower's and other Amherst voices in my head I didn't feel the need, as she did, to seek out Richards. But Vendler's speaking of poetry's "complexes of words" as both "radiant and annihilating" should give us interesting pause. Annihilating of what? Perhaps Richards's own writing provides a clue, if we remember what he once said about the final moment from *Antony and Cleopatra* when Octavius Caesar gazes down at the dead Cleopatra and observes that

> She looks like sleep,
> As she would catch another Antony
> In her strong toil of grace.

After quoting once more the final line—"In her strong toil of grace"— Richards asked "Where in terms of what entries in what possible dictionary, do the meanings here of *toil* and *grace* come to rest?" This is a question not to be answered by neat measurement, and one provoked, I think, by the way a particular complex of words, used by a master of language, can be "annihilating" of boundaries and limits as defined by the dictionary, or by the teacher intent on fixing a character or the play within some "meaningful" scheme of his own.

Most Amherst students who elect to take a poetry course with me expect that we will be centrally concerned with "complexes of words" as they are laid into lines and stanzas. But when fiction rather than poetry is the subject, such an assumption about focus is less common. In Modern Satiric Fiction we read many books during the semester—about one a week—so that there isn't time to pay the kind of respectful and detailed attention to language one can afford a lyric by Hardy or Yeats. Does that mean that attention must, initially or ultimately, be turned somewhere else than toward language? There are different ways to view this issue, and one critic (Marvin Mudrick), whose major interest was in fiction rather than poetry, has warned us that "in the beginning of poetry is the word; in the beginning of fiction is the event." Mudrick argues that the words of a work of fiction needn't be so precise and special as the words of a poem, and that fiction's words should not arrogate to themselves too much precision or "radiance" (Vendler's word). Perhaps so; yet the characters and events in a novel are perceived—are constructed by the reader—only through language. If some novelists, Dreiser say, or Dostoyevsky, ask to be considered in terms other than for their "precise and special use of words," there are others, James or Proust or John Updike, who as far as I can see stake everything on their "verbal complexes," on their styles.

In any case, I find that students in my fiction class are often puzzled as to what, in their papers, they should be writing about. I remember vividly how one member of the class who had done poorly on his first essay came to talk to me about this matter: what did I, in the famous word, "want"? I may have been somewhat evasive, but finally he asked, point blank, "You mean you want us to write about the language?" Remaining calm, I said that this didn't seem a bad idea to me; sure, why not try writing about the writing, rather than about the truth, or American society, or male-female relationships. No doubt the student left my office figuring that he'd pegged *me* as one of those aesthetes interested in technique rather than substance. What he didn't know, and what I couldn't tell him at that point, was that "technique" is more mysterious and even "annihilating" of clearly marked boundaries and dictionary definitions than he might have thought. Once more Eliot provides the useful formulation: "We cannot say at what point technique begins or where it ends."

Writing well about writing—whether that writing is poetry, drama, or fiction—means that the student must be helped to listen well; so, in a recent term of Reading Fiction, I invited the class which had just completed works by Dickens, Trollope, and George Eliot (the latter two items were fairly short, and I assigned only half of Dickens's *Pickwick Papers*) to see what would happen if they practiced some of Frost's "ear-reading" with respect to a particular sequence from one of these writers. They were to select a passage, quote it at least in part (such focus localizes attention to individual sentences), and then—in a deliberately vague question I often resort to—try to describe their "interest" in the sequence or passage. One student quoted some sentences from Eliot's short novel, *Amos Barton,* in which the clergyman's wife Milly is introduced: "a lovely woman—Mrs. Amos Barton: a large, fair, gentle Madonna, with thick, close chestnut curls beside her well-rounded cheeks, and with large, tender, short-sighted eyes." The student felt, rightly, that such language contrasted rather sharply with Eliot's comic and satirical presentations of other characters—most notably, the Rev. Amos Barton himself—in previous chapters. Where on earth, asked the student, did "this gentle Madonna" with her "placid elegance and sense of distinction" come from?

> Is she perhaps instead a divine being descended directly from the heavens? Somehow it is too much to swallow without chok-

ing a bit. Are we to believe that the sly wit so skillfully exhibited
on the preceding pages can perform such an abrupt about face?

He went on to quote more of Eliot's picture of Milly as possessing the
"soothing, unspeakable charm of gentle womanhood; which supersedes all
acquisitions, all accomplishments. . . . You would even perhaps have been
rather scandalized if she had descended from the serene dignity of *being* to
the assiduous unrest of *doing*."

All this, the student felt, was too much. Was it possible, he wondered,
that Eliot, "a highly intelligent and sensitive woman in a society dominated by the male sex," felt contempt for the "regard" in which women
were held? Could indeed the description of Milly be understood as "a parody of the skewed, romantic, Christian notion of the 'ideal woman' current at the time"? Could Eliot, in going so far as to write the following
sentence—"Happy the man, you would have thought, whose eye will rest
on her in the pauses of his fireside reading" —be deliberately mocking the
conception of woman as pure and sacrosanct, a conception given much
currency by male poets and novelists?

Whether his speculations and inferences are wholly correct or need to
be adjusted and qualified needn't concern us here, though they were of
concern when we discussed his paper in class. The point is that the student
gave us something to argue about and did so by beginning with George
Eliot's "technique": with matters of voice, diction, and intonation—words
brought off the page and to life in an imagined utterance. We can't say
where technique begins or where it ends, proof of which statement is there
in the student's move from small, local matters of hearing and noticing, to
speculations about male and female in nineteenth-century England—large
matters indeed. But the respect paid to Eliot's art is both evident and admirable. This is an "English" paper, a piece of literary criticism rather than a
sociological or political argument.

One further example of how practice in listening to, in constructing
and describing the "sound" of a particular novelistic moment may lead to
results that couldn't otherwise have been achieved. The climactic chapter
of Jane Austen's *Persuasion* is one in which the heroine, Anne Elliott, and
her lover-husband to be, Captain Wentworth, become fully aware of their
love for one another. Anne is engaged in conversation with a mutual friend
of hers and Wentworth's, Captain Harville, while Wentworth sits nearby,

writing a letter, but in fact eavesdropping on the conversation. Anne and Harville get into a friendly argument about the differences between men and women, and which sex has the stronger capacity for feeling, for "loving longest" especially "when existence or when hope has gone." (Anne and Wentworth, through her decision, were separated years previously and she has never ceased to grieve for him.) Anne claims the privilege for women, but Harville, somewhat teasingly reminds her that "all histories are against you, all stories, prose and verse." He tells her that

> "I do not think I ever opened a book in my life which had not something to say upon woman's inconstancy. Songs and proverbs, all talk of woman's fickleness. But perhaps you will say, these were all written by men."
>
> "Perhaps I shall. —Yes, yes, if you please no reference to examples in books. Men have had every advantage in telling their own story. . . . I will not allow books to prove any thing."

Since throughout this particular book Anne has been characterized as a very serious reader, exceptionally responsive to fiction and poetry, her forbidding any reference to books has a sharp ring to it. The discussion continues with her own voice gradually becoming firmer and more poignant as, without ever mentioning his name, she indirectly confesses to the ever more attentive Wentworth the faithfulness and durability of her love for him.

In the exercise I gave my students I said that this passage in *Persuasion* could be studied for what it might reveal about Jane Austen's attitude toward the sexes. But, I suggested, it might be studied—at least *read*—for something else, and I asked them to try to describe that something. I had in mind the way, as Anne assumes the ascendancy and moves toward a quite glowing affirmation of her love, she responds to Harville's polite admission that, since the evidence he alludes to comes from books which were all written by men, she is justified in denying their authority as foolproof indication of female inconstancy: "But perhaps you will say, these were all written by men." Then, with no narrative indication of how Anne says them (vigorously, teasingly, scornfully, determinedly?) we are given her three words back at Harville: "Perhaps I shall—." My point was that in this wonderful moment Austen is inviting, indeed compelling individual readers to do something, to "hear" these three words in a particular way—

or at least to entertain some different ways in which they might be spoken. Whether the reader opts for calm certainty on Anne's part or a sudden seizing of the reins as the opportunity presents itself; whether she makes a humorous, eye-twinkling riposte to Harville or settles into a righteous affirmation of her claim's virtue—the three words need to be heard as rendered other than in a monotone. It is a moment in a dramatic sequence, in a conversation that has a before and after; it is progressive; it issues in something beyond itself. Returning to Frost once more: "The ear does it; the ear is the only true writer and the only true reader." My mildly polemical point in the exercise was that a reader interested only in what Jane Austen "thinks" about the sexes (in fact she thinks lots of things, contradictory ones even) is engaged in eye-reading merely, and is losing the best part of the experience of art.

* * * *

"I'd no more set out in pursuit of the truth
than I would in pursuit of a living unless
mounted on my prejudices."
                              –Robert Frost

Kingsley Amis, one of the most entertaining novelists currently at work, once said with regard to a question of English usage: "I sometimes feel I have shifted a good way to the right in this matter over the years, but I feel no less often that (as in other matters) I have stayed more or less where I was while nearly everybody else has shifted to the left." There are a number of matters involving teaching, colleagues, students, and curriculum where Amis's observation strikes home to me. Some are trivial; others perhaps less so. For instance: I still call students by their last name (Miss Jones, Mr. Smith) in class; still give a two-hour final examination in my courses. I dislike catalog descriptions by colleagues that go on for too long, or use "critique" as a verb ("students will critique each other's papers") or show an over-fondness for words like "problematizing." I look with a wary eye on courses that appear to have a political agenda with a view to replacing presumably unexamined student prejudices with "correct" left-liberal ones—though sometimes I think the left-liberal ones are correct. (It will of course be pointed out to me that the claim to have no political agenda is but another sort of political agenda. My withers are unwrung.) Although my department offers serious courses in film, I would prefer that students chose to study Shakespeare or Romantic poetry first, just as I want them to read and study literature before they take a course in literary theory, if they ever do. And at a time when the cry is for "opening up" what is termed the literary "canon" so as to include within it (or substitute for it) works by recently discovered or rediscovered female and minority, non-Western, nonwhite male writer, my interest is in going deeper into the canon as currently perceived. Or rather, in exposing students to the canonical works few of them are even acquainted with.

Some years back I had occasion, in a required course for English majors, to ask the class what it thought of this notion of opening up the canon; to a man and woman they replied that it seemed like a fine idea. I then threw out some names of well-known works and authors from the unopened canon—Marvell's "Horatian Ode," Wordsworth's "Resolution and Independence," Samuel Johnson, John Henry Newman, Anthony Trollope, Bernard Shaw. Not just the majority but virtually the entire class of intelligent and articulate Amherst College students had no sense at all of these writers and their work. Admittedly this fact isn't about to impress teachers dedicated to opening things up. But it brought home to me that, in these days of "pluralistic" (to use the dignified word for it) approaches to the teaching of English—days in which, more or less, anything goes— it might be adventurous to teach the canon. Accordingly over the past few years I have offered old-fashioned "period" courses in English poetry from Spenser to Pope, or Wordsworth to Tennyson, and I plan to offer further ones involving eighteenth-and nineteenth-century British novelists and prose writers. In an important sense this is a selfish act on my part, since I'm serving my own need to explore further an already established list of writers and to share my discoveries with an audience. (It is easy, by the way, to forget how important students are in providing ears—sometimes responsive ones—for talk about writers, Marvell or Wordsworth or Samuel Johnson, on whom you'd have trouble focusing the conversation at a dinner or cocktail party.)

How much does my resistance to some of today's going concerns have to do with being one of the tiny number of Amherst graduates who currently teach on its faculty? (There are four extant, three of us in our late fifties.) I do know that I'm strongly prejudiced against the notion that education at Amherst has improved over the past few decades as a result of gradual liberation from a required curriculum—The New Curriculum. Those who delight in Amherst's current pluralism have been known to characterize the learning atmosphere of that old New Curriculum as an "intellectual boot camp." On the other hand, nobody has suggested that the U.S. Marines were not well trained, and there is a case to be made for the kind of learning that, sometimes, went on in Amherst between 1946 and 1966. Still, the teacher-alumnus must also distrust his own affection for an undergraduate experience he may well be idealizing. The last two lines of Randall Jarrell's "In Those Days" put the case with proper ambiguousness—"And yet after so long, one thinks / In those days everything was better." "One thinks" that everything was better back then, when in fact things were, perhaps not worse, but certainly different. And to a nostalgic eye like my eye, the very fact of difference, of something that was once and is now retrievable only in memory and imagination, imperceptibly elides itself from "different" into "better."

An unskeptical eye may also view the profession of English studies in rather more glamorous colors than are appropriate to the case. A useful critic of such glamorizing, Richard Poirier, has written of what he calls the "illusions" under which many academics labor—

> the illusion, first, of the necessity, and second of the enormous importance of literary studies. These illusions, shared in some degree by anyone occupationally involved, are difficult but necessary to resist. They intrude themselves because the study is confused with the subject, and teaching confused with the thing taught, the teacher, very often, with the author, whom he is "making available" to the young and to himself. It's a heady experience, after all, to have a direct line to Shakespeare, especially when it's assumed there's only one.

The warning is worth heeding, and yet—as Poirier himself admits—anyone who teaches English has to share such illusions "in some degree." Who knows when a line of poetry, read aloud in the classroom or to oneself in one's dormitory room, may come home to roost? More than once I've received testimony from a student about how—fifteen, twenty years after the fact—something Yeats wrote in a poem (a poem read sophomore year at Amherst) suddenly made sense. There is a poignant moment in Saul Bellow's *Seize the Day* when its hapless protagonist, Tommy Wilhelm, on the edge of failure and disaster, recalls involuntarily some words from a

Shakespeare sonnet—"love that well which thou must leave ere long." Wilhelm begins to think about his college days and "the one course that now made sense" —"Literature I":

> The textbook was Lieder and Lovett's *British Poetry and Prose,*
> a black heavy book with thin pages. Did I read that? he asked
> himself. Yes, he had read it and there was one accomplishment
> at least he could recall with pleasure. He had read "Yet once
> more O ye laurels." How pure this was to say! It was beautiful.
> Sunk though he be beneath the wat'ry floor . . .

For all his clunkishness, Wilhelm has got it right, and the rightness involves his listening to a voice—Shakespeare's or Milton's or his own buried one—that suddenly surfaces with something momentous. Here, it seems to me, "the enormous importance of literary studies" (Poirier's words) becomes not illusory, but real and inescapable.

"Teaching what we do"—my "doing" in this essay may well sound too simple and schematic in its dwelling rather exclusively on matters of voice and listening as my focus in the classroom and in the papers I ask students to write. I might have gone on at some length about the mutually enhancing relationship I feel between the teaching I do in class and the writing I do outside of it. Or, if it were not an impossibly self-regarding occupation, I could have written about my teaching style as a humorous one. "If it isn't any fun, don't do it," D. H. Lawrence once advised; as I grow older I grow less interested in classes where there's no laughter. "Humor is the most engaging form of cowardice," was Frost's inventive definition, and it's clear to me that, with the exception of one or two transcendent geniuses like Milton or Wordsworth, few poets and novelists live without engaging us in humorous ways (in fact the poetic behavior of both Milton and Wordsworth can be the occasion for a good deal of fun in the classroom). So the teacher—and the student as well—needs to speak back to the work in a comparably fresh and enlivening manner. The most awkward moment in any class term is that first meeting, in which any pronouncement, no matter how outrageous, is likely to be met with total, if not totally respectful, silence. To make that silence come to life is part of the fun and point of any academic term. One of my best recent students wrote me a note at the end of a semester, saying that her sister was planning to take a course of mine in the fall, and that she had advised her sister to read the books carefully, write honestly on the papers, and listen hard for my jokes. If it's true that "the ear really does it," then her final bit of advice was a particularly good one.

—*Teaching What We Do: Essays by Amherst College Faculty.*
Amherst College Press, 1991.

Novelists

Glorious Trollope

IS THERE ANYTHING more to say about Trollope beyond confessing one's addiction? And doesn't that merely characterize one as a throwback or curmudgeon, resisting contemporary fevers and frets on the cutting edge of nouvelle critique (the way we live now) in favor of a simpler time when a gentleman was a gentleman and things were called by their right names? My departmental colleagues on or near the cutting edge aren't likely to spend many hours reading Trollope (the two faculty colleagues who seriously read him are a philosopher and a mathematician), and although there have been a number of solid books written about him over the past couple of decades, he remains far from the centers of critical debate. There are of course Trollope scholars, one of the foremost of whom is N. John Hall. Ten years ago he gave us a beautifully annotated edition of Trollope's letters in two volumes; now he has published an extremely readable biography. It's not the sort of book that is going to make anyone reconsider his or her opinion about Trollope, but that may just be in the nature of things so far as this eminent Victorian is concerned.

One of Trollope's very best books is his autobiography (innocently titled *An Autobiography*), so a biographer is going to have to decide just how to place himself in relation to it. Mr. Hall's frequent practice, not altogether a satisfactory one I think, is to construct his own narrative by splicing together bits from Trollope's, as in the following treatment of the incipient novelist as a young post office employee sent out to investigate the delivery of letters in rural Ireland. Here is Trollope on the subject:

> I have often surprised some small country postmaster, who had never seen or heard of me before, by coming down upon him at nine in the morning, with a red coat and boots and breeches, and interrogating him as to the disposal of every letter which came

into his office. And in the same guise I would ride up to farm-houses, or parsonages, or other lone residences about the country, and ask the people how they got their letters, at what hour, and especially whether they were delivered free or at a certain charge. . . . In all these visits I was, in truth, a beneficent angel to the public, bringing everywhere with me an earlier, cheaper, and much more regular delivery of letters. But not infrequently the angelic nature of my mission was imperfectly understood.

He goes on to explain how his abrupt style of interrogation often caused suspicion and consternation in the parties interrogated. Hall retells it in this manner:

Sometimes he was a peculiar sight, dressed in red coat, boots, and breeches, swooping down at nine in the morning on a country postmaster demanding to know the disposal of every letter that arrived in his office. And often similarly attired, he would surprise farmers, parsons, lone country residents and their wives by suddenly appearing and asking questions about the delivery of their letters. . . . He considered himself "a beneficent angel to the public," even though the public did not always understand how this was so.

And so on in this vein, perfectly acceptable as long as you don't compare it to, as it were, the original. When you do, you see what's been lost: the understated comedy with which Trollope portrays himself as the brash interrogator, "coming down" (Hall soups it up to "swooping down") out of nowhere; or the nice touch, quite lost in Hall, of the beneficent angel whose angelic mission is "imperfectly understood" by his audience. In the main Hall is not a very humorous writer; Trollope is often so, and that makes a difference.

Hall is, however, a scrupulous provider—as was Trollope himself—of the financial details surrounding each of the writer's books; and he does a good job in evoking the misery of Trollope's childhood, in tracing the course of his career in the Post Office, first in Ireland, then in the West of England, and later on in following Trollope on his indefatigable travels. Among other countries Trollope visited the West Indies, the United States (five times!), Australia (twice), and New Zealand, South Africa, and Iceland (he wrote books about four of these places). Nor was there anything perfunctory about these visits: in Australia he didn't just go to New South Wales, but to all the remaining colonies including Tasmania, approaching his travels—as he did everything else—combatively:

> His sometimes circuitous routes took him thousands of miles by ship, rail, and coach; he went great distances in buggies, over the bush roads, and trails which in England would have not been considered roads; he also travelled much on horseback, sometimes managing "forty, fifty, and even as much as sixty-four miles a day"; he covered hundreds of miles through forests and mountains "so steep it was often impossible to sit on horseback."

In Tasmania he had himself lowered 150 feet down the mine shaft of a gold mine "with his foot in the noose of a rope," in order to explore the stalactite caves toward which he "made his way for a mile underground. . . . crawling, creeping, wading in waist-deep water." At this time he was in his later fifties; a couple of decades earlier, investigating postal conditions in the West Indies, he once rode so many miles on a bad horse and saddle that, in his discomfort, he thought of giving up the project. But, as he later told his brother Tom, that night he ordered two bottles of brandy, poured the contents into a large basin, and sat in it. After brief agony he was in shape to proceed on his mission.[1]

This was also the way he went about his writing, up and at his desk by 5:30 A.M., a half hour spent reading over what he'd written the previous day, then two and a half hours in the attempt, usually successful, to write a page every fifteen minutes: total, ten pages—after which it was time to dress or breakfast and repair to his other job in the postal service. Not to write was not to be alive, and Trollope kept himself alive by keeping himself writing. The piles of reports he produced about how to improve conditions in this or that postal district played directly, so he claimed, into his novel writing: "If a man knows his craft with his pen, he will have learned to write without the necessity of changing his words or the form of his sentences. I had learned so to write my reports that they who read them should know what it was that I meant them to understand." Just as with the pages of a novel where, without undue fussing about word and image, character and event could be so lucidly presented as to be thoroughly understood. Once a man really got going there need be no limit to the different narratives he could keep in motion. Noting that at one point in his career he was writing two full-length novels *(Castle Richmond* and *Framley Parsonage)* at the same time, he assures us that

> when the art has been acquired, I do not see why two or three should not be well written at the same time. I have never found myself thinking much about the work that I had to do till I was doing it. I have indeed for years almost abandoned the effort to think, trusting myself, with the narrowest thread of a plot, to work the matter out when the pen is in my hand.

"When the art has been acquired": once you know how to do it, you'll be able to do it, and do it without undue "thinking." It brings to mind T. S. Eliot's provocative question about Shakespeare: "Did Shakespeare think anything at all?"—a question Eliot answered by asserting that Shakespeare "was preoccupied with turning human actions into poetry." Each morning Trollope preoccupied himself with turning them into prose, as naturally and effortlessly, so it seems, as did Macaulay in his great history. (Trollope praises Macaulay, in the *Autobiography,* for the assistance his example has given to writers of prose.)

Hall observes that there has been little agreement about the best and worst of Trollope's novels, pointing out by contrast that "No one thinks that *Barnaby Rudge* is Dickens's greatest work, or *Philip* Thackeray's or *Romola* George Eliot's." This may mean that, compared to theirs, Trollope's work is extraordinarily even in quality, containing relatively no peaks or valleys. But it means also that when English novelists of the period are ranked, Trollope brings up the rear, a solid fourth behind the more distinguished threesome. Both Henry James and Tolstoy agreed on this ranking, James stating that Trollope's talent "was of quality less fine than theirs" —a judgment Tolstoy evidently concurred in, although he said in 1865, after reading *The Bertrams,* that "Trollope kills me with his virtuosity. I console myself that he has his skill and I have mine." Condescension to Trollope may have reached its limit with Leavis's *The Great Tradition* in which he is dismissed as a lesser Thackeray (not that Leavis has much to say for Thackeray either) and, in a particularly demeaning sentence, is contrasted to George Eliot and Henry James who are "great novelists above the ruck of

Gaskells and Trollopes and Merediths." It's that ugly word "ruck" and the assumption that Trollope and Meredith are equally undistinguished goods that especially infuriate.

Hall is not out to question anybody's ranking, and perhaps a biographer shouldn't be concerned with such matters. Trollope, though, was much concerned to explain, in the *Autobiography,* why he ranked Dickens third to Thackeray and Eliot (Dickens's characters were too stagey and artificial). In that spirit, it may be appropriate that, rather than joining the fan club of Trollopians, one should push the case for Trollope as great novelist more strongly than it is usually pushed. I would do this not by a comparison with the original genius of Dickens, but by raising the possibility that, taken in the large and over the course of years, Trollope is a more repaying novelist than either Eliot or Thackeray. This is not to deny that *Middlemarch* is a great book, a peak the height of which Trollope could never reach.[2] But whatever one thinks of *Daniel Deronda* (my thoughts are decidedly mixed), Eliot's earlier novels, *Silas Marner* excepted, are not things one looks forward eagerly to rereading. With Thackeray there is the peak of *Vanity Fair,* again perhaps unattainable by Trollope. But there is also the windiness and affectation of *Pendennis,* the sheer overweight of *The Newcomes,* the datedness of *Henry Esmond* and its historical furniture (Trollope thought it the best English novel ever written, superior even to *Pride and Prejudice* and *Ivanhoe*), not to mention the Thackeray novels I haven't read. What I'm arguing is that *Barchester Towers, The Last Chronicle of Barset, The Way We Live Now, The Prime Minister,* and *The Duke's Children,* along with darker horses like the gloomy *He Knew He Was Right* and the sparkling *Ayala's Angel* plus numbers of other highly entertaining, expertly managed narratives *(The Claverings, Can You Forgive Her?, The Vicar of Bullhampton),* are enough to call for nothing less than the highest claims for their creator.

In the course of his great essay on Trollope published in 1883, the year after Trollope died, Henry James has provided probably the most astute comparison of him to his novelist contemporaries, both in England and in France. One tends to remember from the essay—because it is so often quoted—James's censuring of Trollope for his "suicidal satisfaction in reminding the reader that the story he was telling was only, after all, a make-believe." But of far more use as a rich indicator of Trollope's art are the following sentences from a very long paragraph:

The striking thing to the critic was that his robust and patient mind had no particular bias, his imagination no light of its own. He saw things neither pictorially and grotesquely like Dickens; nor with that combined disposition to satire and to literary form which gives such "body," as they say of wine, to the manner of Thackeray; nor with anything of the philosophic, the transcendental cast—the desire to follow them to their remote relations—which we associate with the name of George Eliot. Trollope had his elements of fancy, of satire, of irony; but these qualities were not very highly developed, and he walked mainly by the light of his good sense, his clear, direct vision of the things that lay nearest, and his great natural kindness. There is something remarkably tender and friendly in his feeling about all human perplexities; he takes the good-natured, temperate, conciliatory view—the humorous view, perhaps, for the most part, yet without a touch of pessimistic prejudice.

After judging that his later works do savor of some bitterness, particularly *The Way We Live Now,* James returns to positive appreciation:

[Trollope] represents in an eminent degree this natural decorum of the English spirit, and represents it all the better that there is not in him a grain of the mawkish or the prudish. He writes, he feels, he judges like a man, talking plainly and frankly about many things, and is by no means destitute of a certain saving grace of coarseness.

The phrase that sums it all up and forms the paragraph's first sentence is rightly famous: "His great, his inestimable merit was a complete appreciation of the usual." I would argue that even while James ranks Trollope below his three English contemporaries, the very strength and justness of his claims make a case for Trollope's greatness that James never made for Dickens, or Thackeray, or George Eliot.

Trollope's "robust and patient mind," wrote James, had no "particular bias." In fact James wasn't the first to perceive this, since an unsigned notice in *The Times* some years previously had pointed out, generalizing from *He Knew He Was Right,* that Trollope's writings "have no aesthetic purpose; they mean nothing more than they say; they are not written *at* the reader; the author thinks of nothing but how his work may be made a correct copy, complete and minute." This is a move toward defining the novelist as realist. In what looks to me the most adventurous and original of recent critical books about Trollope, Walter Kendrick, using the language of post-structuralist discourse, ingeniously describes the difference between Trollope's realism and the mode of other kinds of writers such as poets, the "sensation" novelists (who were his contemporaries), and Post Office employees who make a first draft of a report with the intention of improving it subsequently:

> These writers have in common . . . that they put on paper words that are not exact—whether the form be a plot outline, an early version of a poem, or a first draft of a report. All of them are willing, then, to transform this writing by means of other writing—filling in the outline, refining meter and metaphor, polishing phrases. Such nonrealistic writers treat words as words; they deal with words in their interrelations, apart from their connections to the things they signify. For the Trollopian realist, writing is valuable only because it is necessary to make the reader's experience of the characters as similar as possible to the novelist's experience of them before he begins to write. But there is no value in intertextuality. Indeed, there is less than no value in it, because the admission of an intertextual relation does harm to the achievement of equivalence that is the goal of the whole novel business. If any participant in that business considers a text as a text, then reality has been compromised. All the opponents of Trollopian realism . . . share the antirealistic habit of admitting that writing has value as writing, rather than as the pure conveyance of what is other than itself.[3]

Accordingly Kendrick understands the authorial intrusions of which Henry James complained as Trollope's attempts to "degrade" the text, the better to enhance the "equivalence" between the novelist's apprehension of reality and reality itself (Trollope knew what that was).

Even when Trollope's prose calls attention to itself for its more than usual density, the novelist assures us that in fact we really don't need his words. In an extraordinary passage from *The Prime Minister* when the villainous Ferdinand Lopez—whose machinations Trollope manages to make continuously interesting—is about to throw himself under a train, the site of his suicide is introduced this way (Lopez is at Euston Station, bound presumably for Birmingham on business):

> After a while he went back into the hall and took a first-class return ticket, not for Birmingham, but for the Tenway junction. It is quite unnecessary to describe the Tenway junction, as everybody knows it.

But you must *show*, not *tell*, cries the neophyte Creative Writer, and even though everybody knows what the Tenway is like, Trollope will describe it anyway, no big deal:

> From this spot, some six or seven miles distant from London, lines diverge east, west, and north, north-east, and north-west, round the metropolis in every direction, and with direct communication with every other line in and out of London. It is a marvellous place, quite unintelligible to the uninitiated, and yet daily used by thousands who only know that when they get there, they are to do what some one tells them. The space occupied by the convergent rails seems to be sufficient for a large farm. And these rails always run one into another with sloping points, and cross passages, and mysterious meandering sidings, till it seems to the thoughtful stranger to be impossible that the best trained engine should know its own line. Here and there and around there is ever a wilderness of waggons, some loaded, some empty, some smoking with close-packed oxen, and others furlongs in length black with coals, which look as though they had been stranded there by chance, and were never destined to get again into the right path of traffic. Not a minute passes without a train going here or there, some rushing by without noticing Tenway in the least, crashing through like flashes of substantial lightning, and others stopping, disgorging and taking up passengers by the hundreds.

Wonderfully caught up in the place he's describing which "everybody knows," Trollope finally informs us that "over all this apparent chaos there is presiding a great genius of order," but isn't so immodest as to admit that the genius is himself. The best way succinctly to demonstrate the differ-ence between Trollope and Dickens is to compare this passage about the Tenway junction with Dickens's equally brilliant creation of the railway junction that has replaced Staggs's Gardens in the London of *Dombey and Son*. For all that Trollope's presentation of Tenway stands out from the less memorable character of his usual prose, it still issues in what James called a "complete appreciation of the usual" —after all, everybody knows about Tenway junction. What Dickens does to the junction that's replaced Staggs's Gardens is to write it up into the noticeably unusual through para-graphs of fantastic figuration.[4]

In other words, Dickens is always noticeable in his writing, always the resourceful performer endlessly deploying his bag of tricks. By contrast, Trollope brings off his effects without inviting us to be conscious of the way he writes them up. Ford Madox Ford placed him in the company of Chaucer and Jane Austen as, before all things, a "snooper," and Ford uses the testimony of Trollope's nephew, a Mr. Synge, to weave a picture of the novelist as clubman-snooper:

> Trollope was extraordinarily unnoticeable. Wherever he was, it seemed to be absolutely natural that there he should be. . . . When he entered a club smoking-room no one interrupted his conversation; when he shot no one noticed his bag. Synge said that, occasionally, when Trollope was the last member in the lounge of the old Club, St. George's Hanover Square, the wait-ers would put out the lights, not noticing Trollope, although he was under their eyes.[5]

Ford goes on to surmise that therefore he must have heard more "gossip"—the best gossip in the world—than any writer except perhaps Jane Austen. He calls Trollope "the greatest of all specifically English novelists," and, in one of Ford's shrewdest sentences, notes that "he is less of an artist than she but he is male, and that counts." What "counts" is of course male privileges such as being allowed to snoop at the club in Hanover Square.

Style, said Robert Frost once, is the way a person carries himself toward his ideas and his deeds. In speaking of Trollope one wants to add that such carrying is done, essentially, through a narrative voice. It's doubtless unconscionably vague to speak about "voice" and how getting to recog-nize and love Trollope's over the course of time is such a rewarding activity.

But an early reviewer of *Barchester Towers* struck the right vocal emphasis when he said that Trollope sounded "like one's father should sound." And this father was willing to put himself on the line by speaking about basic human values. Trollope said about the Pallisers—Lady Glencora and her husband Plantagenet ("Planty Pal," the Duke of Omnium, the once Prime Minister)—that they were "safety-valves by which to deliver my soul." He delivered it most movingly in The *Prime Minister,* a novel which, mysteriously, was met with disdain—"worse spoken of by the press than any novel I had written," wrote Trollope regretfully in a footnote to the *Autobiography.* This book and its successor, *The Duke's Children,* seem to me to constitute the peaks of Trollope. Coming near the end of his career (1876 and 1880), they refute James's verdict on the inferiority of the later works.

Trollope resigned from the Post Office in 1867 and George Eliot warned about the consequences: "I cannot help being rather sorry. . . . But it seems to me a thing greatly to be dreaded for a man that he should be in any way led to excessive writing." But Trollope lived by writing excessively, and in the fifteen years left to him produced some of his very best novels. He was excessive as well about the consumption of cigars, at one point, in a letter to Eliot, generously offering to share the 8,000 cigars, which had just arrived from Cuba, with Eliot's common-law husband, G. H. Lewes. His love of hunting also remained unabated, as we learn in a passage from the *Autobiography* which gives us the Trollope voice about as clearly as we ever hear it. He tells us that he's never been able to analyze to his own satisfaction his delights in this amusement and that in fact he knows very little about hunting (remember that he begins the book by calling himself "an insignificant person the details of whose private life would naturally bear little interest to readers"):

> I am too blind to see hounds turning, and cannot therefore tell whether the fox has gone this way or that. Indeed all the notice I take of hounds is not to ride over them. My eyes are so constituted that I can never see the nature of a fence. I either follow some one, or ride at it with the full conviction that I may be going into a horse-pond or a gravel-pit. I have jumped into both one and the other. I am very heavy, and have never ridden expensive horses. I am also now old for such work, being so stiff that I cannot get on to my horse without the aid of a block or a bank.

What's left then? Nothing less than everything:

> But I ride still after the same fashion, with a boy's energy determined to get ahead if it may possibly be done, hating the roads, despising young men who ride them, and with a feeling that life cannot, with all her riches, have given me anything better than when I have gone through a long run to the finish, keeping a place, not of glory, but of credit, among my juniors.

Among his juniors, the novelists who came and come after him, his place is not of credit merely, but of glory.

—*Hudson Review*, Spring 1993.

Notes

1. It wasn't all painful, though. In New Zealand he went one dark evening with a friend to bathe in a hot spring, already occupied by three Maori women. With pats on his back, they encouraged Trollope to come bathe, and after a time in the water he remarked to his companion, Gilbert Mair, that "he wished he had something to lean against." Whereupon Mair whispered this "to a fine young woman of splendid proportions . . . who immediately set her capacious back against him, whereat he exclaimed, 'Well, Mair, this is very delightful, don't you know, but I think I did wise in leaving Mrs. Trollope in Auckland.'"
2. In a letter to Trollope, Eliot called his books "pleasant public gardens, where people go for amusement and, whether they think of it or not, get health as well."
3. Walter Kendrick, *The Novel-Machine* (Baltimore, 1980).
4. "To and from the heart of this great change, all day and night, throbbing currents rushed and returned incessantly like its life's blood. . . . The very houses seemed disposed to pack up and take trips. . . . Night and day the conquering engines rumbled at their distant work, or advancing smoothly to their journey's end, and gliding like tame dragons into the allotted corners grooved out to the inch for their reception, stood bubbling and trembling there, making the walls quake, as if they were dilating with the secret knowledge of great powers yet unsuspected in them, and strong purposes not yet achieved." (*Dombey and Son*, Chapter 15)
5. Ford Madox Ford, *The March of Literature.*

Anthony Powell's Serious Comedy

THE MOST HEARTENING, if uncelebrated, literary event of recent months is the publication by the University of Chicago Press of Anthony Powell's masterwork, *A Dance to the Music of Time,* in anticipation of Powell's ninetieth birthday. Each volume of three novels makes up one "movement" in the twelve-novel sequence. Each features on its cover a detail from Poussin's painting in the Wallace Collection, "A Dance to the Music of Time," with black-and-white reproduction of the painting inside the cover. The books are well bound; their type is large and reader-friendly; they look as if they will be around for some time.

A Dance to the Music of Time began to unfold in 1951, when Powell published *A Question of Upbringing,* largely concerned with the life of the narrator, Nicholas Jenkins, at "school"—Eton and Oxford, though neither of them is named. The novel introduces us to a number of characters who will play significant or minor roles in the sequence to come, among them Nick's roommates, Peter Templer and Charles Stringham. Even as a young man Templer is good with the ladies, not much with the books; Stringham, ironic and literary, is already detaching himself from conventional social expectations. We also meet figures who will surface later on, "characters" such as Nick's housemaster, the hellenizing LeBas and his stock of bad Victorian verse, and Nick's relative, Uncle Giles, "a bit of a radical" (as he likes to think of himself) who always turns up at the wrong time. But the figure with whom—after a short prologue—the novel begins is that of Kenneth Widmerpool, another school acquaintance. Except for Nick himself, Widmerpool will play the most significant role in *Dance,* turning up in each successive volume, never less than substantially.

We are introduced to him as he is taking "a run" —something he does voluntarily every afternoon—"in a sweater once white and cap at least a size too small, hobbling unevenly, though with determination, on the flat heels of spiked running-shoes." Nick continues:

> It was on the bleak December tarmac of that Saturday afternoon . . . that Widmerpool, fairly heavily built, thick lips and metal-rimmed spectacles giving his face as usual an aggrieved expression, first took coherent form in my mind. As the damp, insistent cold struck up from the road, two thin jets of steam drifted out of his nostrils, by nature much distended, and all at once he seemed to possess a painful solidarity that talk about him had never conveyed.

Thus "stiffly, almost majestically, Widmerpool moved on his heels, out of the mists."

Dance concluded in 1974 with *Hearing Secret Harmonies,* Jenkins now living, as Powell has for decades, in the country, observing and commenting with his usual wit and dispassion, on the social, political, and sexual turbulences in the early 1970s. Previous novels in the sequence have taken Nick through the years between the wars as he works in publishing, then screenwriting, publishes a couple of novels, gets married, lives in London. He serves as an officer in the army during World War II and afterwards participates in the London literary scene. Meanwhile all about him characters appear, disappear, then—like Widmerpool—once more rise up out of the mists, usually causing a surprise when they do.

The presiding metaphor of a dance is set forth in two opening paragraphs to the whole sequence, as an anonymous narrator encounters some road repair work in which a number of workmen, taking a break, are gathered round a bucket of coke burning in front of their shelter. Snow begins to fall; the workmen go back to work; the day draws in. Gradually the narrator begins to emerge, being reminded first of the ancient world ("legionaries in sheepskin warming themselves at a brazier"), then of Poussin's painting, "in which the Seasons, hand in hand and facing outward, tread in rhythm to the notes of the lyre that the winged and naked greybeard plays." There follows an often-quoted piece of writing in Powell's high style that gives eloquent expression to the project on which he and we are about to embark:

The image of Time brought thoughts of mortality: of human beings facing outward like the Seasons, moving hand and hand in intricate measure: stepping slowly, methodically, sometimes a trifle awkwardly, in evolutions that take recognizable shape: or breaking into seeming meaningless gyrations. while partners disappear only to reappear again, once more giving pattern to the spectacle: unable to control the melody, unable, perhaps, to control the steps of the dance.

At which point "classical associations" remind him of his days at school and the narrative proper launches itself.

Twenty years after the dance so launched was brought to its close, it should be possible to arrive at an estimate of Powell's literary contribution. To an extent he is a cult figure, admired by an informed and devoted group of Anglo-American readers able at a moment's challenge to distinguish a character named Bithel from one named Borrit (I once failed to do this), or not to confuse Lady Anne Stepney with her sister Lady Peggy. But that cult status makes it harder to decide how much Powell counts. To be the sort of writer whose work invites guidebooks in which characters, plots, births, deaths, and marriages may be charted at length, is to risk accusations of triviality—just the thing that Anglophiles get carried away by. The reader who doesn't get on with *Dance* is put off by the worry or the certainty that it's all just gossip, and gossip about a particular social stratum at the end of its tether: the English upper-class, public school, privileged network of old boys and the girls they do or don't marry, 1920-1970. (It's interesting that, though a similar devaluation could be made of Proust on the grounds that he inspects a privileged class in *A la recherche,* it is not made—Marcel's intensities and the magic of Proust's name evidently making any such demurring impossible.) For those who don't get on with Powell, Marvin Mudrick will have said the last word when he mocked the sequence as "the most interminable soap-opera since Australopithecus": "Powell's method of getting on with the story must be the most ponderously inefficient of all time," Mudrick began, noting that when a character is introduced, the narrator, Jenkins, spends a few pages speculating on the probable nature of this figure who, it may be, "is blond, has small ears, and wears a black raincoat." Later on, as the character turns up more than once, Jenkins will proceed, says Mudrick, to add further uninteresting though precise details to the portrait. Mudrick called this procedure less a narrative method than "a spreading tumor of speculation," and said that Powell suffered from "an elephantiasis of the will, making harrumphing preparations for something that never happens."

There is no point surely in "arguing" with such a colorful onslaught; there is point in noting that, by never descending to quoting anything from the novel, Mudrick assumes (or assures us) that no one could be interested in *listening* to the narrator's speculating voice as it slyly presents and protracts character in action. But if slyness is attributable to Powell the novelist, it does not at all describe the blend of modestly thoughtful and intimate speculation that characterizes Nick Jenkins's voice. Nick is perhaps the least aggressive, least willful, most reasonable narrator ever to show up in a novel; by contrast, even the self-effacing apologies of Fitzgerald's Nick Carraway are memorably eloquent. Jenkins's virtue, or limitation, is to avoid self-dramatizing theatrics, indeed to make reticence about private matters a mark of character. When, in an especially charged moment, he lays eyes for the first time upon Isobel Tolland, one of a large number of brothers and sisters in an aristocratic family, he addresses us with a question: "Would it be too explicit, too exaggerated, to say that when I set eyes on Isobel Tolland, I knew at once that I should marry her?" Never did a question more invite the negative answer, and we hear virtually no more about Isobel at this or subsequent moments. She marries Nick, has children by him, shares a joke or a quiet exchange with him now and then, but that's all. Although it would be misleading to call Nick reticent in his dealings with and speculations about other characters, those speculations always feel tentative, capable of revision, not to be laid in stone. The more offensive and egregious are the words or behavior of someone, like Widmerpool, with whom Nick has to deal, the more he will bend over backward to insist that there's perhaps something to what Widrnerpool is saying. Nick is very good at seeing what there is to be said in defense of even the most indefensible person or attitude; he provides us with the kind of detached consideration of the foibles of others which, in life, we're scarcely able to manage. Much of the time, since this is a work of comedy, his perspective on things, the tone in which he registers them, is open, watchful; if not amused, at least interested in what's going on.

Consider a moment from *A Question of Upbringing* in which a practical joke misfires. Nick is visiting his roommate Peter Templer, at whose father's house the guests include a somewhat disagreeable man named

Jimmy Stripling, married to Templer's older sister Babs, and a rather more attractive one named A. Sunderland ("Sunny") Farebrother. One evening Farebrother attempts to demonstrate a handy gadget for turning white shirt collars, thus saving money. Stripling offers one of his collars for demonstration, and eventually the contraption manages to tear, dirty, or ruin several of them. In revenge, Stripling plans a trick on the night before Farebrother's departure, after the party has returned from a dance. A load of baggage outside the latter's door—suitcases, fishing rod and landing net, a gun case—includes a leather hatbox containing the bowler required for Sunny's business in the City. As Nick and Templer's sister watch, Stripling appears, approaching Farebrother's closed door, carrying a small green chamber-pot in his hand, the plan being to substitute it for the hat:

> My immediate thought was that relative size might prevent this plan from being put successfully into execution; though I had not examined the inside of the hat-box, obviously itself larger than normal (no doubt built to house more commodious hats of an earlier generation), the cardboard interior of which might have been removed to make room for odds and ends. Such economy of space would not have been out of keeping with the character of its owner. In any case it was a point upon which Stripling had evidently satisfied himself, because the slight smile on his face indicated that he was absolutely certain of his ground. No doubt to make an even more entertaining spectacle of what he was about to do, he shifted the china receptacle from the handle by which he was carrying it, placing it between his two hands, holding it in front of him, as if it were a sacrificial urn. Seeing it in this position, I changed my mind about its volume, deciding that it could indeed be contained in the hatbox. However, before this question of size and shape could be settled one way or the other, something happened that materially altered the course that events seemed to be taking; because Farebrother's door suddenly swung open, and Farebrother himself appeared, still wearing his stiff shirt and evening trousers, but without a collar. It occurred to me that perhaps he knew of some mysterious process by which butterfly collars, too, could be revived, as well as those of an up-and-down sort, and that he was already engaged in metamorphosing the evening collar he had worn at the Horabins'.

There the long paragraph ends, a new one beginning with this short sentence: "Stripling was taken completely by surprise." Farebrother remains silent, only raising his eyebrows a little; whereas Stripling's features, as he strides on down the hall, "looked not so much angry, or thwarted, as in actual physical pain." "With an air of being hurt, or worried," Farebrother quietly shuts his door; the narrator, feeling uncommonly tired, also retires. And that is that. Mudrick might call it a perfect example of harrumphing aimlessly, as Nick's cautious, even pedantic deliberations unfold: he hadn't examined the inside of the hat-box, isn't sure the chamber-pot will fit—though perhaps this box, built for former "more commodious" hats, and with its cardboard removed, may do the trick. Yes, he decides as Stripling holds it up urnlike in front of him, the chamber-pot *will* fit.

In one sense all this fussing has nothing to do with the fact that Farebrother opens the door and catches Stripling in the act of behaving, as he thinks, very oddly, In a more important sense, however, the fussing, the qualification and requalification, the leisurely focus, are the whole point of such comic writing. After all, Powell has read his Proust and knows that his readers most likely will have done so as well. Are there not satisfactions in writing post-Proust about chamber-pots and hat-boxes as if they constituted the stuff of imaginative recapture, the remembrance of things past? Although Powell's humorous writing is often compared with Evelyn Waugh's, it has more affinities with early Samuel Beckett, especially the Beckett of *Murphy* who, at the beginning of his literary career, wrote a monograph on Proust. Beckett's comedy is louder, more slapstick, but it unfolds like Powell's, through the narrator's mock-pedantic treatment of his subject. If one doesn't take the trouble to listen to Beckett's or Powell's sentences as the voice unrolls them, the writing will provoke not pleasure but active annoyance.

Assuming, though, that you are pleased rather than provoked by the hatbox incident, you may become curious to hear more about the potential victim turned conqueror, Sunny Farebrother. We come immediately to the second great pleasure of *Dance*—second only to its narrative voice: the disappearance and reappearance of characters who, facing outward like Poussin's Seasons, are "moving hand in hand in intricate measure." The following morning Nick finds himself on the same train to London with Farebrother who, in puzzlement, tells Nick about Stripling's strange behavior—"Marching down the passage holding a *jerry* in front of him as if he were taking part in some ceremony." What could he have been doing, and was it a joke? Nick plays the innocent. Sunny finally decides that it wasn't a joke, since "we are always hearing that his health is not good." In other words, Stripling's involvement with the "jerry" might be accounted for by serious intestinal problems. At any rate. Farebrother concludes with a vague and pleasantly irrelevant reflection about Stripling: "Coupled with the rest of his way of going on . . . it made a bad impression." Farebrother's futile attempt to make sense of Stripling's behavior stands on its own with minimum narrative comment, Powell taking care not to spoil the comedy by explicit underlining. Abruptly the section ends:

> We passed on towards London. When we parted company Sunny Farebrother gave me one of his very open smiles, and said: "You must come and lunch with me one of these days. No good my offering you a lift as I'm heading Citywards." He piled his luggage, bit by bit, on to a taxi; and passed out of my life for some twenty years.

From time to time, in the novels that follow, Farebrother is briefly thought of in connection with Stripling's attempted joke. In *The Soldier's Art* (book eight) he reappears in person, skirmishing with Widmerpool, both of them now officers in the army. Finally, in *Hearing Secret Harmonies,* Nick recalls meeting Farebrother, now nearly eighty, in the tube, coming back from Kensal Green cemetery where Farebrother has attended the funeral of none other than Jimmy Stripling. He makes a point of going to funerals, Farebrother confides, "because you always meet a lot of people at them you haven't seen for years, and that often comes in useful later." Stripling's, however, was the exception to this rule, the turnout embarrassingly small, the assembly a poor lot ("I shall never expect to set eyes on mourners like his again, Kensal Green, or anywhere else"). Preparing to depart the train, Nick asks after Sunny's health and Sunny replies, "Top-hole form, top-hole. Saw my vet last week. Said he's never inspected a fitter man of my age." A widower now, he invites Nick and his wife to come and see his roses ("I can always manage a cup of tea. Bless you, Nicholas, bless you"):

> As I walked along the platform towards the Exit staircase the train moved on past me. I saw Farebrother once more through the window as the pace increased. He was still sitting bolt

upright, and had begun to smile again. At the visit to which he had himself referred, the time when Stripling's practical joke had fallen so flat, Peter Templer had pronounced a judgment on Farebrother. It remained a valid one.

"He's a downy old bird."

Whatever, exactly, a downy old bird might look like, we have undeniably met him in the person of Sunny Farebrother.

Farebrother's quirky memorableness, like so many other figures that populate the pages of *Dance,* is grounds for reflection on the novelist's technique of characterization, especially since. as the individual books appeared, reviewers fell into the habit—encouraged by Nick's own commentary—of classifying characters either as representing the Will or the Imagination. Men of the Will are power-hungry, like Widmerpool, or the critic J. G. Quiggin, or the industrialist, Sir Magnus Donners; men of Imagination like Stringham, or Nick's composer friend Hugh Moreland, or Nick himself, care about poetry, art and music, are sometimes careless of their own best interests—at least in the eyes of others. This distinction between will and imagination is harmless and true enough, but it doesn't go far toward reminding us that, as his treatment of Farebrother may suggest, Powell's art is importantly an art of the surface, insofar as it asks us to be interested in what the character *is* rather than what he or she represents. After all, Poussin's Seasons are facing outward, not inward. Powell, who admired the Wyndham Lewis of *Tarr* and *The Wild Body* stories, has his own predilection for "external" art, a predilection to be noted especially in his brilliant prewar novels *Afternoon Men* (1931) and *From a View to a Death* (1933). But the external treatment is to be found in *Dance* as well. The essential things about Farebrother are his smile, his roses, his expressions ("jerry," "Top-hole," the doctor as a "vet"), and of course his name itself. In response to those who call Powell's characters and their world superficial, there is Eliot to quote on Ben Jonson: "We cannot call a man's work superficial when it is the creation of a world; a man cannot be accused of dealing superficially with the world which he himself has created; the superficies *is* the world." This is not the whole story of Powell's art, but it's an important part of it.

In calling *Dance* the most interminable soap opera since Australopithecus, Mudrick must have thought he'd scored a good hit, since what is more damning to art than a comparison to trash? But Powell's art is not necessarily undone by the comparison. As with daily episodes in a soap opera, you could skip parts of any particular novel from *Dance* and still be able to locate yourself well enough in its successor. For although both *Dance* and the soap have plenty of plots, they lack an overall Plot. A master plot would imply a conclusion, when in fact the show aspires to run on forever. Powell has said that he conceived of *Dance* because he didn't think he was especially good at making up plots that would begin, develop, and conclude themselves in 225 pages. To write a twelve-novel sequence is, time and again, to defer conclusion. *Dance* eventually concludes, but we don't read it with the excited sense that we're following an action that's working itself out.

It is also possible to develop kinds of affection for and interest in a character, whether in novel or in soap opera, that depend upon acquaintance developed over the long haul. Experiencing the self-contained characters of *Dance,* with their amusing, often striking surfaces, their distinctive idioms and vocabularies, their styles of address, is a more complex version of the way we get to know long-enduring characters in a soap. Of course the psychology of a soap character's "inner life" is laughable, sketched only in the crudest of fashions; but over the course of time spent watching, we build up a pleased recognition as characters reappear, sometimes even come back from the dead, once more to do their thing. Increased acquaintance with rather than deeper knowledge about these characters is the name of the game. So it is with most, if not all, of the personages in *Dance.* But, unlike the effect of a soap, the illusion of Powell's art is to make us feel that, oddly enough, the more we're acquainted with a character, the more his ultimate inaccessibility to us and to the narrative understanding that presents him becomes apparent. For the reader who takes Powell seriously, there are of course innumerable other aspects and qualities of the work with which to be concerned: the rendering of period details from the twenties to the seventies; the pervasive mythological, historical, and occult lore that deeply fascinates some of the characters and in a playful way Powell himself; the unusual pungent sexual language ("I only stuffed her once," says Bob Duport of the notorious Pamela Flitton, "Against a shed in the back parts of Cairo airport, but even then I could see she might drive you round the bend"). Questions of literary value might be raised as well: does the sequence reach its high point in the three war volumes, then fall away somewhat in the last three, or are those final volumes an intensification of earlier ones? Is the abject death of Widmerpool in *Hearing Secret Harmo-*

nies a believable metamorphosis or an example of what, with reference to Milton's treatment of Satan in *Paradise Lost,* A. J. Waldock called the "technique of degradation"?

Rather than exploring such matters, I want—by considering some examples of it—to touch on an enduring pleasure of *Dance* not enough remarked on by critics of Powell's work. This pleasure comes from the densely allusive way in which poems, hymns, and popular songs pervade the sequence. (The going word for it these days is "intertextuality," a term that would doubtless afford Powell some amusement.) An appealing instance is found in the character of Ted Jeavons, second husband of the Lady Molly whose name gives the fourth novel its title. Jeavons was wounded in the stomach in the First World War and has suffered ever since ("I feel bilious most of the time"). Given to long silences, he has no visible employment, but is interested in various gadgets and attempts without success to interest others in them. Every so often Jeavons needs to kick up the traces and go out on his own for a night of serious drinking (incapacitating himself for days thereafter), perhaps flirt with a "tart" or two. His finest moment comes at the end of *The Kindly Ones,* just half-way through *Dance,* at the point where England has gone to war with Germany and Nick is trying to get commissioned in the army. At the end of a small party, Nick is sitting with Ted and his brother Stanley in the Jeavonses' South Kensington flat, the room blacked out in response to German air raids. Ted Jeavons is wandering about in his mackintosh and pajamas and Stanley, who "evidently found his brother's life inexplicable," has given Nick a useful lead on getting into an infantry regiment. Whereupon Ted Jeavons

> moved towards the table where the beer bottles stood. Suddenly he began to sing in that full, deep, unexpectedly attractive voice, so different from the croaking tones in which he ordinarily conversed:
>
>> There's a long, long trail a-winding
>> Into the land of . . . my dreams,
>> Where the night . . . ingale is singing
>> And the white moon beams.
>> There's a long, long night of waiting,
>> Until my dreams all . . . come true . . .

He broke off as suddenly as he had begun. Stanley Jeavons began tapping out his pipe again, perhaps to put a stop to that refrain.

"Used to sing that while we were blanco-ing," said Jeavons. "God, how fed up I got cleaning that bloody equipment."

At which point Nick says good night and makes his way home. Abrupt, inexplicable, unexpectedly attractive, mysterious in its point of ending as well as its motive for beginning, the moment makes Ted Jeavons stranger as well as more familiar to us.

What difference does it make if one knows the tune to "There's a long, long trail . . ."? All the difference, insofar as we can perform in our head the heightened, sentimental execution of a song that calls out to be suitably lingered over, drawn out mightily in an exaggerated style. (My father used to embarrass me by singing "The Sweetheart of Sigma Chi" in such a style.) By the same token, it helps to know the song "South of the Border" if we are to experience properly the moment in *The Valley of Bones* (book seven) when Nick, joining his regiment in Wales, with his mind full of Celtic lore and thoughts of the Seven Churches of Asia (one of which, Sardis, is the name for the cavelike "tabernacle" where his company is billeted), views the "asymmetical rows of double-decker bunks upon which piles of grey-brown blankets were folded in regulated manner." As he looks, he hears from the far end of the "cave"

like the anthem of the soloist bursting gloriously from a hidden choir, a man's voice, deep-throated and penetrating [that] sounded, rose, swelled, in a lament of heartbreaking melancholy:

That's where I fell in love
While stars above
Came out to play;
For it was *mañana,*
And we were so gay,
South of the border,
Down Mexico way . . .

My 1939 sheet music of "South of the Border" reveals a couple of words out of place ("For it was fiesta," is correct), so either the soldier or Powell erred slightly. No matter, for nothing could be more incongruous than this song that surfaced briefly on "Your Hit Parade" and, I had thought, disappeared forever. How odd to have it called up decades later by an English novelist! But then, incongruity is the reigning principle in *Dance,* to be accepted as perfectly appropriate, the way life is:

> The mournful, long-drawn out notes died for a moment. Glancing round, I thought the singer, too, was praying then saw his crouched position had been adopted the better to sweep under one of the bunks. . . . Rising, he burst out again with renewed, agonized persistence:
>
>> . . .The Mission bell told me
>> That I mustn't stay
>> South of the border,
>> Down Mexico way. . .
>
> The message of the bell, the singer's tragic tone announcing it, underlined life's inflexible call to order, reaffirming the illusory nature of love and pleasure.

And Nick girds his own loins for the new professional life of the soldier he has embraced. As always at memorable moments in *Dance,* the pleasure lies in the complex mixture of feeling, the narrative "tone" that constitutes Powell's unique blend of things. The soldier who was singing may have adopted a tragic tone, but the vehicle doesn't quite measure up to tragedy—however attractive, in its faded recall, "South of the Border" is to us. To speak grandly, as Nick does here, of "the illusory nature of love and pleasure" may suggest that Powell is inviting us to reach into the depths with such a grand formulation. But in fact the formulation won't bear much thinking about—you can't do anything interesting with it. What we do instead is take pleasure in the vivid juxtaposition of the banal tune and lyric with whatever feelings—deep or shallow—the singing soldier is giving expression to.

Finally I want to suggest, by way of a more lengthy example, the kinds of allusive satisfactions *Dance* provides and the way the book, at one such moment, touches upon greatness. These satisfactions are splendidly present in the six-and-a-half pages of *The Military Philosophers* (book nine) when Nick attends the service of General Thanksgiving in St. Paul's to commemorate the end of World War II. In these pages we give ourselves

over to the meanderings of an intricate if reticent sensibility as it responds
to various lines and passages from the Bible and from English poetry, while
becoming itself densely poetic in its associations. After the Royal Party is
seated there are prayers, then a hymn:

> Angels in the height, adore him;
> Ye behold him face to face;
> Saints triumphant, bow before him
> Gather'd in from every race.

Nick thinks that, whether saints or no, under the great dome are gathered together, in the various Allied representatives, every race. He remembers how Stringham, dead in a Japanese POW camp in Singapore, used to
quote hymns because they "described people and places so well." Thoughts
of Stringham bring to mind others dead in the war, like his old roommate
Peter Templer and his cousin George Tolland.

The minister begins to read from the book of Isaiah about how, in the
new dispensation "the wilderness and the solitary place shall be glad for
them; and the desert shall rejoice, and blossom as the rose." Mention of
"the wayfaring men" who "though fools, shall not err within," makes Nick
wonder who these "fools" are: one would surely be the drunken, endearing
Bithel (whom Widmerpool had sacked from the Mobile Laundry). But
what about the perennially unsatisfied Borrit, another of Nick's wartime
companions? Borrit once told of marveling at how, traveling in Spain on
business, he noticed honeymoon couples being shown to their bedrooms,
then not being visible for a fortnight ("They've got their own ways, the
Spaniards"). We remember that Borrit was sexually disappointed; that, as
he put it once, he "never had a free poke in his life. Subject doesn't seem
to arise when you're talking to a respectable woman." Now Borrit, too, is
dead, and Nick wonders whether he ever got that "free poke" before the
grave claimed him.

More prayers, a psalm, a dull bit of preaching by the Archbishop, then
all rise to sing Blake's *Jerusalem*:

> Bring me my bow of burning gold;
> Bring me my arrows of desire;
> Bring me my spear; O Clouds unfold!
> Bring me my chariot of fire!

Was that also about sex, Nick wonders, and if so why are they singing it at the victory service? He thinks about Blake, "a genius, but not one for the classical taste. He was too cranky." Further reflections on changes in poetic fashions and on Blake's phrase "arrows of desire" makes Nick think of Cowley, a once famous poet who didn't survive his own age but (unlike Blake) is buried in Westminster Abbey. Nick recalls Pope's question about the man ("Who now reads Cowley?") and his "Pindarique art." Yet, remembering some witty lines from Cowley about lust ("Thou with strange adultery / Doest in each breast a vigil keep; / Awake, all men do lust for thee, / And some enjoy thee when they sleep"), Nick decides that the poet who wrote them shouldn't be forgotten. He compares them favorably with lines from "poor old Edgar Allan Poe" on a similar theme, Poe having recourse to "ethereal dances" and "ethereal streams." Yet it was the lines from Poe, Nick reflects, that used to run in his head when many years previously he was in love with Jean Duport.

The audience stands to sing "Now thank we all our God" —was this hymn of German origin chosen by design or inadvertence? Finally comes the national anthem and Nick decides that its second verse ("O Lord our God arise / Scatter his enemies, / And make them fall. / Confound their politics / Frustrate their knavish tricks"), is the best part, since "the verbiage of high thinking had not yet cloaked such petitions." But then and finally, in one of those gestures that permeate *Dance,* where a formulation is slightly taken back, criticized, and qualified, Nick questions his own verbiage:

> Such a mental picture of the past was no doubt largely unhistorical, indeed totally illusory, freedom from one sort of humbug merely implying, with human beings of any epoch, thraldom to another. The past, just as the present, had to be accepted for what it thought and what it was.

So ends the service and Nick's accompanying monologue, whose concluding sentence is a fine and moving example of the cast of Powell's mind. Nick and his creator resist the temptation to take a nostalgic view of history, to believe that back there somewhere people and song lyrics said what they meant, without "the verbiage of high thinking." Such a view of the past is rejected by what appears to be a theoretical idea that goes deeper into things, that explains and accounts for them; but the idea is a formula that doesn't quite formulate, since it leaves us with both past and present "to be accepted for what it thought and what it was." The surface of things, of history and character, is too much itself to be gone behind, to be violated by something less real than the way words and things look and feel and say. Like Henry James's mind according to Eliot, the narrative poise of *Dance* is so fine that no idea can violate it. So the only thing to do is reread, something any lover of Powell will do abundantly.

At the service in St. Paul's, Nick calls Blake "a genius, though not one for the classical taste. He was too cranky." Compared to Powell, the other two central writers of English comedy in recent decades, Evelyn Waugh and Kingsley Amis, seem, for all their brilliance, cranky rejecters and mockers of modern civilization. In his registration of different people, different historical periods—including the present one—Powell by contrast offers something that might be called classical. Or call it neo-classical, as summed up in Pope's fine couplet: "Let the strict life of graver mortals be / A long, exact, and serious comedy."

—*New Republic*, August 19 and 26, 1996.

Elizabeth Taylor's Otherness

OVER THE LAST couple of decades I can't exaggerate the number of people I've tried, successfully or not, to introduce to "the other" Elizabeth Taylor's fiction. Along with this proselytizing directed at worthy individuals, I've taught some of her novels to undergraduates who knew even less of her than they did of other twentieth-century novelists on the syllabus. I even managed to encourage a gifted senior, bound for law school, to write her honors essay on Taylor; and I took the opportunity, when Virago Press in England republished many of her books in the 1980s, to write a short appreciative essay about her virtues. From time to time others have tried too; most notably in a recent piece by the *Atlantic's* literary editor, Benjamin Schwarz, there have appeared attempts to sing her not-heralded-enough virtues, always to little avail. Now we have a full and fully sympathetic biography, which tells us things we—certainly I—had no inkling of. The occasion is a propitious one for some reappraisal.[1]

Elizabeth Taylor died of cancer in 1975, having over the preceding thirty years published eleven novels and four volumes of stories. (Her posthumous novel, *Blaming,* appeared the year after she died.) Nicola Beauman, who has written a biography of E. M. Forster and I presume has been living with the Taylor project for a long time, tells us she waited to publish it until Taylor's husband, John, died two years ago. To readers like myself, who accepted the picture of the devoted wife and mother sitting in her armchair writing the books, only to be interrupted periodically when family duties intervened, it seemed that the life of such a dutiful, private person would be pretty hard to make interesting. Nothing could be further from the truth, at least about the first thirty-three years of Taylor's life that preceded her first published novel, *At Mrs Lippincote's,* in 1945.

Beauman's main discovery, which gives central life to her narrative, was that not only did the married Taylor have a long-term affair with a man, Ray Russell, who belonged, as she did for many years, to the Communist Party, but that Russell was alive at age ninety and willing to share a large cache of letters from Taylor to him. (Beauman provides an affecting picture of the aged Russell observing her as, in an upstairs room at his domicile in Hull, she reads the letters and copies out passages from them.) Taylor's affair with Russell would continue intermittently for ten years, some of them years when he was interned in a prison camp during World War II. She never seriously contemplated running away with him, Beauman says, because of her two children and the agreeable conditions for writing that her husband's social and economic situation provided (John Taylor was a successful manufacturer of sweets). In the letters to Russell she alternated vague promises that sometime in the future they would live and work together (he was a furniture designer) with hopes that he will meet someone "cheerful and normal and get married." She assures him that "we are both awkward and difficult sods & understand one another as other people never have understood us. We see unguessed things in each other." The affair brought with it two abortions, after the second of which her husband insisted that she break things off with Russell. She did, the same summer that her first novel was published.

Born as Betty Coles, Taylor was sent by her parents, beginning in 1923 when she was eleven, to the Abbey School in Reading, a highly regarded institution where each year she won the top prize in English, eventually receiving 99 percent on her School Certificate English paper, the highest ever at the school. (Since no one's handwriting was perfect, she was denied a 100 percent mark.) She also delighted in history and especially Greek; alas, she failed maths, and this failure meant that any prospects of a university education were dead. Beauman gives us a poignant few sentences from her diary, apropos of her final days at school:

> I shall never forget my Greek lessons and how they excited me and it was a great grief to take my books out of my desk for the last time. Everyone else knows what they are going to do except me. I only want to write what I want to write. This evening I tried to read some of the Alcestis but it didn't seem the same. I feel as if my life is over, and I don't know what to do. Perhaps someone will marry me.

For the next fifteen years she would work as a tutor and a librarian. She found her first love in a stone- and wood-carver artist named Donald Potter, associated with the sculptor Eric Gill, at whose communal home—Piggotts Hill, near High Wycombe, Buckinghamshire—she spent much time. (She would make use of the Gill commune in her novel *The Wedding Group.)*

Beauman fills in richly the years between Taylor's graduation from Abbey School and her entry into publishing. In 1932 she wrote a fan letter to Virginia Woolf ("Dear Miss Virginia Woolf") saying how much she had admired *The Waves,* which she'd read twice: "So rarely, in prose, is anyone so keenly appreciative of individual words. It is like a symphony. Suddenly the English language is translated into fluid music, like Greek." (Woolf replied, but the letter is lost.) Taylor was quite right in pointing to the musical, symphonic effect of *The Waves.* But—and we can be thankful for it—her own novels, especially as she developed, would eschew the kind of high-pitched swoon that Woolf's novel displays. On the contrary, Taylor's fiction at its best is cool, ironic, even sardonic in its view of things, therefore much less "accepting" than the Woolfian purview in *The Waves* and elsewhere.

Looking back on her earlier self in a letter to Ray Russell in 1938, she had made up her mind that she was "naturally frigid and would never marry and have children." Neither condition turned out to be the case: in 1934, after she had joined the Communist Party, she met John Taylor, a fellow actor in the Naphill Village Players and son of the mayor of High Wycombe. A year after the birth of his and Elizabeth's son, she would begin the affair with Russell. There are some salient descriptions of her appearance and manner in her mid-twenties. One of her friends described her as not so much pretty as very beautiful; while Oliver Knox, a gifted pupil whom she tutored (he was the nephew of the prelate Ronald Knox), wrote forty years later of "her diffidence the thinnest of veils covering a decisiveness, a positiveness, even a detached sense of cruelty." This sense of cruelty can be felt—and perhaps had been by Oliver Knox in his later years—in many passages from her fiction.

From the letters to Russell we get a sense of Taylor's definite tastes and prejudices concerning her literary predecessors: the "big" novels and novelists—Dostoyevsky, Hardy, Dickens, George Eliot, D. H. Lawrence—counted for little compared to the following ones she listed in a letter: "It is easy to see who is behind me: Jane Austen, & Chekhov & E. M. Forster ["I respect this man more than any other writer now living," she wrote to

Russell] & Virginia Woolf." Of her contemporaries, Ivy Compton-Burnett and Elizabeth Bowen stood out; she seems to have been relatively uninterested in or unresponsive to American writers; at least she doesn't refer to them. As to the situation of the woman writer, she wrote as follows:

> I feel instinctively that women who have children can't write. A certain single-mindedness is denied to them. In the end, children and writing suffer. Guilt is bound up with this. Women writers do not have children—Sappho, Jane Austen, George Eliot, Miss Mitford, Fanny Burney, the Brontës, Virginia Woolf, Gertrude Stein.

Historically, this was surely the truth, and the list she compiles is a daunting one for a woman writer to flout. She flouted it nonetheless by giving up single-mindedness to focus on children as well as writing. Beauman doesn't make much of the possibility, but it may have been that having it both ways, a situation in which "children and writing suffer," was also the richly challenging enterprise that kept her going.

This is perhaps enough to suggest that the biographical part of Nicola Beauman's book is full, sympathetic, even-handed. As a critic of Taylor's fiction, she seems to me much less satisfactory, at least as far as her preferences among the twelve novels. One might say this doesn't matter, tastes differ, and readers can make up their own minds. But if a reader looked to be guided toward the peaks of her novels, he or she would, I think, be misled by Beauman's pointings. Briefly, her take seems to be that Taylor's early novels, especially the first one, *At Mrs Lippincote's,* and (even better) the fifth one, *A Game of Hide and Seek,* represent the consummation of her art and do so "because their heroines, Julia and Harriet, are her *(Madame Bovary, C'est Moi)."* This is crude, and bringing in Flaubert doesn't help matters. Aside from demurring about any fictional character being indistinguishable from its creator, we should note that by this standard any attempt on a novelist's part to imagine a protagonist substantially different from the novelist (assuming that we know what that novelist is Really Like) would be misconceived. In later references to this matter, Beauman tends to hide behind the plural in order to gather support for her opinion, as when (referring to *A Game of Hide and Seek*) she writes: "What many, this writer included, consider her masterpiece (and what some consider her last great novel)"; or says, about the same novel, it "would be seen by some as

one of the great novels about love in the English language." I see no indication, in published criticism of Taylor's works, that anyone except Beauman
considers *A Game of Hide and Seek* to be a "great novel" of any sort; indeed,
it would be a somewhat odd and dissatisfying career for a novelist to write
a great novel as she was starting out, then decline from it throughout the
remainder of her work. Beauman's solution to the problem is an attempt to
rescue Taylor's "greatness" from diminishment by holding up the short stories she had begun to publish, mainly in *The New Yorker.* So—and here is
that "some" again—"some of Elizabeth's readers may feel that after she had
written . . . *A Game of Hide and Seek* . . . that her greatness lay in her short
stories." The biographer's conviction about this is such that she uses it to
justify her description, in detail, of each one of the fifty or so stories. No
reader is likely to submit willingly to being dragged through what happens
here and there in stories that, unless one rereads them on the spot, will
elude even an agile memory.[2]

My assessment of Taylor's novels is the reverse of Beauman's, since I
judge her best to be *In a Summer Season* (her eighth) and her final two,
Mrs Palfrey at the Claremont and *Blaming. The Wedding Group,* another of
the later ones, should also be up there, and *Angel,* distinct in its subject
and treatment, must not be missed. But before turning to them briefly, a
word about the early ones Beauman admires. Taylor's debut in *At Mrs Lippincote's* is impressive, with fine presentations of the lively heroine, Julia,
as she lives with her conventional husband, Roddy, and sister-in-law in a
rented house near a military base. (Taylor lived for a time in Scarborough,
in the north, when John Taylor was stationed there.) At the novel's end,
Julia, having discovered Roddy's infidelity, tells him that "We are still the
same people. Why look like that?" Then the narrator explains: "But Roddy
wanted love only where there was homage as well, and admiration. He did
not merely want to be reckoned at his own worth." Such heavy narrative
underlining takes the zip out of Julia's subsequent declaration: "I have
never admired you, Roddy, in the ways in which you expected admiration.
In which women are supposed to admire men." The livelier things in *Mrs
Lippincote* are incidental ones, details of housekeeping and cookery, with
plenty of arrowroot mold and lemon curd and egg sandwiches as English
wartime fare.

The novel is best when Taylor's ironic humor comes into play, as it seldom does in the four novels following. *Palladian* is a sort of Gothic parody
of *Jane Eyre* and takes some effort to get through. So does, even more so, *A*

View from the Harbour, the only novel of Taylor's I failed to finish. *A Wreath of Roses,* she herself accurately characterized as having "nothing funny, no wit, no warmth, no children, no irony—it is *deadly serious.* Horribly sad, Cold, Everyone will hate it." "Everyone" didn't, but her assessment stands. These novels followed each other rapidly, between 1945 and 1950; then comes Beauman's favorite, *A Game of Hide and Seek* (1951), which game is played by the heroine, Harriet, who as a young girl fell in love with a feckless young man named Vesey. She goes on to marry a more conventional man, has a child, but is not enlivened by the "solid" life she shares with her husband. Vesey reappears, still feckless (though less healthy), and they begin a series of illicit meetings, although sex between them never quite materializes and the novel ends inconclusively. William Maxwell liked the book enough to publish its first chapter in *The New Yorker,* and at one moment in that chapter the narrator addresses a character whose life before the First World War had been idyllic. Things had fallen off since and the narrator muses:

> If we do not alter with the times, the times will alter us. We may stand perfectly still, but our surroundings shift round and we are not in the same relationship to them for long; just as a chameleon, matching perfectly the greenness of a leaf, should know that the leaf will one day fade.

This seems to me the polite laboring of a pretty unadventurous thought, uttered in a solemn, poetical tone that creeps in at other places in the book. Harriet thinks about her lover in contrast to the marital round:

> But now she flouted what she had helped to create—an illusion of society; an oiling of wheels which went round but not forwards; conventions which could only exist so long as emotion was in abeyance.

Other such passages might be adduced in which is absent the saving humor Taylor would later often employ. If, as Beauman claims, the heroine of *A Game of Hide and Seek* is equivalent to Elizabeth Taylor, then it is a less capacious and wily Taylor than we will encounter in the novels to come.

About no novel of hers is critical opinion more divided than *Angel,* written in a narrative mode unlike the others. It is a "historical" novel about a novelist based on the career of bestselling Marie Carelli, and Taylor takes Angelica Deverell from rags to riches, then, as she falls off in popularity, to the grotesque. Angel is a monster of humorless egotism; the novels she so relentlessly turns out are trumpery fantasies of high life or of Grecian romance, by a writer devoid of any self-consciousness and remorseless in subjecting others to her will. Her literary opinions are priceless—"I quite like Shakespeare . . . except when he is trying to be funny"—indeed she prides herself on not reading. As Beauman points out, she is Taylor's "doppelganger," everything awful and popular that her creator was not. But, as may be suggested by Angel's opinion about Shakespeare, this is exactly what makes her fascinating, a woman you love to be appalled by, and—as opposed to the Harriet protagonist in *A Game of Hide and Seek*—presented with a sardonic wit largely absent from Taylor's handling of figures in earlier books, whose heroines were more "like her." Beauman quotes Paul Bailey, a good critic of Taylor's work, who thought *Angel* her "boldest conception" but adds that because of the "truly desperate sincerity" with which the Marie Corelli figure is endowed, Taylor's treatment never becomes "derisive or satirical." Derisive, no; but satirical, I think, must be allowed, given the range of that word.

It was Kingsley Amis who was instrumental in directing me to Taylor's work and who thought *Angel* the best thing she had produced except for her final two novels. His review of one of them, *Mrs Palfrey at the Claremont,* contains a wonderfully succinct paragraph in which Amis calls her

> one of those novelists who look homogeneous, as if working within a single mood, and turn out to be varied and wide-ranging. There is a deceptive smoothness in her tone, or tone of voice, as in that of Evelyn Waugh; not far-fetched comparison, for in the work of both writers the funny and the appalling lie side by side in close amity.

In speaking of Taylor's final novel, *Blaming,* Amis noted what he called "Taylorian digs," "tiny bolts of a malice that almost rises to a kind of gleeful affection." I should say no "almost" about it, especially with regard to her gallery of pious, awful, sometimes pitiable women. A novel Amis underrates—at least he doesn't mention it—is *In a Summer Season,* which has as its centerpiece an extended dinner party in which everything goes wrong. Given by the heroine, Kate, married to a younger, handsome, self-destructive second husband named Dermot, the dinner consists of Kate's children, her aunt, father-in-law, and assorted others; it is perhaps her most brilliant dramatizing of a domestic event treated with malice well seasoned with affection. On a similar note, Brigid Brophy once identified in Taylor's work what she called "a moral cattiness deepening into irony." This seems a good way to suggest how Taylor turns funny and appalling life into art.

In a Summer Season has a moment when Kate's daughter Lou, responding to her aunt's saying "Perhaps we ought not to discuss people behind their backs," replies, sensibly, "We can't very well discuss them in front of them." One of Taylor's problems as a writer, which she doesn't always handle smoothly, is how to combine what someone says about "people" both in front of and behind their backs. One example among many from *In a Summer Season* occurs when the cook/housekeeper, Mrs. Meacock, inquires after Kate's mother-in-law, whom Kate has just visited in London: "'I hope you found Mrs Heron Senior well,' she said. . . . Not that I'd care twopence if she dropped down dead, she thought." There is a similar, related tendency for the novelist to exercise too easily her expert wit at the expense of a defenseless character. *Mrs Palfrey at the Caremont,* which is set in a hotel for aging citizens smack on London's busy Cromwell Road, has moments highly amusing, yet making us feel a bit guilty at how helpless are the citizens in the hands of an all-knowing narrator. Sunday dinner at the Claremont is over:

> "Well, another Sunday nearly gone," Mrs Post said quickly, to cover a little fart. She had presence of mind.
> "Now don't you wish your life away," warned Mrs Burton; but she tapped her bright finger-nails against her teeth, from boredom; and she yawned and yawned until she thought her poor jaw would give way.

The somewhat high-and-mightier Mrs. DeSalis arrives at the Claremont after convalescence in a nursing home, assuring the occupants she will not be with them for long: "She was a bird of passage as she put it, was looking for a flat in London—Cheyne Walk, she stipulated; or Little Venice. 'I love to look out over water,' she declared, looking out over the Cromwell Road." That Mrs. Palfrey herself is too kind-hearted and unmischievous for such observations makes her own vulnerable and worsening situation the more poignant.

Taylor was dying of cancer as she completed her last novel, *Blaming,* which Beauman calls a "coda" to her previous work although it stands on its own as a moving book about widowhood and loneliness. Still, it is filled with what Amis called "Taylorian digs" and a heroine who doesn't let herself off easily in her loneliness, as in thinking of her dead husband: "And I used to feel bored, she thought, and long for something bracing, even dangerous, to happen. And if he could return, I should be bored again, just the same." Amis had written to her that he planned to review the novel by way of saying "that you're a marvellous writer, among the three or four best of our time, and that your books will be admired and enjoyed as long as people can read our language." As Beauman points out, she never during her lifetime received an award. Her closest chance came when *Mrs Palfrey* made the short list for the Booker Prize, among the judges of which that year was, most famously, Saul Bellow. The chairman of the committee, John Gross, told Beauman that their first meeting began with Bellow remarking about *Mrs Palfrey,* "I seem to hear the tinkle of tea-cups." (The prize went to V. S. Naipaul.) One sees why Bellow would say this, condescending and wrong-headed as it is on the part of the great overstater. Even now, almost thirty years after *Mrs Palfrey,* and with the impetus of Nicola Beauman's admirable labors, justice will not be done to the writer whom A. N. Wilson called "in her understated way . . . among the English giants of the twentieth century." My recent trip through the novels confirms me in the conviction that, in comparison to Elizabeth Bowen and Ivy Compton-Burnett, the two contemporaries Taylor most admired, her books are more human, less cluttered and remote than Bowen's, while striking a human sympathy Compton-Burnett was not interested in pursuing. Readers are encouraged to pick up the novels and test this judgment for themselves.

—*Hudson Review,* Autumn 2009

Notes

1. *The Other Elizabeth Taylor,* by Nicola Beauman (Persephone Books, 2009). My essay about Taylor, "Almost Austen," is in *Playing It by Ear* (University of Massachusetts Press, 1994). The Benjamin Schwarz appreciation may be found in *The Atlantic,* September, 2007.
2. Among the stories I have read from Taylor's four volumes, the following stand out: "Spry Old Character" (*Hester Lilly and Other Stories*) ; "The Dedicated Man" (*The Dedicated Man*); "The Devastating Boys," and "The Fly-Paper" (*The Devastating Boys*).

Evan Connell's *Mrs. Bridge*

THE RECENT DEATH of Evan S. Connell prompts reflection on an American original who over a lifetime of steady work—many volumes of novels, stories, biography, essayistic speculations—left as his permanent contribution to letters one brilliant, memorable book: the novel *Mrs. Bridge*, published fifty-four years ago. To be sure, Connell's other work notably contained an imaginative biography of General Custer *(Son of the Morning Star)*, an account of the Crusades *(Deus lo Volt!)*, many readable short fictions, and *Mr. Bridge*, his revisiting of the Bridge family, this time from the husband and father's point of view. But nothing he subsequently wrote can match the exquisite humor and sadness of *Mrs. Bridge*. (*Mr. Bridge* is not quite in its class.) The critic Cyril Connolly once declared that the only function of a writer was to produce a masterpiece. This Connell did, and never came close again.

The novel sold well, even made the bestseller list for a respectable number of weeks, and has stayed in print over the years since. Looked at historically, and thinking of other end of-the-fifties, urban, family-oriented works that have survived, there is Philip Roth's first book, *Goodbye, Columbus* (1959), John Updike's first novel, *Rabbit, Run* (1960), Richard Yates's dark hymn to suburbia in his first novel, *Revolutionary Road* (1961), and John Cheever's stories from the period. But all of them are set in the American midcentury present; Connells novel is firmly anchored in the 1930s and early 40s, with World War II as a terminus. Nor are the other books constructed in the special way Connell made up for himself: two hundred and some pages broken up into 117 "chapters," each titled in a terse, usually humorous way. In an afterword to a recent reprint of *Mrs. Bridge*, James Salter tells us that the novel was turned down by nine publishers before Viking accepted it, and surely its unconventional form must have roused doubts, as did perhaps the less than heroic location of the action in Kansas City, Missouri, where Connell himself grew up.

Mrs. Bridge, whose odd first name is India and who never gets used to it—"It seemed to her that her parents must have been thinking of someone else when they named her" —is married to Walter Bridge, an overworking lawyer. Their three children, Ruth, Carolyn, and Douglas, are evenly spaced apart in age and over the course of the book grow up and leave the nest empty, with Mrs. Bridge desperate to fill up the days. The novel's epigraph is from Whitman's "Facing West from California's Shores": "But where is what I started for so long ago? And why is it yet unfound?" Mrs. Bridge's increasing preoccupation with the question reminds us that Connell's novel predates the second wave of feminism (Betty Friedan's *The Feminine Mystique* appeared in 1963). The novel could be viewed as evidence about the plight of married American women, whether in the 1930s or 1950s, without much life outside a kitchen full of the latest appliances. Relatedly, it might be thought of as documenting the repressed, compliant spouse, dependent for her opinions on her husband's authority and subservient to his will.

Yet to speak in this knowing way takes away the charm of Connell's presentation. For example, at one point Mrs. Bridge decides that what she needs is psychoanalysis and one night near bedtime tremulously announces this to her husband as he is reading about the stock market. "Australian wool is firm," he mutters, then looks "inquisitively" at her: "'What?' he demanded. 'Nonsense,' he said absently, and he struck the paper into submission and continued reading." There is a cool touch in the novelist's treatment of a potentially poignant confrontation that tilts things toward the aesthetic, if ever so slightly.

John Updike once denied that his relation to his characters was a satirical one; since he created them, why should he laugh at their follies? An overstatement, but useful in suggesting why it's a mistake to treat Connell's relation to his heroine as a satirical one—putting "the literary scalpel to the suburban skin," as one of his critics described it. In the first place it would not be much of a feat to score points off so unprotected and uncertain a figure as India Bridge; in the second, closely connected place, the book is simply too rich in its inventions to be so reduced. When Mrs. Bridge and her lady friends attend a stage performance of *Tobacco Road,* a once-reputed "earthy" novel by Erskine Caldwell, the ladies agree that they didn't much like the play. Mrs. Bridge doesn't see why such a play is "necessary," yet it has its effect. One hot morning she forgoes wearing stockings, then is embarrassed when two elderly widow sisters come to call: "'My goodness,' cried Mrs. Bridge as she greeted them at the door. 'I look like something out of *Tobacco Road!*'" Connell then begins a new, very short chapter with perhaps the book's longest sentence: "Having been repelled by *Tobacco Road* to the point where it obsessed her, she employed it as a pigeonhole: whatever she found unreal, bizarre, obnoxious, indecorous, malodorous or generally unsavory, unexpected, and disagreeable henceforth belonged to *Tobacco Road,* was from there, or should have been there." If this is "satire" it is of the sort T. S. Eliot once called "creative" rather than "critical"; it emanates not from an animus directed at some piece of human folly, but from an impulse to enhance the folly, rather than reduce it. So Mrs. Bridge becomes the focus of a complicated, densely witty construction rather than something to be scornfully dismissed.

Perhaps the greatest pleasure in reading *Mrs. Bridge* is the way it confirms things we've forgotten about—like Guest Towels (title of chapter thirteen). These are put out for visitors but never used, neither by them nor by members of the Bridge family. When Mrs. Bridge goes round to collect the "little pastel towels" she finds one missing, then discovers it in her son Douglas's bathroom, filthy. It has obviously been used by him, whom she finds sitting in a tree in the adjacent vacant lot and who admits to having dried his hands on it. "'These towels are for guests,' said Mrs. Bridge, and felt herself unaccountably on the brink of tears." As Douglas climbs higher into the tree she begins to feel foolish, waving the towel and addressing someone who is invisible to neighbors who might possibly be watching. The scene is perfect in its compression, concluding with her repeating that guest towels are for guests, as Douglas climbs higher in the tree.

Then there is the problem of how far to go in decorating one's house at Christmas. Mrs. Bridge (like my mother) believes in making the home "festive without being ostentatious." This she does unfailingly, and on one holiday occasion takes the children for a ride in the car to look at the Christmas decorations of others. One house, outrageously, has an enormous cutout of Santa Claus on the roof, "six reindeer in the front yard, candles in every window and by the front door an enormous cardboard birthday cake with one candle. On the cake was this message, "HAPPY BIRTHDAY, DEAR JESUS." How might an inventive writer end this chapter, titled "A Matter of Taste"? By having his heroine declare, thoughtfully, "My word, how extreme . . . Some Italians must live there."

As a professor of literature I have "taught" the novel many times (though it never feels like teaching) and always wonder what part of it to conclude with. Late in the book Mr. Bridge presents his wife with a Lincoln automobile, the size of which intimidates her. In trying to parallel park it she remembers that Douglas, in a fit of measuring things, has determined that the Bridges' pantry is approximately two cubic feet smaller than the Lincoln. But this does not assist Mrs. Bridge as she struggles to park the car, thinking "that it would have been easier to park the pantry." At the novel's end she is sitting helplessly inside their garage, the Lincoln's motor having died, without room for her to exit the vehicle. This is of course a metaphor for the lonely confinement of her life that the death of her husband and the departure of her children has brought on. It is an affecting close, but maybe too painful a note for the professor to end on.

I choose instead another moment of the woman's defeat, but one that Connell has surrounded with more than enough literary compensation. Mrs. Bridge, determined to surprise her husband with a favorite dish she hasn't made in a long time, mixes up a batch of pineapple bread to accompany the less than thrilling casserole that is dinner. "'Oh-ho!' said Mr. Bridge, rubbing his hands together, 'What have we here?'" As directed, he cuts into the fragrant-smelling loaf:

> The first slice fell down like a corpse and they saw bubbles of dank white dough around the pecans. . . . Mrs. Bridge covered it with the towel and carried it to the kitchen. Having disposed of the bread she untied her little ruffled apron and waited quietly until she regained control of herself

Returning to the dining room with a loaf of grocery store bread, she smiles and says, "It's been a long time, I'm afraid." It may have been tempting for Connell to stop right there, one more bit of pathos to be added to the ever-growing list. Instead he ends this way: "'Never mind,' said Mr. Bridge as he removed the lid of the casserole, and the next day he brought her a dozen roses." My sense is that student readers in 2013 are as touched and pleased by this scene as their parents and grandparents may be imagined to have been. Connell's art in this novel is geared to a time period, but is also timeless.

— *The Weekly Standard*, February 25, 2013.

Poets and Poetry

The Hermeneutical Mafia or,
After Strange Gods at Yale

TWENTY AND MORE years ago William F. Buckley burst upon the scene with a book telling the world how Yale professors were Godless and Keynesian, believed in neither religion nor the further rise of capitalism. At present we observe, in the same academic sanctuary, comparable attempts to frisk students of their principles as naive or enthusiastic readers by proposing new, it may well be revolutionary, ways of reading poetry and criticism. In their New Haven precincts at least, literary study is no longer the relaxed appreciating of good books à la William Lyon Phelps or William DeVane (author of *A Browning Handbook*); nor the devoted explications of irony and paradox by Cleanth Brooks or Maynard Mack. The titles of these recent books by Geoffrey H. Hartman and Harold Bloom suggest that very big game is being stalked, nothing less than the fate of reading, literature, the agonizingly problematical nature of poetry and its interpretation. Since the most common adjective used to describe their work is "brilliant," I shall accept that term as fair enough. But I propose here to look at a few of the brilliant sentences and paragraphs that make up their latest as well as earlier books, then to draw some conclusions about the world they invite us to enter and the style through which they engage it.

In reviewing Hartman's new book, Richard Poirier (*New York Times Book Review*, April 20, 1975) advised us that, along with his previous ones, particularly the essays collected in *Beyond Formalism* (1970), it asks to be "taken as part of a community enterprise meant to constitute the most significant challenge to literary studies since Northrop Frye and, before that, I. A. Richards." Besides Hartman's colleague Harold Bloom, the most prominent members of that community enterprise are two other colleagues, Paul de Man and J. Hillis Miller, whose works are equally well known and who are often to be found giving papers and addresses at

meetings of the M.L.A., the English Institute, and other professional orga-
nizations. When Poirier at one point in his review asks who the imagined
audience is for Hartman's book, one barely suppresses the thought that
members of this community seem to be writing and speaking above all to
each other.[1] This is understandable: they share a passion for comparative
literature and Continental philosophical, psychological and literary speculation; they read Derrida, Poulet, Lacan, and Blanchot; structuralism is
mother's milk to them; eristics, hermeneutics, and propadeutics no more
than ordinary language at ordinary evenings in New Haven. And except
for de Man, about whose preference I'm not sure, the supreme modern
poet, the last word on all thing visible and invisible is their necessary angel,
Wallace Stevens.

Yet, and to confine things for the moment to Hartman's essays, this
reader often feels desperate, wondering how he could possibly remake his
life so as seriously to be touched by the problems the critic sees as troubling
and exciting. In his lead essay ("The Interpreter") to the new book Hartman provides us with paragraphs about the excitements and dangers of
"interrupting" a "text" (the Yale people always deal with texts, never mere
books) and then discusses the "alternate" or "*déjà lu*" theory of describing
our responses to individual works. Interpretation as "interruption" can be
understood as "a shadowy double of the work of art," or, in the alternate
theory

> act and shadow are considered of equal dignity. Both, that is,
> reflect the possibility of a Heavenly City of Mutual Discourse.
> At the same time the reactive or *a posteriori* character of inter-
> pretation, which includes its dependence on source texts, is
> questioned. The hermeneutic universe now envisaged is no lon-
> ger a closed system, with Classics at the center, spin-off works
> as satellites, and the critic-interpreter either encouraging such
> spinoffs by denying exhaustive centrality to certain books (and
> so keeping the system expanding) or discouraging them (and
> inviting closure), "The stubborn center must / Be scattered . . ."
> (Shelley).
>
> There are disadvantages too, in terms of literary-critical *praxis*.
> (I do not try to judge the theory except in this light.) By dimin-
> ishing the book-centeredness of literary discourse you bring it
> closer to philosophical discourse and run the risk of homogeniz-

ing it. True, you may still have "texts" rather than "books"—but what constitutes a text is a slippery thing to define, and the tendency of Heidegger to excerpt freely, of Derrida to use a highly repetitive or snippety canon, and of Lacan to meld everything into his prose by inner quotation produces an intensely frustrating *clair-obscur*. Theology also fragmented scripture into prooftexts, yet the literal text remained, and the discrepancy between letter and figurative development was the very space of revisionary shock or "hermeneutic reversal." Now, however, the *facticity* of a book, or the *force* of a "dialectical lyric" like Hölderlin's "Der Rhein" or Shelley's "Mont Blanc" or Kierkegaard's *Fear and Trembling* may be lost.

Hartman has just referred, in his preface, to a certain group of critics that "justifies everything by the pragmatic test of the classroom, as if the world had to pass through that needle's eye, or as if a pedagogy accommodated to the pressures of a particular community were the best we could hope for." Nobody wants to be a miserable pragmatist, but I think the test of the classroom—of a good classroom, that is, since they vary—would be less of a needle's eye than the aperture Hartman has constructed for us to get through in the above paragraphs. That is to say, anyone who spends any time in class with students is aware that whether you call the thing in front of you (or wherever it is) a "book" or a "text," you will be dealing with a slippery thing, and you will find it wise not to "define" it for more than a minute or two lest someone should interrupt you to say, no that is not it at all. We learned this pretty early along, as teachers or students, just as we learned that words are not things, art not life, the "unmediated vision" (the title of Hartman's first book) what isn't around to be had, or is to be had only in a world of abstraction. Hartman's abstracting is off-putting because of the style in which it's conducted: reactive spin-offs on the one hand, hermeneutics and closure on the other (or is it the same hand?), with a line from Shelley vainly stabbing at uniting them. To say nothing of *praxis* (practice?) and *clair-obscurs* and *facticity* (equaled only by Bloom's favorite, *rhetoricity*). Taken together these, like other and even more striking overreachings in Hartman's style, make up *clair-obscurs* that are intensely frustrating. Stop for a moment and ask yourself who in the world of readers—classroom or otherwise—"may" ever lose the facticity of Hölderlin's or Shelley's poems. Who ever had the facticity of Kierkegaard's difficult meditation to lose anyway? But we refer now to ordinary readers rather than these extraordinary troubled men of Yale.

Perhaps not all that troubled. Most of the time Hartman seems the opposite of anguished and not overburdened with, as he calls it, the fate of reading. *Beyond Formalism* contained a thick swatch of overwhelmingly learned essays on aspects of poetic language in Milton, Marvell, Blake, Wordsworth, Hopkins; the new book continues these interpretative performances with ones on Smart, Keats, Goethe, and Valéry. I respect, and at times receive, genuine pleasure and illumination from such essays, even though I find them written in never much less than a daunting style, and though the level at which they operate is refined perhaps beyond the point not merely of desirable but of civilized practice, in or out of the classroom. Still, such essays have a specifiable audience, one of academics whose favorite magazines are *New Literary History, ELH,* and others less well known to me. In this league, and it is a big enough league, Hartman is one of the very best players of the interpretive game; although if you are going to play it with him you must prepare yourself to read a footnote like the following to an essay on Akenside's "Ode to the Evening Star":

> The preposition "to" in st. 1 foregrounds itself so strongly that, to subordinate it, one is tempted to read it on the pattern of "to-night" (i.e., proclitically) and so bring it closer to the bonded preposition "sub" in *supply, suppliant* (a near pun, anticipating the reversal mentioned above) and even *suffer.* Compare the syntax of st. 6; also the "prefer" of 1.19 which makes "vows" both its direct and indirect object. It draws attention once more not only to the prepositional but also to the syntactical bonding of one verse-line with another. All this fosters a sense of the discontinuous or precarious path followed by the verses' "feet." It is interesting that in Christopher Smart's *Song to David* (1763) the problem of hierarchy, subordination (hypotaxis), and prepositional-syntactical bonding reaches an acute stage.

This is not quite a grammarian's funeral but it sounds like it, and Hartman's most strenuous engagements with verbal matters (his earlier essay "The Voice of the Shuttle" shows them at their best) are forbiddingly couched so as to resist all but the most devoted reader—and of Dr. Mark Akenside to boot. And so when, in the title essay to *The Fate of Reading,*

Hartman announces things like the following—"This indifference, an apathy or arbitrariness of emotional reaction, or an orgasmic shuttle of both together, remains a complex phenomenon"—the reader may very well conclude he'd rather be in Philadelphia. Whose indifferent apathy or arbitrary emotional reaction combined into which shuttle is he supposed to care about? In case you accuse me of quoting out of context, be assured that the reference is to, in the preceding paragraph, "the activist potential of articulated or publicized thought, in whatever form."

In his review Poirier refers to Hartman's "sometimes gleeful unintelligibility," and the other review I've seen (Denis Donoghue's in *T.L.S.*, August 29, 1975) also admits to unhappiness with the critic's style. Both of them, though, are more forgiving of these lapses and more generous in their appreciation of Hartman's virtues than I can find myself to be; and neither reviewer evidently finds more than trivial faults, since neither mentions them, Hartman's misquoting of lines and his heavyhanded attempts at lightness of touch. "I admit to a variable style, which consists mainly of a playful dissolving of terms and abstractions . . ." he winks at us; but without systematic checking of his quotations my ear caught the following dissolvings of lines originally written otherwise. The examples are from his two books of essays, and I specify the poet misquoted: "As flies to wanton boys, so are we to the gods" (Shakespeare); "The forward Youth that would appear / Must forsake his muses dear" (Marvell); "blanket of the night" (Shakespeare); "a road not taken" (Frost); "The best lack all conviction, and the worst are full of passionate intensity" (Yeats); "Soldier, there is a war between the mind and the sky" (Stevens); plus the invention of Stevens-titles like "The Snowman" and "L'Esthetique du Mal." I don't mean to claim that Hartman is in Stephen Spender's league in the misquoting stakes (see the latter's *Love-Hate Relations* for the champion book in this respect), but what these errors suggest to me is that his ear for the rhythm and tone of individual lines of poetry is a good deal less secure than his formidable ability to spin words around them. He gives us the ritual or Continental business about how "complex" it is "to decide where a text ends or begins," then seems to find it similarly complex to decide whether accurate quotation is worthwhile.

His "playful" style is even more bothersome: "Is criticism a yea, yea, nay nay affair, best conducted in as dry a prose as possible?" No, professor, it is not, but the alternative to dryness needn't be the following bit of liveliness from "History Writing as Answerable Style": "Our hearts are sad at the culture supermarket; packaged historical reminiscences meet us everywhere; the Beatles' *Yellow Submarine* is a moving toyshop of topoi." Hartman's invoking of 1960s pop has the effect of too-eagerly assuring us that an erudite fellow like him can relax too. And like pop like feminism: "It is proper to recall here Pope's wittily sexist observation that 'Women have no character at all.'" But of course it is highly improper, because Pope never wrote a line close to the one Hartman invents, nor did the author of "Epistle to a Lady" make (like Johnny Carson, say) "wittily sexist" remarks. "But let me damp my superciliousness," he nervously intrudes into his essay "On the Theory of Romanticism," and in the acknowledgments to *The Fate of Reading* salutes his wife who "occasionally tried to chasten my style." Mrs. Hartman must have desisted or nodded during the title essay when her spouse got on to the following conceit: "The point is . . . that sexuality is simply a pointing. If you don't get the point, there is little one can do. You fear castration, and you hover compulsively, emptily, near that point. 'Omne tulit punctum' said horny Horace. A promiscuous metaphor is better than a faceless literalism. So Freud moves on, winning his point!" Such depressing high jinks are, I'm convinced, a consequence of Hartman's desire to expatiate on all sorts of nonsubjects (like The Fate of Reading) we can well live without investigating. At any rate the playful style has its grim corollary in the unanswerable one, as when the historical space between Hegel and Greece "is less the space of mystery than of interpretation: it is hermeneutic as well as pneumatic. Hegel stands here on the threshold of the passage from *Geistergeschichte* to *Geistesgeschichte*." "No man is an island (except some Englishmen)," he wittily remarks at one point, and I rejoin, standing there on the threshold with the abominable Hegel and his hermeneutics, Give me Leavis, nay give me Grigson, nay give me Clive James even. Or just give me an American like William James who said in 1882 that "Hegel's philosophy mingles mountain-loads of corruption with its scanty merits."

But let us turn instead to Harold Bloom, introducing him through Hartman's summary of Bloom's argument in *The Anxiety of Influence* (1973). Since I do not believe, as Bloom claims in his dedication, that the new *A Map of Misreading* should be understood as "an antithetical completion" to the earlier book, I take Hartman's description to be still accurate:

> [Each essay from] . . . this dense, eloquent and experiential
> brooding . . . defines what is called a "revisionary ratio," that is,

a specific type of "misreading" which helps poets to overcome the influence of previous poets. Influence is understood as dangerously preemptive (hence the anxiety), as an in-flowing that tends to become a flooding, so that for the later poet to survive means to wilfully revise (euphemistically, "correct") his precursor. . . . Bloom seeks "a wholly different criticism" which would transfigure source-study by revealing in each poem, or in the poet's corpus as a whole, echoings of a precursor, imitations as complex as those by which the child wrests his life-space from parents.

Assuming most readers of this magazine will by now be somewhat familiar with this argument, at least in its compressed form, and because the bypaths Bloom pursues can't be adequately paraphrased or charted (is he not, his own terms, a Strong Poet?), I shall inquire instead whether Bloom's "wholly different practical criticism," as practiced by himself, delivers the goods so loudly promised by his theoretical performance.

First, though, it is silly to pretend that anyone comes to Bloom's work with a wholly open mind, ready somehow objectively to weigh the evidence, then "agree" or "disagree." From the beginning of his productions as a critic he has made no pretense to open-mindedness or fairness. Like Robert Graves in only one respect (Graves who was reprimanded by his Oxford tutor for preferring some books to others), Bloom has from the start been polemical, even pugilistic. My own reading of him began with *Shelley's Mythmaking* (1959), an intemperate, exaggerated defense of Shelley against which I had to examine my inert received notions (received from Leavis, alas) of how Shelley's poetry would not do at all. More recently Bloom's book on Yeats energetically combated received opinion about the Yeats canon and his status as a great poet. And *The Ringers in the Tower* (1971) contained strongly argued essays on Keats, Shelley, appreciations of Ruskin and Pater as literary men, good accounts of Robinson, Hart Crane, and an extremely useful one of Stevens's "Notes Toward a Supreme Fiction."

On the basis of his published work, then, Bloom seems most himself and most engaging as a proselytizer for neglected, misvalued or imperfectly understood creative work—mainly poetry—produced by English and American writers—mainly since 1800. As a provocative spokesman he needs constantly to be argued with, but this is good for a reader's faculties and provides an experience different in kind from most academic assays.

And there are passages in Bloom's latest books where he indulges in sweeping annoyances which seem to me to make for health and life—as when in *Anxiety of Influence* he excoriates "the anti-humanistic plain dreariness of all these developments in European criticism that have yet to demonstrate that they can aid in reading any one poem by any one poet whatsoever." He is also, at moments, less than absolute for his own theory, suggesting at the beginning of *Map of Misreading* that the theory's truth may be irrelevant to its usefulness for practical criticism; though perhaps this disclaimer permits him all the more to be extravagant in unqualifiedly setting forth the reader's situation: "Reading, despite all humanist traditions of education, is very nearly impossible, for every reader's relation to every poem is governed by a figuration of belatedness." Is there any point in saying that some of us old-fashioned humanists thought coming late to the poem— sometime well after it was written—was what made reading *possible* as well as necessary? But with "very nearly impossible," the bold formulation takes itself back just enough for safety's sake.

Of course one feels less than magnanimous in asking such common-sense questions since, as Bloom has said in *Anxiety,* "strong poets can only read themselves. For them, to be judicious is to be weak, and to compare, exactly and fairly, is to be not elect." From his writing, I presume Bloom has taken this admonition to heart, and that strong critics also must abjure these weaker virtues. How it applies to style is revealed through his quoting, of all people, the Elizabethan rhetorician George Puttenham on the "far-fetcher" trope—"as when we had rather fetch a word a great way off than to use one nearer hand to express the matter aswel and plainer . . . so . . . leaping over the heads of a great many words, we take one that is furdest off, to utter our matter by. . . . " An example from the new book, in which Bloom proposes to consider "a Post-Enlightenment crisis-lyric of major ambitions and rare achievement, wholly in the abstract," must suffice to illustrate how faithfully he has followed up Puttenham's tip:

> Applying the Lurianic dialectics to my own litany of evasions, one could say that a breaking-of-the-vessels always intervenes between every *primary* (limiting) and every *antithetical* (representing) movement that a latecomer's poem makes in relation to a precursor's text. When the latecomer initially swerves (clinamen) from his poetic father, he brings about a contraction or withdrawal of meaning from the father, and makes/breaks his

own false creation (fresh wandering or error-about-poetry). The answering movement, *antithetical* to this *primary*, is the link called *tessera*, a completion that is also an opposition, or restorer of some of the degrees-of-difference between ancestral text and the new poem. This is the Lurianic pattern of *Zimzum→Shevirath ha-kelim→Tikhun*, and is enacted again (in finer tone) in the next dialectical pair of ratios, *kenosis* (or undoing as discontinuity) and *daemonization* (the breakthrough to a personalized Counter-Sublime).

The paragraph (and the "analysis") goes on, but I cease to quote, only admitting that Bloom in one of his many maddening incorporations of Wallace Stevens's lines into his own prose calls what he is doing here "the accomplishment of an extremist in an exercise." Hartman finds these terms "exuberantly eclectic," and I suppose one might revel in the high spirits of such extremity, since there is certainly no point in objecting to what looks like deliberate devilishness. Yet when later on Bloom confides (to whom? the elect?) that "I will try to remember that the common reader cares little to be taught to notice tropes or defenses," it may well be hazarded that this common reader, not necessarily to be despised, would more willingly submit to such instruction if it were expressed in English.

When Bloom gets round to considering post-Enlightenment crisis-lyrics in the concrete they still sound pretty abstract. An important exhibit is Wordsworth's Immortality Ode and its relation to the precursor, Milton. Here is a sample from Bloom's commentary on stanzas I-IV of the poem:

> The first part begins with images of absence, the realm of 'there was a time!' There is an *illusio* here, for though Wordsworth actually fears that a Glory has passed away from himself, he says it has passed from the earth. As a defense, this reaction-formation wards off instinctual impulses by means of that mode of self-distrust that creates the superego. Poetically, instinctual impulses are internalized influences from a precursor-fixation, and Wordsworth's selfdistrust reacts therefore to Milton's strength. "Intimations" in the title means something very like "signs" or "tokens" and the title therefore suggests that the poem is a searching for evidences, almost a quest for election. The precursor poem, in a deep sense, is Milton's *Lycidas*, and

> Wordsworth's Ode also is intended primarily to be a dedica-
> tion to the poet's higher powers, a prolepsis of the great epic
> he hoped still to write. But that intention, though it will deter-
> mine the poem's final attempt at a transumptive stand towards
> Milton, seems largely negated by much of the poem's first two
> movements.

This writing veers uneasily from loose, "ordinary" language—Wordsworth
"reacting" to Milton, the poem "almost" a quest for election (all Romantic
poems are of course, for Bloom, Quests), *Lycidas* being the precursor "in a
deep sense" —to psychoanalytic paraphrase, for which the ideal reader is
clearly Vladimir Nabokov, and finally to the shiny terms wheeled out for
inspection—transumption and prolepsis and more to follow. But there is
precious little about the "movements" of Wordsworth's poem at the level
of voice and diction, and nothing about them at the level of sound, pace,
rhythm—the level at which everything is heard. The "strong" way of writing about poems is often a barbarous and sometimes a bathetic way. "I am
myself an uneasy quester after lost meanings," says the on-stage troubled
critic, sinking as he speaks.

Moreover, to be strong is to bully, and especially there to be bullied
is that common reader who needs to be told who is better than whom.
For example: Browning, we learn from Bloom's headnote in the *Oxford
Anthology of English Literature,* surpasses not only his rival Tennyson but
all modern poets "including even Yeats, Hardy, and Wallace Stevens, let
alone the fashionable modernists whose reputations are now rightly in
rapid decline." What must be said to this is Nonsense, Eliot's reputation is
in decline of no sort, except in Bloom's head; and nonsense it is too to talk
about Browning's "surpassing" the other moderns we care most about and
whose work helped us shuck off Browning. (This is heresy, I am aware; I
have also read Browning recently with some care, and he surpasses neither
these modern poets nor Tennyson.) But at the least such big talk should be
backed up by practical criticism of Browning's work; instead Bloom offers
us in the new book yet a further analysis of "Childe Roland" —he had ana-
lyzed it twice before, once in *Ringers,* once in *Anxiety*—proving once more
to his own satisfaction that it is a great quest poem.

The large-mannered motions Bloom makes in the directions of poems
often seem not very practical criticism at all, indeed not very critical. I
could not begin to quote the numbers of times lines or phrases from Wal-

lace Stevens are woven into Bloom's sentences, as they are into Hartman's, the allusions never ironic (as in the one I committed just above) but rather celebratory and reverential. Though not quite as "great" as Browning, Stevens now seems to be beyond any attention other than devoted construing and quoting as "proof" of the critic's high argument. So even a minor, pleasant little poem like "The Rabbit as King of the Ghosts" becomes (in *Anxiety*) an example of poetic *askesis* which "compensates for the poet's involuntary shock at his own daemonic expansiveness. Without askesis, the strong poet, like Stevens, is fated to become the rabbit as king of the ghosts." And after quoting some lines which end with "You become a self that fills the four corners of night," Bloom adds "Humped high, humped up, the poet will become a carving in space unless he can wound himself *without further emptying himself of his inspiration.* He cannot afford another *kenosis.*" Proceeding in this vein, Bloom turns what I as common reader had thought was Stevens's indulgence of the rabbit's momentary grandeur into (it turns out to be instead) a cautionary tale for the modern strong poet who needs a good dose of askesis to counteract his kenosis. In the process, not only has the individual poem been ransacked, its pleasantly odd language ("Humped high, humped up") wrenched out of the poet's context into the critic's (the word "carving," which doesn't occur in the Rabbit poem, may have been borrowed for the occasion from "The Auroras of Autumn" where "The necklace is a carving, not a kiss") and the whole business humped very high indeed.

Space forbids my pursuing further examples of what strikes me as huffing and puffing rather than demonstration. But I will refer to an instance of such in *Misreading* when Hardy's final book, *Winter Words,* is put forth as a "superb volume" to which "few books of twentieth-century verse . . . compare . . . in greatness." This would be marvelous if true, and I can only ask the student of Hardy's verse to read through *Winter Words* and see if with the best of intentions and loving respect for the old poet he can find Bloom's statement to be more than hyperbolic and misleading (misreading, if he'd prefer). But, and again, no practical criticism of the poems is provided; rather Bloom has his eyes on the precursor Shelley, on "The Return of the Dead" [Apophrades], on "the chastened return of High Romantic Idealism." If you accept Bloom's systematic theorizing it *does* make a difference after all, for whether or not it's true you will begin to see the last poems of Hardy to which it's applied become portentous, exemplary, and therefore great.

As for his taste with regard to contemporary writers, Bloom finds Robert Lowell "anything but a permanent poet . . . mostly a maker of period-pieces from his origins until now." John Ashbery, however, because he expresses the American Counter-Sublime and follows on from the deified Stevens, is a "radiant" poet ("an inevitable comfort in our current darkness," says Bloom, darkly, elsewhere). "Radiance" is one of Bloom's favorite good words, and I am not able quite to fathom what richnesses it portends. A. R. Ammons is also extremely radiant, but Norman Mailer is extremely flawed, while Saul Bellow really isn't all that satisfactory, and Bloom prefers Pynchon to Mailer, but. . . . At which point someone says, don't you see that he is a *romantic?* to which I answer, yes and I see also why he should have spent much energy in castigating T. S. Eliot and the "churchwardenly critics" (Bloom's phrase, proving he himself is no sissy) who were supposedly crippled by their priest. For Eliot pointed out in *The Sacred Wood*, apropos George Wyndham, that "Romanticism is a short cut to the strangeness without the reality" and that Wyndham employed it "to complete the varied features of the world he made for himself." So, Eliot concluded, the only cure for Romanticism was to analyze it. To be cured of his own Romanticism Bloom, and Hartman too, would need to draw upon modes of self-irony, possibilities for a comic perspective on things (and here they could take a lesson from their admired Kenneth Burke), which they are surely not about to do. Listen to Bloom on Blake's Tyger: "Hartman acutely points out that 'fearful symmetry' in *The Tyger* should be read as 'fearful ratio,' since *The Tyger's* speaker is the ephebe and the Tyger's maker the precursor. The Tyger, as Hartman suggests, is thus a Spectre or Covering Cherub, imposed by the late-comer imagination upon itself." Let it be pointed out then that there are, still are, other people listening to, reading, reading Yale professors in hopes of extending their literary-critical imaginations, but they may not find it in them to stay much longer at this exclusive hermeneutical shindig.

—*Hudson Review*, Winter 1976.

Notes

1. *Beyond Formalism* was dedicated to Bloom; Bloom's collection of essays *The Ringers in the Tower*, to Hartman. Hartman's new collection contains a review of Bloom's *Anxiety of Influence* ("this dense, eloquent, and experiential brooding"), while his previous one had a backcover blurb from Hillis Miller ("This admirable book, a subtle and long-mediated version of literary history"). Paul de Man, the subtlest analyst and best writer of the community, publishes relatively little compared to the others. Particularly unforgettable are moments in which one of the giants confronts another; I remember an English Institute meeting at Colombia when, in the discussion period following Bloom's talk, Miller rose to ask a question and was recognized by Bloom in some such terms as "my great antagonist" (or was it "mighty opposite"?"). At such moments other academics in the room felt kind of humble and kind of proud.

Talking Back to Emily Dickinson

THE BOLD TITLE has a personal reference, since in decades of reading and teaching English and American poetry, I've largely managed to avoid talking back to, indeed talking *about,* Emily Dickinson. My occasional attempt to engage one of her poems in class hasn't been markedly successful; visits to the Homestead in Amherst, with some curious out-of-towner in tow, never yielded much; not even the just-effected presence of a piece of sculpture in a little park near the Homestead (in which she is presumed to be in "colloquy" with Robert Frost, another piece of Amherst sculpture facing her) could propel me into serious reading of her. Only the invitation to speak to this audience was strong enough to launch me on a three-month crash course in the poems and some of what has been written about them. Any interest these remarks have must come, then, from a non-Dickinsonian, even a nonbeliever's immersion in a bewildering body of verse.

Bewildering, in that the more I read her and about her, the more uncertain I become about questions of value, of just how much—as F. R. Leavis used to say—the achievement "weighs" and what kind of achievement it is anyway. More than a hundred years ago, W. D. Howells began his review of the Todd-Higginson first selection by referring to "the strange *Poems of Emily Dickinson.*" A century later, in his Dickinson chapter in *The Western Canon,* Harold Bloom has recourse to the same word—"as strange as Dante or Milton"—he also drags in the fashionable "uncanniness"—then asserts that strangeness is the prime requirement for entry into the canon. In opening the door for Dickinson, Bloom praises her "extraordinarily cognitive power," her display, again and again, of "tough writing and hard thinking" that puts her in league with Dante, Milton, and William Blake. Bloom's student Camille Paglia is equally enthusiastic about her in the fifty pages that, with a flourish, conclude *Sexual Personae:* for Paglia,

Dickinson is Amherst's Madame de Sade, a denatured vampire whose masculine, sadistic poetic speech and brutal metaphors unite her with Blake and Spenser in "helping 'pagan' Coleridge defeat Protestant Wordsworth." For Paglia, not only does nature betray the heart that loves her, nature does so with wonderfully satisfying violence: "Wham! Chop! Faster than a speeding spear, the Dickinson ear demolishes a hapless heart, which is like a piece of liver hewn by the cook's cleaver." (This in relation to the final stanza of poem #1764—"An ear can break a human heart / As quickly as a spear, / We wish the ear had not a heart / So dangerously near" — an utterance that seems to this reader something less than a wham-chop operation.)

Of course neither Bloom nor Paglia ever understated anything, their mode of literary commentary being heated, strident, excessive, and sometimes very entertaining. Still, it's possible Dickinson's is the kind of poetry one can say almost anything about without being arrested and hauled into court. It is extremely hospitable, that is, to readings, interpretations, valuations that are quite at odds with one another. To some extent this is true of any poet, but a lot more so of Dickinson than, say, Ben Jonson, or William Cowper, or Byron, or Philip Larkin—poets with whom, to my knowledge, she has never been compared. This up-for-grabs quality has importantly to do with my Dickinson problem, if perhaps not yours, the problem of explaining why I've had trouble "talking back to Dickinson" or—in the words of a recent book title—why I have "the trouble with genius."

Let me begin not with some patently problematic poem to which critical response has been uncertain, but with one universally admired. "Because I Could Not Stop for Death" first appeared in the Higginson-Todd selection of 1890, was written about by the New Critics Allen Tate and Yvor Winters and by many since. I have no fresh reading of the poem to offer, nor would I suggest it is any less powerful than readers have found it to be. Yet a clear account of it, of its value, is not easy to provide:

> Because I could not stop for Death—
> He kindly stopped for me—
> The Carriage held but just Ourselves—
> And Immortality.
>
> We slowly drove—He knew no haste
> And I had put away

My labor and my leisure too,
 For His Civility—

We passed the School, where Children strove
 At Recess—in the Ring—
We passed the Fields of Gazing Grain—
We passed the Setting Sun—

Or rather—He passed Us—
The Dews drew quivering and chill
For only Gossamer, my Gown—
My Tippet—only Tulle—

We paused before a House that seemed
A Swelling of the Ground—
The Roof was scarcely visible—
The Cornice—in the Ground—

Since then—'tis Centuries—and yet
Feels shorter than the Day
I first surmised the Horses' Heads
Were toward Eternity—

                    #712

Todd and Higginson changed the opening of stanza 3 to "We passed the school where children played / Their lessons scarcely done" (so as to rhyme with "sun"); they omitted the fourth stanza, made the Cornice of the penultimate stanza a "mound" (so as to avoid the Ground / Ground rhyme), and rewrite "and yet / Feels shorter" in the final stanza to "but each / Feels shorter."

An early reviewer in the *Boston Evening Transcript* was in no doubt about what the poem meant nor that he admired it: "Clearly, Death is here regarded . . . as a benignant and friendly being; the poet was not allowed voluntarily to seek him out, so he kindly waited for her and introduced her to Immortality, where a thousand years are as one day." This reviewer was the first of many to admire the personified "gazing grain," and he recommended learning the poem by heart. Tate's pioneering essay of 1932 was even more certain of its high value: "One of the most perfect poems in English"; "one of the greatest in the English language." Tate admired its images as they were fused into a central idea, also the "subtly interfused erotic motive" and the way the terror of death "is made ironically to serve the end of Immortality." He said the poem presented, but didn't resolve, a typical Christian theme: "There is no solution of the problem; there can be only a presentation of it in the full context of intellect and feeling." A few years later Winters also found it a "beautiful poem" whose subject was "the daily realization of the immanence of death." He thought however that its final statement was "not offered seriously" and that insofar as it attempted to experience "the death to come," it was "fraudulent." But as a presentation of the life being left behind, the poem was "wholly successful."

More recent critics have found it says a number of different things: Clark Griffith discovers "psychological ambivalence" and declares that when "Dickinson thinks about her own death she can not honestly make up her mind about what her feelings and attitudes are." Sharon Cameron finds a "dialectic in which the self comes to terms with its impulse for fusion and identic relationship, and with the loss attendant upon realizing that such fusion is truly illusory." Vivian Pollak says that it "enacts the death of her quest motif" and that Dickinson is suggesting that "life contains many such deaths." Cynthia Griffin Wolff finds in it a victory, "the poet's victory over time and mortality." Judith Farr is convinced that when Dickinson arrives at her grave, she "also realizes she has been buried for many years" (for Farr, the "Ground/Ground" rhyme shows Dickinson's complete assurance that the grave is "an airless vacuum, out of Nature") and finds the dash at the poem's end a declaration that "unending immortality has been achieved," that the poem "is thus her supreme assertion of the continuance of the self or soul." Jane Eberwein is convinced, on the contrary, that not Dickinson but "the speaker mistakes Death for a human suitor," and that by the poem's end the deluded woman has ended up "with eternity as an inadequate substitute for either Immortality or Mortality."

These statements by Dickinson scholars about what happens in "Because I Could Not Stop for Death" are set forth with a minimum of qualification and uncertainty. For all the aggressive reading they display, they have little to say about what, in other poets, would engage us—matters of tone, of verse movement, of compelling imagery. (The field of "Gazing Grain" is admired, but what of the Gossamer Gown and "Tippet—only Tulle," which sounds a bit to these ears like the Belle of Amherst?) Some have found it amusing that Dickinson's poems in common meter like "Because I Could Not Stop" can be sung to the tune of "The Yellow Rose of Texas" (I have heard it performed by a chorus). Should an account of it engage the question of how or whether Dickinson's rhythms subtly play off against the metrical grid? How should the drama in the poem—if indeed it is a "dramatic" lyric—be described, and in what sort of tone should it be delivered? (Randall Jarrell once described the opening address as something like "We have a nice hotel room. The girl, myself, and the Sphinx.") Rather than talk back to Dickinson's poem, critics tend to talk *for* her by bringing out, usually at length, what it is she's implying, not just stating, in the poem. The Russian poet Marina Tsvetaeva once called the short lyric poem "a catastrophe. It's hardly begun when it's already come to be ended. The cruelest self-torture." Critics of Dickinson's short poems seem to be in the business of prolonging, by drawing them out into coherent statements that bear only obliquely on the poem as experienced.

One further response to "Because I Could Not Stop" and, by extension, to a significant part of Dickinson's poetry: This was Philip Larkin's, when with reference to "the Day" of her surmise in the poem's final stanza, Larkin wondered whether it was the day Dickinson realized that "love was not for her, but only death." He quickly dismisses his query as useless, saying that she was determined to keep hidden the nature of her preoccupations, "that her inspiration derived in part from keeping it hidden," and that the price she paid "was that of appearing to posterity as perpetually unfinished and willfully eccentric." Then, in a formulation that has stayed with me, Larkin says that "too often the poem expires in a teased-out and breathless obscurity."

Larkin was talking back to Dickinson out of his own practice as a poet who took the greatest pains to avoid obscurity, breathless or not, and who did so partly through a technique of extended specification and delicately nuanced tone. I shall return to his charge, indirectly, later on but consider now another famous Dickinson poem, perhaps her best-known one about the soul. Are we clear what happens in it and do we need to be?

> The Soul selects her own Society—
> Then—shuts the Door—
> To her divine Majority—
> Present no more—
>
> Unmoved—she notes the Chariots—pausing—
> At her low Gate—

Unmoved—an Emperor be kneeling
Upon her Mat—

I've known her—from an ample nation—
Choose One—
Then—close the Valves of her attention—
Like Stone

#303

In early editions it was titled "The Exclusion" and reviewers cited its first stanza as an example of Dickinson's "reticent" or "nun-like" behavior. Recent commentary concurs to some extent, as Eberwein says in a flash of understatement, "Evidently, Dickinson found most people unrewarding." Griffith in a similar vein decides that "she worships only at an inward shrine" and effects "a spiritualization of the total self." Charles Anderson, on the one hand, finds various possibilities for the "One" chosen, speculating that it "may be muse rather than lover." On the other hand, "as suggested by the capitalization," the "One" may be God. (But should one try to make *anything* out of Dickinson's capitalization?) Wolff, however, finds her rejecting the deity and choosing "One other with herself," a choice, she claims, that is signaled by the final line, "a two-word spondee." Shira Wolowsky decides that the "One" chosen might, like Emerson's or Whitman's, "still include all," although this "One" seems to be "just herself." There's a question, then, of just how exclusive is this exclusion; I see no definitive way to answer the question.

A traditional way of trying to answer it—at least since I.A. Richards and the New Critics—was to direct us to matters of tone and voice, the relation of speaker to listener. When Archibald MacLeish came to Amherst's bicentennial in 1960 to speak about "Emily" (as he called her) he put all his eggs in the tonal basket: "It is the tone rather than the words that one remembers afterwards." And what were the main characteristics of that tone? It was a "wholly spontaneous" one in which "Something is being *said.*" Moreover, what is being said, or spoken, speaks to *you*—there is an intensely direct relation between poet and reader. MacLeish quoted bits from poems to illustrate this "spontaneous" immediate tone, but—perhaps wisely—did not attempt to describe or characterize what, in the individual instance, it sounded like: after all, if the Tone was "wholly spontaneous," why should any particular description of it be useful or accurate?

What *is* there to say about the tone of the first stanza: "The Soul selects her own Society / Then—shuts the Door— / To her divine Majority— / Present no more—"? Can it be called declarative and annunciative? Or should it be contrasted with the relative confidentiality and informality of "I've known her—from an ample nation— / Choose One"? In the chapter titled "Tone" from *T S. Eliot and Prejudice*, Christopher Ricks offers the following: "Tone has been called the expression on the face of the words; you may know exactly whose face your eyes are meeting but may still need reassurance as to just what expression is on that face." I need more than reassurance as to just what expression is on the face of Dickinson's words at the climactic moments of "Because I Could Not Stop" and "The Soul Selects"; and though exceptions can be produced ("How dreary to be somebody / How Public—like a Frog") her poems in the main don't invite the sort of rhetorical tonal analysis we give to Donne or Keats or Frost or Elizabeth Bishop. Attempts to present Dickinson as a "dramatic" poet might consider the extent to which the drama is dependent on, or somehow takes place without, strong tonal indications. "Never if you can help it," wrote Frost in a letter, "write down a sentence in which the voice will not know how to posture *specially.*" My sense is that there are plenty of those sentences in Dickinson's poetry. Punctuation is sometimes a help in determining tone, but the dashes in this over-dashed poem don't help, indeed make the tone harder to specify. (Of course, by way of justifying the dashes, there is Wendy Martin in the *Columbia Literary History of the United States:* Dickinson's "dashes signal an urgent immediacy that under-cuts the possibility of an absolute cultural hegemony. Her phrases referring simultaneously backward and forward permit the reader to make connec-tions and create the ambiguity necessary to create new modes of percep-tion." Clear on that, are we? And the capitalizations?)

Another, somewhat less talked-about one of her soul poems may tell us something about the nature of the Dickinson performance:

> Of all the Souls that stand create—
> I have elected—One—
> When Sense from Spirit—files away—
> And Subterfuge—is done—
> When that which is—and that which was—
> Apart—intrinsic—stand—
> And this brief Drama in the flesh

Is shifted—like a Sand—
When Figures show their royal Front—
And Mists—are carved away,
Behold the Atom—I preferred—
To all the lists of Clay!

#664

Commentators are pretty much agreed that this is a salute to "the invisible spirit," to an immortality "purified of all but created soul," although one of them says rather wistfully that "the reader finds no promise of beholding this fascinating atom until eternity brings its revelations," so that "speculation naturally ensues." But the nature of this, and other Dickinson performances, is such as to not make me want to speculate at all. I recall a graduate school classmate, standing next to his kitchen refrigerator, reciting "Of All the Souls" aloud from memory and asking me if I didn't think it a wonderful poem. I said I did, and I still do—especially that fine line in which the dashes are perfectly justified—"Apart—intrinsic—stand". A great poem to "perform" in the sense that I discharge it, execute it, begin and end it with a flourish. But if Dickinson the poet is satisfyingly on display, the performance is not such as to make me care about the character—the "I" of the poem. Indeed I'm not much interested in her, have no yearning to behold the "Atom" she prefers, am not much taken up with what used to be called "the dramatic situation." For there's little drama here, little variety of interest in the tone that shows forth the expression on the speaker's face—in fact I don't know *what* she looks like. For all the poem's images—of sand and mists, filing and carving—there is something unignorably *abstract* about the proceedings. David Porter says, justly, that in reading her we are often "caught in the bright but indefinite lights of a highly figural style." Bright lights the highly figural style of "Of All the Souls" most certainly gives off; maybe "indefinite" too, insofar as, while I'm more than satisfied in reading it aloud, I'm not further tempted to explore its definiteness, its definities.

In her recent, accomplished book *The Passion of Emily Dickinson,* Judith Farr, before launching a case for the overwhelming importance, to the poems, of Dickinson's love for her sister-in-law, Sue Gilbert Dickinson, disposes of critics like me who would attempt to stay, for better or worse, with the words on the page. Farr concedes that, yes of course, one *could* regard the poems as "études in poetic . . . form" merely, but that such a "severely formalistic" procedure "seems a solipsistic avoidance and even unhelpful in studying an art that is so clearly post-romantic." It is a "fantasy," she continues, to think that great artists write without directly experiencing "what is called 'life.'" And the life Dickinson lived, the people she cared about, influenced the language she made poems out of. What Farr doesn't consider, in her sharp opposition between solipsistic formalists and healthy post-Romantics who believe in "life," is the extent to which Dickinson experienced "what is called 'life'" —how directly, or indirectly, it entered her poetry. Compared to poems by post-Romantic contemporaries, most of whom she admired—Tennyson's *In Memoriam*, Browning's "By the Fireside," Elizabeth Barrett Browning's sonnets, Christina Rossetti's poem to her brother, "By Way of Remembrance," or Arnold's "Stanzas from the Grand Chartreuse," Dickinson's poems typically don't set up lines of easy commerce between themselves and life. "Depersonalization," as Eliot infamously praised it in his "Tradition" essay, is more appropriate to characterize her poems than theirs. Just exactly what experience, what people, went into the forming of "My Life had stood—a Loaded Gun"?

I don't think of my procedures as a reader of Dickinson's poetry as "severely formalistic," and I have introduced various critical readings and explanations of three anthology favorites by way of suggesting there may be another way of reading her than one that works mainly at getting the right interpretation of an individual poem. When I teach her in an introductory course, about to begin next week, I shall at all costs avoid laying out strenuous readings demonstrating how one or another poem of hers is the product of genius. Rather I hope the students will get well-lost in her, as I have done this summer. David Porter says that after reading her work "other poetry seems hesitant and slack in comparison." While not in favor of slackness, I should stress the *relief* with which I put down her poems and read, oh, parts of Cowper's *The Task* or Byron's *Don Juan*, poems which, compared to hers, look slack. Her preceptor Higgins having visited her, said, "I never was with anyone who drained my nerve power so much. Without touching her, she drew from me. I am glad not to live near her." And Paglia ends her essay by calling Dickinson "frightening." Excessive, but in a milder way I have been illustrating the difficulty of "talking back to Dickinson" —to a poet who (in contradiction to MacLeish's account of her voice) is much of the time *not* speaking to me; who much of the time is doing without the social and dramatic atmospheres and conventions that sustain me in Donne or Ben Jonson, Frost or Philip Larkin.

When she sustains me, it is through the sumptuous destitutions of language Richard Wilbur found in her:

> There is a finished feeling
> Experienced at Graves—
> A leisure of the Future—
> A Wilderness of Size.
>
> By Death's bold Exhibition
> Preciser what we are
> And the Eternal function
> Enabled to infer.
>
> #856

Is this "slight" or not? I at any rate am made "preciser" by such a wholly finished poem with its oblique rhymes (Graves/Size; We are/infer) and its offbeat alliterative swing, from "finished" to "feeling" to "Future" to "function" to "infer." And I don't need further instruction in Dickinson's of life, or of death, or of other people, in order to read it with satisfaction.

The "finished feeling" of this poem is an important aspect of many others in her work: but if the emphasis is put instead on her strangeness, or her great cognitive power, or the multiple possibilities or ambiguities held out by the teasing voice, less exciting virtues may be overlooked, and the poems in which they occur will be treated as minor compared to those of "major" difficulty. Sometimes the poem is so finished and inescapable that we suspect it of too-easy resolution:

> The Sky is low—the Clouds are mean.
> A Travelling Flake of Snow
> Across a Barn or through a Rut
> Debates if it will go—
>
> A Narrow Wind complains all Day
> How some one treated him
> Nature, like Us is sometimes caught
> Without her Diadem.
>
> #1075

Did Frost or Hardy write that? Is it "merely" charming, not up to the tragic Dickinson standard? I'm suggesting that, when with relative ease and comprehension we are taken by one of her lyrics, we feel guilty, as if such ease were a substitute for a worthier difficulty and uncertainty.

On at least one occasion, a sequence of stanza is so easeful, finished, and elegant, that the poem's conclusion can't live up to it, as in the early one titled by Higginson and Todd "Indian Summer":

> These are the days when Birds come back—
> A very few—a Bird or two
> To take a backward look.
>
> These are the days when skies resume
> The old—old sophistries of June—
> A blue and gold mistake.
>
> Oh fraud that cannot cheat the Bee—
> Almost thy plausibility
> Induces my belief.
>
> Till ranks of seeds their witness bear—
> And softly thro' the altered air
> Hurries a timid leaf.
>
> #130

The line about the old sophistries of June was really written by Lorenz Hart or Cole Porter; the fourth stanza beautifully anticipates A. E. Housman's great tribute to nature's deception, "Tell me not here, it needs not saying." After such brilliances, the concluding fifth and sixth stanzas just sound earnestly exclamatory, for what that matters.

Randall Jarrell, who was meditating an essay on Dickinson at the time he died, made up, as was his wont, a list of her best and next-best poems—his way of talking back to Dickinson. Looking respectfully at the oeuvre of Dickinson criticism that has accumulated over the past decades—responsible, resourceful, ingenious as much of it is—I would welcome more subjectivity, more list makings by individual readers of the fine and not-so-fine poems. This might help in sharpening appreciation and making criticism of her less a sacred act of homage conducted under solemn rubrics like

Love, Death, Election, the Woman Question, the Fate of the Soul. As a very small beginning here are two poems that don't make the anthologies or get written about much, but say everything that needs to be said in the smallest space. The first is positive, recuperative, introduced to me by a friend who had come out the other side of desperation and found himself:

> A Death blow is a Life blow to Some
> Who till they died, did not alive become—
> Who they had lived, had died but when
> They died, Vitality begun.
>
> #816

The second is mischievous, even wicked, mocking, seeing-through-everything; yet like the one just quoted, exuberant in its formulation, its wild way with words:

> Finding is the first Act
> The second, loss,
> Third, Expedition for
> The "Golden Fleece"
>
> Fourth, no Discovery—
> Fifth, no Crew—
> Finally, no Golden Fleece—
> Jason—sham—too.
>
> #870

Sharon Cameron calls it a "poem about disillusionment," which makes the important connection only after it is too late. But not for the reader whose last act, as with "Vitality begun," is a very satisfying finding indeed.

—Talk given at the second annual conference of the Association of
Literary Scholars and Critics, Boston, September 1996.

Larkin's Presence

"I THINK IN one sense I'm like Evelyn Waugh or John Betjeman, in that there's not much to say about my work. When you've read a poem, that's it, it's all quite clear what it means." Thus Philip Larkin, parrying an interviewer's asking whether he had profited from reading criticism of himself. One takes the point: this is a poet who made every effort, and successfully, not to write poems that—as he said Emily Dickinson's too often did—"expire in a teased-out and breathless obscurity." And even though relative obscurity can occasionally be found in Larkin's poetry, especially in earlier work like "Dry-Point" and "Latest Face" from *The Less Deceived*, his poems typically have "plots," are narratives with beginning, middle, and end, spoken by a voice that invites trust (though not all speakers in his poems are trustworthy), and seeks what Frost said good poems issued in—a "clarification of life." Not necessarily, as Frost went on to say, "a great clarification, such as sects and cults are founded on," but "a momentary stay against confusion."

Larkin's remark about his poems being so clear in what they mean that there's not much to say about them should not however be dismissed—like Waugh's responses to interviewers—as merely a way of eluding questions. Not that he's above discomfiting the questioner, as when, asked what he had learned from his "study" of Auden, Yeats, and Hardy, he snapped back with "Oh, for Christ's sake, one doesn't *study* poets! You *read* them, and think, That's marvellous, how is it done, could I do it?" (The best riposte to one of his parryings was Auden's. After asking Larkin how he liked living in Hull and having Larkin reply that he was no unhappier there than any other place, Auden clucked at him "Naughty, Naughty.") But a glance at criticism of the poems doesn't reveal interpretive disputes about them or strikingly divergent notions of which are the best ones. It seems generally agreed that his poetic output, if small, was distinguished; that whether his range is thought to be relatively narrow or wide as life itself, the poems are like nobody else's. If there are readers of poetry in England and America who don't at all share these sentiments, they have kept quiet about their dissent. But if indeed there's "not much to say" about the poems—as there is, for example, a great deal to say about James Merrill's poems: charting allusions, sizing up the tone of a line, proposing and correcting particular "readings"—there may yet be something of interest to be said about the challenge Larkin's work presents to contemporary ideas about poets and poetry. This would require an attempt to characterize the reader of Larkin who feels that this challenge is a splendid thing to have occurred. And with Larkin more than with most poets the challenge is one the reader takes personally: why does this body of work matter so much to *me?*

More than thirty years ago Randall Jarrell said in a letter to James Agee that writing poetry involved one in struggling "both against the current of the world and the current of the World of Poetry, a small world much more interested in Wallace Stevens than in Chekov, Homer, and Wordsworth combined." Looking around him, shortly before the publication of Ginsberg's *Howl* and the domestic poems of Lowell's *Life Studies,* Jarrell saw in American poets under forty (he had just turned that corner) what he called "the world of Richard Wilbur and safer paler mirror-images of Richard Wilbur"—the era of "the poet in the grey-flannel suit." Three years later, looking through an anthology of English and American poets under forty, he saw little to contradict his picture of poets and poems that didn't take enough chances: *New Poets of England and America* (ed. Hall, Pack, and Simpson) mainly presented—and seems three decades later still to present—work for which the word accomplished comes all too readily to mind. Yet in that anthology Jarrell found and read with pleasure seven poems by Philip Larkin, including "Church Going," "Poetry of Departures," and "At Grass," from *The Less Deceived.* (The book had not yet been published in America, but serious readers of poetry knew about it in the late 1950s, when it could be ordered from England for ten shillings and sixpence.) Lowell, then well into his *Life Studies* poems in the new style—he included a version of "Skunk Hour" in a letter to Jarrell about the anthology—told him that he had been reading Larkin since the previous spring and liked him better than anyone since Dylan Thomas, indeed liked him better than Thomas. He was not only the most interesting of

the "movement" poets, but "unlike our smooth younger poets says something." In reply, Jarrell said he was "delighted" with the remark about Larkin, since he himself was "crazy about him."

I mention this little episode in literary history to point out that for all
the critical tendency to patronize Larkin as a wistful ineffectual angel ("He
is plain and passive . . . a sympathetic figure as he stands at the window,
trying not to cloud it with his breath"), his voice in its early manifestations
struck two of the best American poets as a fresh accent, put to the service
of saying something, as in the opening of "Poetry of Departures":

> Sometimes you hear, fifth-hand,
> As epitaph:
> *He chucked up everything*
> *And just cleared off,*
> And always the voice will sound
> Certain you approve
> This audacious, purifying,
> Elemental move.

The voice's accent commands not only a lively, slangy idiom in which
chuckings up and clearings off are at home, but in addition a cool Latinate superiority to people who get so excited about that idiom that they
can't imagine anyone hearing it in a different way. Having so deftly laid
down those ironic adjectives—"audacious," "purifying," "elemental"—so
as seemingly to kill any pretensions to value the "move" might have, Larkin then changes perspective, appearing to entertain a second thought and
what follows from it. For the rest of the poem it's impossible to consider
stanzas separately since the voice moves through and over them with quietly dazzling changes of pace:

> And they are right, I think.
> We all hate home
> And having to be there:
> I detest my room,
> Its specially-chosen junk,
> The good books, the good bed,
> And my life, in perfect order:
> So to hear it said

He walked out on the whole crowd
Leaves me flushed and stirred,
Like *Then she undid her dress*
Or *Take that you bastard;*
Surely I can, if he did?
And that helps me stay
Sober and industrious.
But I'd go today,

Yes, swagger the nut-strewn roads.
Crouch in the fo'c'sle
Stubbly with goodness, if
It weren't so artificial,
Such a deliberate step backwards
To create an object:
Books; china; a life
Reprehensibly perfect.

In reading the poem aloud or typing it out, one discovers just how perfect an object it is, though not "reprehensibly" so. Although I don't propose to talk about Larkin's rhyming, it should at least be acknowledged as the operation that makes everything come together and cohere (as it does with his early master Yeats and his later master Hardy). In "Poetry of Departures" there are full rhymes usually at the end of a stanza (approve/move; bed/said; stay/today), Audenesque off-rhymes (there/order; think/junk; if/ life), and comic-looking or -sounding ones that vary depending on your Anglo or American pronunciation (epitaph/off; stirred/bastard—in his recording of the poem Larkin pronounced it bah-stud, which makes for a wholly engaging ring).

For all its talk of undone dresses and bastards, "Poetry of Departures" recalls no modern poet more than Frost, not just because Larkin refuses to trade in "a deliberate step backwards" for the call of the wild (Frost wrote a poem titled "One Step Backward Taken"), but for the way both poets need to plant themselves firmly some place so that they can compellingly imagine some place else. Frost's charming poem about Henry Hudson ("I stay; / But it isn't as if / There wasn't always Hudson's Bay") is titled "An Empty Threat," but the threat of departure, however empty, is enough to fill a poem with detail after imagined detail. The same for Larkin, whose little poem of departure plays with the notion of walking out on things, something he can imagine doing only when he has his feet still in the middle of them. Frost is one of the poets from this century, along with Hardy, Sassoon, Edward Thomas, Betjeman, and Wilfred Owen, whom Larkin said he kept within reach of his working chair (no Auden? no Graves?), but it is important that their affinity not be seen to consist in the way they both expunge romantic possibilities from their consciousness. They may have expunged them from their lives—or at least Larkin did—but only the better to entertain them in their writing.

John Bayley, who has written about Larkin with his usual perceptiveness, calls this temperamental inclination by the title of a poem from *The Whitsun Weddings,* "The Importance of Elsewhere," and calls Larkin also, with Keats and Yeats in the background, the last Romantic. As with Keats—and probably Yeats too, as it was for D. H. Lawrence, who made up the phrase—Larkin's was a case of "sex in the head," or so he would have us believe from the things he said in print. For him, says Bayley, "The erotic is elsewhere and evaporates on consummation." And with Keats's "Lamia" and Larkin's first novel, *Jill,* in mind, Bayley suggests that "the man who creates and contemplates romance is extinguished by its realization or fulfilment." Larkin uses that last word at the end of "No Road," one of a number of poems in *The Less Deceived* that speak, with an unmistakably personal ring, about a relationship between two people which didn't pan out and after which, the poet imagines, time will obliterate the already disused road between them:

> To watch that world come up like a cold sun,
> Rewarding others, is my liberty.
> Not to prevent it is my will's fulfilment.
> Willing it, my ailment.

The poems he wrote were good for what ailed him. Another way of making the same point about life was to reply, as Larkin did when asked if he were happy, that yes he was but that one couldn't write poems about being happy: "Deprivation is for me what daffodils were for Wordsworth," was his happy formulation. In other words, you can and cannot know me through my poems.

Along with sex, the richest "elsewhere" in Larkin's experience was American jazz, even as he listened to plenty of it. For him and Kingsley Amis as Oxford undergraduates,

> Russell, Charles Ellsworth, "Pee Wee" (b. 1906), clarinet and saxophone player extraordinary, was, *mutatis mutandis,* our Swinburne and our Byron. We bought every record he played on that we could find, and—literally—dreamed about similar items on the American Commodore label.

This was no charming exaggeration; Larkin and Amis may have had better ears than any other recent English writers (or is it just that my own ear is tuned to them?), and I can't believe it had nothing to do with how much jazz, Pee Wee Russell and the rest, they listened to. The whole of English poetry was available there in the Bodleian, yet think of all those American Commodore jazz records that were elsewhere, the ones they hadn't heard. Although at Oxford, as in other places, jazz was and is a minority taste, its being more exciting than poetry surely had to do with this relative inaccessibility. Anyone who once yearned to possess sides or albums the record companies had let go out of print (things are better these days) knows what the excitement of such an elsewhere can feel like.

But it wasn't only the music that interested Larkin. Even before he discovered jazz he had listened to dance music, dance bands, and said that he must have learned "dozens of dance lyrics" about which he said to an interviewer that

> I suppose they were a kind of folk poetry. Some of them were pretty awful, but I often wonder whether my assumption that a poem is something that rhymes and scans didn't come from listening to them—and some of them were quite sophisticated. "The Venus de Milo was noted for her charms / But strictly between us, you're cuter than Venus / And what's more you've got arms" —I can't imagine Mick Jagger singing that; you know, it was witty and technically clever.

The lines about the Venus de Milo, from "Love Is Just Around the Corner," seem to have been favorites since he mentions them more than once, and the influence of dance lyrics may be observed, not merely in the fact that

Larkin's poems rhyme and scan, but in how they sound, the way—line by line—they swing. There is no better place to observe such a movement than in the opening poem from *The Less Deceived*, the one that thirty years ago introduced this reader to Larkin. "Lines on a Young Lady's Photograph Album" says more about looking at photographs than any poem I know, and it also investigates what it means to pore over the snapped stages of someone whose past you care about:

> My swivel eye hungers from pose to pose—
> In pigtails, clutching a reluctant cat;
> Or furred yourself, a sweet girl-graduate;
> Or lifting a heavy-headed rose
> Beneath a trellis, or in a trilby hat

> (Faintly disturbing, that, in several ways) —
> From every side you strike at my control,
> Not least through these disquieting chaps who loll
> At ease about your earlier days:
> Not quite your class, I'd say, dear, on the whole.

The movement of these stanzas is of course more complicated and "unsingable" than dance tunes can afford to be—consider the pauses within the lines, the way cat/graduate slightly off-rhymes, the parenthetical irony. Yet there are also memorable solo lines that seem to have come out of some Golden Treasury of Popular Song: "From every side you strike at my control" or "Not quite your class, I'd say, dear, on the whole"—surely Fred Astaire sang them in some 1930s movie? And there is a distinctly Cole Porterish feeling in a later stanza, which, after insisting that the photographs have persuaded him "That this is a real girl in a real place," goes on to speculate about whether and how much the truth of those images is dependent on their original being no longer present:

> In every sense empirically true!
> Or is it just *the past?* Those flowers, that gate.
> These misty parks and motors, lacerate
> Simply by being over; you
> Contract my heart by looking out of date.

Witty and technically accomplished certainly, but also poignant the way a gorgeous line can be, this last one delivered, again, with the wistful elegance of an Astaire, maybe a Billie Holiday. (And note the wonderful bonus provided by the double sense of "contract.") When Louis MacNeice died in 1963, Larkin wrote a short appreciation for the *New Statesman* in which he called MacNeice a "town observer" whose poetry was the poetry of everyday life. But beyond that poetry's treatment of shopwindows and lawn mowers and its "uneasy awareness of what the newsboys were shouting," MacNeice, he wrote, "displayed a sophisticated sentimentality about falling leaves and lipsticked cigarette stubs: he could have written the words of 'These Foolish Things.'" A lovely tribute which might well be paid to Larkin himself, especially in his earlier poems.

All the best ones from *The Less Deceived*, including of course the best known of all, "Church Going," are poems of tenderness directed at something that is now elsewhere. Their need is nothing so clearly identifiable as nostalgia; nobody who took Larkin's sardonic, unillusioned view of his own childhood can be accused of that:

> By now I've got the whole place clearly charted,
> Our garden, first: where I did not invent
> Blinding theologies of flowers and fruits,
> And wasn't spoken to by an old hat.
>
> "I Remember, I Remember"

He doesn't write poems out of the feeling that—as in a line from Jarrell—"In those days everything was better." It is rather the difference between now and then (most affectingly expressed in "MCMXIV" from *The Whitsun Weddings*) that moves him and animates a poem. In speaking about something that is elsewhere—maybe past and gone but not quite—Larkin achieves an extraordinary intimacy of tone, both in relation to that subject and to the implicated reader, who, it is assumed, will care just as much about it as the poet does. (His rhetoric never insists on how really splendid something is, in fact.) Think of this passage about a married woman's maiden name:

> Now it's a phrase applicable to no one,
> Lying just where you left it, scattered through

> Old lists, old programmes, a school prize or two,
> Packets of letters tied with tartan ribbon—
> Then is it scentless. weightless, strengthless, wholly
> Untruthful? Try whispering it slowly.
> No, it means you. Or, since you're past and gone,
>
> It means what we feel now about you then:
> How beautiful you were, and near, and young,
> > > > "Maiden Name"

Jarrell once wrote that "the poem is a love affair between the poet and his subject, and readers come in only a long time later, as witnesses at the wedding." Such a poetry has its sudden intimacies of tone ("No, it means you"), and—in case there are people who think Larkin's voice lacked passion—its certifiable intensities of feeling, of love, are witnessed by us.

Unlike the almost forgotten maiden name Larkin writes a poem to revive, a name can live on while the bearer of it is forgotten, and Larkin can right that balance too, as in the final poem from *The Less Deceived* about once-famous racehorses now subsided into something else. "The eye can hardly pick them out," "At Grass" begins, but by the fourth stanza Larkin has achieved a beautiful feeling for his subject, those horses that are wholly unaware of his questioning of them:

> Do memories plague their ears like flies?
> They shake their heads. Dusk brims the shadows.
> Summer by summer all stole away,
> The starting-gates, the crowds and cries—
> All but the unmolesting meadows.
> Almanacked, their names live; they
>
> Have slipped their names, and stand at ease.

The touch is so sure that one almost misses the point that those horses shake their heads not to assure the poet they're impervious to memory but merely to twitch away the flies that are plaguing them. About the surprising "unmolesting," as modifying the meadows, faithful in their way to the otherwise deserted horses, one can only say with Larkin, who, when asked how he'd arrived at an image in his poem "Toads," answered, "Sheer genius."

These poems and others from *The Less Deceived* speak to the reader's own need to be less deceived—the need to be intimate with the past and with loss (of a maiden name, of how one used to look, of a horse's once thoroughbred performance) by seizing them through the poet's words. There is little to be done about the present except to endure it as it erodes us; Frost's lines from "Carpe Diem" say what there is to be said on the subject:

> But bid life seize the present?
> It lives less in the present
> Than in the future always,
> And less in both together
> Than in the past. The present
> Is too much for the senses,
> Too crowding, too confusing—
> Too present to imagine.

And when Larkin decides to live for a bit in the future, the consequences are predictably grim, the end of England foreseen:

> For the first time I fed somehow
> That it isn't going to last,
>
> That before I snuff it, the whole
> Boiling will be bricked in
> Except for the tourist parts—
> First slum of Europe: . . .
> > "Going, Going"

But on occasion he succeeds magnificently in imagining the crowding, confusing present by writing a poetry of becoming, of flux, and by exulting in the process rather than lamenting it. "Wedding-Wind" (an early, Lawrentian poem) and "Coming" from *The Less Deceived*, "Here" and "Water" from *The Witsun Weddings,* are examples of such imaginings. And in the second section of "Livings," from *High Windows,* an unidentified speaker, evidently a lighthouse keeper, raptly contemplates a vividly present scene:

Seventy feet down
The sea explodes upwards,
Relapsing, to slaver
Off landing-stage steps—
Running suds, rejoice!

Rocks writhe back to sight.
Mussels, limpets,
Husband their tenacity
In the freezing slither—
Creatures, I cherish you!

It is a remarkably early-Audenesque telegram in which the importance of elsewhere is subordinated to the here-and-now:

Radio rubs its legs,
Telling me of elsewhere:

Barometers falling,
Ports wind-shuttered,
Fleets pent like hounds,
Fires in humped inns
Kippering sea-pictures—

Keep it all off!

Without the author's name attached, no one would guess this was Larkin; its language revels in the attempt to live up to, even outdo, the invigorating chaos of the world it embodies.

A similar, and similarly rich, satisfaction—though most mutedly expressed—occurs when a scene or place in the present engages him because the life has gone out of it, has gone elsewhere. Yet, as with Wordsworth looking at London from Westminster Bridge before anyone is stirring, the place now offers its essential being, seen as if truly for the first time. In "Friday Night in the Royal Station Hotel,"

Light spreads darkly downwards from the high
Cluster of lights over empty chairs

That face each other, coloured differently.
Through open doors, the dining-room declares
A larger loneliness of knives and glass
And silence laid like carpet. A porter reads
An unsold evening paper. Hours pass,
And all the salesmen have gone back to Leeds,
Leaving full ashtrays in the Conference Room.

In shoeless corridors, the lights burn. How
Isolated, like a fort, it is—
The headed paper, made for writing home
(If home existed) letters of exile: *Now*
Night comes on. Waves fold behind villages

I suppose that down through the line comparing the hotel to a fort one
might call the poem merely expert, the sort of thing one comes to expect
from Larkin-on-emptiness. But where on earth did the italicized message
come from, imagined to be written home by the imaginary exile? It moves
the poem beyond expertise into the surprising, unsettling creation Larkin
at his best is capable of.

"Livings" (part II) and "Friday Night in the Royal Station Hotel" offer
us, if you will, glimpses of the Sublime; but sometimes Larkin invites us
into a present, at least for a moment, by achieving what a student of mine
cleverly called The Tacky Sublime. In "The Large Cool Store" we are shown
how most of the "cheap clothes" match the workday habits of the working-
class people who buy them. Then there is a surprise:

But past the heaps of shirts and trousers
Spread the stands of Modes For Night:
Machine-embroidered, thin as blouses,

Lemon, sapphire, moss-green, rose
Bri-Nylon Baby-Dolls and Shorties
Flounce in clusters . . .

Yet this satiric vision of loveliness leads not to further satiric treatment, but
rather to a serious meditation on how hard it is to say something conclusive about women and love.

Some of Larkin's best work is to be found in each of the three books of poetry he published at ten-year intervals (I am excluding his early *The North Ship* as not the real thing), and the finest of the three is the last, *High Windows.* Perhaps, with T. S. Eliot in mind, he scoffed at the notion of a poet's "development" (to Ian Hamilton in an interview he quoted Oscar Wilde's line about only mediocrities developing). But *High Windows,* with only twenty-four poems, is the quintessence of all the books and contains four of his richest and most ample works: "To the Sea"; "The Old Fools"; "The Building"; and "Show Saturday" (with Yeats-like stanzas of nine, twelve, seven, and eight lines respectively), Along with his final poem, "Aubade," "The Old Fools" and "The Building" are the darkest, most death-oriented poems he wrote; the other two are equally life-affirming in their blessings on two rituals—going to the beach, going to the fair. "Show Saturday," with its elaborately rhymed stanzas that enjamb themselves one into the next, concludes in a burst of—for Larkin—positively positive thinking, saluting with alliterative energy the "dismantled Show," now concluded but to return next year, same time:

> Let it stay hidden there like strength, below
> Sale-bills and swindling; something people do,
> Not noticing how time's rolling smithy-smoke
> Shadows much greater gestures; something they share
> That breaks ancestrally each year into
> Regenerate union. Let it always be there.

Larkin is not, of course, exactly "there," nor is he one of the bathers in "To the Sea" who persist in making another kind of annual show:

> If the worst
> Of flawless weather is our falling short,
> It may be that through habit these do best,
> Coming to water clumsily undressed
> Yearly; teaching their children by a sort
> Of clowning; helping the old, too, as they ought.

These are the sort of people an Auberon Waugh recoils from in disgust; Larkin gives them his considered respect.

As for the dark poems, "The Building" and "The Old Fools" lose none of their original terror—it is not too strong a word—on rereading. The first is an improvisation, in the mode of Kafka or Fellini, on this unnamed structure (to call it a hospital would be to commit the Jamesian sin of weak specification) which signals that "something has gone wrong":

> It must be error of a serious sort,
> For see how many floors it needs, how tall
> It's grown by now, and how much money goes
> In trying to correct it. See the time,
> Half-past eleven on a working day,
> And these picked out of it; see, as they climb
>
> To their appointed levels, how their eyes
> Go to each other, guessing; on the way
> Someone's wheeled past, in washed-to-rags ward clothes:
> They see him, too. They're quiet. To realise
> This new thing held in common makes them quiet,
> For past these doors are rooms, and rooms past those,
> And more rooms yet . . .

The neutral tone belies the hopeless subject: it is as if Larkin has to keep writing in the hope that, for the space of the poem, he can help us fend off the hopelessness. By contrast, "The Old Fools" is more compact and more tonally aggressive, especially in its first two stanzas, at the expense of age's incapacity to know what's happening to it ("Do they somehow suppose / It's more grown-up when your mouth hangs open and drools, / And you keep on pissing yourself, and can't remember / Who called this morning?"). But by the third stanza, in a moment of sympathetic identification the poet makes up for his would-be callousness, giving the old fools some metaphors with which to see themselves:

> Perhaps being old is having lighted rooms
> Inside your head, and people in them, acting.
> People you know, yet can't quite name; each looms
> Like a deep loss restored, from known doors turning,
> Setting down a lamp, smiling from a stair, extracting
> A known book from the shelves; or sometimes only
> The rooms themselves, chairs and a fire burning,

The blown bush at the window, or the sun's
Faint friendliness on the wall some lonely
Rain-ceased midsummer evening. That is where they live:
Not here and now, but where all happened once.
　　　　This is why they give

An air of baffled absence, trying to be there
Yet being here . . .

It is, I think, Larkin's most handsome stanza (comparable to it are the
final ones from "The Whitsun Weddings" and "Dockery and Son"), and
it encloses perhaps the most beautifully realized and affecting sequence in
all his work. The poem doesn't quite end there, and the horror of enduring this "whole hideous inverted childhood" returns, now with the poet
including himself in it: "Well, we shall find out." It is the last answer, if
another were needed, to Browning's salute to age in "Rabbi Ben Ezra,"
and not just one further voice in an argument about growing old but a
crushing unanswerable statement of fact. Perhaps too crushing, one might
argue—too sweeping, too exclusively grim in its portraiture; yet it has a lot
of truth going for it. As Lowell remarked, a poem by Larkin "says something." "The Old Fools" says something final about what was always his
ultimate subject.

For if Larkin was driven to write about love consummated elsewhere,
the young in one another's arms—"Sexual intercourse began / In nineteen
sixty-three / (Which was rather late for me) –"—then age and the death
about which "we shall find out" was even more irresistible as a subject to be
fetched from elsewhere and entertained in the poem. Larkin "developed"
into the poet who wrote "The Old Fools" by taking life—as Frost said
poetry should—by the throat, exaggerating both his disgust at old-age horrors and his sympathetic tenderness for those people with lighted rooms
inside their heads. It issues in a memorableness that has nothing in common with A. Alvarez's calling him the poet of "suburban hermitage . . . and
all mod con." "Death kills a man; the idea of death saves him," said Forster
in *Howards End* perhaps too chirpily, at least too much so for Larkin, who
wasn't about to talk about salvation in any terms. There is testimony in
Andrew Motion's fine memorial poem about him, "This Is Your Subject
Speaking," that he refused to talk about salvation as being somehow possible through art. In that poem Larkin, visiting Motion for supper, comes

across a book-mark which says "Some say / Life's the thing, but I prefer reading," and snaps back:

> *Jesus Christ what balls.* You spun
> round on your heel to the table
> almost before your anger took hold . . .

Later, cooled down, "Larkin" goes on to say:

> *You see, there's nothing to write*
> *Which is better than life itself, no matter*
> *how life might let you down, or pass you by . . .*

This speaking up for life might have taken a sharper edge as he saw his own powers as a poet disappearing. In 1982 he ended his *Paris Review* interview with the terse declaration: "It's unlikely I shall write any more poems" (not many, *any)* and at another moment in Motion's poem he says to the younger man

> *Don't ask me*
> *Why I stopped, I didn't stop. It stopped.*
> *In the old days I'd go home at six*
> *and write all evening on a board*
>
> *across my knees. But now . . . I go home*
> *and there's nothing there. I'm like a chicken*
> *with no egg to lay.*

His last egg, as it were, was one of his very best. "Aubade," published December of 1977, was written as death in its elsewhereness seemed closer, staying in the poem's words "just on the edge of Vision":

> I work all day, and get half drunk at night
> Waking at four to soundless dark, I stare.
> In time the curtain-edges will grow light.
> Till then I see what's always really there:
> Unresting death, a whole day nearer now.
> Making all thought impossible but how

And where and when I shall myself die.
Arid interrogation: yet the dread
Of dying, and of being dead,
Flashes afresh to hold and horrify.

Here, unlike "The Old Fools," the personal edge is felt at the very beginning and only deepens over the poem's five stanzas. It is nothing more than
mere total emptiness that horrifies him— "nothing more terrible, nothing
more true"—and in the third stanza, with a touch of the younger, slangier
Oxford iconoclast, he sees through the religious consolation:

That vast moth-eaten musical brocade
Created to pretend we never die,
And specious stuff that says *No rational being
Can fear a thing it will not feel,* not seeing
That this is what we fear—no sight, no sound,
No touch or taste or smell, to think with,
Nothing to love or link with,
The anaesthetic from which none come round.

The voice rises, with pressing excitement, to "correct" the blindness of
consolatory wisdom that doesn't know the half of it, of the "Waking to
soundless dark" at 4:00 A.M. which he has just undergone and which is
his undressed rehearsal for the grave. Since "Death is no different whined
at than withstood," the poem ends in a getting up, a coming back without
illusion to life, which like death had better not be either whined at or withstood, but rather just met:

Slowly light strengthens, and the room takes shape.
It stands plain as a wardrobe, what we know,
Have always known, know that we can't escape,
Yet can't accept. One side will have to go.
Meanwhile telephones crouch, getting ready to ring
In locked-up offices, and all the uncaring
Intricate rented world begins to rouse.
The sky is white as clay, with no sun.
Work has to be done.
Postmen like doctors go from house to house.

Those three single-line concluding sentences, in which the "intricate rented world" is faced (and what a stroke that "rented" is), are the point in his work beyond which Larkin was not to go, and perhaps for strong reasons. If a poet has to stop writing there is justice for it happening in coincidence with his subject: to maul slightly Emily Dickinson's line, Larkin's work could stop for death. "Most poets have nothing to write about," James Dickey once confided. Larkin knew what he had to write about and when he had done it.

One's response to his death in December of 1985 was then, for all the sense of loss, not a sense that had he lived he would have gone on to write poems he had not quite yet grown into writing. (It would be nice to have been wrong and to have seen him live and write on so as to prove it.) For essentially his work felt complete—as Jarrell's did after *The Lost World* or Bishop's after *Geography III,* or as Lowell's did perhaps even before he published *Day by Day.* On the face of it nothing could be more absurd than to compare the four slim volumes Larkin gave us (counting *The North Ship* this time) with the eight individually much larger ones of his ancestral favorite, Hardy; yet if Hardy's emergence as a poet is dated from *Wessex Poems* (1898), both he and Larkin (dating from *The North Ship,* 1945) had some thirty years of production. We know that Larkin put himself on record as not wishing Hardy's vast collection a single poem shorter, and as calling his work "many times over" the best body of poetry in the century. One of the pleasures in rereading Hardy is of course the discovery of poems one had previously missed, or only half-read: compared, say, to Eliot, he seems inexhaustible. How many rereaders of Larkin's books have a similar feeling? I think I know his poems as well as those of any postmodern poet; still, to reread is to be struck not by there being fewer than 100 poems all told in *The Less Deceived, The Whitsun Weddings,* and *High Windows,* but by the density and weight of the ones there are.

How much this has to do with their being poems of great formal craft, especially (and frequently) in their often elaborately schemed rhyme and stanzas, is hard to specify. My feeling is that the craft has a great deal, maybe everything, to do with it. When compared to two very different contemporary poets of reputation, John Ashbery and Adrienne Rich, the difference Larkin's adherence to traditional metric, stanzas, and rhyme makes is patent. Ashbery may well possess, as David Bromwich has declared, the "original idiom of our times," but as his prolific output testifies it may not take quite as much care or time to write a poem if one doesn't require rhyme and stanza, and if one is more concerned with nonsense than with sense. (I can't believe that Larkin was not making pointed mischief when he said—explaining why his bad hearing kept him from traveling to America—"Someone would say Ashbery, and I'd say, I'd prefer strawberry, that sort of thing.") And it is hard to imagine Adrienne Rich discovering that her poetry had just dried up, that (in the phrase from Motion's poem about Larkin) she had become a chicken with no egg to lay. There will always be some new or old issue of gender and power on which to exercise her poetic will in various free forms. Ashbery and Rich have written many books of poetry; we may see Larkin's relatively few against the background of the formal tests he set for himself in drawing the figures of poems.

The craft, the elegance, the ceaseless wit—how could anyone say, as W. J. Bate and David Perkins do in their recent anthology of British and American poets, that Larkin writes "the poetry of personal statement and dreary realism"? Although thirty years ago Jarrell hailed him as the antidote to "the world of Richard Wilbur," it is Wilbur, born just a year before Larkin, to whom he can be compared in his command of syntax and suppleness and tone. Larkin might not have liked the comparison, might have felt Wilbur more of a high-toned formalist than he. But for all the American poet's fastidious good manners (those who don't much like him call it primness), Wilbur's poetry from *Ceremony* through *The Mind-Reader* unmistakably reveals a distinct presence, a person whose character and inclinations we get to know very well. If Wilbur, in Brad Leithauser's phrase, is "one of the few living American masters of formal verse," then Larkin was its most recent English master of such verse. And for all its difference from Wilbur's, his poetry shows a person at least as distinct in his outlines, his tastes, the clarity of his idiom. Either of them could have written the next to last poem in Larkin's last book:

> Cut grass lies frail:
> Brief is the breath
> Mown stalks exhale.
> Long, long the death
>
> It dies in the white hours
> Of young-leafed June
> With chestnut flowers,
> With hedges snowlike strewn,

White lilac bowed,
Lost lanes of Queen Anne's lace,
And that high-builded cloud
Moving at summer's pace.

In the fewest possible words, "Cut Grass" says much, surely enough to serve as a poet's epitaph.

— *Raritan*, Spring 1987.

Elizabeth Bishop: Poems, Prose and Letters

ELIZABETH BISHOP died in 1979 and immediately ascended to the heaven inhabited by dead poets—George Herbert, John Keats, and Emily Dickinson—whom everyone venerates. In a review of Alice Quinn's edition of Bishop's unfinished poems, William Logan put the following question apropos of Bishop's ascendancy: "Why has our age become so enamored of a poet who almost to the end of her life required a special taste?" Logan doesn't quite answer that question, though he does suggest what is probably undemonstrable—that readers "adore themselves for adoring her." Nor can I demonstrate that the poets listed above are indisputably ones whom everyone venerates; but they share a winning vulnerability to the assaults of life, a vulnerability that many sorts of readers find deeply appealing, indeed irresistible. By contrast, two poets who ascended to another part of heaven, John Donne and Robert Lowell, for all their dramatizing of vulnerability ("Batter my heart three-personed God"; "I hear my ill spirit sob in each blood cell"), beat—in Lowell's words from a letter to Bishop—the "big drum" so forcefully that they seem scarcely in need of our sympathetic concern. At any rate, it is undeniable that Bishop's reputation has been untouched by anything like adverse criticism, and it is no surprise that she is the first twentieth-century woman poet to be included in the Library of America.

With the exception of Robert Lowell, it would be difficult to find a poet who, with her first book, *North & South*, got off to a more smashing start. She had met Randall Jarrell in January 1947—he was spending a year as literary editor of *The Nation*—and he introduced her to Lowell, with whom she would have a rich, sometimes troubled friendship that lasted until Lowell's death. (Her beautiful poem "North Haven" is dedicated to his memory.) Both Lowell and Jarrell reviewed *North & South* briefly but trenchantly. Lowell called her poems, in the tripartite clusters of adjectives he was addicted to, "unrhetorical, cool, and beautifully thought out," also praising her "large, controlled and elaborate common-sense." Already, in her first book, she is "one of the best craftsmen alive." Jarrell said that all her poems had written under them, "*I have seen it*," and called "Roosters" and "The Fish" "two of the most calmly beautiful, deeply sympathetic poems of our time." There would follow over the years, and as future volumes were published, accolades from poet-contemporaries such as James Merrill, John Ashbery, Anthony Hecht, and Richard Wilbur, as well as from younger ones like Frank Bidart, Robert Pinsky, Mark Strand, and (one of the coeditors of this volume along with Robert Giroux) Lloyd Schwartz. David Kalstone's 1989 book, published after his death, explored Bishop's relation to Marianne Moore and to Lowell; there have also been a biography by Brett Millier and a number of useful critical studies, Thomas Travisano's being the first comprehensive one.[1] Books and essays will continue to appear, with "readings" of individual poems proliferating until a weary reader returns gladly, once more, to the poems themselves.

Bishop's poems and translations make up about a third of the Library of America's thousand pages; the other two-thirds consists partly of stories, most of them set in the Nova Scotia landscape where Bishop spent part of her childhood. There are also essays and reminiscences, including a memoir ("Efforts of Affection") of Marianne Moore, and a very amusing piece titled "The U.S.A. School of Writing," about a correspondence school in New York City where Bishop worked for a short time after graduating from Vassar. Some "Literary Statements and Reviews" in this collection are mostly brief, and the volume ends with a selection of her letters, the most interesting of them to Lowell. But it is the poems that count and that will be considered here.

The four volumes of them she published during her life are evenly spaced out in roughly ten-year periods: *North & South* (1947); *A Cold Spring* (1955); *Questions of Travel* (1965); and *Geography III* (1976). *The Complete Poems* (1983) appeared after her death, and the volume of unfinished poems and fragments (*Edgar Allan Poe and the Juke-Box*, 2006), welcomed by some, was strenuously condemned by Helen Vendler on the grounds that, considering Bishop's scrupulousness about what she published, she could not have looked favorably on resurrecting into print stich unpublished items. In their questioning, exploratory, nonauthoritarian way of proceeding, her poems are extremely hospitable to critics, who are unlikely to be "wrong" about some particular interpretive scheme to which they are inclined. Similarly, from my classroom experience with her poems I can say that students don't feel intimidated by them and are relatively unworried that they have missed something big. This is all to the good, insofar as it encourages them to give plenty of time to the poem's surface; it presents a problem when, in writing, a critic substitutes, for Bishop's patient procedures, his or her own probably less delicate and qualified effort. In other words, professional academic criticism may be tempted to say too much, go on for too long, in the attempt to reach language adequate to Bishop's effects.

An example of such straining can be seen in the following commentary on a crucial sequence from her much-admired "In the Waiting Room;" the first poem in *Geography III*. In this poem the almost seven-year-old girl accompanies her aunt to the dentist, and while the aunt is in the dentist's chair, the little girl sits in the waiting room full of grown-up people. She reads an article in *National Geographic* and looks at its pictures of a volcano erupting, of a dead man, of babies, and of black, naked African women whose breasts are "horrifying." Suddenly a cry of pain comes from inside the dentist's office, precipitating in the little girl a sensation of identifying with the voice and of "falling off the round, turning world / into cold, blue-black space." Nothing stranger has ever, could ever happen to the child, who thinks

> Why should I be my aunt,
> or me, or anyone?
> What similarities—
> boots, hands, the family voice
> I felt in my throat, or even
> the *National Geographic*
> and those awful hanging breasts—
> held us all together
> or made us all just one?
> How—I didn't know any
> word for it—how "unlikely". . .

Here are some words from a three-page commentary on the poem by a practiced critic of modern poetry:

> A shocking experience of identification, as we have seen, creates a simultaneous loss of original identity, and this loss is

never overcome. The inscrutable volcano, the inside of the child's mouth, the dentist's chamber, are all figures for the abyss the child has discovered, and as she peers into it she is full of questions, another and another—why? what? how?—until she is thrown back into the exclamatory "how 'unlikely,'" and it is clear that they will never be answered. But the transformation of question into exclamation does create a sense of recognition, even if it is the permanently strange that is recognized. We get only a "sidelong glance," not fulfillment or total recognition. Yet, for a moment, this glance does begin to organize the dualities toward some unutterable simplicity. The questions mediate between absolute difference and undifferentiation, between stillness and total flux, and in this way, however fleetingly. accommodate the self most.[2]

It cannot be said about these sentences of Bonnie Costello's that they fail to notice this or that about the poem's language, or misstate the dramatic situation of "In the Waiting Room." At the same time, they feel overburdened and heavy-handed—not helping a reader make a more successful entry into the poem. What might be accepted as useful clarifications and identifications of a poem by Yeats or Pound or Stevens seem beside the point when the language is as free of difficulties to be puzzled out or extravagances to be described as Bishop's in these particular lines. She loved George Herbert. but does not attempt his witty conceits and doublenesses. Admittedly the poems in the late *Geography III* are different, in their achievement of a phrasing that is natural and breathlike (she used these adjectives about Lowell's *Life Studies*), from the complicated, "surrealist" wit of early ones like "The Man-Moth," "The Weed," or "The Monument," which seem better candidates for explicative commentary. But for most readers, I think, the later poems represent the summit of Bishop's poetic arc, and they present a special and formidable challenge to the critic who aims at relevant notation.

When a precocious senior at Vassar, Bishop published (in *The Vassar Review*) a first-rate essay on the poet who, along with Herbert, ranked at the top of her "favorite" list. The essay on Gerard Manley Hopkins bears the subtitle "Notes on Timing in His Poetry," and its opening paragraph calls attention to what would be a central preoccupation in her own work. Since, she begins, poetry is motion, it is essential to consider "the releasing,

checking, timing, and repeating of the movement of the mind according
to ordered systems." For her, at least,

> an idea of *timing* in poetry helps to explain many of those
> aspects of poetry which are so inadequately expressed by most
> critics; why poets differ so much from each other; why using
> exactly the same meters and approximate vocabularies two poets
> produce such different effects; why some poetry seems at rest
> and other poetry in action.

Hopkins's poems need to be considered in such terms, and she mentions
among other things, as central aspects of his technique, "abundant use of
alliteration, repetition, and inside rhymes" as "characteristics which place
firm seals upon his words, joining them, at the same time indicating the
sound relationships in the same way that guide lines, or repeated forms
might, in a drawing." Attention to such matters is crucial in responding
properly to any poet, but seems especially so when Bishop's work is the
subject.[3]

One of her most motion-filled poems is "Sandpiper" (in *Questions of
Travel*), a detached (compared to "In the Waiting Room") contemplation
of a bird on a beach. "Sandpiper" features the alliteration, repetition, and inside rhymes she speaks about in her Hopkins essay as central in creating the
"timing" of a poem. Here are the first three stanzas of the five-stanza poem:

> The roaring alongside he takes for granted,
> and that every so often the world is bound to shake,
> He runs, he runs to the south, finical, awkward,
> in a state of controlled panic, a student of Blake.
>
> The beach hisses like fat. On his left, a sheet
> of interrupting water comes and goes
> and glazes over his dark and brittle feet.
> He runs, he runs straight through it, watching his toes.
>
> —Watching, rather, the spaces of sand between them,
> where (no detail too small) the Atlantic drains
> rapidly backwards and downwards. As he runs,
> he stares at the dragging grains.

The only allusion in these stanzas, indeed in the whole poem, is to the first line of Blake's "Auguries of Innocence" ("To see the world in a grain of sand"), since this is a Blakean sandpiper in its awkward but controlled panic. Robert Lowell once remarked sardonically that no one, except for St. Anthony or a catatonic, wants to see the world in a grain of sand, but this little sandpiper seems wholly committed to the project. A reader who listens to the poem and follows the curve of its developing voice will encounter pleasing surprises (Bishop thought that surprise was the *sine qua non* of any poem). The movement of its first line ("The roaring alongside he takes for granted") is extended in the thirteen-syllable second line, as the "r" sound builds up ("roaring," "granted," "every," "world"). We are given not just one "runs" but two, with its pause after the third line's first foot, both awkward and controlled. "Shake," "south," and "state" aren't exactly internal rhymes but perhaps close enough to count. The third line hiccups after "he runs," then pulls itself up (as the bird veers to the south) with the unobvious but perfect "finical," and with "awkward" pointing toward the "state of controlled panic" (that last word picking up "finical"). The stanza completes itself with the cool rhyming of "shake" and "Blake," and there will be more of the same in stanzas that follow.

Perceptions about a poem's "timing," such as the remarks above, do not make for sentences one takes great satisfaction in writing, or that a reader is likely to warm to. What they remind me of is how much more rewarding it is to deal with a Bishop poem in the classroom, by reading aloud, by rereading a line with a different emphasis on this word, that syllable. If this could be said about any poet, it seems especially to the point with someone who continually and subtly exploits the resources of voice, the natural or breathlike sounds of a Herbert, a Hopkins, a Frost. (It may also help explain why previous to this I have never attempted to write about Bishop's poetry.)

From Randall Jarrell on down, every critic has praised her for regarding. like the sandpiper, "no detail too small." Jarrell's italicized *I have seen it* was taken as conferring upon her an unambiguous compliment. Yet a passion for detail may have its possible overkill. The critic James Wood, writing about prose fiction, notes that while he relishes and consumes "detail," he also chokes on it. "Overaesthetic appreciation of detail" (Wood's words) in a post-Flaubertian world can stifle as well as stimulate. So it is possible to have mixed responses to the plethora of detail in certain Bishop poems; for example, the very first one in *North & South*, "The Map," which begins

Land lies in water; it is shadowed green.
Shadows, or are they shallows, at its edges
showing the line of long sea-weeded ledges
where weeds hang to the simple blue from green.
Or does the land lean down to lift the sea from under,
drawing it unperturbed around itself?
Along the fine tan sandy shelf
is the land tugging at the sea from under?

Very delicate, scrupulous, fastidious—yes, but there is a part of me that says, in responding to "Shadows, or are they shallows," oh, *you* decide, *I* really don't care. "Is the land tugging at the sea from under?" Well, it could be, poet, please let me know. She wrote in 1964 to her first biographer and critic, Anne Stevenson, that so far she had produced "what I feel is a rather 'precious' kind of poetry, although I am very much opposed to the precious." This is well said, and it shows that she was aware of possibly sounding just too, too. . . . Another letter, to Lowell in 1960, wondered whether "I'm going to turn into solid cuteness in my poetry if I don't watch out—or if I do watch out." Again we see how clearly she was aware of her gift, also aware of its possible abuse, its manner becoming—as Jarrell said happened to Auden's in the 1930s—"bureaucratized," formulaic.

 With hindsight, and doubtless some simplification, it appears to me that the "surreal" mode on display in many of the poems from *North and South* was something Bishop needed to develop out of; that is, out of the highly worked fantasies of such impressively built poems as "The Monument" and "The Man-Moth" that can also be charged with the inclination toward preciousness, even cuteness. (The final directive of "The Monument," "Watch it closely," has always seemed to me a shade cute.) Jarrell was right to single out "Roosters" and "The Fish" as the two "deeply sympathetic" poems in which a more resonant, not at all fussy, voice takes command. It is a voice that will emerge again in the final section of "At the Fishhouses," as the narrator confronts the water ("Cold dark deep and absolutely clear, / the clear gray icy water") and imagines dipping her hand in and tasting it:

If you tasted it, it would first taste bitter,
then briny, then surely burn your tongue.
It is like what we imagine knowledge to be:
dark, salt, clear, moving, utterly free,

drawn from the cold hard mouth
of the world, derived from the rocky breasts
forever, flowing and drawn, and since
our knowledge is historical, flowing, and flown.

What is "seen" here is something far beyond the visual, as it is at the end of "The Armadillo"—the Bishop poem that meant so much to Lowell—when in the italicized final stanza, after observing the fire balloon and its effects on the small animals it disturbs, the anonymous voice speaks for everyone:

> *Too pretty, dreamlike mimicry!*
> *O falling fire and piercing cry*
> *and panic, and weak mailed fist*
> *clenched ignorant against the sky!*

The too pretty, dreamlike mimicry at which the voice exclaims may well refer to the preceding un-italicized stanzas describing the emergence of the owls from their burned nest, the rabbit "with fixed ignited eyes" and the "glistening" armadillo himself, "a weak mailed fist" against the sky. At any rate it is a visionary moment (the overused word still seems appropriate) created by the narrator's rising to a pitch of statement, exclamatory in "The Armadillo" but correspondingly intense in "At the Fishhouses," moving the utterance out of or beyond any particular tone. To the extent that Bishop moves, and moves us beyond "tone," such apostrophes resist paraphrase by making interpretive efforts feel somehow beside the point, crude or callow. She wrote May Swenson in 1955, "I think myself that my best poems seem rather distant, and sometimes I wish I could be as objective about everything else as I seem to be in and about them. I don't think I'm very successful when I get personal,—rather sound personal." Such depersonalizing occurs in these sequences from "At the Fishhouses" and "The Armadillo," but they would hardly be so effective—breathtaking, even—without the breathed, nuanced, varied tone and tones in the earlier parts of each poem.

Bishop once provided Anne Stevenson with a capsule account of her own temperament. She said she had never liked Emily Dickinson much, but after reading through the collected edition found many poems to admire "though not the oh-the-pain-of-it-all" ones. She admits to snobbery about "the humorless Martha-Graham kind of person who does like

Emily Dickinson": "In fact I think snobbery governs a great deal of my taste. I have been very lucky in having had, most of my life, some witty friends—and I mean real wit, quickness, wild fancies, remarks that make one cry with laughing." Most of her friends, such as the aunt she liked best, her partner Lora de Macedo Soares, Marianne Moore, E. E. Cummings, were very "funny" people: "Perhaps I need such people to cheer me up." A moment in her poetry that seems to me quintessential "real wit," a truly wild and "funny" stroke, occurs in "Arrival at Santos," the first poem in *Questions of Travel* (although she had printed it previously in *A Cold Spring*). Its ten quatrains, with their rollicking, offbeat cadences and seemingly catch-as-can rhymes, present the speaker, about to debark into the port city of Santos, for customs inspection. She notes that despite this new environment, she will encounter familiar things, like a "flag,"

> And coins, I presume,
> and paper money; they remain to be seen.
> And gingerly now we climb down the ladder backward,
> myself and a fellow passenger named Miss Breen,
>
> descending into the midst of twenty-six freighters
> waiting to be loaded with green coffee beans.
> Please, boy, do be more careful with that boat hook!
> Watch out! Oh! It has caught Miss Breen's
>
> skirt! There! Miss Breen is about seventy,
> a retired police lieutenant, six feet tall,
> with beautiful bright blue eyes and a kind expression.
> Her home, when she is at home, is in Glens Fall
>
> s, New York. There. We are settled.

An important, though not the only, reason why I find this sequence so satisfying—so satisfyingly *funny*, to use Bishop's word—is that I once heard James Merrill read the poem aloud. His wonderfully nuanced voice did an especially fine job with "Watch out! Oh! It has caught Miss Breen's / / skirt!" —exclamations he delivered in a mock-horrified, somewhat campy mode that Bishop herself would surely have loved. Merrill would speak, in a tribute written just after she died, of her poems as "wryly radiant, more touching, more unaffectedly intelligent than any written in her lifetime." That phrase "wryly radiant" is as good as any I've found to catch the mixture of wit and wonder that was hers in so many of the poems. To be wryly radiant is to be something quite distinct from what Frost liked to call, with a condescending twist in his voice, "poetical." In a rather unbuttoned conversation she had with an interviewer in 1966, when she had begun to teach writing at the University of Washington, Bishop said she had told her class that the poems they'd handed in contained "a disproportionate number of *haikus*" and were "not very well written either," "more like the sort of thing one might jot down when one is feeling vaguely poetic." She mused upon the students in that class,

> with their trusting eyes and their clear complexions. Have you seen the expensive cars that some of them drive? . . . Most of them look quite well fed and rather well off. And what do they write about in their poems? *Suffering*, of all things!

She told the students they should come to Brazil and see what real suffering was like, then perhaps they wouldn't write so "poetically" about it.[4]

North & South has thirty poems; *A Cold Spring*, eighteen; *Questions of Travel*, twenty. The last book Bishop published in her lifetime, *Geography III*, consisted of only ten poems. This is extraordinary, and becomes more so when, in the Library of America edition, we note roughly 150 pages of uncollected, unpublished poems and translations, some of which are perfectly good work that most poets would not have held back. *Geography III* has been widely admired and praised, and seven of its ten poems are among the best ones she ever wrote. "In the Waiting Room" has had more than its share of attention, and "Crusoe in England" is surely as original a creation as she produced. "The Moose" seems to me, even more affectingly, to contain the surprise Bishop felt essential to any good poetry, most beautifully in the sequence that moves from the bus passengers "Talking the way they talked / in the old featherbed," as sleep comes over them, only to be startled by the great animal, "Towering, anterless, / high as a church, / homely as a house / (or, safe as houses)." As for her villanelle "One Art," Brad Leithauser wrote recently that, along with Dylan Thomas's "Do not go gentle into that good night;" it figures as a poem "that might have taken the elaborate stanzaic arrangement even if the Italians hadn't invented it three hundred years ago." "The End of March," in its serious play, is also top-grade Bishop. My own two favorites—maybe not the two "best" ones—turn out to be "Poem" and "Five Flights Up," and I will say just a word about their superb endings by way of one more gesture at Bishop's originality.

"Poem," the most modest and accurate of all Bishop's titles perhaps, is about the small painting by an uncle ("About the size of an old-style dollar bill") passed down to her as a "minor family relic" of seventy years back. The course of "Poem" enacts the quickening of interest as the emerging Bishop-figure recognizes houses, elm trees, a church steeple, tiny cows, and two white geese. In fact it's not just a Nova Scotian landscape but one closer to home ("Heavens, I recognize the place, I know it!"), even though, she confides to us, "Those particular geese and cows / are naturally before my time." From these appealing, even chatty reflections, she moves into an identification of Uncle George's "view" (as shown in his painting) and her own, memory-imperfect sense, when a young child, of the "life" he had rendered into art: "our looks, / two looks: / art 'copying from life' and life itself, / life and the memory of it so compressed / they've turned into each other." "Which is which?" she asks, then moves into a concluding tribute as moving in my judgment as anything she ever wrote:

> Life and the memory of it cramped,
> dim, on a piece of Bristol board,
> dim, but how live, how touching in detail
> —the little that we get for free,
> the little of our earthly trust. Not much.
> About the size of our abidance
> along with theirs: the munching cows,
> the iris, crisp and shivering, the water
> still standing from spring freshets,
> the yet-to-be-dismantled elms, the geese.

What a model of not saying too much but just enough—of "radiance," twisted enough to be wry, yet gracefully so. Once more it is "timing" that is central: the crucial repetitions of "dim," of "Life and the memory of it," of "the little . . . the little." The really astonishing effect occurs after the reflection about our "abidance," a slightly remote and dignified word for the earthly dwelling we share "along with theirs"—the natural and animal inhabitants denoted in the painting. "Theirs" is what fills up the last three and a half lines, individual items separated only by the neutral, nondiscriminatory comma and concluding in the most unspectacular of ways with (merely) "the geese."

Merrill also wrote a poem in homage to Bishop ("Overdue Pilgrimage to Nova Scotia") of five connected sonnets, the third of which begins, "In living as in poetry, your art / Refused to tip the scale of being human / By adding unearned weight." These lines fit perfectly the human scale ruefully celebrated in "Poem." In her own life she was not likely to add "unearned weight" to the scale; writing to Pearl Kazin in 1953, she remarks in a throwaway sentence, "It is a little hard to get used to being happy after forty-two years . . . of being almost consistently unhappy." The final poem in *Geography III,* "Five Flights Up," assesses the human scale in its daily resumption, by contrasting it with the sounds of little animals heard upon waking:

> Still dark.
> The unknown bird sits on his usual branch.
> The little dog next door barks in his sleep
> inquiringly, just once.
> Perhaps, in his sleep, too, the bird inquires
> once or twice, quavering.
> Questions—if that is what they are—
> answered directly, simply,
> by day itself.
>
> Enormous morning, ponderous, meticulous;
> gray light streaking each bare branch,
> each single twig, along one side,
> making another tree, of glassy veins . . .
> The bird still sits there. Now he seems to yawn.
>
> The little black dog runs in his yard.
> His owner's voice arises, stern,
> "You ought to be ashamed!"
> What has he done?
> He bounces cheerfully up and down;
> he rushes in circles in the fallen leaves.

Obviously he has no sense of shame.
He and the bird know everything is answered,
all taken care of,
no need to ask again.
—Yesterday brought to today so lightly!
(A yesterday I find almost impossible to lift.)

In his review of *North & South*, Jarrell wrote that Bishop's poems instead of crying "This is a world in which no one can get along" show that "it is barely but perfectly possible—has been, that is, for her." At the end of "Five Flights Up," in that juxtaposition of the exclamatory wonder at what the bird and the dog know ("everything is answered, / All taken care of"), and the final, confiding murmur within the parentheses, the getting along of a new day seems possible—but just barely. Here the "human scale" is all but overtaken by the weight of the burden.

She wrote Jarrell a wonderful letter in 1965, the year he published his last book, *The Lost World,* and the year of his death. Whatever her reservations about Frost and his poetry ("a malicious old bore," she called him in one of her letters), she must have heartened Jarrell by calling him "the real one and only successor to Frost," not the folksy-wisdom side of Frost, but "all the good, the beautiful writing, the sympathy, the touching and real detail, etc." She says she could almost write a piece about this if she were a more skillful critic: "You're both [Jarrell and Frost] very sorrowful, and yet not the anguish-school that Cal [Lowell] seems innocently to have inspired— the self-pitiers. . . . It is more human, less specialized, and yet deep." However truly it fits the best of Jarrell, she was also, in these sentences, writing her own epitaph.

— *Hudson Review*, Summer 2008.

Notes

1. Reviews of Bishop may be found in *Elizabeth Bishop and Her Art*, ed. Lloyd Schwartz and Sybil P. Estes (Ann Arbor: University of Michigan Press, 1983). David Kalstone's book is *Becoming a Poet* (New York: Farrar, Straus, and Giroux, 1989). Brett Millier's biography is *Elizabeth Bishop: Life and the Memory of It* (Berkeley: University of California Press, 1995). Thomas Travisano's book is *Elizabeth Bishop: Her Artistic Development* (Charlottesville: University of Virginia Press, 1988).

2. Bonnie Costello, "The Impersonal and the Interrogative in the Poetry of Elizabeth Bishop," in *Elizabeth Bishop and Her Art*, 119-32.

3. The best account of Bishop's poetic rhythm is Penelope Laurans, "Elizabeth Bishop, 'Old Corespondences': Prosodic Transformations in Elizabeth Bishop," *Elizabeth Bishop and Her Art*, 75-95.

4. In *Conversations with Elizabeth Bishop*, ed. George Monteiro (Jackson: University Press of Mississippi, 1996), 41.

James Merrill Collected

ALTHOUGH 2001 has some months to go, the literary event of the year has occurred with the publication of James Merrill's *Collected Poems*. Collected rather than complete, since not included is his volume-length epic, *The Changing Light at Sandover*. But it contains enough to keep a reader busy for months, years: ten volumes, ranging from *First Poems* published in 1951, four years after his graduation from Amherst College, to *A Scattering of Salts*, brought out soon after his death in 1995. In addition there are about two hundred pages of material only the Merrill expert will be familiar with—translations, uncollected and unpublished poems, including a final few written when he was near death. As a physical object, the nine-hundred-page volume is a beauty: handsomely bound and sewn, with black pages separating the individual collections and with Thomas Victor's photo of Merrill wrapped around the spine of a mostly black dust-jacket on which appears the poet's name in large, lavender letters. The lavender motif—alluding to Merrill's homosexual preference—is extended to the opening and closing pages and to a silk bookmark, all in all a state-of-the-art project designed by the resourceful Chip Kidd. In a time when one is invited to plunk down twenty-five dollars for any old novel, the forty-dollar pricing of *Collected Poems* is a bargain.

In fact, the book is priceless. For what immersion in Merrill's life work of poems brings us is the conviction that, taken together, the volumes of beautifully wrought verse he gave us make up what we must call—vaguely but unmistakably—a world, one capacious enough to allow endless opportunities for moving around in, for surprise, for continued discovery. About the creation of that world, Merrill was astonishingly prophetic when, in his early thirties, he wrote "A Tenancy," the concluding poem in *Water Street* (1961), the book in which we hear for the first time the deepened range of a poetic voice. The poem begins with Merrill recalling a March afternoon in 1946 when, having turned twenty, he proposes a "bargain with—say with the source of light":

> That given a few years more
> (Seven or ten or, what seemed vast, fifteen)
> To spend in love, in a country not at war,
> I would give in return
> All I had. All? A little sun
> Rose in my throat. The lease was drawn.

"A Tenancy" ends with the now "leaner veteran" of fifteen years later being visited by three of his friends and contemplating his identity as a poet:

> If I am host at last
> It is of little more than my own past.
> May others be at home in it.

This pledge of hospitality offered the reader was to be observed for the next thirty-four years, as the world of Merrill's poetry expanded and complicated itself but never ceased to imagine a listening reader, someone who cared enough to tune in to the unfailingly regular broadcasts.

The best critic of Merrill's work has been Helen Vendler (her collected reviews of him would make an excellent book), who has more than once spoken to the "Mozartian" spirit of his work. She is referring to its comic nature, comedy of course being a most serious matter; indeed Alexander Pope wanted life to be "a long, exact, and serious comedy," and Vendler names as Merrill's three great precursors in English verse Pope, Byron, and W. H. Auden. These poets may well be the greatest technicians of our language (we don't think of Shakespeare or Wordsworth as technicians, even though their employment of words is brilliant). It's also on record that Merrill's contemporary, Richard Wilbur, has called him "the most dazzling technician we have"—this compliment paid by a fellow graduate of Amherst who might himself with equal justice be called the most dazzling technician we have. But the word is dangerous, since it can invite the demeaning adjective "mere" (a "mere" technician, "merely" technique), so to rescue Merrill from the impeachment we should recall T. S. Eliot's observation that "we cannot say at what point 'technique' begins or where it ends." In other words, it won't do to hive off the dazzling employment of words from anything supposedly more serious.

By way of suggesting how impressive a technician James Merrill was and how fully that technique served to create a compelling human presence, I will adduce a single poem, "The Victor Dog," published in *Braving the Elements* (1972):

> Bix to Buxtehude to Boulez,
> The little white dog on the Victor label
> Listens long and hard as he is able.
> It's all in a day's work, whatever plays.
>
> From judgment, it would seem, he has refrained.
> He even listens earnestly to Bloch,
> Then builds a church upon our acid rock.
> He's man's—no—he's the Leiermann's best friend,
>
> Or would be if hearing and listening were the same.
> *Does* he hear? I fancy he rather smells
> Those lemon-gold arpeggios in Ravel's
> "Les jets d'eau du palais de ceux qui s'aiment."
>
> He ponders the Schumann Concerto's tall willow hit
> By lightning, and stays put. When he surmises
> Through one of Bach's eternal boxwood mazes
> The oboe pungent as a bitch in heat,
>
> Or when the calypso decants its raw bay rum
> Or the moon in *Wozzeck* reddens ripe for murder,
> He doesn't sneeze or howl; just listens harder.
> Adamant needles bear down on him from
>
> Whirling of outer space, too black, too near—
> But he was taught as a puppy not to flinch,
> Much less to imitate his bête noire Blanche
> Who barked, fat foolish creature, at King Lear.

Still others fought in the road's filth over Jezebel,
Slavered on hearths of horned and pelted barons.
His forebears lacked, to say the least, forbearance.
Can nature change in him? Nothing's impossible.

The last chord fades. The night is cold and fine.
His master's voice rasps through the grooves' bare groves.
Obediently, in silence like the grave's
He sleeps there on the still-warm gramophone

Only to dream he is at the première of a Handel
Opera long thought lost— *Il Cane Minore.*
Its allegorical subject is his story!
A little dog revolving round a spindle

Gives rise to harmonics beyond belief,
A cast of stars . . . Is there in Victor's heart
No honey for the vanquished? Art is art.
The life it asks of us is a dog's life.

It is one of the poems ("Matinees" and "The *Ring* Cycle" are others) in which his inwardness with music is patent. It is learned and difficult, but not obscure, and it has elicited surprisingly little comment, perhaps because—misleadingly, I think—critics deem it so light-spirited as to be the opposite of profound. "The Victor Dog" is a poem of forty lines, in ten stanzas rhyming ABBA. It is spoken by the Poet, the one on whom nothing is lost, who knows and sees and hears all, and to whom it is our privilege and pleasure to listen. If the lines quoted earlier from "A Tenancy"—the poem in which Merrill pledged himself to his art—are gravely thoughtful, those in "The Victor Dog" crackle with witty fireworks, to describe which the adjective "playful" is woefully inadequate. "Bix to Buxtehude to Boulez" is, for openers, a line no one came close to writing previously, showing an aural quickness of association, which, once "Bix" is sounded, moves inevitably to "Bux[tehude]" then (with the sound of "hude") to "Bo*u*lez." There is a sheer pleasure in pronouncing the names of these three B's of the composer-performer world.

Merrill's own performance in the first three stanzas seems especially packed with what Frost named as the essential constituents of poet-ry—"this thing of performance and prowess and feats of association." Merely to note the ABBA rhyme pattern suggests nothing about how delightfully "off" are the first and fourth line-rhymes of these stanzas: Boulez / plays; refrained / friend; same / *s'aiment.* Auden was expert at slanting his rhymes, but Merrill's rhyming is even more inventive, more fun (especially in the same / *s'aiment* rhyme where the words look so very different). Then there is the pacing: Frost said he was interested in how he could "lay" sentences into lines of verse; Merrill's three stanzas contain seven sentences—of, respectively, three, one, one, two, two, a half, and two and a half lines—with the effect of keeping us off-balance, surprised at the way a line does or doesn't conclude itself in a full-stop period. These off-beat happenings help generate changes of voice: from the mock-casual "It's all in a day's work, whatever plays" (the play on "work" / "play" is so casual as to be scarcely discernible); to the mock-thoughtful "From judgment, it would seem, he has refrained"; to the deadpan coupling of the Chris-tian church's laying its foundation on a rock " *Tu es Petrus"*) with the 1970s acid rock that the dog refrains from judging, just listens to. My favorite moment is the mock correction of phrase in "He's man's—no—he's the Leiermann's best friend," the reference here being to the final song in Schubert's *Winterreise,* a strange, ghostly one about a hurdy-gurdy man.

As always with lines from Merrill's poems, there is more to be said, and I refrain from further lunges at explanation. (But what about "the Schumann Concerto's tall willow hit / By lightning"? Do we need to hear the opening theme in the third—or the first—movement?) Yet the poem is more than one devilishly clever stroke after another, since it also has a development, a little narrative that broadens into an exquisitely touching finality of statement:

> The last chord fades. The night is cold and fine.
> His master's voice rasps through the grooves' bare groves.

That is what it is like to hear the record-player's needle having come to the end of the piece and moving through "grooves' bare groves" as they revolve. Suddenly we are precipitated into the lovely conceit of the little dog's dream; involving discovery of the hitherto undiscovered opera *Il Cane Minore* (slant-rhymes with story), at which point the poet, caught up in the dream ("life's allegorical subject is his story"), is moved to state the ultimate mystery of how going round and round the spindle produces the splendors and sadness of music. Such "harmonies beyond belief" that call forth a mid-line breaking-off (. . .) and a poignant question not to be answered: "Is there in Victor's heart / No honey for the vanquished?" Or rather, answered only by the bare truths that end the poem:

Art is art.
The life it asks of us is a dog's life.

Merrill went to his writing desk every morning, led the dog's life of writing, in order to give us the richness of his music.

Merrill's art is to give rise to harmonies beyond belief without ever raising his voice—as Eliot, Yeats, Robert Lowell raised their voices. He once said on the subject that "If you were taught that it's not polite to raise your voice, it's very hard to write like Whitman," and we may be grateful that he didn't attempt the barbaric yawp. In this restraint he most resembles that other "technician," Wilbur, who has also avoided loud affirmations or negations, believing (in the words of Merrill's "The Thousand and Second Night") that "Form's what affirms." Merrill and Wilbur, along with Anthony Hecht, all roughly the same age, seem to me our great formal poets, each brought up on high modernist predecessors, but also responsive to the quieter voicings and ceaseless wit of a Frost, an Elizabeth Bishop. Like Frost and like Bishop, these successors are committed to narrative, to writing poems with a "plot," a development that, however difficult it is to track (and with Merrill it is often extremely difficult if not impossible), is committed to making something we call, for lack of a better word, *sense*. (Here the three poets differ from their contemporary John Ashbery, who just goes on in his merry way making nonsense.)

Merrill's poems have denouement; they twist and turn in the motion of an imagination working something out. His practice and subjects as a poet have been remarkably continuous: one does not talk of "development" in the twenty-three years of work that followed "The Victor Dog." We may recall Oscar Wilde, declaring that only mediocrities develop, but note as well that unlike, most impressively, Robert Lowell's, Merrill's art is not made out of the dramatic presentation of self-struggle, action and reaction, the taking on of successive Yeatsian masks. He claims furthermore never to have thought of his homosexuality as an "issue," either in the poems or outside them. As the social stigma lessened or disappeared altogether in the

1970s, Merrill was not on the battlements: "I stood still and the closet disintegrated," he remarked: "I don't believe in being the least militant about it." His final three volumes, published after the closet disintegrated (*Late Settings, The Inner Room,* and *A Scattering of Salts*), are books this reader has scarcely begun to assimilate), and they contain some of his very best poems.

Perhaps, in the manner Randall Jarrell liked to employ when dealing with a poet's life work, it is permissible to name about twenty-five poems for which in my judgment Merrill should be most remembered. In more or less chronological order, then: "The Black Swan," "The Country of a Thousand Years of Peace," "Mirror," "An Urban Convalescence," "For Proust," "Getting Through," "Annie Hill's Grave," "A Tenancy," "The Thousand and Second Night," "Time," "The Broken Home," "Matinées," "Up and Down," "The Victor Dog," "Lost in Translation," "Clearing the Title," "Days of 1941 and '44," "The House Fly," "Santorini: Stopping the Leak," "Investiture at Cecconi's," "Farewell Performance," "Nine Lives," "The *Ring* Cycle," "Family Week at Oracle Ranch," "164 East 72nd Street," "Overdue Pilgrimage to Nova Scotia," "Self-Portrait in Tyvek™ Windbreaker." Add to these two of the last poems he wrote that conclude this volume, "Christmas Tree" and "Days of 1994."

To call these last poems rehearsals for death puts it too bluntly only if the moving affirmations in which they end are ignored. "Days of 1994," the last of many "Days of" poems he wrote, concludes with the notion of waking in a tomb "Below the world" and enumerates some of "the thousand things / Here risen to if not above / Before day ends":

> The spectacles, the book,
> Forgetful lover and forgotten love,
> Cobweb hung with trophy wings,
> The fading trumpet of a car,
> The knowing glance from star to star,
> The laughter of old friends.

And—if possible—even more movingly because more wittily, there is "Christmas Tree," an account by the tree of being "brought down from the cold mountain," "warmly" taken in and dressed by the world, put under the spell of love and human hospitality. But the tree knows how different is what lies ahead, and seamlessly the speaking voice becomes the poet's from his hospital bed ("a primitive IV / To keep the show going"). He imagines "the stripping, the cold street, my chemicals / Plowed back into the Earth for lives to come." But it is too much to be dwelt on and the voice ends instead with "No dread. No bitterness," naming its surroundings even as they vanish:

> Dusk room aglow
> For the last time
> With candlelight.
> Faces love lit,
> Gifts underfoot.
> Still to be so poised, so
> Receptive, still to recall, to praise.

The tenancy, drawn up in 1946, was about to expire; the tenant remained in his lines, ever poised, receptive, recalling and giving praise.

(Full text of "Christmas Tree" appears on the next page.)
—*Amherst,* Summer 2001

CHRISTMAS TREE

*

To be
Brought down at last
From the cold sighing mountain
Where I and the others
Had been fed, looked after, kept still,
Meant, I knew—of course I knew—
That it would be only a matter of weeks.
That there was nothing more to do.
Warmly they took me in, made much of me,
The point from the start was to keep my spirits up.
I could assent to that. For honestly,
It did help to be wound in jewels, to send
Their colors flashing forth from vents in the deep
Fragrant sables that cloaked me head to foot.
Over me then they wove a spell of shining—
Purple and silver chains, eavesdripping tinsel,
Amulets, milagros: software of silver,
A heart, a little girl, a Model T,
Two staring eyes. The angels, trumpets, BUD and BEA
(The children's names) in clownlike capitals,
Somewhere a music box whose tiny song
Played and replayed I ended before long
By loving. And in shadow behind me, a primitive IV
To keep the show going. Yes, yes, what lay ahead
Was clear: the stripping, the cold street, my chemicals
Plowed back into the Earth for lives to come—
No doubt a blessing, a harvest, but one that doesn't bear,
Now or ever, dwelling upon. To have grown so thin.
Needles and bone. The little boy's hands meeting
About my spine. The mother's voice: *Holding up wonderfully!*
No dread. No bitterness. The end beginning. Today's
Dusk room aglow
For the last time
With candlelight.
Faces love-lit,
Gifts underfoot.
Still to be so poised, so
Receptive. Still to recall, to praise.

Critics, Criticism

Johnson's *Lives*

W<small>E SHOULD BEGIN</small> with the title in full: *The Lives of the Most Eminent English Poets; With Critical Observations on Their Works*, by Samuel Johnson. The author once remarked to Boswell that he was engaged in writing "little Lives, and little Prefaces, to a little edition," an enterprise set in motion by a consortium of London booksellers. The "little edition" was to consist of fifty-two English poets in an anthology designed to fend off competition from a Scottish publisher, John Bell, who had brought out a comparable anthology. Johnson's accompanying "lives" or prefaces—he used both terms to describe his contributions—would be a key attraction in the competition. It took him four years to complete the task, and in 1781 the *Lives* were first published independently of the poems and poets they introduced. Now the remarkable Roger Lonsdale, already a distinguished eighteenth-century scholar, has, as a crowning achievement, edited them for Clarendon Press in a four-volume boxed set for which the cliché "magisterial" scarcely begins to suggest the project's immensity.[1]

Its dimensions deserve to be enumerated. Running to 1,981 pages total, the editor's commentary and textual notes easily outstrip Johnson's own pages, especially in the fourth volume (190 pages of Johnson, 327 of Lonsdale), where the "Life of Pope" is especially heavily annotated. Lonsdale's admirable predecessor as an editor of *Lives of the Poets* was George Birkbeck-Hill, who in 1905 brought out, also under the Clarendon Press imprint, a three-volume edition. The main difference between the earlier and the latest edition is that Birkbeck-Hill—to whom Lonsdale records his debt—placed his footnotes at the bottom of each page with numbers in the text to tell us when we might look down for further illumination. Birkbeck-Hill also placed marginal numerals to mark the beginning of each of Johnson's new paragraphs, as does Lonsdale. But Lonsdale places his notes at the end of each volume so one is not directed at specific points to consult a note. And though he gives no explanation for this decision, it may be that since he annotates each and every one of Johnson's paragraphs—usually to the teeth—he is inviting us always to turn to the back.

So a reader of *Lives* in its entirety has to decide how much attention to give the always pertinent annotation. Eager to learn more about Milton or Dryden, I'm not so eager about William King or Richard Duke, the latter of whose poems, Johnson wrote, "are not below mediocrity; nor have I found much in them to praise." Duke is dispatched by Johnson in less than a page; Lonsdale, in much smaller print, provides two pages of commentary in his standard format: Composition, Sources, Publication, Modern Sources—and gives notes, as always, to each paragraph of the seven Johnson wrote. The proportion of annotation to text is navigable in such a tiny compass, but becomes not such clear sailing when Abraham Cowley's forty-one pages receive forty-nine of annotation. The "Life of Cowley" was thought by Johnson to be his best, since he was proud of the lengthy set-piece in which he adversely criticizes the Metaphysical Poets (especially Cowley and Donne). But the once-alive Cowley is now dead as a poet. "Who now reads Cowley?" asked Alexander Pope, rhetorically, a half-century after Cowley's death. Who now is impelled to attend to forty pages of commentary on a poet no one reads?

Further indications of the scope of Lonsdale's undertaking: volume one consists of 400 pages, only a quarter of which are made up of the first three lives—Cowley, Denham, and Milton—in Johnson's series. The volume is kicked off by a masterly introduction of 185 pages, which surely rivals (in length) any introduction to any book I'm aware of. It is occupied mainly with the project's origin; with the alternately dilatory and rapid pace at which Johnson composed the essays; with the persons who were his editorial assistants and the main sources he consulted. Lonsdale proceeds "to outline the trajectory of the *Lives* and to trace Johnson's explicit and implicit assumptions and preoccupations." This involves a chronological run-through of the whole list of poets by way of qualifying the received notion that Johnson was unambiguously devoted to celebrating the "elegance" and "correctness" that emerged in the Restoration and reached its apex in the poetry of Pope. Persuasively, Lonsdale finds that Johnson did not simply hold such an assumption; that rather he was

> haunted, first, by a growing suspicion that some older kinds
> of poetic "vigour" and mental "comprehension" had simul-

taneously been sacrificed, and, secondly, by an awareness that the civilized poetic qualities he himself valued had unaccountably come to seem insipid and outdated to his younger contemporaries.

It is an interesting coincidence to note that the year 1783, when the final, revised version of *Lives* was published and Johnson's six-year labor ended, is also the year in which William Blake published his first book—his only conventionally produced one—of poems. The last poem in *Poetical Sketches,* "To the Muses," looked sadly at contemporary poets and addressed them reprovingly:

> How have you left the ancient love
>   That bards of old enjoy'd in you!
> The languid strings do scarcely move!
>   The sound is forc'd, the notes are few!

Blake was preparing to move the strings to notes not yet heard.

Viewing the list of fifty-two poets from Cowley to Lyttleton, we might ask how, even two and more centuries ago, this could have passed as a reasonable list of the most eminent English poets. The official answer is that no poet who wrote before the Restoration was included (no Donne, no Spenser) nor any poet still alive (no Cowper, no Chatterton). Johnson's friend, Oliver Goldsmith, had died but was omitted for reasons of copyright; the satirist Charles Churchill, praised by Yvor Winters but otherwise unread, was also omitted, either for the same reasons or because, as Mrs. Thrale claimed, Johnson didn't want him in. So essentially these most "eminent" English poets were selected by the booksellers from a span of about a hundred years, and it is hardly surprising that most of them are unknown to serious readers of poetry in 2007. No women are represented, not even Anne Finch, Countess of Winchilsea, or Lady Mary Wortley Montague, scourge in her verse of both Swift and Pope. (Lonsdale has edited an Oxford edition of eighteenth-century women poets.) One of the longest lives here is also the earliest written, Johnson's sixty-nine-page account of his friend of youthful days, Richard Savage. The "Life of Savage," longer than any of the others except Dryden's and Pope's, has, unsurprisingly, a personal, autobiographical note absent from the other lives—except for the one of William Collins, which contains the lovely sentence "Such was the fate of Collins, with whom I once delighted to converse, and whom I yet remember with tenderness."

Johnson's *Lives,* written as he tells us "in my usual way, dilatorily and hastily, unwilling to work and working with vigour and haste," has come down to us as in effect the great writer's last will and testament. It is his supreme attempt to put in convincing order, as his own life drew to a close, his thoughts about the meaning of a literary career and the significance, or insignificance, of the English poets whose inheritance was his. Roughly a hundred years later, Matthew Arnold wrote a little-known essay on Johnson in which he put forward a possible use that contemporary readers, especially younger ones, could make of the *Lives.*[2] Arnold's essay was an introduction to a volume that consisted of the six most substantial lives— in his opinion, Milton, Dryden, Addison, Pope, Swift, and Gray—and is opposed, in principle, to Lonsdale's magnificent edition. Arnold's idea was that in reprinting the six lives without encumbering notes and commentary, the selection would provide what he called an admirable *"point de repère,* or fixed centre" for the student of English literature. The lives of these six important authors, as told by a great man, would, Arnold hoped, lead students to acquaint themselves with some of the leading and representative works of each. Except for Milton, Arnold had less than the highest opinion of the authors as poets, especially Swift and Addison. He saluted the Restoration and eighteenth century as the great age when English prose became a natural, viable, and adequate vehicle for thought, as it had not been in the earlier seventeenth century and before. ("Inconvenient" and "obsolete" are words he uses to characterize the prose of such seventeenth-century writers as Milton and George Chapman.) Although Arnold was relatively uninterested (as was Johnson, often) in the facts and dates of biography, and although he disagreed with Johnson's high valuation of Dryden and Pope, as well as with his dismissal of Milton's *Lycidas* and his thorough downgrading of Thomas Gray (except for "Elegy in a Country Churchyard"), Arnold believed his selection from the *Lives* would give a "compendious story" of an important age in English literature, and would itself be "a piece of English literature of the first class." Like his much-abused "touchstones"—great passages from Homer, Dante, Shakespeare, and Milton that would, as we recalled them, save us from overvaluing some contemporary lines from a lesser poet—Johnson's *Lives* provided a similar fixed center from which the life of literature could be contemplated.

T. S. Eliot, who never missed an opportunity to snipe at Arnold, nevertheless also used Johnson's *Lives,* specifically the "Life of Cowley," as a "fixed centre" when he closed his introduction to *The Sacred Wood* with a note that began thus:

> I may commend as a model to critics who desire to correct some of the poetical vagaries of the present age, the following passage from a writer who cannot be accused of flaccid leniency, and the justice of whose criticism must be acknowledged even by those who feel a strong partiality toward the school of poets criticized.

There follow two paragraphs from the "Life of Cowley" in which, having convicted the Metaphysical "school" of far-fetched conceitedness, Johnson turns on himself and says something in favor of the poets he's been criticizing: "Yet to write on their plan, it was at least necessary to read and think." Years later in his rich and lengthy essay "Johnson as Critic and Poet," Eliot addressed himself to the problem of Johnson's "ear" for poetry, or his lack of it, by noting that readers of the *Lives* remember most strongly the strictures against the Metaphysicals (including Donne) and against *Lycidas,* "of which the diction is harsh, the rhymes uncertain, and the numbers displeasing." Even more surprising than these strictures against poetry we take to be canonical was Johnson's silence about Shakespeare (in the "Preface to Shakespeare") as a writer of verse whose diction and movement—to apply the terms Arnold used in "The Study of Poetry" —were exemplary. But rather than deploring Johnson's ear, Eliot explains it historically by implying that, as it were, Johnson was unable to read Eliot's "Tradition and the Individual Talent," in which is set down the "obvious fact" that "art never improves, but that the material of art is never quite the same." On the contrary, Johnson felt no need for the "renewal" of literature, as Eliot did in renewing his own verse by way of seventeenth-century English poets and nineteenth-century French symbolists. For, Eliot wrote, "the age in which Johnson lived, was not old enough to feel the need for such renewal: it had just arrived at its own maturity. Johnson could think of the literature of his age as having attained the standard from which literature of the past could be judged."

At about the time Eliot's essay appeared, F. R. Leavis also criticized Johnson's ear as a critic of poetry, but in a less far-seeing way.[3] While admiring of Johnson's greatness as a writer of prose and verse, Leavis dwelt on the limitations revealed in his criticism of Shakespeare's poetry, his inability to appreciate "the Shakespearean creativeness," "the exploratory creative use of words upon experience" that "we" (Leavis and other enlightened modern readers) find in the verse of Shakespeare's tragedies, or—in another example Leavis adduces as beyond Johnson's appreciative power—in the fourth book of Pope's *Dunciad*. For Johnson, Shakespearean "complexity" was not to be marveled at, but rather explained as (in language from the "Preface to Shakespeare") "the writer becoming entangled with an unwieldy sentiment, which he cannot well express, and will not reject." So that, for example, Johnson felt it incumbent upon him to unpack Hamlet's famous "To be or not to be" soliloquy by translating it into clear, discursive prose.[4] At first glance Leavis's point seems final; but Eliot in his discussion of the same Johnsonian "limitation" manages to make something more positive out of it. If Johnson lacks the historical sense, is unable to understand "archaic" rhythm and diction such as is found in the Metaphysicals and in Shakespeare's poetry, then it was, Eliot writes, "not through lack of sensibility but through specialization of sensibility." He enlarges on this:

> If the eighteenth century had admired the poetry of earlier times in the way in which we can admire it, the result would have been chaos: there would have been no eighteenth century as we know it. That age would not have had the conviction necessary for perfecting the kind of poetry that it did perfect. The deafness of Johnson's ear to some kinds of melody was the necessary condition for his sharpness of sensibility to verbal beauty of another kind.

This seems to me on Eliot's part a wonderfully capacious and generous use of the historical sense that, more than any other twentieth-century critic, he helped bring into awareness.

■ ■ ■ ■

Unlike Arnold, who sponsored a pared-down "essential" *Lives of the Poets,* Eliot insisted that they be read entire if Johnson's achievement were to be appreciated. (Eliot also insisted the same thing with respect to Shakespeare, Ben Jonson, George Herbert, and Baudelaire.) I read through the *Lives* in order—they are arranged by date of the author's death—turning frequently but not invariably to Lonsdale's commentary. Doubtless I flagged, blurred, and failed to take in some of the less memorable Johnsonian sentences, and I skipped the occasional Latin epitaph which, in the case of the forgotten seventeenth-century poet George Stepney, takes up half of the two-page life. Occasionally I marked, then typed out, utterances that made me smile, like the beginning of the "Life of Otway": "Of Thomas Otway, one of the first names in the English drama, little is known; nor is there any part of that little which his biographer can take pleasure in relating." Lonsdale calls this "Johnson's most sombre opening to a literary biography," but I should have called it not devoid of mischief. By way of making a point against the over-explicit long-windedness of Cowley's imagery in his twelve-book poem *Davideis,* Johnson quotes Cowley's description of the angel Gabriel:

> He took for skin a cloud most soft and bright.
> That e'er the midday sun pierc'd through with light,
> Upon his cheeks a lively blush he spread,
> Wash'd from the morning beauties deepest red;
> An harmless flattering meteor shone for hair,
> And fell adown his shoulders with loose care;
> He cuts out a silk mantle from the skies,
> Where the most sprightly azure pleas'd the eyes;
> This he with starry vapours sprinkles all,
> Took in their prime ere they grow ripe and fall,
> Of a new rainbow, ere it fret or fade,
> The choicest piece cut out, a scarfe is made.

Johnson comments:

> This is a just specimen of Cowley's imagery: what might in general expressions be great and forcible, he weakens and makes ridiculous by branching it into small parts. That Gabriel was invested with the softest or brightest colours of the sky, we might have been told, and been dismissed to improve the idea in our different proportions of conception; but Cowley could not let us go till he had related where Gabriel got first his skin, and then his mantle, then his lace, and then his scarfe, and related it in the terms of the mercer and taylor.

Excellent! Of Sprat, the historian of the Royal Society and a less than impressive poet: "He considered Cowley as a model, and supposed that as he was imitated, perfection was approached." So much for Sprat. Although Edmund Waller's "petty compositions" are less hyperbolical than the "amorous verses" of some other poets, still

> Waller is not always at the last gasp; he does not die of a frown, nor live upon a smile. There is however too much love, and too many trifles. Little things are made too important; and the Empire of Beauty is represented as exerting its influence further than can be allowed by the multiplicity of human passions, and the variety of human wants.

Here is the Johnsonian proportion and sanity. I raised my eyebrows when told that one of Waller's sons, Benjamin, was "disinherited, and sent to New Jersey, as wanting common understanding." I pictured poor Benjamin Waller as exiled to somewhere in the vicinity of Newark, perhaps Bayonne, until Lonsdale assured me that Johnson was speaking of Jersey, a colony in the West Indies. The brief "Life of William King" is concluded by Johnson's noting that "if his verse was easy and his images familiar, he attained what he desired." Well and good, then Johnson qualifies: "His purpose is to be merry; but perhaps, to enjoy his mirth, it may be sometimes necessary to think well of his opinion." A sentence that has thought and thought well about its own opinion.

I quote these examples of satisfying sentences, representative of many more, not for any larger significance they have in *Lives* overall, but because they are the other, humorous, side of Johnson's enterprise. As to the larger significances, Paul Fussell three decades ago named it in language that hasn't been improved on, placing the *Lives* within the tradition of a number of great eighteenth-century works of English prose and finding it, preeminently, "concerned with the nature, and more importantly, with the limits of human experience." Fussell sees the "Life of Savage," in its mordant and sympathetic account of that poet's ills and depredations, as giving an overall tone to the book whose "subject is the pathos of hope and the irony of all human and especially literary careers." Johnson scholar Greg Clingham has spoken of the writer's distinctive combination of criticism and biography as discovering "in human limitations and the historical realm a dignity and grace."[5] In other words, *Lives of the Poets* is the final investigation of matters Johnson has been exploring in various forms throughout his career: in the periodical essays from the *Rambler;* in the prefaces to the Dictionary and to Shakespeare; in *Rasselas;* and in "The Vanity of Human Wishes" and the poem to Dr. Levet.

But it is finally at the level of style—of the sentence, the paragraph— where we engage with Johnson most fully and unmistakably. Lonsdale speaks well in his introduction when he says that whatever Johnson's critical limitations and idiosyncrasies, his "energy and trenchancy" are always evident, particularly in passages from the *Lives*—"in which his prose evokes, and even competes with, the qualities of the poetry he is describing." This may be true of any great critic, but Johnson's trenchancy—usually informed by irony—is often such as to obviate the necessity of saying anything further about the literary work under consideration. Any reader of the *Lives* will encounter passages that aptly illustrate this critical power, and in limiting myself to three examples I'm aware of ignoring much. The first is from the "Life of Dryden," when Johnson, surveying the plays, has this to say about *The Conquest of Granada,* Dryden's over-the-top two-part heroic drama of 1672:

> The two parts of the *Conquest of Granada* are written with a seeming determination to glut the public with dramatick wonders; to exhibit in its highest elevation a theatrical meteor of incredible love and impossible valour, and to leave no room for a wilder flight to the extravagance of posterity. . . . Yet the scenes are, for the most part, delightful; they exhibit a kind of illustrious depravity, and majestick madness: such as, if it is sometimes despised, is often reverenced, and in which the ridiculous is mingled with the astonishing.

Johnson's two-mindedness about Dryden's spectacle is nicely concentrated in the oxymoron, "illustrious depravity." How is any future critic of the play to top that, and why should he or she try?

From the paragraphs about Pope's *Essay on Man* the following sequence suggests Johnson's less than fully admiring attitude toward the poem, "certainly not the happiest of Pope's performances." But as one paragraph turns into the next, we see the perspective moving from denigration to a somewhat reluctant admiration:

Having exalted himself into the chair of wisdom, he tells us much that every man knows, and much that he does not know himself; that we see but little, and that the order of the universe is beyond our comprehension; an opinion not very uncommon; and that there is a chain of subordinate beings *from infinite to nothing,* of which himself and his readers are equally ignorant. But he gives us one comfort, which, without his help, he supposes unattainable, in the position *that though we are fools, yet God is wise.*

This Essay affords an egregious instance of the predominance of genius, the dazzling splendour of imagery, and the seductive powers of eloquence. Never were penury of knowledge and vulgarity of sentiment so happily disguised. The reader feels his mind full, though he learns nothing; and when he meets it in its new array, no longer knows the talk of his mother and his nurse.

Such is the power of the "new array" in which Pope garbs his commonplaces that genius, dazzle, and seductive eloquence are the results.

The third and final example is one of Johnson's most quoted pronouncements. The "Life of Gray" was originally to have concluded the whole series, but George, Lord Lyttelton was added subsequent, thus ending things on an anticlimax. Johnson was severe about the body of Gray's poetry, particularly the Odes, and especially "The Bard," whose "puerilities" and "obsolete mythology" Johnson condemned ("I do not see that 'The Bard' promotes any truth, moral or political"). Near the end of the life, he sums up his distaste for Gray's Odes, which he says

are marked by glittering accumulations of ungraceful ornaments; they strike, rather than please; the images are magnified by affectation; the language is laboured into harshness. The mind of the writer seems to work with unnatural violence. *Double, double, toil and trouble.* He has a kind of strutting dignity, and is tall by walking on tiptoe. His art and his struggle are too visible, and there is too little appearance of ease and nature.

Then follow two short paragraphs somewhat modifying the censure, after which Johnson abruptly directs attention to Gray's most famous poem, almost catching us by surprise:

In the character of his Elegy I rejoice to concur with the common reader; for by the common sense of readers uncorrupted with literary prejudices, after all the refinements of subtilty and the dogmatism of learning, must be finally decided all claim to poetical honours. *The Church-yard* abounds with images which find a mirrour in every mind, and with sentiments to which every bosom returns an echo.

He singles out four stanzas for special praise, then writes the great final sentence: "Had Gray written often thus, it had been vain to blame, and useless to praise him." This deference to the "common reader" is so graceful and assured that we almost forget to ask whether there weren't at that time a number of such readers whose bosoms returned an echo to the Odes of Gray. In the two pages of commentary Lonsdale devotes to that final paragraph, he aptly quotes Lawrence Lipking, who wrote about its final sentence, "Johnson resigns his authority—and also asserts it, by merging the public judgment into his own."[6] Lipking adds, with an understandable flourish, that "his whole career had led up to this moment." If so, Johnson knew—once more and most memorably—exactly what should be said.

—Hudson Review, Spring 2007.

Notes

1. Samuel Johnson, *The Lives of Poets*, with an introduction and notes by Roger Lonsdale, 4 vols. (Oxford: Claredon Press, 2006).
2. Matthew Arnold, "Johnson's Lives," in *Essays in Criticism*, Third Series (Boston: Ball, 1910).
3. Eliot's essay may be found in *On Poetry and Poets* (New York: Farrar, Straus, 1959); Leavis's "Johnson and Augustanism" is in *The Common Pursuit* (New York: George W. Stewart, 1952).
4. Johnson's note begins, "Of this celebrated soliloquy, which bursting from a man distracted with contrariety of desires, and overwhelmed with the magnitude of his own purposes, is connected rather in the speaker's mind, than on his tongue, I shall endeavour to discover the train, and to show how one sentiment produces another."
5. Paul Fussell's *Samuel Johnson and the Life of Writing* (New York: W. W. Norton, 1971) is still the best introduction to Johnson's work. Greg Clingham's words are in his *Johnson, Writing, and Memory* (New York: Cambridge University Press, 2002), 98.
6. Lipking's excellent chapter on *Lives of Poets* may be found in his *Samuel Johnson: The Life of an Author* (Cambridge, MA: Harvard University Press, 1998), 259-94.

What to Do with Carlyle?

IN ONE OF his letters, Robert Frost defined "style" as "the way a man carries himself toward his ideas and deeds," then gave some examples of how different writers such as Stevenson, Swinburne, and Emerson carried themselves stylistically. The only example to receive a bad grade was Thomas Carlyle's, whose way of taking himself, Frost said, "simply infuriates me." Surely Frost's is a reasonable response to the most intractable and cantankerous of Victorian sages. I first encountered Carlyle through snippets from a double-columned anthology of Victorian prose (Harrold and Templeman) that didn't help to make him appealing. But since I was in search of facts I needed to master for a Ph.D. oral, I read Carlyle's chapters on the No and Everlasting Yea, from *Sartor Resartus,* and took careful notes on what he "meant" by those terms. Further pages followed, as I remember, from *The French Revolution, Past and Present,* and—as an example of the later Carlyle—"Shooting Niagara." All sputter and invective and self-righteousness, I decided: a most infuriating writer indeed.

In his readable new biography of the sage, Simon Heffer is convinced that Carlyle is a heroic and indispensable figure whose trajectory since his death in 1881 been "a long and damaging fall from the pedestal he occupied." Carlyle cries out, as Heffer sees it, for "rediscovery and reappraisal," especially with regard to his writings and their contribution to political thought. Heffer's introduction stresses Carlyle's humorousness and his kindness toward his family, and the biographer sums things up as follows: "If he is estranged from polite society today it is because his humour is misunderstood and his candour undervalued in a world based on avoiding truths wherever those truths are uncomfortable." This immediately struck me as unconvincing, since I know of no "polite society" from which Carlyle is estranged: surely academic society, where he is discussed at times, can't be construed as "polite." To blame "the world" for undervaluing Car-

lyle because that world seeks to avoid unpalatable truths, while not understanding the sage's humor, seems an abstract and unuseful way of blaming
anything but Carlyle himself.

Is it true that Carlyle's fall from the pedestal is any more radical than
those of his three great Victorian contemporaries—Ruskin, Newman, and
Arnold? (Mill has continued to get a good press, especially for *The Subjec-
tion of Women*.) Carlyle was the subject, as the others were not, of a great
biography by J. A. Froude to which Heffer pays generous tribute. Most
recently Fred Kaplan has provided a fully scrupulous, though quite unhu-
morous, account of the life, which had been earlier told, most succinctly
and entertainingly, by Julian Symons, a master of the biographer's trade.
Kaplan makes no mention of Symons's book; Heffer mentions neither
Kaplan nor Symons; one wonders whether these omissions are made in the
fear that one's own biography will seem less groundbreakingly unique. In
fact, Heffer's new one has nothing, that I can see, to add to the facts of Carlyle's life; his commentary on the work is however—like Symons's—lively
and pertinent (Kaplan does little with Carlyle's writings). But perhaps it is
enough justification for a new biography if it can bring us to fresh engagement with its subject. *Moral Desperado* most surely succeeds in doing that.

Of course any biographer of Carlyle must take his bearings in relation to
Froude's biography, and not only the biography but the books he brought
out after Carlyle's death in 1881: first the *Reminiscences,* containing Carlyle's
agonized reflections put down after his wife, Jane Welsh Carlyle, had died
and he had discovered, in looking over her letters, how much she suffered
during the course of their marriage—how much, in his inattention and
silent withdrawal, he was responsible for that suffering. The *Reminiscences*
(1881) were quickly followed by the first two volumes of Froude's biography
(covering Carlyle's years in Scotland); then, in 1883, *Letters and Memori-
als of Jane Welsh Carlyle,* with notes by both Carlyle and Froude; finally,
the second half of the biography, detailing the London years and Jane's
increasing unhappiness. As the well-known story has it, Carlyle's descendants were outraged by what they felt to be Froud's partiality toward Jane,
his suggestion that Carlyle was impotent, and his willingness to write the
sort of "warts-and-all" biography Carlyle himself desired. Froude defended
himself ably enough, but the counterattack continued.[1] Though Simon
Heffer doesn't get caught up in the old quarrel, his sympathies clearly lie
with Froud's portrait of the Carlyle marriage; and since Carlyle himself,
after Jane's death, contributed so much to filling out the painful picture,

it's impossible not to feel strongly toward this forty-year marriage of two extraordinary gifted sufferers. Yet in some heartless way, for all our sympathetic vibrations to each of them, we wouldn't have had it otherwise.

A good place to begin reading Carlyle is a review of two books of philosophy he published in the *Edinburgh Review* in 1831, not long after he came to live in London. Titled "Characteristics," it is less a review than a bold attempt at characterizing the spirit of the age, containing in embryo all Carlyle's later religious and political ideas. In fact, it is a mistake to speak as if "ideas" in Carlyle's writing were something that could be abstracted from the prose and studied at leisure. As John Holloway shrewdly observed, in his still useful book *The Victorian Sage,* rather than being presented with an argument to which one does or doesn't assent, "the reader is hurried, as if by an all-pervading and irresistible violence, from one problem to another." It's the violence and the hurry that, one suspects, must have infuriated Frost, who was unlikely to have read "Characteristics," where Carlyle proceeds with relative calm and clarity:

> The healthy know not of their health, but only the sick: this is the Physician's Aphorism; and applicable in a far wider sense than he gives it. We may say, it holds no less in moral, intellectual, political, poetical, than in merely corporeal therapeutics; that whatever, or in what shape soever, powers of the sort which can be named *vital* are at work, herein lies the test of their working right or working wrong.
>
> In the Body, for example, as all doctors are agreed, the first condition of complete health is, that each organ perform its function unconsciously, unheeded; let but any organ announce its separate existence, were it even beautifully, and for pleasure, not for pain, then already has one of those unfortunate "false centres of sensibility" established itself, already is derangement there. The perfection of bodily well-being is, that the collective bodily activities seem one, and be manifested, more-over, not in themselves but in the action they accomplish.

He goes on to treat England as a very unhealthy place indeed, cataloguing with some relish the various derangements under which it suffers. In "Characteristics" and in "Signs of the Times" (published a year or so earlier), Carlyle's first significant assault on "machinery," materialism, and the utilitarian calculus, we have, as Heffer notes, "the foundations of his outlook and principles" set forth in accessible, vigorously stated prose.

At a basic enough level, one could even say that these essays said what he had to say about modern civilization. But Carlyle was a *writer*, and writers once they get launched tend not to stop the flow: the early essays and reviews were succeeded by two unique examples of Genius Carlyle: *Sartor Resartus* (1834) and *The French Revolution* (1836). In these two immoderate books he exploited to the full the famous Style toward which readers would have such mixed feelings. In responding to critics of the way he used language in *Sartor*, Carlyle replied that "if one has thoughts not hitherto uttered in English Books, I see nothing for it but that you must use words not found there, must *make* words." From a more disinterested source, Julian Symons, comes the best description of this "making" I know of:

> The style of Carlyle remains unique in English. It is at once breathlessly colloquial and full of elaborate metaphors; connectives are eliminated to gain force; words become displaced in the sentences, as it seems by accident, but always with the effect of increasing power and urgency of expression; the parts of speech abandon their usual functions, and move into new and fantastic patterns. . . . It brings together in a single paragraph, sometimes in a single sentence, neologisms and compound words, strange nicknames like Teufelsdröckh, and fantastic metaphors: the whole informed with a humour at once extravagant and clownish, obscure yet overflowing with vigour.

Carlyle extinguished, so Symons argues, classical diction in prose.

For at least this reader, the genius of Carlyle's achievement in *The French Revolution* comes through in memorable scenes where the historian's own excess and exhilaration "breathlessly" animate characters and settings. Not the least attractive of Carlyle's appeals is his occasional willingness to confess how much beyond even *his* mortal powers as a writer is the immense subject. Preparing to describe the siege of the Bastille, he pauses, asserting that it "perhaps transcends the talent of mortals. Could one but, after infinite reading, get to understand so much as the plan of the building!" But he plunges on undaunted, after winning us over by his confession of defeat. For all its huffings and puffings, and partly because of *The French*

Revolution has an attractive, you-are-there feel to it that bears out Carlyle's claim to Mill, who had been critical of Carlyle's stylistic excesses, that "the great business for me, in which alone I feel any comfort, is recording the presence, bodily concrete coloured presence of things."

But the other "genius" book of Carlyle's youth—*Sartor Resartus*—can't similarly be rationalized and justified, at least for one who butted his head unrewardingly against this monstrous work. In a recent introduction to *Sartor* in the World's Classic series, its editors offer it to us, with some seriousness, as "essentially a work of imaginative fiction that demands a more sensitive and complex response than that in which its formal and stylistic husks are stripped away to reveal the doctrinal kernels." They also recommend it by pointing to Emerson's sponsorship of it, as well as to its influence on Melville's *Moby Dick* and Whitman's *Song of Myself.* Well and good, and surely the days have past when "doctrinal kernels" like the Everlasting Yea (which Christopher Ricks suggests may have been succeeded in our own day by the Everlasting Yeah), the Centre of Indifference, or The Dandiacal Body are to be lifted out of what the editor in *Sartor* calls "the enormous, amorphous Plumpudding, more like a Scottish Haggis," which Herr Teufelsdröckh "had kneaded for his fellow mortals, to pick out the choicest Plums." There remains the question of just how satisfying, as imaginative fiction, *Sartor* turns out to be in the reading. In response to Mill's worry that its "mode of writing, between sarcasm or irony and earnest" might not have been too unrelievedly employed, Carlyle conceded Mill's point, and said the mode probably had something to do with not knowing "who my audience is, or whether I have any audience" —thus the "Devil-may-care principle" informing the book. And he added, saliently, "Besides I have under all my gloom genuine feeling of the ludicrous; and could have been the merriest of men, *had I not been the sickest & saddest.*" Contemporary readers—assuming they pick up the book at all—must decide for themselves whether and how often Caryle's "ludicrous" mode is all that funny, especially when compared with his acknowledged ancestors, Swift's *Tale of a Tub* and Sterne's *Tristram Shandy.* To my eyes and ears, *Sartor* feels, by comparison with those satirical operations, heavy-footed and haranguing, even as it tries to be madcap and devil-may-care. But then, John Stuart Mill, soberest of critics, eventually came round to reading it with keen delight.

These two works from the 1830s were—with the exception of the later *Reminiscences*—Carlyle's most "literary" performances. More than once—

and increasingly—in later years he would contemptuously express his alienation from the world of literature: in a letter from the 1840s to James Spedding, he announces that "I begin very greatly to despise the thing they call 'Literature'." And even when, in his early reviews, he took on literary figures, he had little to say about their literary qualities. The essay on Croker's edition of Boswell's *Life of Johnson* is very funny about Croker, very appreciative of Boswell's character, but tells us nothing about why Johnson is a great writer. The review of Lockhart's Scott gives us no insight into why Scott as a novelist should be read. And the pages on Shakespeare in *Heroes and Hero-Worship* ("The Poet as Hero"), while full of adulation for the poet's strength, greatness, morality, intellect, what-you-will, have nothing to say about his achievement with words. In a moment like our present one, when the head of Dartmouth College's English department warns us, primly, that we must not "deify" Shakespeare, it is good to read out in response Carlyle's thunderous deification of him: "Such a calmness of depth; placid joyous strength; all things imaged in that great soul of his so true and clear, as in a tranquil unfathomable sea!" But beyond that, there's little to be got from the lecture. Where Carlyle is superb, though in very brief compass, is in his portrait of Coleridge on Highgate Hill (in *The Life of John Sterling),* or of Wordsworth (in *Reminiscences);* what's superb is the evocative portraiture rather than any literary-critical judgment delivered. You can *argue* with Samuel Johnson's extended setting out of Shakespeare's virtues and defects in Johnson's preface to his edition of the poet; with Carlyle one beats the empty air, as one does if one looks to find out, in *Past and Present,* about what "Hero-Worship" should properly consist in, and is given the following: "it is the summary, ultimate essence, and supreme perfection of all manner of 'worship,' and true worships and noblenesses whatsoever." No doubt, but where do we go from there?

By the late 1840s Carlyle was turning out the rancorous essays that would be published as *Latter-Day Pamplets*—to which "The Nigger Question" provided a fittingly unpleasant introduction. He had originally titled it, more politely, "The Negro Question," then when informed that people were outraged by it, proceeded to retitle to make it more offensive. Heffer remarks that Carlyle was "making a career out of being ill-natured in the most entertaining way, albeit often unintentionally." But "The Nigger Question" may not qualify as bona fide entertainment, and even "racism" is an inadequate word for Carlyle's attitude toward black people, whom he tolerated as long as they remained slaves, docilely eating pumpkins and drinking rum: "A swift, supple fellow; a merry-hearted, singing, affectionate kind of creature, with a deal of melody and amenability in his composition." (Carlyle may have figured this was a genially entertaining touch of style.) It was about this time that Mill, appalled by some of the things Carlyle was saying, ended their relationship: Carlyle professed not to understand why Mill had so taken offense. The habit of fixing on a colorful phrase, then beating the reader to death with it, more and more substituted for analysis and argument. In "Shooting Niagara" (1867), for example—usually taken as the final exercise in Carlylean negation and despair—he coins the word "swarmeries" to indicate superstitions that hold man in delusive wastefulness. Such is, prominently, literature, "what they call Art or Poetry, and the like . . . that inane region, fallen so inane in our mad era." Art or Poetry is nothing but "a refined Swarmery; the most refined now going; and comes to us in venerable from, from a distance of above a thousand years." Convinced he is seeing through nothing less than everything, Carlyle abandons his mind and his prose to frenzied dithyramb. Here was the moral desperado Matthew Arnold disliked, even as—his biographer points out justly—the "authoritarian" tone in Arnold's own *Culture and Anarchy* owed much to Carlylean doctrines.

Around his house in Chelsea, the moral desperado was also in evidence. Here the witness is Jane Carlyle, who succinctly characterized Carlyle's physical and emotional state: "as usual, never healthy, never absolutely ill—protesting against 'things in general' with the old emphasis—with an increased vehemence just at present." This was in the 1840s, and things would only get worse when Carlyle embarked upon the deadening thirteen-year project of a life of Frederick the Great—Jane would die before he had completed it. "This man of mine will absolutely do nothing but write books and be sick," she had written earlier to John Forster, Dickens's biographer, but the chipper tone is belied by her own prolonged illnesses. The seeds of what Heffer calls "self-flagellatory, self-pitying guilt" that followed her death and informed Carlyle's notes to his portrait of Jane in *Reminiscences* were well-sown early on. His devotion to Lady Harriet Ashburton, his high attentiveness to female aristocratic temperaments even as he managed to devote precious little attention to Jane, made things all the worse: "My husband always *writing*, I always *ailing*," as she neatly put it. Her letters are filled with wonderful sequences in which she manages, through gifts of style and wit, to make the intolerable into something less threatening, indeed amusing, as in an early letter to her aunt written just after the publication of *Sartor:*

> And then there is a young American beauty—such a beauty! "snow and rose-bloom" throughout, not as to clothes merely, but complexion also; large and soft, and without one idea, you would say, to rub upon another! And this charming creature publicly declares herself his "ardent admirer," and I heard her with my own ears call out quite passionately at parting with him, "Oh, Mr. Carlyle, I want to see you to talk a long time about—Sartor!" "Sartor" of all things in this world! What could such a young lady have got to say about "Sartor," can you imagine? And Mrs. Marsh, the moving authoress of "The Old Man's Tales" reads "Sartor" when she is ill in bed; from which one thing at least may be clearly inferred, that her illness is not of the head. In short, my dear friend, the singular author of "Sartor" appears to me at this moment to be in a perilous position, inasmuch as (with the innocence of a sucking dove to outward appearance) he is leading honourable women, not a few, entirely off their feet. And who can say that he will keep his own? After all, in sober earnest, is it not curious that my husband's writings should be only completely understood and adequately appreciated by women and mad people? I do not know very well what to infer from the fact.

This is marvelous, and one can see how Carlyle, coming across even such a composed piece of discontent, could have used it as more grist for his self-accusatory mill.

Readers unfamiliar with Carlyle's reminiscence of his wife should not, however, think that it is one long gloomy paean emanating from a suffering widower. Parts of it are animated by fierce humor, as in the following sketch of a "Catholic sick-nurse" brought in (but only briefly!) to care for Jane during one of her illnesses. One night Carlyle is awakened (his room was above Jane's) by her violently ringing the bell: the French nun had tried to minister to Jane with "ghostly consolations" such as, perhaps, "Blessed Virgin" or *Agnus Dei.* The nun is dismissed next morning "never to reappear, she or any consort of hers," and Carlyle adds:

> I was really sorry for this heavy-laden, pious or quasi-pious and almost broken-hearted Frenchwoman, —though we could perceive she was under the foul tutelage and guidance, probably of some dirty muddy-minded semi-*felonious* Proselytising Irish Priest: but there was no help for her, in this instance; probably, in all England, she could not have found an agonised human soul more nobly and hopelessly superior to her and her *poisoned-gingerbread* "consolations."

Here it is the poisoned-gingerbread conceit that vitalizes, in a typical manner, Carlyle's writing, as for a moment regret and guilt are put aside in favor of forceful abuse (that "semi-*felonious*" Irish priest is a particularly fine stroke).

Whatever Simon Heffer meant in his introduction by claiming that Carlyle is now in bad repute partly because his "humor" is misunderstood, it's true that, in a broad sense, Carlyle's humorous ways, and not just in writing, are what make him an appealing subject for biography: his long late-night evening gallops about London on his horse Noggs (named for a character in *Nicholas Nickleby*); or his visiting Stonehenge with Emerson on the latter's second trip to England when, Emerson writes in *English Traits*, after "they walked round the stones and clambered over them" they "found a nook, sheltered from the wind among them, where Carlyle lighted his cigar"; or his penchant for deterring oncoming colds by plunging himself into a freezing bath, evidently to successful effect—the ultimate Boy Scout maneuver.

In his late years he was summoned, along with Browning and a couple of others, to meet the queen, and wrote afterwards to his sister how she "gently acknowledged with a nod the silent deep bow of us male monsters." He described Victoria as a "comely little lady" than whom it was "impossible to imagine a politer little woman: Nothing the least imperious; all gentle, all sincere-looking, unembarrassing, rather attractive even; —makes you feel too (if you have sense in you) that she is Queen." Her response to him, as recorded in her journal, went as follows: "a strange-looking eccentric old Scotchman, who holds forth, in a drawling melancholy voice, with a broad Scotch accent, upon Scotland and upon the utter degeneration of everything." Yes, we feel, they had each other right.

The hero of Wyndham Lewis's novel *Tarr* is characterized as a sort of anti-Quixote whose "sardonic dream of life" brought him "blows from the swift arms of windmills and attacks from indignant and perplexed mankind." Tarr possesses, is inflicted with, we are told, "the curse of humour . . . anchoring him at one end of the see-saw whose movement and contradiction was life." Carlyle was, in the same manner, humorously cursed, and never got off the see-saw until he died at eighty-five, having exhibited, so his brother-in-law commented, "such tenacity of life and vitality" as he had never observed in any human being. My single favorite moment from his writing is one in which he registered comparable tenacity in another human being, namely Wordsworth in old age, wearing his protective green eyeshade at a London dinner party amidst an atmosphere of "babble" and "cackle," "heartily unimportant to gods and men," so Carlyle judges it. Seated far away at the table from Wordsworth, Carlyle suddenly looks up and sees the poet:

> there, far off, beautifully screened in the shadow of his vertical green circle . . . sat Wordsworth, silent, in rock-like indifference, slowly but steadily gnawing some portion of what I judged to be raisins, with his eye and attention placidly fixed on these and these alone. The sight of whom, and of his rock-like indifference to the babble, quasi-scientific and other, with attention turned on the small practical alone, was comfortable and amusing to me, who felt like him but could not eat raisins.

The curse of dyspeptic humor, turned—especially through the raisins—into a wonderful moment of sympathetic identification, is something even the most unconvinced reader of Carlyle can admire.

—*Hudson Review*, Summer 1997.

Notes

1. In *Keepers of the Flame: Literary Estates and the Rise of Biography from Shakespeare to Plath* (London: Faber and Faber, 1992), Ian Hamilton has an entertaining chapter on the warfare between supporters and detractors of Froude's work on Carlyle. Christopher Ricks, in his essay "Froude's Carlyle," has provided a sensitive defense of Froude's biographical and critical procedures (*Essays in Appreciation* [New York: Oxford University Press, 116]).

John Churton Collins:
Forgotten Man of Letters

W HEN WAS THE following credo written
and by whom?

> I believe, for the reasons already explained, that Belles Lettres are
> sinking deeper and deeper into degradation, that they are grad-
> ually passing out of the hands of their true representatives, and
> becoming almost the monopoly of their false representatives,
> and that the consequences of this cannot but be most disastrous
> to us as a nation, to our reputation in the World of Letters, to
> taste, to tone, to morals. It is surely a shame and a crime in any
> one, and more especially in men occupying positions of influ-
> ence and authority to assist in the work of corruption.

Jonathan Swift? William Wordsworth? John Ruskin? F. R. Leavis? The
credo contains sentiments that each of them on more than one occasion
endorsed. But in fact these words were set down a hundred years ago, by
a man of letters whose name a century later is scarcely known, even to
academics in English studies. For John Churton Collins is one of the great
secrets of belles lettres in English, a prophet without honor even in the
writings of those—such as Leavis—who might have recognized him as a
forebear and fellow spirit in the fight to make the criticism of literature a
serious and valuable activity. The reasons for Collins being buried so deep
in the ranks of those forgotten should be enquired into.

Insofar as he is remembered at all, it is as an irascible, if well-equipped,
attacker of his contemporary men of letters. Foremost of these attacks is
the one on Edmund Gosse, whose Cambridge Clark Lectures, published
in book form as *From Shakespeare to Pope* (1885), were taken to pieces by

Collins as a tissue of factual error and incompetent judgments. The review begins famously:

> That such a book as this should have been permitted to go forth to the world with the *imprimatur* of the University of Cambridge, affords matter for very grave reflection.

The forty pages to follow document the charge, citing chapter and verse. And Collins provided similar dismantlings of what he called dilettantism—loose, impressionistic commentary on literary works—in books by John Addington Symonds, George Saintsbury, and other lesser-known belletrists. The attack on Gosse is understood to have provoked Gosse's friend Tennyson—about whom Collins had already written essays that displeased Tennyson—to call him, picturesquely, "a Louse on the locks of Literature." In fact, as Christopher Ricks and, later, Gosse's biographer Ann Thwaite have pointed out, Tennyson employed the less picturesque "Jackass" by way of characterizing Collins.

Dilettantism was one-half of what Collins saw as the besetting sin of literary studies; the other half was philology, the discipline that controlled that study at both Oxford and Cambridge. His plea for the detaching of literature from philology as a legitimate subject of study was forcefully and scornfully made in the first part of a three-part essay titled "English Literature at the Universities" *(Ephemera Critica)*. Collins describes philology's resistance to any attempt to widen and extend the audience for literature by making it a subject for "liberal" study. On the contrary, he says of philologists:

> In their eyes the Universities are simply nurseries for esoteric specialists, and to talk of bringing them into touch with national life is, in their estimation, mere cant. Their attitude toward Literature, generally, is precisely that of the classical party toward our own Literature: they regard it simply as the concern of men of letters, journalists, dilettantes, and Extension lecturers.

Collins goes on to admit that philology is a branch of learning "of immense importance," but also declares that as a science "it has no connection with Literature." He believed that the "instincts and faculties" of the study of philology, compared to the student of literature, were radically dissimilar, and that until the study of literature became separated from philological investigation, it would lack integrity.

Collins himself was an extension lecturer, perhaps the busiest and most devoted of them who ever lived. In the appendixes to the memoir *Life and Memoirs of John Churton Collins,* his son L.C. Collins tells us that his father began his career in the University Extension Society in 1880, continuing for twenty-seven years, by which time he had delivered over three thousand lectures. He possessed, we are told, a remarkable memory for prose as well as verse, and a flair for the dramatic, with the result that he was enormously popular and much in demand. L.C. Collins notes, "As his memory was so good, he was able to dispense for the most part with the use of his notebooks, and on this account the lecture was rendered more pleasing for its air of ease and spontaneity; he displayed, too, a genuine and never lacking enthusiasm in his subject and this usually became infectious." Yet for most of those twenty-seven years, despite repeated applications, Collins had no university post (he eventually received one at the University of Birmingham in 1905), which surely fueled his conviction that he was an outsider; while inside the universities lived philologists (and perhaps some dilettantes as well) resisting any attempt to open up the study of English to more systematically critical operations.

His hero was Matthew Arnold, whose great essay "The Study of Poetry" appeared the year Collins began work as an extension lecturer. But satiric urbanity of the sort Arnold deployed in that essay, when he treated Dryden and Pope as classics of prose, rather than of poetry, from our "excellent and indispensable eighteenth century," was not Collins's usual style. Arnold could deftly and smoothly expose the awkwardness of Francis Newman's translation of Homer, or the banalities of Mr. Roebuck and Sir Charles Adderley in the famous "Wragg is in custody" passage from "The Function of Criticism at the Present Time." By contrast Collins's attacks were the opposite of feline, and "urbane" would be scarcely the right adjective for their comportment. Consider sentences from his evisceration of Gosse in the *Quarterly Review,* 1886:

> There is not a chapter—nay, if we except the Appendices and index, it would be difficult to find five consecutive pages which do not swarm with errors and absurdities. And the peculiarity of Mr. Gosse's errors is, that they cannot be classed among those to which even well-informed men are liable. They are not mere

slips of the pen, they are not clerical and superficial, nor such as, casually arising, may be easily excised, but they are, to borrow a metaphor from medicine, local manifestations of constitutional mischief. The ignorance which Mr. Gosse displays of the simplest facts of Literature and History is sufficiently extraordinary, but the recklessness with which he exposes that ignorance transcends belief.

And he proceeds, damningly, to lay out the evidence.

This vigorous no-holds-barred relentlessness with which Collins prosecuted his victims has been unfortunate for his reputation, insofar as when critics recognize his work at all it is to focus on its demonstrable excesses. Rather than attention being paid to the truth or falsity of Collins's charges, it is directed at the psychology of the charger: thus Collins, rather than his victim, becomes the subject of analysis. For example, Phyllis Grosskurth, the biographer of John Addington Symonds, speaks of the "paranoiac envy and irascibility that characterized his [Collins's] work." Although she admits that Collins's rebuttal to Gosse's response to the attack on him was "far more specific about actual inaccuracies and incomparably better organized as a whole than Gosse's effort," we are left with the impression that Collins's effort proceeded from motives somewhat dishonorable, certainly less than the "disinterested" criticism Arnold had called for. Ann Thwaite, in her biography of Gosse, goes even further along this line, admitting that Collins was quite right in his pointing out Gosse's errors, but also calling Collins "a fanatic and a pedant," thereby undermining his worth.

In a similar vein, Grosskurth points to Collins's demonstration of how much Tennyson's poetry owed to his predecessors—how adept and inveterate a borrower was the poet—as a covert slur on Tennyson. She credits Collins's "fantastic memory, his ability to find allusions and parallels behind nearly every phrase of Tennyson's." But when she comes to Collins's declaration that his tracing of allusion was "offered as commentaries on works which will take their place beside the masterpieces of Greek and Roman genius," she finds that declaration to be "intoned sanctimoniously" and that what really happened was that "Collins had tasted blood." The significant fact that Collins's way of noting sources, allusions, and indebtednesses to his predecessors in Tennyson's poetry would be drawn upon and practiced in Christopher Ricks's great edition of his works seems to go for naught—at least when compared to the analyzing and demoting of the less than worthy motives out of which Collins's practice supposedly issued.

In *The Rise and Fall of the Man of Letters,* John Gross has some pages on Collins that give a more sympathetic picture of his contribution. But Gross too is bothered, at least slightly, by what he calls Collins's "licensed ferocity" as a critic. Gross admits that the errors Collins uncovered in other critics ought not to have been let pass, and that "other reviewers in the same situation might well have delivered equally unfavorable verdicts." But, Gross goes on to qualify, "he did bring to the task of demolition a peculiar intensity, which was over and above the call of scholarly duty, and which suggests the brooding assassin rather than the judge." This is fair enough, but leaves us to decide for ourselves just how attractive this peculiar intensity that goes beyond "the call of scholarly duty" remains for us today.

By drawing on his son's memoir we can suggest the nature of Collins's "intensity," then observe it in the literary work of a critic whose legacy is richer and more various than the demolition jobs on his contemporaries for which he is mainly remembered. Everyone was in awe of his wonderful memory—"the greatest since Macaulay," testified a Philadelphia host of Collins, who had been invited to lecture there in 1893 by the American Society for the Extension of University Teaching. He was not just good at quoting *poems* from memory, as his host, Mr. Miles, testified when Miles's son asked Collins where he could find a good description of a great battle. "In Napier's Peninsular War, Vittoria for instance," was the answer.

> "Of course, Mr. Collins," I said *in jest,* you can recite the whole of it?" Whereupon, he reeled off fifteen pages of Napier without a pause, or hesitation, to the great delight of the youthful Basil and all of us. He followed this, a little later, with the whole of Manzoni's hymn to Napoleon, *in Italian!*

Collins's familiarity with languages was also phenomenal: he could read Greek, Latin, French. Spanish, Italian, and, in his later years, German. He was especially devoted to Italian and issued a vigorous protest when the Civil Service abolished it from its examinations on the grounds that it was too easy to "get up." As for the classics, his campaign to bring English and Classical curricula into some kind of harmony went along with a number of practical suggestions in his *The Study of English Literature,* in his edition of Matthew Arnold's *Merope* along with Sophocles' *Electra,* and in his post-humously published series of lectures, *Greek Influence on English Poetry.*

The intensity of Collins's literary pursuits can be observed in the pattern of his daily activity. His son quotes from his father's notebook: "Have just completed, 3 a.m. a respectable feat. I have carefully annotated the whole of Pope's Essay on Criticism. I began it on Sunday midday, August 9th and have finished it at 3 a.m. on August 12th, 1896." The three a.m. end to the workday was not an isolated instance. At one point he speaks of "the most frightfully laborious six weeks I have ever known," in which he frequently worked sixteen or seventeen hours a day. In 1903, completing a month's visit to Oxford, where he had been working on a long article on nineteenth-century American poets, he says he has avoided "*deep* depression," though has had "a good deal of the milder kind." And he enumerates a typical day: "Always a plunge in the river at 8.30: then breakfast 9.15: work from 10.30 to 5 as a rule: then bicycle ride: then dinner 7.30: then rest: then work 9.30 to 3 a.m. nearly every day." Even for a nineteenth-century man of letters, this must be extreme. Saintsbury, after all, had his wine cellar for diversion; whether Collins felt anything about wine is unrecorded. L.C. Collins tells us that his father cared nothing for the theater or for picture galleries, and that he was especially bored "by music in any shape or form." He did take an active interest in criminology, and he loved cemeteries, which, his son tells us, were always the first places he visited in a new town.

Although prey to depression throughout his life, his physical constitution was strong and he scarcely missed a single one of the ten thousand or so lectures he was to deliver over his career. The depressions, which could last for months, were inexplicable, and they came and went. His marriage seems to have been a happy one, though it is hard to see what sort of time he could have spent with his wife and the seven children she bore him. His death, under mysterious circumstances—his body was found in a dike in the English countryside, a bottle of sedatives nearby—could have been intentional or accidental, or some blurry combination of these. Although it can't be proven by demonstration, he appears to have been an essentially solitary being in the midst of the domestic and educational society in which he was involved. An entry from his notebook suggests how he contrived to see himself in relation to other people, to society: he writes that our character seems to have been given us at birth ("*what* a man is *that* is he born") and that so far as the foundations of character are concerned, education has little or perhaps no weight. I cannot call to mind a single human being who has had *the slightest* influence on me. My *intense* love of literature was inspired by no one, encouraged by no one, influenced by *no one*. It awoke suddenly and spontaneously—my life, my deeper life, has been *essentially* and permanently *solitary*. At school, at College and since it has been quite apart from my surroundings.

This is really an extraordinary claim to make for oneself, with the italicized words pumping up the intensity, and it's no wonder that such a man should fail to be rewarded in his attempts at public, institutional success. At the beginning of the last century, he launched a campaign to found a scholarship at Oxford for the comparative study of classical and English literature. He found a philanthropist named John Passmore Edwards who expressed interest in the project; then Collins solicited many letters from leading intellectuals in the culture (Arnold, Jowett, Gladstone, John Morley). Eventually the project did succeed—the money came through and was accepted by Oxford. But at one point it looked as if the benefactor was pulling out, and Collins confided the following to his notebook; that it was "one more of the many illustrations of the ill-fortune which has pursued me through life":

> I have never succeeded in anything except as a lecturer, everything that I have essayed has broken down, even when there seemed every chance of my succeeding as here. Bitter indeed has been the disappointment. I had set my heart on this and it seemed so likely to succeed.

It almost must have been difficult for him, after things righted themselves in this instance, to grant an exception to the blanket wailing over himself as a perfect failure in everything.

Yet Collins succeeded in the most important way a literary man can be said to succeed: he produced a substantial number of commentaries on poets and critics that are permanently valuable examples of intelligent criticism. And he provided a passionate, still relevant example of a way of thinking about the study and teaching of literature. This is to make no claim for his endurance as someone whose writings will be consulted, looked up for critical insights: his books are out of print and will remain so. In a sense it could be argued that he didn't really write *books,* but essays rather, which he then cobbled together into his most important volumes of criticism, *Essays and Studies; Studies in Poetry and Criticism; Ephemera Critica.* His biographical works—studies of Bolingbroke and Swift, an account of Voltaire, Montesquieu, and Rousseau in England—are, though readable and clearheaded, perhaps the least original of his productions. But his work as an editor of texts, the plays of Cyril Tourneur (the introduction to which T.S. Eliot singled out for praise) and of Robert Greene (the editorial part of which was taken to task by a later scholar, W. W. Greg), were honorable projects that deserve at least mention. And his Clarendon Press editions, with introductions, of More's *Utopia* and Sidney's *Apologie for Poetry* are elegant little monuments to memorable texts.

But his most original work consisted in the critical commentaries on subjects he cared about with his peculiar intensity, and in his splendid polemic, *The Study of English Literature: A Plea for Its Recognition and Organization at the Universities.* To take up the latter first: Collins argues that when literature has been recognized at all as a subject for teaching in the universities) it has been done in a spirit similar to that in which classics has been taught:

> It has been regarded not as the expression of art and genius, but as mere material for the study of words, as mere pabulum for philology. All that constitutes its intrinsic value has been ignored. *All* that constitutes its value as a liberal study has been ignored. Its masterpieces have been resolved into exercises in grammar, syntax and etymology. Its history has been resolved into a barren catalogue of names, works, and dates. No faculty but the faculty of memory has been called into play in studying it. That it should therefore have failed as an instrument of education is no more than might have been expected.

This passionate declaration, issued we must remember from a man who had been lecturing for eleven years in the university extension program; who had been attempting to demonstrate to non-university audiences all over England the "intrinsic value" of literary masterpieces; and who believed—as Arnold believed—that poetry was a criticism of life and that the task of literary criticism was to elucidate (in Arnold's terms) how that poetry shows "a power of forming, sustaining, and delighting us as nothing else can." The study of literature in the universities was instead an exercise in how not to do things: "We have absolutely no provision for systematic critical training," declared Collins; the interpretation of literature, of "verbal analysis, analysis of form and style, analysis of sentiment, ethic, and thought," was not being performed. Instead, philological investigation took its place. Collins's strictures on philology, after he grants it a place in the academic groves, are pretty severely unqualified in their negative estimate:

> It must not be confounded with Literature. . . . Up to the present time, it has, in consequence of this confusion, been allowed to fill a place in education altogether disproportionate to its insignificance as an instrument of culture. As an instrument of culture it ranks—it surely ranks—very low indeed. It certainly contributes nothing to the cultivation of the taste. It as certainly contributes nothing to the education of the emotions. The mind it neither enlarges, stimulates, nor refines. On the contrary, it too often induces or confirms that peculiar woodenness and opacity, that singular coarseness of feeling and purblindness of moral and intellectual vision, which has in all ages been characteristic of mere philologists.

He remembers suggesting to Mark Pattison, and receiving Pattison's approval, that Pope's lines from *Dunciad IV* should be inscribed over the doors of the Classical Schools:

> Since man from beasts by Words is known
> Words are man's province, Words we teach alone.
> When Reason doubtful, like the Samian letter,
> Points him two ways, the narrower is the better.
> Plac'd at the door of Learning, youth to guide,
> We never suffer it to stand too wide
> . . . .
> Whate'er the talents, or howe'er designed,
> We hang one jingling padlock on the mind.

Collins's conviction that the philological study of literature frequently directs attention to "unprofitable topics" is substantiated by his quoting from a university "paper" on *Macbeth,* which consists of questions like the following (I am compressing them):

> 1. What reasons are there for believing that this play has been interpolated? Point out the parts probably interpolated.
> 2. What emendations have been proposed in the following passages? [There follow seven passages.]
> 3. Give the meanings and derivations of the following words. In what context do they appear?
> 4. Illustrate from the play important points of difference between Elizabethan and modern grammar.

Collins points out that the only mental faculty appealed to is that of memory, and that nothing in the questions "indicates the existence of what constitutes the life and power of the work." In like manner he adduces editions of Shakespeare and Milton from Oxford's Clarendon Press that, solid though their scholarly editing is, insist on regarding the work as a monument to language merely; on dwelling "with tedious and unnecessary minuteness" on that which is of interest only to philologists, and of confining themselves oppressively to these matters. As with the paper on *Macbeth,* Collins quotes from the editorial notes that accompany these editions.

Yet for all philology's anti-liberal pedantry, it is to Collins's mind a lesser evil than dilettantism. One of philology's arguments against "literary" rather than linguistic study of works was that it would too easily turn into vague, impressionistic remarks ("chatter about Shelley") testifying only to the professor's or student's pleasure or lack of it in a particular instance of art. How do you grade such "subjective" responses whose rightness or wrongness can't be measured the way interpolations to *Macbeth* can? Collins himself worries about the matter, especially when the subject is lyric poetry, and he admits that the "spectacle" of a lecturer with one of Tennyson's poems in hand ("Tears, Idle Tears," or "Mariana") attempting to show "what is graceful, what is fanciful, what is pathetic," would be "ludicrous and repulsive"; yet, he adds, anything can be ridiculed, and so long as the lecturer remembers that his task is "the interpretation of power and beauty as they reveal themselves in language"—so long as he remembers, with Arnold, that poetry is the criticism of life—he will be performing his proper function as a teacher, as a critic. (In an appendix to *The Study of English Literature* Collins provides, under various headings—historical, comparative, critical—sample questions that a serious, "liberal" study of literature might involve.)

Decades later, in the essays gathered together in *Education and the University* (especially "Literary Studies" and "A Sketch for an 'English School'"), F. R. Leavis would expand on some of the ways a literary-critical training might be conducted. "It is plain that in the work of a properly ordered English School . . . the training of reading capacity has first place. By training of reading capacity I mean the training of perception, judgment and analytic skill commonly referred to as 'practical criticism'—or, rather, the training that 'practical criticism' ought to be." By that time, with philology no longer so preeminent, Leavis took up arms against "literary history, as a matter of 'facts about' and accepted critical (or quasi-critical) description and commentary." Leavis called such history worthless unless the student could, as a critic, as "an intelligent and discerning reader," approach literature with a reading capacity trained in the practical criticism of language. Leavis was not given to generous recognition of his forebears in the fight to recognize "English" as a legitimate subject of study, but Collins deserves an important place among that number.

If Leavis should have given Collins a mention, so might have T. S. Eliot, who praised his introduction to the plays of Tourneur but appears not to have noticed how similar to Collins's are his, Eliot's, own strictures on impressionistic criticism. In the two essays that open *The Sacred Wood,* "The Perfect Critic" and "Imperfect Critics," Eliot was concerned to distinguish what he saw as appropriate "objective" criticism from the more subjective sort practiced by two of his predecessors, Swinburne and Arthur Symons. Eliot notes in Swinburne's critical essays important "faults of style," such as "the tumultuous outcry of adjectives, the headstrong rush of undisciplined sentences" that are "the index to the impatience and perhaps laziness of a disorderly mind." The resultant "blur" Eliot sees as continuous with Swinburne in his poetry. As for Symons, whose book on Symbolist poetry Eliot testified to having been influenced by, he is content to give us his sensations about *Antony and Cleopatra* ("the most wonderful, I think, of all Shakespeare's plays") without moving beyond those sensations to generalization, analysis, construction—"*ériger en lois ses impressions personnelles,*" as Eliot liked to quote from Remy de Gourmont.

Thirty-five years previously, in "The Predecessors of Shakespeare," Collins proceeded to give his own accounts of those playwrights, but first took to task John Addington Symonds—whose book on them occasioned the essay—and Swinburne, for the impressionistic excesses of their prose. Collins admits that Swinburne possessed a "powerful and accurate memory" but that this is his sole qualification as a critic (note the overlap with philology as also memory-oriented):

> His judgment is the sport sometimes of his emotions and sometimes of his imagination. A work of art has the same effect on Mr Swinburne as objects fraught with hateful or delightful associations have on persons with sensitive memories. The mind dwells not on the objects themselves, but on what is accidentally recalled or accidentally suggested by them. . . . Criticism is with him neither a process of analysis nor a process of interpretation, but a "lyrical cry." . . . What seem to be Mr. Swinburne's convictions are merely his temporary impressions.

Collins finds a continuation of Swinburne's hyperbole in J. A. Symonds's "wild and whirling verbiage, his plethora of extravagant and frequently nauseous metaphor," and he quotes a number of passages where Symonds has even outdone his master in such stylistic vices and deformations. Now of course—as with the evisceration of Edmund Gosse—it is possible to see these adverse reflections on Swinburne and Symonds solely as examples of Collins's destructive motives. (Especially with Swinburne, who had encouraged and supported Collins in his editing of Tourneur, we feel the feeding hand being bitten.) The alternative, one more appreciative of Collins, is to see these attacks, like those Eliot mounted decades later, as undertaken in order that stronger, more telling critical operations might proceed—operations that both Collins and Eliot practiced with impressive results.

As always seems to be the case with people who write about Collins's work, these pages have concentrated on his efforts as an adversarial critic of bêtes noires like philology and impressionistic criticism, and on some representative practitioners of them. What to my knowledge no one has remarked about his achievement overall are the number of pages devoted to "positive," that is, encomiastic, criticism of writers: Shakespeare, Milton, Dryden, Chesterfield, Wordsworth, Crabbe, Byron, Arnold, and others, including (surprisingly) nineteenth-century American poets. The best of these show him operating in a manner his master Arnold (with

Sainte-Beuve in mind) liked to call flexible and varied (*ondoyant et divers*), combining historical "placing" of the writer and his works with vigorous making of judgments on the relative virtues of those works and of the writer's rank compared to contemporaries and predecessors. In the range and openness of his taste, he compares favorably to Arnold who (as Eliot noted in *The Sacred Wood*) succumbed to the temptation "to put literature into the corner until he cleaned up the whole country first." Eliot wished Arnold had given us more judgments and analyses of particular writers; for all Collins's absorption in the "idea" of how literature should properly be taught, he seized plenty of occasions for exercising his more purely literary discriminations.

This is not to say that he doesn't present limitations that we are conscious of, from the standpoint of a century and more later. Two of these limitations are probably related. For all Collins's belief in the analysis and interpretation of a poet's words, he seldom if ever comes to particular grips with them the way his twentieth-century successors—I. A. Richards, Empson, Leavis, and the American New Critics—have shown us can be exciting. He doesn't attempt to enter into passages of poetry by describing (in words Arnold used in "The Study of Poetry") their diction and movement. (In fact Arnold didn't do much of such "entering" himself, preferring to stay back and remain external to the poetry, even as he pronounced it sound or unsound, great or not so great.) Related to this absence in Collins is his tendency to substitute for discussion of the poem's language an insistence on its soundness, its goodness as a moral statement. This tendency is particularly marked in the volume of essays his son published after Collins's death—lectures, most of them, with plenty of passages quoted but too often simply affirmed as noble. The essay on Wordsworth, significantly titled "Wordsworth as a Teacher," is one of his weaker efforts, since it consists too frequently of such affirmations about various Wordsworthian passages of poetry. In these respects we can say, without complacency or finger-shaking, that Collins was of his age rather than ahead of it.

He never wrote better than in the four long essays published in the *Quarterly Review* between 1878 and 1892, which, along with a shorter one on Menander, were gathered to make up *Essays and Studies,* his best book. Along with the essay on Shakespeare's predecessors, with its attack on Symonds, are ones on Dryden, Lord Chesterfield, and Lewis Theobald—"The Porson of Shakspearian Criticism," as Collins calls him in the essay's title. In his book on Collins, Anthony Kearney speaks of his "tendentious" use of Dryden as a support for Collins's own fight against the excesses of late Victorian impressionism in criticism. Tendentious or not—and the word did not occur to me as I read the essay—this ninety-page trip through Dryden's life and major works is a triumph of clear-eyed criticism, unafraid to make its preferences and judgments known. Its opening paragraph, running to nearly three pages, is a magisterial summary of Dryden's "services" to literature, sentence after sentence of which begins "He had rescued," "He had brought home to us," "He had given us," "He had shown us," as we are moved through Dryden's contributions in poetry and the criticism of poetry. Collins doesn't offer a new "take" on Dryden; his essay is continuous with Walter Scott's fine "Life" in his edition of Dryden, and with the accounts that were to follow by Saintsbury and Mark Van Doren (the latter precipitating Eliot's essay of 1920). But the distinguishing touch of his readerly sensibility is always evident.

A single example must suffice: late in the essay he comes to discuss Dryden's *Fables, Ancient and Modern,* and immediately tells us we must discriminate between the successes and failures of these translations. He finds Dryden to be essentially a "rhetorical" poet, and although Collins notes the lack of affinity between Dryden's temperament and Virgil's, he can with qualification praise Dryden's "re-writing" of the *Aeneid* as substituting a "masterpiece of rhetoric for a masterpiece of poetry." But such was not possible with Chaucer, where Dryden's failure is, to Collins, egregious:

> All Chaucer's *naiveté,* simplicity, freshness, grace, pathos, humour, truth to nature and truth to life, all that attracts us in his temper, tone, and style, have not merely disappeared, but, what is much worse, have been represented by Drydenian equivalents. Where Chaucer is easy and natural with the easiness and naturalness of good breeding, Dryden is simply vulgar. It may be doubted whether there is a single touch of nature which Dryden has not missed or spoilt, or a single pathetic passage which he has not made ridiculous.

Illustrations follow, after which Collins names a number of "passages which admit of rhetorical treatment," in which, by contrast, Dryden is extremely successful. What *is* worth noting here and characteristic in general of Collins's criticism, is the willingness to speak harshly about parts of a poets achievement that are unsatisfactory to the critic's eyes and ears.

These adverse judgments make more convincing the praising of other work by Dryden, and make more telling the essay's concluding salute to "the manifold energy of that vigorous and plastic genius, which added to our literature so much which is excellent and so much which is admirable."

The distinction between the rhetorical and the truly "poetic" was an important one for Collins, and he uses it again in another of his best critical performances, "The Works of Lord Byron" (*Studies in Poetry and Criticism*). Singling out parts of the work where Byron's rhetorical or "falsetto" note is most heard (the dramas, the first two cantos of *Childe Harold,* he distinguishes them from the poems, or parts of poems, in which Byron is sincerely moved—in which he truly becomes Byron the poet:

> It is when we compare the dramas with *The Vision of Judgment* and *Don Juan,* that we measure the distance between Byron the rhetorician and Byron the poet, between degrees of talent and the pure accent of genius. A large proportion, perhaps two-thirds, of Byron's poetry resolves itself into the work of an extraordinarily gifted craftsman, with a rhetorical talent as brilliant and plastic as Dryden's, working on the material furnished by an unusually wide experience of life, by sleepless observation, and by a marvelously assimilative and retentive memory, incessantly if desultorily adding to its store.

But in *The Vision of Judgment* and in *Don Juan* we have something that goes beyond talent and reveals "the true, full man," reveals the "amazing versatility and dexterity of his genius for comedy and satire." Collins's account of Byron's poetry, in its fullness and particular discriminations, supplies what Matthew Arnold, in his own essay on the poet, signally failed to give us, since Arnold was so busy comparing Byron to Wordsworth and Leopardi that he managed never once in the entire essay to mention either *Don Juan* or *The Vision of Judgment,* those poems Collins rightly saw as the peak of Byron's achievement.

In suggesting briefly the often invigorating character of Collins's criticism (as well as the sheer reading pleasure of the sentences as he lays them out), I should mention his eighty-page survey of American poetry, "Poets and Poetry of America" (*Studies in Poetry and Criticism*). He opens it by claiming that American poetry is underestimated in England, and his essay, published in 1905, is the first serious attempt of an English critic to recognize and come to critical grips with poets across the water. In his survey Collins does, among other things, the following: he singles out Philip Freneau as someone whose too voluminous work nevertheless presents "a few flowers"; he praises Bryant as America's first poet of distinction, mentioning "Thanatopsis" and "To a Waterfowl" especially; he calls Emerson one of the greatest American poets, but finds that claim best substantiated in Emerson's prose, since although the poetry is "absolutely original," it frequently shows Emerson's defective ear and unmusical blank verse. Collins anticipates Yvor Winters in having a good word to say for Jones Very, while he finds the more popular Whittier deficient in "high poetic quality." As for what are now called the Fireside Poets—Holmes, Longfellow, and Lowell—Collins calls them "genial, polished, and most accomplished men" but also judges that "from men so constituted and tempered great poetry we cannot hope to find." Poe, on the other hand, gives us a poetry that is both new and original, though his most famous poems are tours de force or "tuneful nonsense." Emily Dickinson is faulted for being "in her jerky transcendentalism and strained style, too faithful a disciple of Emerson," but Collins finds much real merit in her work. And Whitman, a figure of "monstrous and ludicrous egotism" (anticipating D. H. Lawrence's essay soon to come), is also in his art an "astute showman," able to "collect a crowd for a show which, in some respects, is well worth seeing."

Collins concludes his survey in a curious manner, pronouncing gloomily that the "future of American poetry is as dark as that of our own," and although in 1905 it would have been understandable to have such thoughts about the mainly genteel American products appearing, it is of a piece with Collins's inability to look at the future of literature with anything but low hopes. The few contemporary poets he wrote about—William Watson, Gerald Massey, Stephen Phillips—were hardly the bringers of a new style or point of view. Indeed it may be that as an omnivorous reader of everything—at least all the poetry and poetic drama—written prior to, say, 1885, Collins was a sufferer from the Burden of the Past. Knowing how much had been written and how much of it was good, he couldn't imagine there was anything notable to come. At any rate he was not the man to discover what Leavis was to call "new bearings" in English or American poetry.

These judgments, culled from his American poetry survey, are not produced to prove Collins's indisputable rightness as a critic of those poets, but to suggest that, as is always the case, his judgments—however summary and undemonstrated through particular analysis—are worth considering, qualifying, amending. In a word, Collins is an *interesting* voice to have in the conversation. And with respect to American poets, the conversation, at least in England, hadn't proceeded very far by the beginning of the last century.

It would be unprofitable, and perhaps unnecessary, to take up for discussion various of Collins's other essays: these pages have made, I hope, a case for his historical but also for his continuing value for us as a writer about literature. Instead I will close by quoting briefly, from two of his best essays, sentences that, ostensibly about the subject under examination, have also unmistakable application to the examiner. The first, longer, one is from his essay on Chesterfield, an impressive exercise in setting that writer in relation to Cicero, La Bruyere, La Rochefoucauld, and Voltaire and comparing him in intellectual honesty and moral candor to Montaigne and Swift. At a certain point in the essay, describing Chesterfield's importance, his particular message and value, Collins puts him in the class of the work "of men out of touch and out of sympathy with their surroundings, separated by differences of character, temper, intellect from their fellows, viewing things with other eyes, having other thoughts, other feelings—aliens without being strangers." He says that the judgments of these men provide the "tests of national life":

> They put to the proof its intellectual and moral currency. They call to account its creeds, its opinions, its sentiments, its manners, its fashions. For conventional touchstones and standards of their own, derived, it may be ideally from speculation, or derived, as is much more commonly the case, from those of other nations . . . they are the upholders of the Ideal and of the Best.

If we substitute "national literature" for "national life," Collins would qualify as one of these men; at least, the peculiar intensity of his prose in this passage, in conjunction with his self-born, self-created myth quoted earlier ("My intense love of literature has been inspired by no one, encouraged by no one, influenced by *no one*"), encourages us to think of him as an "alien" like the Chesterfield he is writing about.

A similar affection for the outsider who has been reviled, at least his achievement underappreciated, shines through in the conclusion to "The Porson of Shakspearian Criticism," his convincing attempt to rehabilitate Lewis Theobald as a great textual critic of Shakespeare. Theobald, once of *The Dunciad* and a name thereafter dogged with the imputation of pedantry and obfuscation, is for Collins a hero, the first great editor of Shakespeare who provided a "settled text" that deserves the gratitude of mankind. Collins's words about Theobald—"He belonged to a class of men who are or ought to be the peculiar care of the friends of learning"— serve well as Collins's own epitaph.

A SELECT COLLINS BIBLIOGRAPHY

Illustrations of Tennyson (1891)

The Study of English Literature: A Plea for Its Recognition and Organization at the Universities (1891)

Essays and Studies (1895)

Ephemera Critica: or Plain Truths about Current Literature (1901)

Studies in Poetry and Criticism (1905)

L. C. Collins, *Life and Memoirs of John Churton Collins* (1912)

Anthony Kearney, *John Churton Collins: The Louse on the Locks of Literature* (1986)

—*Yale Review*, October 2002.

Edmund Wilson's Permanent Criticism

WHEN LEWIS DABNEY's long-awaited biography of Edmund Wilson was finally published, it provided the occasion for sustained reflection on the man's life—his relations with women, with alcohol, with Vladimir Nabokov and other writers. Mr. Dabney, who has provided the notes for these two welcome Library of America volumes,[1] paid ample attention in his biography to Wilson's writing, particularly the three longer books—*Axel's Castle, To the Finland Station,* and *Patriotic Gore*—that many consider the core of his achievement. Yet splendid as those books are, the Wilson who provided the most memorable and lasting critical stimulus for some of us is to be found, I believe, in the mostly literary essays from three decades, the 1920s through the 1940s (including the ones in *Axel*). It is then more than appropriate that the compact, legible, and affordable form of these two volumes, a form Wilson himself first imagined in his attack on the MLA and its cumbersome scholarly editions, should become an indisputable part of the American writing he cared so much about and that he celebrated in his anthology, *The Shock of Recognition.*

My own reading of Wilson began in graduate school some three years after *The Shores of Light,* his collection of essays and reviews from the twenties and thirties, appeared. I took the opportunity of its republication, along with the other books, to read in pretty much chronological order Wilson's literary work of three decades in an effort to see how much "permanent criticism" (the phrase is Clive James's about Wilson) they contain. Wilson was contemptuous toward the academy, especially toward English professors, thus it may be fitting that he occupies no place in the going literary curriculum of the twenty-first century.[2] He himself did virtually no teaching, except for short stints at the University of Chicago and at Harvard. I remember less than enthusiastic comments from graduate students who enrolled in his Harvard seminar; one guesses that being a charming and "lively" teacher interested him scarcely at all—he was interested rather in doing the reading and writing for *Patriotic Gore;* yet the educative value of his writing for myself and others has been enormous. Here are a few observations about Wilson's practical contribution to literary studies.

Probably the fullest and most adverse treatment he ever received from another critic was Stanley Edgar Hyman's chapter on him in *The Armed Vision* (1948). In what was the first significant survey of important twentieth-century critics of literature, Hyman took us by not-so-easy stages through the work of twelve of them, ranging from ones he had mainly distaste for (Wilson, Yvor Winters, T. S. Eliot) to the four who to him represented the apex of New Criticism—R. P. Blackmur, William Empson, I. A. Richards, and (Hyman's especial hero and Bennington colleague) Kenneth Burke.[3] Each chapter in *The Armed Vision* had a subtitle, Wilson's being "Translation in Criticism." Hyman's argument was that Wilson should be considered primarily as a provider of "synopses" of difficult modern writers like Proust, Joyce, and Eliot. These translations or synopses were of the work's "content," Wilson—in Hyman's estimation—having no interest in "form" except as a packaging that must be unwrapped in order to get at what lay inside or behind it. Although Hyman conceded that when *Axel's Castle* appeared in 1931 it was useful to have summaries of difficult modernist writers like the ones named above, such translation had become unnecessary and obsolete as academic treatments of the writers proliferated. Furthermore, Wilson's method often consisted—and Hyman instanced his dealings with Pushkin and Henry James in *The Triple Thinkers*—of "straight plot summary, incident by incident, like an undergraduate précis." If this sounds like a damning indictment, it gives in fact a quite false idea of the experience of reading through Wilson's "plot-summaries" of works by Pushkin or Proust. Hyman also accused Wilson of being a bad, uncomprehending critic of poetry in his reviews and in his essay "Is Verse a Dying Technique?" Hyman was willing to grant that he "writes clearly and readably," but never entertains the possibility that there is usually an art to Wilson's writing that is deeper and ultimately as rewarding as the high-wire performances of a Blackmur or an Empson.

The charge that Wilson was an uncomprehending critic of poetry is based in part on what is sometimes seen as a grudging response to the major American poets of the last century. Yet the brief reviews from the 1920s in *The Shores of Light* are never less than shrewd, whether he is writing in praise or something less than praise of the poet in question. He judges Edwin Arlington Robinson to be "a poet of regrets and failures" who is "the last and probably the greatest of the line of New England Poets." Although he doesn't admire Robinson's then-popular longer poems ("they seem to me among the flattest of later blank verse deserts"), he says they could only have come from "a distinguished and original mind." He shakes his head about Pound's "patchwork" translations and impersonative poems, but honors him for "having failed in so high a cause." Reviewing *Harmonium*, he notes Wallace Stevens's "curious ironic imagination" and richness of verbal display, but finds that in the book as a whole they issue often in a certain aridity: "Emotion seems to emerge only furtively in the cryptic images of his poetry, as if he had been driven, as he seems to hint, into the remotest crannies of sleep or disposed of by being dexterously converted into exquisite amusing words." Granted this is not the way Stevens is regarded today, but it is a provocative, plausible, and thoughtful testimony to the distinctly odd impact *Harmonium* made on its first readers. As for E. E. Cummings (whom he reviews along with Stevens), Wilson calls him "a genuine lyric poet at a time when there is a great deal of writing of verse and very little poetic feeling." In response to Hart Crane's *White Buildings* he says that Crane commands a "diapason," one "of which the phrases are anything but clearly outlined, the images anything but definite." He registers Crane's "remarkable style" even as he finds it in excess of its subjects, whatever they are. He finds good things to say about the "Tennessee" poets—John Crowe Ransom, Allen Tate, and Robert Penn Warren. By contrast, his lifelong dislike for Archibald MacLeish and his work began when he found this poet "of the age of Masefield" now under the influence of T. S. Eliot, so that however admirable his "instrument," "emotionally and intellectually, I fear that a good deal of the time he is talking through his new hat." (Wilson jokes that Eliot's influence is "making the young men prematurely senile.")

I quote these snippets because they are not ones Wilson is usually remembered for and because they demonstrate that, however right or wrong his critical judgments now seem, individual instances of them are never less than intelligently formulated and declared. His sympathetic response to women poets of the time—to Sara Teasdale, Elinor Wylie, and, above all, to Edna Millay—are well known, as is his absolute refusal to say a good word about Robert Frost. Just as his personal relationships with Wylie and Millay surely determined some of his admiration for their work, so his opinions of Frost's poetry ("dull," "overrated") had a good deal to do with disliking Frost the man's showmanship. In 1959, after Lionel Trilling had given the "birthday" speech in which he announced his discovery of Frost as a tragic poet, Wilson, upon reading the speech, wrote Trilling that he, Wilson, thought Frost "partly a dreadful old fraud and one of the most relentless self-promoters in the history of American literature." But he admits that Trilling had made him sound more interesting than Wilson thought, and says he must read the poems Trilling praised. (There is no indication that, if Wilson did, he changed his mind.)

One issue on which he and Frost were in agreement however was the centrality of an auditory approach to poems. Frost's championing of what he called "ear-reading," rather than eye-reading, is echoed by Wilson in "The Muses Out of Work" (1927), where he casts aspersions on the Imagist movement as a "poetry for the eye" that, as practiced by Sandburg, Amy Lowell, and John Gould Fletcher, is wholly inadequate to his (and Frost's) idea of what poetry ought to be. He tells of discussing English poetry with "a number of young men," one of them a practitioner in the Imagist tradition, all of whom agreed in their distaste for Milton. When Wilson confronted them with particular passages from *Paradise Lost,* the young men found in them only obsolete theology and "the affectations of a tortured tongue." In fact, he believes they were tone-deaf to Milton's effects, since they approached his poem only through the eye and the intellect: "They could not *hear* the difference between Wordsworth and Longfellow any more than they could hear the kinship between Wordsworth and Milton." This is tonic, and one wishes he had taken more occasions, in his reviewing of books, to deal with older English poets. There is a rare example of such dealing when, in 1925, he reviewed Lytton Strachey's pamphlet on Pope. Wilson picks out a couplet that Strachey admires—"Lo! where Maeotis sleeps, and hardly flows / The freezing Tanaïs thro' a waste of snows"— which Pope is supposed to have considered the most successful lines he ever wrote. In his *Life of Pope,* Samuel Johnson said he could not understand the reason for Pope's preference; Wilson suggests that in these lines and in others, Pope made something besides the "rocking-horse" aphorisms for which he was denounced by Wordsworth and for which he was still condemned by some:

> These lines, with their self-contained pattern, their frozen coldness and retarded flow, have a perfection of linguistic harmonies and an accurate descriptive brilliance that are typical of Pope at

his best, but in which the romantics, except for Keats, did not as
a rule excel.

He then proceeds, usefully, to compare such harmonies with those of Tennyson. This brief review ("Pope and Tennyson") is a gem of compressed
critical thinking and listening.

It is unlikely that, almost eighty years after *Axel's Castle* was published
(1931), the fledgling reader of Yeats or Eliot will begin by reading Wilson's
chapters on them (Hyman would call those accounts "obsolete"). But
we should bear in mind their historical importance as seminal accounts
of each poet at a certain point in his not-yet-completed career: Yeats up
through *The Tower* and Eliot through "Ash-Wednesday." *Axel's Castle* preceded F. R. Leavis's *New Bearings in English Poetry* by only a year, but,
compared to Leavis's pages on the two poets, Wilson's chapters are more
spacious and (especially in the case of Yeats) more welcoming. They also
give attention to the importance of both poets as writers of prose, Wilson
memorably characterizing Yeats's prose as "like the product of some dying
loomcraft brought to perfection in the days before machinery." He finds
in that prose "a man of both exceptionally wide information and exceptional intellectual curiosity," although—in one of those qualifying con-
nectives that mark Wilson's treatments of most writers—he demurs at *A
Vision*, which (in its 1925 version) "makes us impatient with Yeats." (He
would later express impatience with much of Eliot's later prose.) But it is
the poetry mainly that matters, and Wilson closes his account of Yeats by
quoting the final stanza of "Among School Children" that had been published only a few years previously:

> Labor is blossoming or dancing where
> The body is not bruised to pleasure soul,
> Nor beauty born out of its own despair,
> Nor blear-eyed wisdom out of midnight oil.
> O chestnut tree, great rooted blossomer,
> Are you the leaf, the blossom or the bole?
> O body swayed to music, O brightening glance,
> How can we know the dancer from the dance?

He comments :

Here the actual scene in the convent, the personal emotions it awakens and the general speculations which these emotions suggest, have been interwoven and made to play upon each other at the same time that they are kept separate and distinct. A complex subject has been treated in the most concentrated form, and yet without confusion. Perceptions, fancies, feelings and thoughts have all their place in the poet's record. It is a moment of human life, masterfully seized and made permanent, in all its nobility and lameness, its mystery and actuality, its direct personal contact and abstraction.

To my knowledge no later commentator has substantially improved upon this response to Yeats's stanza.

As for Eliot, Wilson says his critical prose has affected literary opinion since the First World War "more profoundly than any other critic writing English." Its style is very different from that of his poetry, "almost primly precise and sober, yet with a sort of sensitive charm in its austerity— closely reasoned and making its points with the fewest possible words, yet always even, effortless and lucid." "Sensitive charm" is not an inappropriate phrase to characterize the qualities of Wilson's own prose, which is not to be reduced to the "simple and comprehensible English sentences" of Hyman's account. Wilson had reviewed *The Waste Land* in *The Dial* in 1922 (the review is included as one of the uncollected pieces in the Library's volumes), and in *Axel's Castle* he provided one of the first accounts of Eliot's indebtedness in his early poems to Laforgue and Corbière, while he insisted also that, despite its complicated references and quotations, *The Waste Land* was "intelligible at first reading," and that it was not necessary to know anything about Grail legends to find it so. In *Axel's Castle* he shows how certain intelligible sequences from that poem have been constructed by the poet.

It is true that in the 1930s and beyond, he paid increasingly less attention to poetry, his preoccupation with politics, with social upheaval in America, and with various prose writers largely supplanting it. Hyman detects a "constant sniping" at poetry in his reviews and articles, and singles out as proof of this "Is Verse a Dying Technique?" from *The Triple Thinkers* (1938). In fact this essay seems to me one of Wilson's boldest and best, in its breaking down the prose-poetry divide by suggesting how much "poetry" may be found in the prose of various nineteenth- and twentieth-century novelists. He argues that, more and more, prose has taken over material that "formerly provided the subjects for compositions in verse"; so it does not make sense to distinguish poetry from prose, as if the former were something that the latter couldn't contain. Wilson had read Dante and Flaubert at Princeton under the tutelage of his mentor, Christian Gauss. The "comparative" habit he learned from this professor of Romance Languages would make itself felt twenty-five years later when, in "Is Verse a Dying Technique?," he puts Dante and Flaubert together: "One who has first come to Flaubert at a sensitive age when he is also reading Dante may have the experience of finding that the paragraphs of the former remain in his mind and continue to sing just as the lines of the latter do." There is no doubt that Wilson was the "one" who had this experience; Dante may be greater than Flaubert, but the latter "belongs in Dante's class," and Wilson unites them under "poetry," claiming that "by Flaubert's time the Dantes present their visions in terms of prose drama or fiction rather than of epics in verse."

"Is Verse a Dying Technique?" most comes alive when, after juxtaposing Flaubert and Dante, Wilson for good measure brings in Virgil, since, as he tells us, the same "one" spoken of above happened to read Virgil's *Georgics* not long after having read Flaubert:

> If you think of Virgil with Tennyson, you have the illusion that the Virgilian poets are shrinking; but if you think of Virgil with Flaubert, you can see how a great modern prosewriter has grown out of the great classical poets. . . . Flaubert is no less accomplished in his use of words and rhythms than Virgil; and the poet is as successful as the novelist in conveying emotion through objective statement.

He proceeds to put Virgilian lines from the fourth *Georgic* about bees swarming with sentences from *Madame Bovary* in which Emma hears and sees the bees on an April afternoon, and invites us to "compare Virgil's sadness and wistfulness with the sadness and nostalgia of Flaubert." The two or three pages devoted to these comparisons and juxtapositions are alive with a creative glow, the critic having experienced something that he needs to pass on to his readers. Wilson calls Flaubert "the first great writer in prose deliberately to try to take over for the treatment of ambitious subjects, the delicacy, the precision, and the intensity that have hitherto been identified with verse." (There follows a correlative mention of Ibsen's prose as another instance of a medium in which poetry occurs.) His formulations about Flaubert constitute a challenge to an imperfect reader like myself, restless and dissatisfied with *L'Education Sentimentale* (as read in translation). Along with so many other moments in his critical commentaries, they provide incitements to extending ourselves as readers. The overall force of the essay is not that it causes us to answer the question, yes, verse *is* a dying technique as far as conveying all sorts of "poetic" effects for which it was once the only medium. Nevertheless, at his most tendentious, which he often delights in being when he gets on a roll, he can grandly pronounce the end, as it were, of a poetic form: "The trouble is that no verse technique is more obsolete today than blank verse. The old iambic pentameters have no longer any relation whatever to the tempo and rhythm of our lives," he writes, adding that Yeats was the last great poet able to use blank verse convincingly. Not so, we say, noting that if Wilson had been open to such blank verse as had already been written by Frost and Stevens, or could have anticipated it as it would be written by James Merrill or Anthony Hecht, he would have been less certain about its obsolescence.[4] But I think this mistake matters less than the positive force of what the essay brings to life. As a reader of poetry—rather than just verse—Wilson is exciting and provocative.

"Is Verse a Dying Technique?" is the second essay in *The Triple Thinkers,* which in its reprinted (1948) form would consist of twelve essays, almost all of them representing Wilson at his height of critical achievement. In this class may be placed the following: "In Honor of Pushkin"; "A. E. Housman"; "The Politics of Flaubert"; "The Ambiguity of Henry James"; "John Jay Chapman"; "Bernard Shaw at Eighty"; and "Morose Ben Jonson." Two of the essays, "Mr. More and the Mithraic Bull" and "'Mr. Rolfe'" (Alfred Rolfe was Wilson's classics master at The Hill School), exploit the vein of reminiscence found most memorably in his portrait of Christian Gauss. Rereading these essays from *The Triple Thinkers,* some of which I hadn't picked up in a while, enforces the rightness of Isaiah Berlin's judgment—quoted by Dabney in his biography—that this "wonderful book" convinced Berlin that Wilson was a great critic.[5] It is of course impossible to "prove" Berlin was right by rehearsing the arguments and contributions of the essays, but I will mention some aspects of them that make Wilson stand out as a writer and that can be found throughout his work.

Most prominent is his ability to convince us that we absolutely must become familiar with the book or life he is writing about. An exemplary instance of this ability occurs in the Pushkin essay, where Wilson takes us on an eight-page tour of *Eugene Onegin,* a tour that should not be dismissed as merely telling the plot, since every sentence helps to bring out the nuance and tone of Pushkin's poem. This ability to hold in its entirety a piece of narrative, while proceeding through the stages of its unfolding, is a gift not easily come by—as we can see from fiction reviewers who manage to bore us with the novels whose plots they are delineating. (Wilson does this even more impressively in the chapter on Proust's novel in *Axel's Castle.*) Then there is the range and extent of the reading he felt it was necessary to engage in before sitting down to write about a subject. Coming back to these essays made me aware of how much my memory had simplified and distorted them: for example, "The Ambiguity of Henry James" I mainly remembered as a Freudian reading of *Turn of the Screw;* in fact it takes us through most of the phases of James's career as a writer, from his early stories to *The Ivory Tower.* T. S. Eliot liked to say, about writers such as Shakespeare and Ben Jonson, that any particular play could be understood only in relation to their work considered as a whole. Wilson invariably takes on the whole of a writer's work so as better to fit the individual piece into it. "Morose Ben Jonson," one of the essays added to the second edition of *The Triple Thinkers,* was remembered by me as an expose of Jonson as an anal-compulsive hoarder—storing up and withholding, driven by the impulse "to collect and accumulate." But as with the James essay, Wilson is less interested in making Jonson fit a Freudian category than in elucidating the qualities that made him "a great man of letters, if he is not often a great artist." He has read Eliot's classic essay on Jonson, but draws back from some of its claims:

> It is surely, then, misleading for Eliot to talk about Jonson's "polished surface," and to call him a "great creative mind," who "created his own world," and not to warn you of the crudities and aridities, the uncertainty of artistic intention and the flat-footed dramatic incompetence, that you will run into when you set out to read him.

Wilson not only set out to read him but evidently finished the task, since his essay refers not just to the great plays, *Volpone* and *The Alchemist,* but to lesser-known ones like *Cynthia's Revels, The Staple of News,* and *The Devil is an Ass,* works Eliot downplays or ignores in his concentration on Jonson at his best.

Wilson concludes the Jonson essay with an extraordinary list of subsequent English writers who were indebted to him, different as those debts were. He agrees with Jonson's editor, Gifford, that Milton owed something to Volpone's opening address to his gold. Then there is the bravura wit of Wycherley and Congreve, indebted to Jonson, along with the tonal style of Swift's poems to Stella and his "morosely humorous realism" in "A Description of a City Shower." Jonson's comedy of humors, Wilson claims, eventually leads to the novels of Peacock and Aldous Huxley—not to mention Dickens, who loved to act the part of Jonson's Bobadil. Tennyson's *In Memoriam* tetrameter stanza (ABBA) may be found in Jonson's fine elegy "If beauty be the mark of praise." And there are further glimpses of Jonson's presence in Lewis Carroll, in Joyce, and in Ronald Firbank. Granted there is some bravura of Wilson's own on display here, but it is a remarkable calling up of unobvious examples of literary indebtedness, as seen in various English writers from a critic thought by many as predominately a discoverer of not-so-well-known American writers, such as the John Jay Chapman he writes about so brilliantly in *The Triple Thinkers.* Wilson followed the book three years later with another collection of essays, *The Wound and the Bow,* which, except for the now classic essay on Dickens and a pioneering look at *Finnegans Wake,* doesn't equal the "permanent criticism" found in its predecessor.

In concluding this ramble through one man's appreciation of memorable things in Wilson's writing, I want to mention his old-fashioned, belletristic performances that, in their geniality and good-humored openness to experience, contrast so strongly with the crusty, cantankerous, *impossible* person we meet in Isaiah Berlin's essay or in many episodes from Dabney's biography. One of the most delightful and easy to overlook is a short piece from 1927, "A Preface to Persius." It begins with Wilson preparing to dine out alone in New York City and stopping on his way to the Italian restaurant at a bookstore where he buys an eighteenth-century edition of the Latin poet Persius, edited and translated by a man named William Drummond. While at the restaurant he waits for his antipasto he reads Drummond's preface, which leads him to various disparate but related reflections on the differences between the editor and his subject; on E. E. Cummings, whom he catches sight of across the restaurant; on Sacco and Vanzetti, who had been recently executed; and on other matters including the courses of the meal as they arrive and are enumerated: minestrone "with its cabbage, big brown beans and round noodles," chicken and greens, an apple, Brie cheese and a demitasse, and, throughout the meal a bottle of "yellow wine," all of which wine, naturally, Wilson consumes.

Then there are the autobiographical reminiscences with a Princeton venue: the masterly tribute to Christian Gauss, and one in a broadly comic vein on Paul Elmer More, whose recent death reminded Wilson of an occasion when he and Gauss visited More in Princeton, had a discussion of the Mithraic cult, and later attempted to locate in the Princeton Art Museum the Mithraic bull of the essay's title. Princeton also appears centrally in the account of Woodrow Wilson's career as president of the institution. Woodrow Wilson wanted to get rid of the snobbish eating clubs, long an ornament (or blemish) to Princeton life. Edmund Wilson, like Woodrow, is no fan of these heavy and often oppressive institutions, but he points out how strongly some of the alumni feel about them. Or rather, not "points out," but expressively and convincingly evokes their charm by noting that they

> have inevitably become identified with that peculiar idyllic quality which is one of the endearing features of Princeton. It is difficult to describe this quality in any concrete way, but it has something to do with the view from Prospect Street, from the comfortable back porches of the clubs, over the damp dim New Jersey lowland, and with the singular feeling of freedom which refreshes the alumnus from an American city when he goes back to Prospect Street and realizes that he can lounge, read or drink as he pleases, go anywhere or dress anyhow without anybody's interfering with him.

As someone who has, on the basis of a few visits there, steadily remained impervious to the charm of Princeton,[6] let alone the eating clubs, these sentences made me feel how it might be possible to feel as Wilson imagines those returning alumni felt. It is but another instance of the way his power as a journalist and critic has everything to do with his art as a writer.

—*Hudson Review*, Spring 2008.

Notes

1. *Literary Essays and Reviews of the 1920s and 30s: The Shores of Light, Axel's Castle, Uncollected Reviews; Literary Essays and Reviews of the 1930s and 40s: The Triple Thinkers, The Wound and the Bow, Classics and Commercials, Uncollected Reviews,* 2 vols. (Library of America, 2007). The Johns Hopkins University Press has recently brought out, in paper, Dabney's biography, *Edmund Wilson: A Life in Literature* (2007).
2. He is long gone from the *Norton Anthology of American Literature,* where, as an editor, I represented him by some pages from his memoir *Upstate. The Norton Anthology of Theory and Criticism* has room for his now-dated essay "Marxism and Literature."
3. In the abridged second edition of the book, Hyman eliminated the Wilson chapter but kept such forgotten names as Caroline Spurgeon and Maud Bodkin!
4. For an illuminating discussion of blank verse, especially in its twentieth-century manifestations, see Robert B. Shaw's *Blank Verse: A Guide to Its History and Use* (Ohio University Press, 2007).
5. Berlin's essay may be found in *Personal Impressions,* 2nd ed. (Princeton University Press, 1998).
6. Full disclosure: as a callow sixteen-year-old, I applied for admission to the college and was rejected.

Hugh Kenner's Achievement

THE LATE Hugh Kenner's (d. November 2003) contributions to literary studies were immeasurable, but I hope here to make a few measurements, particularly of his rethinking of how to think about poetry in English. Those who know his work know it mainly through his pioneering studies of what he liked to call International Modernism, as it was created by Pound, Joyce, Eliot, Wyndham Lewis, and Samuel Beckett. Viewed in this light, his masterwork is *The Pound Era* (1971), the massive compendium of analysis and anecdote devoted to establishing the centrality of The Men of 1914 (Lewis's name for them) and, as focal point of energy in the literary vortex they formed, the galvanizing presence of Ezra Pound. Yet some readers, including this one, have found it difficult to make the enormous investment Kenner has made in every part of Pound's work. For these less intrepid readers it is impossible to see the *Cantos* as always brilliant, to be admired throughout; or to see Pound's criticism—literary and social—as inevitably shrewd, relevant, useful; or his excursions in the literatures of other times and other lands—Provençal lyric, Confucian analects, Greek tragedy newly translated—as excursions only pedants and timid preservers of the status quo could be less than enthusiastic about.

Attempts to grapple with the whole of Kenner's oeuvre bring out one's readerly limitations. Mine reveal themselves most notably in the failure to take up, or take on, his guide to Buckminster Fuller *(Bucky, 1973)* or his *Geodesic Math and How to Use It* (1976). Sections of *The Pound Era,* notably the ones on China, or on Major C. H. Douglas's economic theories, or on the British biologist D'Arcy Wentworth Thompson's *On Growth and Form*—whose "economies and transformations" Kenner uses to describe, by analogy, Pound's transactions with Latin in *Homage to Sextus Propertius*—these mainly go past my head. Kenner can be downright intimidating, too much for anyone except perhaps his loyal disciple, Guy

Davenport, to assimilate. After all, we learn that as an undergraduate at the University of Toronto he was torn between concentrating in English or in Mathematics, deciding upon the former because (one of his sons has said) he would never be more than a competent mathematician. This particular reader, incompetent as a scientist, is further intimidated by what feels in Kenner's writings like a rich familiarity with physics, with electronics (he assembled his own computer), with "science" generally and particularly. The remarkable thing is that he shows a similar inwardness not just with literature, but with music, fine art, architecture. That he wrote forty-odd columns for the magazine *Art and Antiques* is no more surprising than is his expert fascination with the art of stoic screen comedians like Buster Keaton and W. C. Fields, or his approach to the movie *King Kong* with the help of *Paradise Lost.*

Enough throat-clearing. I can at least recall and describe the impact Kenner made nearly fifty years ago on the sensibility of a graduate student of English at Harvard, circa 1958. In that year Kenner published his first collection of essays—many of them having appeared in *Hudson Review*—titled provocatively *Gnomon: Essays in Contemporary Literature* and dedicated to his friend and colleague at the University of California, Santa Barbara, Marvin Mudrick.[1] *Gnomon* contained a number of pieces about recently published works of Pound's, but what first engaged me was its opening essay on Yeats, in which Kenner put forth the notion that some of Yeats's individual books of poetry should be read as sequentially organized, rather than arranged chronologically or just willy-nilly. To demonstrate, he described the organic continuity exhibited by the first five poems in *The Wild Swans at Coole,* and to introduce that procedure began his essay not in the traditional academic way ("I shall be concerned here to show etc."), but with a dialogue between speakers A and B. In this dialogue, A begins to expound his theory that there is much method to Yeats's placing a poem *here* rather than *there;* after a short while B interrupts him with "Stop, you grow prolix. Write it out, write it out as an explanation that I may read at my leisure. And please refrain from putting in many footnotes that tire the eyes." The ensuing essay does contain three footnotes, not at all hard on the eyes, but unexpectedly witty and arresting, just as was the dialogue that began things. No one at Harvard, certainly no English professor, had told me I should read Kenner; he had been mine to discover, and I was pleased and excited by the discovery.

Gnomon featured useful measurings of Conrad's virtues and limitations as a novelist; of Ford Madox Ford's just reissued *Parade's End;* and of Wyndham Lewis's climactic work, *The Human Age.* It also included a less than reverent look at Freud as he appeared in Ernest Jones's biography ("Tales from the Vienna Woods" was the review's excellent title) and a hilarious survey of nine recent textbook-anthologies of poetry. There were also essays on two contemporary critics, and as a reader brought up to revere William Empson and R. P. Blackmur as consummate analysts of poetry (they had been exalted in Stanley Edgar Hyman's survey of modern critics, *The Armed Vision*), I was surprised, indeed disturbed, by Kenner's less than admiring treatment of them. The Blackmur essay, a review of *Language as Gesture,* began with a flourish:

> Despite his habitual doodling with other men's idioms ("The menace and caress of waves that breaks on water; for does not a menace caress? does not a caress menace?"—p.204) in the hope that something critically significant will occur, Mr. Blackmur has achieved institutional status among the company. not inconsiderable in number, for whom "words alone are certain good."

There follows, after praise of some of Blackmur's early essays on modern poets, a severe but just critique of his fatal fondness for irritating verbal self-displays. Kenner notes that Blackmur "achieves divinations . . . by inspecting the entrails of his own formulations," points out his penchant for "alliterative jingles" and "compulsive repetition of quotations that catch his fancy," and deplores his "intolerably kittenish" essay titled "Lord Tennyson's Scissors," with its "pseudo-wisdom" toying so idly with quotations as to produce "a sort of thwarted poetry": "His hair-trigger pen, tickled by some homonym or cadence, is free to twitch out dozens of words at a spurt." In a word. Kenner is at odds with the "poetry" of a criticism that achieves its effects through words interacting in a closed system, and is to that degree irresponsible and irrelevant to words on the page out there. This was sufficient at least to make me question Blackmur's unshakeable place on the pedestal I had arranged for him.

As for Empson ("Alice in Empsonland"), Kenner begins his review of *The Structure of Complex Words* with another killer sentence that salutes Empson's earlier *Seven Types of Ambiguity,* even as it distances Kenner from its procedures: "In 1930 William Empson published a book of criticism which had the unique distinction of reducing the passivity before poetry of hundreds of readers without imposing—or proposing—a single critical judgement of any salience." Could this be true? As for *The Structure of Complex Words,* a book whose individual chapters I had found myself starting but not finishing, Kenner asserted that for all the impressive lexicographical feats performed in them the chapters were dull, "because the method is wrong for discussing poetry. Long poems deploy a far more complex weight than Mr. Empson appears to suppose. They can't really be reduced to the intricacies of their key words—it is a little like discussing an automobile solely in terms of the weight borne by its ball-bearings." It was surely possible for an admirer of Blackmur or Empson to take issue with Kenner's judgments, but there's no doubt that judgments they were indeed, guaranteed to shake up previous valuations of each critic's work.[2] The jacket blurbs to *Gnomon* included one by Marianne Moore that went like this: "Hugh Kenner, upon technicalities of the trade, is commanding; and when intent upon what he respects, the facets gleam. Entertaining and fearless, he can be too fearless, but we need him." Too fearless in his undeniable penchant for being entertaining? Whatever Moore mischievously meant, she brought out something essential in the aggressive—though good-humoredly so—posture of Kenner's criticism.

In the months that followed my discovery of *Gnomon,* I looked up the three books Kenner had published in a remarkable five-year period from earlier in the decade. These studies, all of which deserve the overused word "pioneering," were devoted to three of the Men of 1914: *The Poetry of Ezra Pound* (1951), *Wyndham Lewis* (1954), and *Dublin's Joyce* (1956). (I failed to locate a copy of his earliest publication, from 1948, *Paradox in Chesterton,* with an introductory essay by Herbert Marshall McLuhan.) The book on Joyce was a rewritten version of Kenner's doctoral dissertation at Yale in 1950, supervised by Cleanth Brooks; the book on Pound, really the first book-length study of that poet's work, was prompted by a visit to Pound at St. Elizabeths he and McLuhan made in 1948. That summer, Kenner tells us later, working at a picnic table overlooking a Canadian lake, he typed out (on a Smith-Corona) in six weeks what became a 342-page book on the poet, including a substantial section on the *Cantos* right down to the recently published Pisan ones. The shorter book on Lewis—156 fully packed pages—was, as with Pound, the first serious book about that controversial writer.

It is no less than astonishing to note that Kenner wrote these books

when he was in his twenties (b. 1923). They show throughout an irrepress-
ible self-confidence in their descriptive and critical pronouncements; one
thinks, by contrast, of Blackmur's and Empson's interest in teasing out and
exploiting the ambiguities they discover in poems, as well as ambiguities
discovered (in Kenner's words about Blackmur) by consulting the entrails
of their own formulations. Kenner, on the other hand, from the beginning
was convinced that, like the created universe, art possessed an intelligible
structure that was there to be revealed by the intelligent reader-critic. His
business was exegesis—explanation and interpretation of the structures
made by significant artists like Pound, Joyce, and Lewis. It is perhaps legitimate to note here that, although he never addressed it explicitly in his
writings, Kenner became a Roman Catholic sometime in his formative
years, and his procedures in scouting out the intelligible forms in works he
admires are as energetic and untroubled by doubts or second thoughts as
appears to be the case with Thomas Aquinas on metaphysics.

A related aspect of Kenner's criticism, evident early on, is its commitment to Eliot's principle, enunciated in "Tradition and the Individual
Talent," that "[h]onest criticism and sensitive appreciation is directed not
upon the poet but upon the poetry." Tutelage under McLuhan, then under
W. K. Wimsatt and Brooks at Yale, could only have confirmed this emphasis; but in Kenner's case it involved a lifelong disinclination (to use a mild
word for it) to practice biographical criticism. The introductory note to his
Lewis book begins with a warning:

> I had better make it clear that this book is not a biography but
> an account of a career, and that the Wyndham Lewis that figures
> in it, not always resplendently, is a personality informing a series
> of books and paintings, not the London resident of the same
> name who created that personality and may be inadequately
> described as its business manager and amanuensis.

This conviction that a too sanguine acceptance of biographical appraisal
would inevitably result in "explanations" of a writer's work that simplified
and distorted it comes out most fully in his less than admiring review of
Richard Ellmann's biography of Joyce, universally lauded when it appeared
in 1959. Needless to say, Kenner never wrote a biography, even as, in later
works like *A Sinking Island* or *The Mechanic Muse*, he is adept at placing his
writerly subjects in various cultural, philosophical, and historical contexts.

Although, in the opening sentence to *Wyndham Lewis* Kenner claims that the Lewis of its pages figures "not always resplendently," his standard practice was to assume an imaginative coherence in Lewis's, Pound's, Joyce's, and, later, Eliot's work as a whole, so that even if some of a writer's books are less highly charged than others, they still demonstrate the emerging pattern of a literary career. In a sense then, the chosen writer can do no serious wrong. and although Kenner judges a minor piece of fiction by Lewis, *Snooty Baronet* (1932), to be "a peppy and pointless novel," it also reveals—in the coldness with which Lewis renders a sex grapple between his hero and a woman—"a technical feat," a prose under "better control" than it was in *The Apes of God,* the novel just preceding *Snooty.* Kenner's "holistic" bent in approaching his writers, each of them treated as heroic in his intransigence and audacity, may be contrasted with that of the man he and Mudrick brought to Santa Barbara to join the English department for a year, Donald Davie. Perhaps the leading scholar of Pound after Kenner, Davie, in his *Ezra Pound: Poet as Sculptor* (1964), a still valuable book about the poet, showed a much more mixed response to Pound's writing than did Kenner. For example, Davie found large portions of the *Cantos* indigestible, raised questions about how *Hugh Selwyn Mauberley* did and did not go together, talked about Pound's ruinous anti-Semitism, and in general—while benefitting enormously from Kenner's book—strove to take a more balanced, more qualified judgment of Pound.

Kenner completed his cycle of books about the Men of 1914 when he published *The Invisible Poet* (1959), his substantial account of T.S. Eliot's literary career. This superb book, still the best overall treatment of Eliot's poetry and prose, has lost none of its freshness four decades and more later. At the time it was notable for its commentaries not only on "Prufrock," on "Gerontion," on *The Waste Land* and *Four Quartets,* but on related matters that hadn't yet been explored: like the significance of Eliot's Harvard dissertation on the philosopher F. H. Bradley, a dissertation that would not be published until 1964; or the importance of anonymity (the invisible poet) in the essays Eliot published as a young critic in the *Times Literary Supplement.* Kenner also brought out, as had no one previously, the incorrigibly humorous character of Eliot's temperament, as displayed, for example, in the fatuous letters he fabricated (in *The Egoist),* written under the following names: J.A.D. Spence, Thridlingston Grammar School; Helen B. Trundlett, Batton, Kent; Charles James Grimble, The Vicarage, Leays.; Charles Augustus Conybeare, The Carlton Club, Liverpool; and Muriel A.

Schwarz, 60 Alexandra Gardens, Hampstead, N.W. Not only the names and addresses but the tones of voice—from high-minded approval to outrage—are fine comic achievements. Here, for example. is the contribution from Charles Augustus Conybeare:

> The philosophical articles interest me enormously; though they make me reflect that much water has flowed under many bridges since the days of my dear old Oxford tutor, Thomas Hill Green. And I am accustomed to more documentation; I like to know where writers get their ideas from. . . .

The book provides a lively and continuous narrative of Eliot's literary life, combined with exegesis ("Comparison and analysis," the tools of the critic, said T.S.E.) and supplemented by glances at relevant events in the world outside Eliot's head. In the views of this particular reader, *The Invisible Poet* stands at the peak of Kenner's critical work, even as it is less ambitious and wide-ranging than *The Pound Era*.

In the same year that *The Invisible Poet* appeared, Kenner brought out his unfortunately short-lived *The Art of Poetry*, a textbook for students and their teachers in introductory poetry courses. I myself used it once in such a course, but as is the case with 99 percent of such textbooks, it soon fell out of print for good. This is unfortunate, since *The Art of Poetry* is notable for its good sense and for the taste with which poems are assembled to form an anthology of illustrative specimens. It contains pithy formulations throughout that stick in the mind, like this one about taste: "Taste is comparison performed with the certainty of habit." Other formulations deal with the notion of "pace"—"the rate at which the poem reveals itself" —or with the reading of poetry generally: "The first requisite is not analytic skill but a trained sensibility." Kenner had no illusions about how easy it was to train sensibilities. In his mainly dismissive survey (in *Gnomon*) of poetry textbooks, he concluded by wondering about the whole enterprise of studying poetry: "To study Poetry requires an unusually tenacious mind, fortified by a wide acquaintance with poems. It is doubtful whether very many people should be encouraged to undertake such a study." The "elitist" ring of this is likely to be troublesome to those teachers of literature who *know* that reading poetry is a good thing and try to sell that line to often unconvinced students.

The clear model for Kenner's textbook was its highly successful predecessor, to be reprinted many times, Brooks and Warren's *Understanding
Poetry*. But Kenner manages to avoid their somewhat humorless and often
relentless tone of instruction. For example, Brooks and Warren devote
three pages to showing the student why a slight poem of Shelley's ("The
Indian Serenade") is hopelessly sentimental, and they point out the dangers of such a state of mind: "We also use the term *sentimentalist* occasionally to indicate a person whose emotions are on hairtrigger. And we
also use it to indicate a person who likes to indulge in emotion for its own
sake." So beware. Kenner's intervening commentary is typically less rigid
than theirs. In an introductory note to the teacher he says wryly, "Much
of the commentary has been kept sufficiently gnomic not to impede the
teacher who wants to modify or dissent from it." Such a note is borne out
by what follows. Every so often, however, he raises a warning finger, as
when suggesting that poetry should be "nutritive": "Some kinds of poetry
are like chocolates, in individual instances pleasant and harmless, but as a
staple diet destructive to the sense, the digestion, and the appetite." This
witty admonition is followed by some lines from Tennyson's "The Lotos-
Eaters" and an example of late Swinburne, "A Ballad of Burdens" ("And
love self-slain in some sweet shameful way. / And sorrowful old age that
comes by night / As a thief comes that has no heart by day"). There follows a one-sentence paragraph: "Probably everyone should read enough
of Swinburne to get tired of him." (We remember Eliot's declaration that
reading the poet gives one the effect of repeated doses of gin and water.)
Kenner's remark holds off the poet a bit but doesn't really disparage him.
Yes, we say, I too should read enough Swinburne to get tired of him.

What is perhaps most engaging and convincing about *The Art of Poetry*
is the way Kenner refuses to encumber "the student" with all sorts of names
and terms that will presumably help in reading poetry. He does introduce a
few useful ones, like the names for poetry's different feet, but pretty quickly
draws back from systematizing by declaring, "With a sufficiently elaborate
system of marks and names it is possible to affix labels to most of the things
that happen in lines of verse, and construct uninteresting models of them,
but the usefulness of this procedure is not evident." Instead he delivers this
terse advice: "*Listen* to the way the verse moves." The emphasis on listening is very much a Poundian one, and the master's voice may be detected
behind the following tip from Kenner:

> Insensibility reveals itself more surely in rhythmic forcing (or
> else in the absence of any rhythmic assurance at all) than in any
> other way. You can tell a live poem from a dead one just as you
> can tell a heart beating from a watch ticking.

His message is, trust your ear to detect the difference between live and
dead work. An unstated corollary is that most of the verse from any
period is immediately disposable—is dead—on grounds of its rhythmic
insensibility.

Trusting the ear goes along, in Kenner's recipe for alert response to
poems, with trusting that the words in a poem mean what they say. In a
section titled "The Image," he points out that much of the time we get
through swatches of printed matter by *not* bothering about the meanings of words—as in the politician's "There exists a solid argument favor-
ing such a course." But when, for example, Shakespeare has Romeo say
"Night's candles are burnt out," we should think of candles. Rather than
enforcing distinctions between metaphor, simile, and other specialized
terms for poetic figures, he adopts the all-purpose "image" to designate
"the thing the words actually name." We are not to think of expression as "a
colorful way of saying something rather commonplace," which may then
be translated into some equivalent; rather, "The poet writes down what he
means. Poetry is the only mode of written communication in which it is
normal for all the words to mean what they say."

More than once in his commentary in the anthology Kenner suggests a
historical view of what happened to English poetry, his suggestion surely
influenced by, though distinct from, Eliot's emphasis on the "dissociation
of sensibility" that occurred in the mid-seventeenth century. Kenner's
warning that some kinds of poetry were, like chocolates, destructive as a
staple diet comes out of a historical conjecture that a relishing of rhythm
and sound for their own sake had roots in "the fact that in its period of
greatest life so much English verse was written to be declaimed from a
stage." This fact he found not to be "wholly fortunate," and indeed, three
years previously, he had addressed the fact more fully in a lecture delivered
in England to the Royal Society of Literature. It was published in *Essays
by Divers Hands* (1958) but never reprinted by Kenner in any of his collections, so it has been somewhat overlooked. Its title, "Words in the Dark,"
alludes to what he called a poetry of "majestic imprecision and incanta-
tion" that originated in the Elizabethan era, more precisely in the great

speeches from Marlowe's and Shakespeare's plays. By way of demonstration he quotes the famous speech from *Doctor Fausus* about Helen of Troy:

> Was this the face that launch'd a thousand ships,
> And burnt the topless towers of Ilium?—
> ....
> O, thou art fairer than the evening air
> Clad in the beauty of a thousand stars;
> Brighter art thou than flaming Jupiter
> When he appear'd to hapless Semele;
> More lovely than the monarch of the sky
> In wanton Arethusa's azur'd arms;
> And none but thou shalt be my paramour!

and says about it:

> These words don't make us see the vision, they are a verbal substitute for the vision. What they achieve by incantation the vision, could we be shown it, would, it is understood, achieve directly. What the audience *saw* was the costumed and painted boy; the words however don't encourage it to examine what can be seen, but to dream away from the visible . . . . A "face" is mentioned but it is not shown; we see ships and towers. And while the words evoke hapless Semele and wanton Arethusa, Helen is not compared to either of them, but to a brightness and a loveliness: the loveliness of the monarch of the sky and the brightness of flaming Jupiter.

What this "parable" shows, in Kenner's view, is that these dramatists were engaged in creating "an illusion more powerful than the testimony of the senses," through words that "sound well in the dark."

By contrast, some different verse of Marlowe's shows that dreaming away from the visible is not the only way for poets to proceed:

> Now in her tender arms I sweetly bide,
> If ever, now well lies she by my side,
> The air is cold, and sleep is sweetest now,
> And birds send forth shrill notes from every bough:

> Whither runn'st thou, that men and women love not?
> Hold in thy rosy horses that they move not.

These lines from Marlowe's rendering of one of Ovid's elegies, lines written 180 years after the death of Chaucer, remind us that in the poetry of Marlowe's predecessors, the "visible" was something to be presented rather than dreamed away from. Such Chaucerian potentialities involved "a close fit between the word and its object and a certain plainness and clarity of sense and definition in the refusal to let every phrase run almost unbidden into metaphor." This last formulation is not from "Words in the Dark" but from Charles Tomlinson's 1989 essay "The Presence of Translation: A View of English Poetry.")[3] There Tomlinson describes how he was struck when Kenner pointed out, in the 1956 lecture, that the poetry of Marianne Moore and William Carlos Williams, neither of whom had made much impact on English readers, might seem difficult to ears coming to poetry with Shakespearean expectations. Since, Tomlinson said, his own poems were being written with the examples of Moore and Williams very much in mind, Kenner's evoking of them was excitingly germane.

"Words in the Dark" would presumably have been part of—probably a key part of—a historical survey of English poetry to be titled *The Night World.* The book never got written, probably because Kenner had so many competing projects in his head that did get written, also perhaps because his interesting idea about the influence of Elizabethan dramatic verse on succeeding poets resisted being worked up into a large-scale argument. (How, for example, Kenner would have handled the poetry of Wordsworth in these terms is a chapter from that unwritten book we would have loved to have seen.)[4] The essays about earlier English poetry he did publish—the introduction to his anthology of seventeenth-century poetry, *The Schools of Donne and Jonson;* a fascinating account of rhyming in Pope ("Pope's Reasonable Rhymes"); an essay on syntax in poetry ("Post-Symbolist Structures") with examples drawn from Ben Jonson, Tennyson, Yeats, and Eliot—provide glimpses of remarkable insights into certain instances of English verse. But it may well have been that he found the three centuries of poetry between Jonson and Yeats to be more various and ungeneralizable about than "Words in the Dark" had suggested.

It's likely, though, that Kenner's rather exclusive attention to certain twentieth-century English and American poets rather than to others— often better-regarded ones—has everything to do with his distrust of language running "unbidden into metaphor" and his admiration for the plain style, the clarity of sense and definition to be found in Chaucer and Ben Jonson, in Pound, Moore, Williams, and some of their more recent descendants. In *A Homemade World* (1975), his survey of last century's American writers—the first in a trilogy of books that includes surveys of Irish and English ones—a major chapter of some length is devoted to American poets who are, to say the least, less than household names. Louis Zukofsky, George Oppen, Charles Reznikoff, Carl Rakosi are the post-Poundian poets who matter to Kenner more than what might be called the descendants of Frost, Stevens, or Hart Crane. Among those descendants are the post-World War II generation of vivid individual talents—Lowell, Bishop, Jarrell, Berryman; and the formalist masters, Richard Wilbur, Anthony Hecht, James Merrill. Kenner's preference for poetry he calls "modernist" (the subtitle of *A Homemade World* is "The American Modernist Writers") rather than what might be called modern / traditional, with its willingness still to risk eloquence in presenting a human dramatic situation, is something of which he is not unaware. On occasion he makes his bias explicit, as when he admits, in the introduction to *A Homemade World,* "There are distinguished bodies of achievement—Robert Lowell's, Robert Frost's—through which the vectors it traces do not run." His study of these "vectors" does not claim to be "a survey nor an honor roll," but his extremely high valuation of modernism earlier in the century means that there will be a falling-off from high achievement into something a good deal lower down. Or so it appears to me the case if (as Kenner does) you ignore Lowell, Wilbur, Bishop, and Merrill in favor of the Zukofsky-Oppen group. *A Homemade World* ends with chapters on these Objectivists and on Faulkner as "the last novelist" whose work shows "the last mutation . . . of the procedures that dominated the novel for many decades." Kenner's references to post-Faulknerian novelists such as John Barth or Thomas Pynchon or William Gaddis are a brief and less than enthusiastic recognition of these deconstructors of the traditional novel. But what, we might ask, of Bellow or Updike or Philip Roth, who write as if that tradition were very much alive? We remember that Kenner's interest in novels focused itself on Flaubert, on Joyce, on Beckett (as studied in *The Stoic Comedians,* 1964, and elsewhere) rather than on Dickens, George Eliot, Henry James, Thomas Hardy: on verbal structures that are comic and satiric, rather than "exploratory-creative" (F. R. Leavis's term) in their tracing of moral issues and human destinies (Leavis's "great tradition").

Even more precipitous is the decline (or sinking) Kenner finds in the Modern English Writers, the subject of *A Sinking Island* (1988). In some ways his most entertaining book, especially in its presentation of different English reading publics at the beginning of the last century, it is also tendentiously and programmatically mischievous, scrupulously "unfair," as Wyndham Lewis said all satire had to be. In Kenner's account, English literature after World War II not only declined, it ceased to exist. Of course there are admirable exceptions, such as Charles Tomlinson and Basil Bunting, the poets with whom the book concludes, but they only prove the rule. This process of disintegration had been going on since the 1930s, when Auden was the rage ("undergraduate callowness merges with unschooled self-esteem"), and the trumpery modernism of *The Waves* confused with the real thing ("Bloomsbury self-congratulation, unreal from end to end, voice after voice finely straining for fineness of perception"). Although Kenner admits in a preface that his treatment of twentieth-century English writers will be "highly selective" (he mentions Ivy Compton-Burnett as an example of one of many "good writers who simply did their job"), the urge to sink the island so infects him as to make his dismissal of or nonattention to modern (rather than modernist) writers blatant, and more revealing of his limitations as a reader than he might have wished. Nonmodernist, un-Poundian poets from earlier in the century fare poorly: Hardy is just barely mentioned; there is no Lawrence (as poet), no Robert Graves, no Louis MacNeice. Philip Larkin is treated as a "portent" of Philistia—Larkin claimed, provocatively, that he didn't know who Jorge Luis Borges was, and Kenner pretends to believe him—and his work is dismissed with the faintest of praise ("Not that his best poems are negligible"). Such grudging admission consorts with other swipes at writers who have in fact pleased many readers not merely susceptible to the whims of fashion. Evelyn Waugh survives, in Kenner's book, on the basis of a single novel, *A Handful of Dust* ("a popular novel for the mid-thirties. Not a great one"). George Orwell does not appear; Anthony Powell's *A Dancer to the Music of Time* is mentioned only to hang the adjective "leaden" on it and to claim (falsely) that no one reads it. Kingsley Amis gets a single mention as one of several "anarchic energies" to have gained applause: "(Yes, Yes, Amis; yes, yes, John Osborne; later yes, yes, *Private Eye*)." So much for those of us who thought Amis as good a comic novelist as ever practiced the trade. One wonders how many of Amis's novels Kenner did or didn't read; then one thinks, how *could* the author of *The Pound Era* have any room in his imagination for the Amis-Larkin disparagement of modernism?

But disagreeing with Kenner's judgments is, after a not very long while, a barren occupation, analogous perhaps to disagreeing with Dr. Johnson's low opinion of *Lycidas,* or with Eliot's judgment about Robert Frost ("his verse, it is regretfully said, is uninteresting"). However major a critic you take Kenner to be, and I take him to be a major one, he is like Johnson and Eliot in that he never writes a sentence that does not show a major style, and that includes "sentences" like the one beginning "(Yes, yes, Amis)." So powerful a style can transform a subject we haven't thought much about— the situation of the Canadian poet, circa 1952—into a memorably creative formulation. A Canadian citizen himself and reviewing an anthology of Canadian poets, he suddenly bursts into a dithyramb on what it is to *be* such a thing as a Canadian poet:

> Situated on a great blank semi-continent whose official culture, as verbalized by the newspapers, isn't a congeries of activities but a kind of *weather* precipitated from extra-territorial cold and hot air—from the most exportable cliches of British and American life: British complacency, lower-class caution, sobriety that makes a cult of mufflers, galoshes, and Sunday; American financial enterprise, urban discipline, and satisfaction in the ownership of "consumer goods."

In these (surprising) terms the Canadian poet is declared to be the most "alienated" in the world. No reader trying to wrap his mind around that sentence is, I think, likely to raise a dissenting hand and claim that, say, the Icelandic or Australian poet is even more alienated. The sentence is just one, admittedly minor, example of what Kenner found distinctive in Joyce's fiction, which is "great, as is much poetry, because the language, which does not merely extend the author but transcends him, has gone into independent action and taken on independent life."

This survey of the work of a voluminous critic—32 books and 856 periodical contributions are listed in Willard Goodwin's heroic bibliography[5]—is too patchy even to qualify as a mini-survey. Indeed, two of Kenner's most original and readable books, *The Counterfeiters* (1968) and *Joyce's Voices* (1978), I haven't even mentioned till now.[6] Instead of doing them justice, I choose rather to close this account of an exceptional writer by noting Kenner's alert generosity to contemporaries he found exceptional. One expects (and receives) handsome valedictions to Eliot, to Williams, to Pound, to Beckett, as they enter the realm of what Dryden called, elegizing Mr. Oldham, "Fate and Gloomy Night." But tributes were not withheld from writers still alive, sometimes unexpected ones like Leslie Fiedler or Tom Wolfe or Norman Mailer ("the most style-conscious, the most *literary* of living novelists"). Each of them was praised in the pages of the *National Review* for the tonic wildness that, it might be said, they shared with Kenner. He admired outlaws when their outlawry was conducted with daring and intelligence. In a review of F. R. Leavis's contribution in *Scrutiny*— which magazine Leavis had referred to as "an outlaw's enterprise"—Kenner saluted Leavis as a writer whom it had been fashionable in many circles to dismiss as a bad writer. No, says Kenner, let us rather seek to record the distinction of those "bad" sentences:

> His expository manner—a fascinatingly taut instrument of registration, like that of an *engagé* Henry James, virtuoso of the trenchant, qualifying clause, the ironically deferred climax, the epithet delicately placed between commas—is like all such complex instruments potentially a body of mannerisms, as I think it became in his late book.

Manner only becomes mannerism, as it were, when it is strong and individual enough to be bureaucratized.

Unfailingly Kenner found original ways to eulogize critics who resembled one another only in being each of them distinctive. John Crowe Ransom, he wrote, "exerted more influence on human learning than anyone in this century. . . . He valued the act of criticism because it can be an occasion for the critic's language to be *about* something it can clarify but not subdue." In a more reminiscent mood he concluded an RIP for his old teacher, Northrop Frye, with whom as a graduate student at the University of Toronto he had taken a Blake seminar: "Oh, 45 years back, the final exam for that graduate seminar was graced with a box of chocolates on the table. Norrie thought we'd earned those at least. What we'd chiefly earned was participation in his intelligence." And in a journal few were likely to see, *Conradiana,* he paid tribute to his old friend, colleague, and professional outlaw, Marvin Mudrick, whose essay "The Originality of Conrad" "drew on a rereading of the whole Conrad canon and a good deal of the major criticism. He reread, as he read, with obsessed intentness, filling flyleaves with pencilled codes that helped him retrieve any beauty, any bathos." Titling his tribute "The Examiner's Eye," Kenner ended by remembering old days with Mudrick at Santa Barbara, also their final meeting in August 1986 when, although "he must have guessed he was dying, he betrayed no sign and was genial as of old: Unable to think how I could have spent better hours than the many consecutive ones I spent in his company, I am greatful to *Conradiana* for a place to light this candle."

More than once Kenner quoted Pound's injunction, directed at Kenner when he visited the poet at St. Elizabeths, to visit the great men of one's own time as a clear duty of one's education. But Kenner added, "it was also part of a duty to such men, who among them comprise the only reason the time, or any time, may be worth remembering, and civilization is memory." I met Kenner only once, and that most briefly, but his work is something the time, our time, should keep remembering.

HUGH KENNER: SELECT BIBLIOGRAPHY

1951 *The Poetry of Ezra Pound*

1954 *Wyndham Lewis*

1956 *Dublin's Joyce*

1958 *Gnomon: Essays on Contemporary Literature*

1959 *The Art of Poetry*

1959 *The Invisible Poet: T.S. Eliot*

1961 *Samuel Beckett: A Critical Study*

1964 *Flaubert, Joyce, and Beckett: The Stoic Comedians*

1968 *The Counterfeiters: An Historical Comedy*

1971 *The Pound Era*

1973 *A Reader's Guide to Samuel Beckett*

1975 *A Homemade World: The American Modernist Writers*

1978 *Joyce's Voices*

1980 *Ulysses*

1983 *A Colder Eye: The Modern Irish Writers*

1987 *The Mechanic Muse*

1988 *A Sinking Island: The Modern English Writers*

1989 *Mazes: Essays*

1990 *Historical Fictions: Essays*
2000 *The Elsewhere Community*

—*Hudson Review*, Autumn 2004.

Notes

1. The Kenner-*Hudson* connection was made to seem ominous, at least shameful, by Irving Howe in his free-swinging essay, "The Age of Conformity" (*Partisan Review*, January 1950). Howe wrote, "When a charlatan like Wyndham Lewis is revived and praised for his wisdom, it is done, predictably, by a Hugh Kenner in *The Hudson Review*." (Howe later wrote for the magazine, so must have had a second thought.)

2. Kenner wrote about Empson on three other occasions, the first being a review of his *Collected Poems,* mainly admiring ("The Son of Spiders," *Poetry*, June 1950); the second a dismissive review of *Milton's God* ("The Critic's Not for Burning," *National Review*, August 28, 1962). In the latter review, Kenner referred to Empson as "The Playboy of the Western Word," the last word of which phrase a typesetter corrected, thinking of Synge, to "World." In *Milton's God* Empson had called Kenner "the American Roman Catholic critic" and "a spanking neo-Christian." In *A Sinking Island* (1988), Kenner quotes from Empson's preface to the second edition of *Seven Types of Ambiguity*—"Whenever a reader of poetry is seriously moved by an apparently simple line, what are moving in him are traces of a great part of his past experience and of the structure of his past judgments" — and says about it, "That is wise, and exact."

3. Collected in Tomlinson's *Metamorphosis: Poetry and Translation* (Manchester: Carcenet Press, 2003, 1-20). Tomlinson's first American book of poems, *Seeing is Believing* (1959), was published by Macdowell Obolensky, with Kenner's urging.

4. In a review of Eliot's *Collected Poems* 1909-1962 (*National Review,* February 11, 1964), Kenner spoke of Wordsworth's poetic procedures—"their evasions, their deliberate blurs of syntax, their odd meditative substantialitives"—and called him the "first specialist in majestically cadenced not-quite-sense." Could this not be Eliot writing about Milton's verse?

5. *Hugh Kenner: A Bibliography*, by Willard Goodwin (Albany, NY: Whitston Publishing, Co., 2001).

6. *The Counterfeiters* contains an especially fine chapter, "The Man of Sense as Buster Keaton," in which Kenner, with the aid of the classic anthology of bad verse *The Stuffed Owl*, shows how one of its exhibits, Cowley's "Ode upon Dr. Harvey," describes Harvey's discovery of the circulation of the blood in a matter so absolutely clear as to be "exquisitely ludicrous."

The Genius of Clive James

WITH THREE LATEST books serving as a capstone to his career as a writer, Clive James is without question the finest, most rewarding literary and cultural journalist in England or America.[1] (I'm tempted to say in the world, since his interests have been global in their reach.) Beginning in 1974, when he published *The Metropolitan Critic,* a collection of essays and reviews mainly literary, he has brought out roughly thirty-five books that show him in a multitude of writerly roles: literary critic, poet, memoirist, novelist, television and film reviewer, television showman, political commentator—you name it. His writings include a substantial number of pieces about matters Australian, the place from which he came to Britain in 1961 in his early twenties. He is incapable of writing a dull or an obvious sentence, and his reading has been ambitious in its inclusiveness: as he once wrote about Aldous Huxley, a comparable polymath, "You name it, and he'd read it. Especially he'd read it when you couldn't name it." More so than Huxley, James's writing is consistently entertaining, thereby making him suspect to whose who insist that a truly significant writer not be too entertaining. But James is never more serious than when joking, and his appeal is always to the ear as well as the eye and the mind. When he admitted recently to trying "not to write anything that can't be read aloud," he was referring specifically to his work as a poet; but the determination extends to everything he writes.

As he takes pains to remind us, James was diagnosed in 2010 with leukemia, emphysema, and kidney failure. In a diary column he wrote for *The Spectator* two years after being diagnosed, he noted that thus far not much of his illness had shown: "So far I've been lucky that way. Various clinics stick needles in me but I look reasonably intact. The major action is going on in the soul. Everything has become personal." Commenting on the recent death of his friend Christopher Hitchens, another polymath, James envies Hitchens's productivity as a writer up until the end, and says that reading his obituaries he was ignobly envious of him: "He had attracted so much love. What would be said of me when I was gone? I almost was. Why not devote myself to the form of writing that has always mattered to me most?" What's behind this question in part is the fact that over the decades James had developed a reputation that threatened any pretense on his part to be a serious poet. In his earlier days, he published a mock epic titled "Peregrine Prykke's Pilgrimage Through the London Literary World," featuring a number of James's pals who were in that world in the 1970s. This clever and amusing poem—given that you knew or cared something about the milieu he was presenting—was a mistake, insofar as it was seen to be less poetry than a species of show business. Thirty years afterwards he wrote that it sealed his fate as a performance poet, a would-be entertainer "like all those American visitors who turned up at the Albert Hall in their overalls. I was an Australian visitor (cue artwork of man in bush hat with corks around the brim) making the same sort of flagrant assault on local reticence." In fact, over the decades, his verse, while not excluding satires and parodies, was pitched toward a higher note, most movingly achieved by his "A Valediction for Philip Larkin," written after the poet's death in 1985. This note is strongly heard in the new volume of poems.

Anyone essaying to write about Clive James must note, if only to clear away some of his more dispensable though always entertaining journalism, a few of the forms it has taken. There are, for example, along with scores of TV reviews, his own television broadcasts, sixty of them, collected in *A Point of View*. There are four volumes of memoirs, the best of which, *North Face of Soho*, about coming to London and establishing himself, is the last of the series. There are five full-length fictions, and there are the song lyrics he wrote for his Cambridge friend Pete Atkin to perform on the guitar. There is a travel book, *Flying Visits*, and verse letters in strict forms to the likes of Martin Amis and Tom Stoppard. Then there is his biggest, most ambitious book, *Cultural Amnesia*, which most certainly deserves not to be forgotten, although its forbidding size and often unfamiliar content puts it in danger of becoming so. *Cultural Amnesia* spans 876 large pages and consists of a hundred portraits (some very short, some quite long) of outstanding heroes and villains—literary, historical, political, what you will—whom James wants to bring back to life. It runs alphabetically from Anna Akhmatova to Stefan Zweig. The oddity of the collection, enhanced by its alphabetical sequence (Camus followed by Dick Cavett, Bened-

etto Croce by Tony Curtis), is in the way it allows James to be both terribly responsible—finding terms for Hitler, Freud, or Kafka—and quite
irresponsible. By "irresponsible" one can instance the thirty-odd pages
presumably devoted to an eighteenth-century German thinker, Georg
Christoph Lichtenberg, pages filled with digressive riffs on Shakespeare,
Toulouse-Lautrec, Terry Southern's *Candy,* and the Australian tennis star
Lew Hoad. It is a book designed in part to make you feel guilty: why have I
not read or even heard of this Lichtenberg, or Dubravka Ugrešić, or Alfred
Polgar? Surely I should take another look at W. C. Fields's *The Bank Dick,*
or Michael Mann—sandwiched between Thomas and Heinrich—who
directed the movie *Heat* with Al Pacino and Robert De Niro.

One marvels at James's ability to move from a specific instance of artistic
achievement, say the music of Duke Ellington, into high generalization
about art in the last century. In the pages on Ellington, James singles out
his great tenor sax man Ben Webster, gives special admiration to his solo on
the 1940 recording of "Cottontail," then contrasts his playing with that of
the tenor man John Coltrane of two decades later. James suggests that after
we hear Webster in "Cottontail," we should listen to Coltrane "subjecting some helpless standard to ritual murder." Then the move to generality:
"Here made manifest is the difference between the authoritarian and the
authoritative. Coltrane made listening compulsory, and you had to judge
him serious because he was nothing else. Webster made listening irresistible." James proceeds to consider the "esthetic component" of twentieth-
century art: "One after another they tried to move beyond mere enjoyment
as a criterion, a move which put a premium on technique, turned technique into subject matter, and eventually made professional expertise a
requirement not just for participation but even for appreciation." As when
laymen, having questioned Le Corbusier's plans for rebuilding Paris, were
told by other architects that they were "incompetent to assess his genius."

James knows he should admire the trumpet player Miles Davis, whose
music perhaps "was speaking for Black America," but can't get over how so
much of his playing was "deliberately parsimonious and oblique, like the
soundtrack of a Noh play that had closed out of town." The comparison
of Ben Webster's tenor playing with that of Coltrane, and the wonderfully
impressionistic accuracy of what Miles Davis's horn sometimes sounded
like, should be enough to establish James's credentials as a listener to jazz.
But a comparable expertise obtains in his remarks about classical composers, for example Schubert, whose C major quintet he awards highest

marks. Even modestly equipped classical music listeners would know this piece; not very many of them could say that their entrance to Schubert's music came through listening to Artur Schnabel's recordings of the three great late piano sonatas. (Since my own entry to Schubert as well as Beethoven piano sonatas was by way of Schnabel's recording of them, I quickly acceded.) About popular song and its singers he is equally impressive. An essay titled "The Hidden Art of Bing Crosby," easy to overlook since it was published in *The Meaning of Recognition*—one of a number of James's books that never made it to these shores—shows not only a fine appreciation of the crooner's art but puts it in a satisfying historical context. The context is established first by contrasting Crosby's nuanced savvy with the microphone and its powers of amplification, with Dick Powell's unsubtle if charming amplifications in those Busby Berkeley musicals from the 1930s. It is further established by considering the Paul Whiteman recordings from the late 1920s in which Crosby and Bix Beiderbecke were often a remarkable team (James cites their performances on "There Ain't No Sweet Man That's Worth the Salt of My Tears"). Then the essay moves into some terrific pages about Frank Sinatra and a host of other singers, both male and female, from popular music up through the 1950s. The perceptions are typically made in a laugh-out-loud string of sentences, as when Dean Martin gets a salute for the way he swallows final consonants:

> For those of us who grew up marveling at Dino's ability to exhale a satiated moan along with the fumes of the third cocktail, here is vivid evidence that our memories are exact: he really did keep missing out on the final "s" as if the olive had got into his mouth along with the gin, and he really did bring English into line with Japanese by eliminating the difference between the singular and the plural. Sometimes the consonant before the "s" vanished along with it: "Make my dree come true." At other points, if you put the "s" back on one word as the sense seemed to demand, it turned out that the rhyme word up ahead of it needed an "s" too. ("Thrill me with your charm / Take me in your arm.") In his own words it was a magic technee. ("When we kiss I grow wee.")

James's three latest books—it would be rash to call them his final ones—total just under 500 pages, but they are packed ones. The slightest of them is *Latest Readings,* a collection put together at the good suggestion of Yale University Press. It consists of short pieces, mostly about novels and novelists James has been rereading: his remarks on Hemingway, Conrad, Anthony Powell, Olivia Manning, Patrick O'Brian, although thoughts on biography, poetry, and music also appear. James has always been what George Saintsbury called T. B. Macaulay, "a leader to reading" (odd but apt phrase). His rereading of Olivia Manning's Balkan trilogy led me to read it for the first time; I found it absorbing, though without the stylistic originality and excitement of other sequences of novels from the last century, Ford Madox Ford's *No More Parades,* Waugh's *Sword of Honour,* and Powell's *A Dance to the Music of Time.* Typically, James's piece about novel sequences begins on the fly, when reading Edward St. Aubyn's latest novel, *Lost for Words,* he realizes he must go back and come to terms with St. Aubyn's earlier Patrick Melrose sequence of five novels. Elsewhere he tells us that his plans to read Conrad entire were unfulfilled, but resulted in pages here on *Lord Jim, Nostromo, Under Western Eyes,* and *Victory.* The pages on *Victory* that come near the end of this book salute it as a culmination of Conrad's work, even as, for James, it feels like a personal kind of culmination. He began it in the "infusion site" at the Cambridge hospital, Addenbrooke's (to whose staff *Latest Readings* is dedicated); he finished reading *Victory* while practicing "ambulation" up and down his own kitchen. (He has been told to exercise, and ambulation seems the most possible mode.) Last summer I had similar plans to read all of Conrad, never managed it, but capped it with *Victory,* my favorite of his novels, though not his "greatest" (*Nostromo,* by common consent, wins that honor). James loves *Victory,* but like anyone who reads the novel faithfully is unconvinced by some of its more "poetic" writing and perhaps by, in James's phrase, the "upright stupidity" of its doomed hero, Axel Heyst. "Conrad should have made the hero as wise as himself," James concludes, "the better to illustrate his thematic concern with how the historic forces that crush the naïve will do the same to the wise, if they do not prepare to fight back." I was moved by the thought of Clive James doing battle with his personal history as, in upright stupidity, he ambulates about the kitchen.

Poetry Notebook is a more substantial collection, much of it made up of columns James wrote for *Poetry* when the magazine was edited by Christian Wiman. From these pieces one gets a pretty clear idea of James's principles as a critic and what he values—or doesn't value so much—in modern poetry. (Most of the essays are about twentieth-century poets.) He is proud to call himself "a diehard formalist," noting that in the old Australian school system "You had to get poetry by heart or they wouldn't let you go home." His emphasis is on the poem as something that should be read aloud, since one hears the force of real poetry in "a phrase, something you want to say aloud." But it's not just pure sound or wordplay that catches us; what we experience in a good poem is "the lightning strike of an idea that goes beyond thought into perception and into the area of metaphorical transformation." As in G. M. Hopkins's sonnet that begins "Nothing is so beautiful as spring" and comes to an electrifying moment in its third line, "Thrush's eggs look little low heavens." Read to its end, "Spring" has performed its task of "living up to the standards of thought and perception set by that single flash of illumination."

As a practitioner of what he calls "kitchen criticism," James is attentive to "the level of manufacture at which the potatoes have to be peeled." Strict formalist that he is, he believes in rhyme and stanza and meter, but rather grudgingly admits that there is such a thing as a successful "informal" poem, since a number of them have been written in the last century, although his preferences among poets from that century's latter half are very much for its formalist masters. Back in the 1960s, when some critics were turning away from the patterns of Richard Wilbur toward something more free, James wrote a piece in praise of Wilbur's early poems. Anthony Hecht, a later discovery, is admired similarly for his strenuous technical procedures in service of thought and perception only to be reached through those procedures. He admires James Merrill's "early formal patterns" in his fine poem "The Broken Home," and pays comparably admiring attention to the poems of Samuel Menashe, of Michael Donaghy, and of an impressive Australian poet new to me, Stephen Edgar. His major dissent from prevailing valuations of Modernism are about the virtues of the later Wallace Stevens, who spent too much time, says James, writing in his own manner. A fuller dissent is registered at the work of Ezra Pound in a quite destructive taking-apart of the *Cantos*, interestingly enough for their lack of "specificity." He quotes from Canto XVII—

With the first pale-clear of the heaven
And the cities set in their hills,
And the goddess of the fair knees
Moving there, with the oak-woods behind her.

—and points out how much more of the same is ladled out by Pound: "Palaces, terraces, marble columns, clouds, green sea, rocks, sea under the rocks, rocks under the sea, columns above the clouds, and so on forever."

The two modern poets he most admires (I was pleased to concur) are Eliot and Frost, "still fighting it out for the spot at the top of the rankings." He has never written at length about Yeats but sees him, on the basis of his later work, as a great poet who will survive if new readers can avoid getting caught up in the scholarship and biography that weighs Yeats down. James has written four essays about Philip Larkin (collected in *As of This Writing*) that provide a splendid introduction to the poet. Invited by the *Wall Street Journal* (yes!) to name his five favorite books of modern poetry, he came up with the following: Yeats's *The Tower,* Frost's Collected Poems, Auden's volume of 1936, *Look, Stranger!,* Wilbur's *Poems 1953-1956,* and Larkin's *The Whitsun Weddings.* His favorite "non-great" poet is probably Louis MacNeice, and his ideal poetry critic is Randall Jarrell. As for the highly reputed John Ashbery, James admires his early poem "Daffy Duck in Hollywood," but, as with his difficulty with the later Stevens, finds him to be the victim of his own formless prolixity: Ashbery's later career as an "arts-factory" led him to "turn out a continuous emission of isotropic mincemeat." The judgment rivals one of Jarrell's, in its figurative brilliance aimed at puncturing overpraise of an idol. If James is fighting some sort of rearguard action, it is done in the service of a passionate belief in the importance of poetry, since rather than being a "revolutionary" activity, "the mission of the poet is to enrich literary history, not to change it." When the academic study of a poet begins to concentrate on his supposedly "game-changing impact on the history of literature, it's time to watch out." Poetry is what it is and not another thing.[2]

Finally we come to James's own poetry, of which *Sentenced to Life* is a culminating book. In *Cultural Amnesia* James writes about Larkin, "For him poetry was a life sentence." It has been so with James, but never so concentratedly as here. He remembers his early days in Sydney, walking around "citing E. E. Cummings to an audience of trees, traffic, and puzzled pedestrians," and wonders at the "phonetic force" that drove Cummings's poems into James's head "like golden nails." Fifty years later, he is still trying to figure out just how the "propulsive energy that drives a line of poetry joins up with the binding energy that holds a poem together." In his poems from the last ten years, he has more than once achieved this energy, for me most evident in a wholly overlooked poem from the collection before this most recent one, *Nefertiti in the Flak Tower*. "Whitman and the Moth" is a poem in seven quatrains about the aged poet in post-Civil War America, sitting, according to the historian Van Wyck Brooks, "by a pond in nothing but his hat." Whitman may be in despair at what is happening to the Union ("turned mean") but purges any grief by imagining America still in process of realizing itself. The final four stanzas are as follows:

> Sometimes he rose and waded in the pond,
> Soothing his aching feet in the sweet mud.
> A moth he knew, of which he had grown fond,
> Perched on his hand as if to draw his blood.
>
> But they were joined by what each couldn't do,
> The meeting point where great art comes to pass—
> Whitman, who danced and sang but never flew,
> The moth, which had not written *Leaves of Grass,*
>
> Composed a picture of the interchange
> Between the mind and all that it transcends
> Yet must stay near. No, there was nothing strange
> In how he put his hand out to make friends
>
> With such a fragile creature, soft as dust.
> Feeling the pond cool as the light grew dim,
> He blessed new life, though it had only just
> Arrived in time to see the end of him.

This beautiful poem is jointed together by syntactical sinew, enjambment, pauses and continuities that surprise us, and a subject that turns out to be profound, ultimate.

The new volume contains thirty-seven poems, mainly written in a sober, strict, and stoic measure, often so austere and abstract in its use of figurative tropes as not even to contain creatures like Whitman or the moth. The opening stanza of the title poem may suggest the prevalent style of the volumes:

> Sentenced to life, I sleep face-up as though
> Ice-bound, lest I should cough the night away,

And when I walk the mile to town, I show
The right technique for wading through deep clay.
A sad man, sorrier than he can say.

The house where he sleeps is in Cambridge, England, his last house pre-
paratory to moving on. What he's "sorrier than he can say" about is having betrayed his wife, their consequent separation and his burden of guilt.
Because he can't say how sorry he is, he has to keep trying to say it—thus
the main motive of these poems. "Holding Court" contains the following
advice to himself in his retreat from the world:

My body sensitive in every way
Save one, can still proceed from chair to chair,
But in my mind the fires are dying fast.
Breathe through a scarf. Steer clear of the cold air.
Think less of love and all that you have lost.
You have no future so forget the past.
Let this be no occasion for despair.
Cherish the prison of your waning day.
Remember liberty, and what it cost.

In this waning day he thinks of his wife, their daughters and granddaughter, then, in four lines of complete sentences, remembers his liberty and
what it cost.

In "Balcony Scene," the first two stanzas in alternating rhyme are
addressed to his wife:

Old as the hills and riddled with ill health,
I talk the talk but cannot walk the walk
Save at the pace of drying paint. My wealth
Of stamina is spent. Think of the hawk,
Nailed to its perch by lack of strength, that learns
To sing the lark's song. What else can it do,
While dreaming of the day its power returns?
It is with all my heart I write to you.

My heart alone is what it always was.
The ultrasound shows nothing wrong with it.

And if we smile at that, then it's because
We both know that its physical remit
Was only half the task the poor thing faced.
My heart had spiritual duties, too,
And failed at all of them. Worse than a waste
Was how I hurt myself through hurting you.

In *Poetry Notebook,* James maintains more than once his determination not to write anything that can't be read aloud. Reading these poems aloud one encounters "packed lines" (James's phrase) that look easier to say than in fact they are; their effect is rather of density, the effort of working hard not to show self-pity that remains only self-pity. Thus the third stanza of "Balcony Scene" follows on the poet's guilty confession with the wife's imagined, sardonic retort—"Or so he says, you think." Still, I can imagine a reader who is put off generally by the poems' recurrent complaint or by their unvarying use of pentameter, often without striking images or arresting turns of phrase. As the remarks above suggest, I am not that reader.

"Death is the mother of beauty," wrote Stevens in "Sunday Morning," and the truth comes alive in one of the book's best poems, "Japanese Maple." The man is struck by the fact that, while his energy is low, "thought and sight remain / Enhanced," by the rain that falls on a small tree in his back garden. The two final stanzas:

My daughter's choice, the maple tree is new.
Come autumn and its leaves will turn to flame.
What I must do
Is live to see that. That will end the game
For me, though life continues all the same:

Filling the double doors to bathe my eyes,
A final flood of colours will live on
As my mind dies,
Burned by my vision of a world that shone
So brightly at the last, and then was gone.

Notes

1. *Poetry Readings, Latest Readings,* and *Sentenced to Life.*
2. In one of the "interludes" in *Poetry Notebook*, he writes about memorizing poems, or rather moments in them of "memorable phonetic force." As illustrative, he quotes from Keats's "Ode on Melancholy," one of his favorite poems: "Then glut thy sorrow on the salt-sand wave," which is in fact wrong (should be "Then glut thy sorrow on a morrow rose / Or on the sorrow of the salt-sand wave.") Unaware of his error, presumably, he admits, "I am always forgetting them as well as remembering," perhaps speaking truer than he knew.

Epistolary

Housman in his Letters

IN 1971 Henry Maas published an edition of A. E. Housman's letters consisting of 883 items out of the 1,500 he traced. He excluded "short notes dealing with appointments and minor matters of business," and he separated the ones on classical subjects from the main body of letters. In his preface, Maas put a damper on any readerly expectation of revelatory material to be found in the letters, saying that although they revealed nothing startling they "at least provide solid materials for the study of his life and character." In other words, they would be useful to scholars and biographers of Housman rather than providing pleasure and profit in themselves. The new edition takes a rather different approach in that Archie Burnett, who in 1997 brought out his definitive edition of Housman's poems, has not only located many more letters but has decided to print all 2,327 of them—three times as many as Maas gave us.[1] The ones on classical scholarship now appear with the others, in chronological order, and no item, however brief ("All right," for example), is excluded. Moreover, Burnett is absolutely forthcoming in his recommendation of Housman's character, finding him on the testimony of these letters to be an "even gentler, more amiable, more sociable, more generous, more painstaking, and altogether more complex person" than previous biographies had found him to be. He concludes his introduction by declaring boldly, "My admiration and my liking for him has increased." This reader, having navigated the two volumes, strongly assents to Burnett's testimony, although perhaps not the "gentler" part.

Burnett's editorial work is, as expected, consummate, most notably in the footnotes to each letter. The only imperfection caught by this imperfect reader was a missed allusion in Housman's reference to "the loquacious clock of Trinity" (vol. II, p. 509). He is alluding to Wordsworth's *The Prelude,* Book III, in which the poet-to-be residing at St. John's College next door, tells us, "Near me hung Trinity's loquacious clock / Who never let the quarters, night or day, / Slip by him unproclaimed, and told the hours / Twice over with a male and female voice." Housman is relieved that the clock has now (in 1935) been silenced between midnight and 7 a.m.

Anyone familiar with Housman's prose knows how sharp is the turn he gives to individual sentences. For example, "If unthinking critics could know how much one is ashamed to answer what they write, they would begin to be a little ashamed of writing it" (note the careful weighing of "begin" and "little"). Frequent encounters with sentences that have a kicker in them predispose us to look in each letter for some original twist of expression. We should not, in our appetite for the "devastating" response, turn Housman into a curmudgeon for all occasions; still, his pleasure in turning sentences in unexpected ways is patent. It may be brought out by contrasting him with his friend and contemporary, Thomas Hardy. Like Housman's, Hardy's letters are often, especially in his later years, very short indeed ("My thanks for your good wishes"), but it is sometimes harder to characterize their tone. Hardy's habit is to work toward an epistolary response that is, or seems, blandly unforthcoming, as when he tells an American journalist who had sent him some articles that they "do not require remark." Should we take this to be an artful dismissal of the journalist, or is Hardy merely stating a fact? Both possibilities are reasonable, and they suggest why, in their evenness of tone, his letters have not much appealed to readers who admire those of Keats, Hopkins, or D. H. Lawrence.

Consider, by contrast with Hardy, the following from a letter to an American, Seymour Adelman, who had inquired about *A Shropshire Lad* and sent Housman a map of Shropshire. Now he asks him about the possibility of reprinting Housman's send-up of mistranslation, "Fragment of a Greek Tragedy." Housman replies: "Your amiable desire to print a limited edition in facsimile is one which I should do everything in my power to thwart." After being lulled by that "amiable" a reader (and perhaps Mr. Adelman?) is jolted by the sentence's end, with its non-amiable "thwart." No chance of wondering about the tone here, and no doubt that Housman has taken pains to write a sentence with a true snap in it; the trap has been baited and sprung almost before we realize it. A related example of terse compactness that surprises can be seen and heard in the following about a classicist who represented what Housman called "the low ebb" of nineteenth-century classical scholarship: "His learning was small, and so was his modesty, but he had common sense, and some of his impudence was sprightly." A seeming upbeat at the end, but only if you are delighted by a scholar's "impudence." Sometimes you can feel him growing more limber as he goes along, as when he tells his sister, Katharine Symons, of their brother Laurence's lecture in Cambridge in 1934. Housman's tone toward Laurence is in general slightly on the condescending side, and the lecture, Burnett tells us, was probably about pacifism, a movement that did not warm AEH's heart:

> Laurence was here for two or three days and his lecture seems to have been lively and much appreciated by the rather contempt-ible audience. These "Summer Meetings" consist of people who should never be allowed to enter a University town, and on this occasion I am told that the majority were foreigners—who to be sure were probably the better educated part.

So the lecture (which AEH did not attend) was a success, just the thing to please a "contemptible audience" that shouldn't anyway have been allowed into Cambridge. Then it gets worse (or does it?) when hearsay reports the foreigners were in a majority; but that those foreigners, who we're ready to believe have even less right to enter Cambridge than do the English, turn out to be "the better educated part" of the audience, therefore perhaps less "contemptible." It's another example of how reading Housman's sentences often means rereading them.

Housman is masterly at apologizing to someone and in the same breath making the apology anything but abject—in fact, making it a fresh occasion for humorous mischief. When Edmund Gosse published a life of Swinburne in 1917, Housman responded with a letter expressing his pleasure in the book, but also confessing surprise that Gosse found much to praise in Swinburne's *Poems and Ballads,* second series. He then made a number of corrections (Gosse was famous for his mistakes, as Churton Collins showed in demolishing his *From Shakespeare to Pope*) that could be incorporated in a second edition. Gosse evidently took it amiss, and Housman responds to him a few days later:

> My dear Gosse,
>
> If you are going to indulge in depression of spirits because I manage to find half a dozen mistakes in 350 pages, you will cut

yourself off from my valued corrections in the future. As for my
finding "little to like," you know perfectly well that you write
delightfully and that your taste and knowledge made you just the
man for the work; and you do not need to hear it from me, especially when all the world is saying it. For my own part I always
feel impertinent and embarrassed when I praise people: this is
a defect of character, I know; and I suffer for it, like Cordelia.
The chief fault of your book is one which I did not mention, that
there is too little of it.

This is notable for its combination of a flattery I suspect Gosse felt flattered
by (all the world is praising his Swinburne book) and a teasing suggestion
that he should buck up or he will receive no more of Housman's "valued
corrections." After all, Gosse had failed to value what the scholarly world
recognized as Housman's brilliant editorial work. But the fine stroke here
seems to me Housman's admission that his inability to praise is a defect of
character, then adding that he suffers for it just like—who of all people—
Cordelia! (Here the editor intrudes unnecessarily with a footnote telling
us who Cordelia was and what she did or didn't say to her father.) For the
fastidious Housman to ally himself with Shakespeare's noblest heroine is a
piece of humor that is also serious. Gosse, like Lear, should have been more
appreciative.

But the correspondence is not all super-sardonic performances within
tightly compressed limits. Some of the most expansive and agreeable of the
letters are ones he wrote to his stepmother Lucy describing the terrain and
attractions of a foreign country, in this instance Zug and Lucerne lakes in
Switzerland on the way to Milan:

The water is a strong opaque blue: the scenery, though it is not the
best sort of scenery, must be quite the best of its sort: any number of cliffs falling straight to the water, pine trees and cottages
adhering to them in impossible places, and narrow white water-
falls streaming all down them with a noise to be heard above the
clatter of the train. After you quit the lake and draw near to the
St. Gothard the country is still interesting and in some respects
beautiful: the valleys are often surprisingly soft and pretty, full
of smooth meadows and orchard trees and foaming streams of
yellowish water; but many of the mountains would be the better

for having their tops taken off them. Some of their tops actually were taken off, so far as I was concerned, by the clouds and mist, and I saw no snow.

Here the wit is at ease within an equable, carefully observed run of things. It looks easier to bring off than one might think, but as a character in Trollope reminds us, easy reading requires hard writing. To note that pine trees and cottages are "adhering to the cliffs in impossible places," and to register the "foaming streams of yellowish water" is to see with the poet's eye (think of the heartbreaking landscape of Housman's "Tell me not here, it needs not saying") and create something of real interest not just to a stepmother. When he reaches Milan, he compares the architecture of its cathedral with French and English examples, mentioning in particular Westminster, York, and Winchester. But previous to the extended comparison, he introduces us to Milan, "the least Italian town in Italy," with the following perfect epitaph: "It considers itself the intellectual capital of the country, and probably hopes to go to France when it dies." Note the careful qualification of "probably."

Four years later he visited Constantinople and wrote Lucy Housman that it was a comfort not to have her along, since "[i]t would have been 'poor doggie' every step of the way, and we should never have got a hundred yards from the hotel." He then expatiates on the creatures

> who all have something the matter with them. They are extremely meek and inoffensive: Turkey is a country where dogs and women are kept in their proper place, and consequently are quite unlike the pampered and obstreperous animals we know under those names in England.

The Turkish dog at night "grows melodious":

> He does not bark over his quarrels so much as English dogs do, and when he does bark it is sometimes rather like the quacking of a soprano duck; but he wails: whether he is winning or losing seems to make no difference, so dejected are his spirits. . . . One night in the dark I trod on a dog lying exactly in the middle of the road; he squealed in a bitterly reproachful tone for a certain time;

when he had finished, the next dog barked in an expostulatory manner for the same period, and then the incident was closed.

Here is the felt obligation, nicely carried out, to make one's observations entertaining. It is worth remarking, however, that after identifying dogs and women as objects of sensible Turkish care, he has nothing more to say about the latter.

Housman continued throughout his life to be serious about travel, taking regular holidays mainly in France and Italy. Some of his remarks thrown off about what he has seen in the art and architecture line reveal him to have been a discerning looker. (By contrast he had no ear for music, and was quite as willing to have people set his poems to it as he was not to have them reprinted in anthologies.) He describes in some detail to his stepmother the Byzantine wonders of St. Mark's, Venice, which he calls, carefully, "the most beautiful, not the grandest, building in the world." A brief, packed observation disposes of two of Ruskin's admired Venetian painters, "the lurid and theatrical Tintoret, whom I avoid, and Paul Veronese, whom one soon sees enough of." On the other hand, he singles out for praise the paintings of Giovanni Bellini and of his pupil Cima da Conegliano, and the "very interesting series" of Carpaccio paintings in San Giorgio dei Schiavone. This tallies with my own memories of some Venetian pictures, as does the following judgment of a Brittany artifact: "Carnac is almost as unimpressive as Stonehenge." When I confronted the stones of Carnac, I did not dare hazard the comparison, but certainly had nothing to say about them.

In his introduction Archie Burnett takes up the charge that Housman was a misogynist and says that it needs to be "heavily qualified," adducing warm letters to his sister Kate, to his godmother Elizabeth Wise, and to wives of various colleagues. This doesn't seem to me to qualify very heavily the fact that not only was Housman's social life entirely male-oriented, but he resisted anything that threatened to make changes in the present order. When the novelist Lucy Thicknesse sent him a copy of her husband's *The Rights and Wrongs of Women*, a pro-women's suffrage argument, Housman wrote to her "My blood boils" and ascribed it to the absurdity of the book to hand:

"She cannot serve on any Jury"; and yet she bravely lives on. "She cannot serve in the army or navy"—oh cruel, cruel! —"except"—

this adds insult to injury—"as a nurse." . . . I have been making marginal additions. "She cannot be ordinated a Priest or Deacon": add *nor become a Freemason.* "She cannot be a member of the Royal Society": add *nor of the Amateur Boxing Association.* In short, your unhappy sex seem to have nothing to look forward to, excepting contracting a valid marriage as soon as they are 12 years old; and that must soon pall.

Was Lucy Thicknesse appalled by such insensitivity? Burnett, in his valuable "List of Recipients" identifying Housman's main correspondents, quotes her as telling Grant Richards, Housman's publisher, after the poet's death that "of the long talks I had with him, I chiefly remember the delicious humour of his descriptions of things and people." So it's possible that she was more amused than her husband may have been at Housman's mockery of *The Rights and Wrongs of Women.*

It would of course be heavy-handed to point out the number of Housman's light verse poems in which members of the female sex come to grief, but we remember the Salvation Army's Lieutenant-Colonel Mary-Jane who "tumbled off the platform in the station / And was cut in little pieces by the train." There follows one of Housman's most inspired rhymes: "Mary-Jane, the train is through ye, / Hallelujah! Hallelujah!" Or there is Morbid Matilda, an overeducated girl who drank a pebble in her tea, which she thinks may have been a pearl, then cried "'Don't call me Cleopatra,' / And jumped into the sea; / And with her latest gasp / Said 'Keep away the asp.'" Not one of his best efforts, certainly not up to the perfection of Amelia's treatment of her mother:

> Amelia mixed the mustard,
>   She mixed it good and thick;
> She put it in the custard
>   And made her mother sick;
> And showing satisfaction
>   By many a loud huzza
> "Observe" said she "the action
>   Of mustard on mamma."

Housman's successor in the line of gleeful violence, often directed at children or women, seems to have been Edward Gorey.

But perhaps the purest and to me most amusing instance of Housman's mischievous gift for creating the ludicrous comes in response to William Rothenstein's sending him a book of poems by Darwin's granddaughter, Frances Cornford. Housman sends back his improvement of some lines from Cornford's poem "To a Fat Lady Seen from the Train":

> O why do you walk through the field in boots
>   Missing so much and so much?
> O fat white woman whom nobody shoots
> Why do you walk through the field in boots
> When the grass is soft as the breath of coots
> And shivering-sweet to the touch?

The note informs us, in case we weren't familiar with Cornford's immortal verse, that her line-ending rhymes were "gloves," "loves," and "doves," which Housman replaced by "boots," "shoots," and "coots." The result was one of the surely great apostrophes to be found in English poetry: "O fat white woman whom nobody shoots" bestows on the lady an immortality finer, we may agree, than anything to be gained by serving on any jury or joining the Amateur Boxing Association. Housman loved such "emendations," especially when a newspaper reported an address of his as "On the Application of Thought to Sexual Criticism," "sexual" of course having replaced "textual."

"It looks to me as if the state of mankind always had been and always would be a state of just tolerable discomfort," he wrote to Gilbert Murray in 1900, when he had already published one of his very best poems, "On Wenlock Edge . . .", in which English yeoman and Roman soldier are made one in their troubled thoughts. He also put those troubles into "I to my perils of cheat and charmer," which ends with "So I was ready / When trouble came." Can one ever be "ready" when the real trouble comes? Certainly Housman may have wondered about this in the final two years of his life, when his heart was failing, his nights often sleepless and followed by "the perpetual recurrence of discomfort" upon arising in the morning. "My life is bearable, but I do not want it to continue, and I wish it had ended a year and a half ago. The great and real troubles of my early manhood did not render those days so permanently unsatisfactory as these," he wrote candidly in 1934, a year and a half before he died. Not even perpetual recurrence of his unfailing routine on each December 31 of "eating any amount of oysters up to 4 doz. and drinking all the stout required to wash them down" could assuage things for long. But the mischief, the malice, the mockery never lost their bite, as when an American wrote him saying that he had spent much time in Cambridge but had never attempted to see Housman. The thank-you note in reply began, "Dear Mr Abeel, My heart always warms to people who do not come to see me, especially Americans, to whom it seems to be more of an effort."

In his affecting memoir of Housman, *A Buried Life,* Percy Withers, the recipient of some of Housman's best letters, aptly characterized his style in writing and speech as one of "fastidious precision." But it went along with a personality that in its great constraint and—in Withers's experience—a kind of "taciturnity" was one that could be deeply unsettling and disturbing. Archie Burnett in his identificatory note calls Withers's memoir "sympathetic but somewhat baffled," which seems to me a just response to Housman's intractability. The vein of terrific mockery informing so many of these letters and of Housman's critical prose has in English letters nothing comparable except for Swift (to whom Edmund Wilson compared him decades ago), who, like Housman, was anything but a well-rounded human being. It is a rare occasion when an utterance comes straight from the heart with no surrounding protection of tone. In this collection it occurs most piercingly in a short letter to A. W. Pollard, announcing the death, in 1923, of their roommate at St. John's, Oxford, Moses Jackson, the lost love of Housman's life. "I had a letter from him on New Year's Day, which ended by saying 'goodbye.' Now I can die myself. I could not have borne to leave him behind me in a world where anything might happen to him." It is one of the letters Burnett prints that is absent from Henry Mass's previous collection, and its presence is but one more reason to be grateful for this superbly conducted enterprise.

—Literary Imagination, 2007.

Notes

1. *The Letters of A. E. Housman,* vols. 1 and 2, ed. Archie Burnett (Oxford: Oxford University Press, 2007).

Impossible

WRITING RECENTLY about Edmund Wilson's journals, John Updike cheerfully remarked that there was something in them to offend everyone. But compared to these letters, by the writer Wilson once called "the only first rate comic genius that has appeared in English since Bernard Shaw," they seem quietly inoffensive. Evelyn Waugh was truly what Wilson (with his curt "Edmund Wilson does not . . ." postcards of refusal) sometimes aspired to be: an impossible person. It was a role that came naturally to him, that he worked hard to perfect over the years, and that eventually didn't feel—and doesn't feel to us—like a role at all, just the truth. Waugh's diaries, published a few years back, are likely—in their eight hundred pages of sometimes monotonous recording and complaining—to defeat any but the most devoted fan. The letters, on the other hand, though not without their repetitions and an occasional patch or two of aridity, are eminently available, especially since they have been splendidly edited and selected by Mark Amory, a friend of the Waugh family who has spared himself no labor in doing a fully responsible job. (A trivial and amusing example of his assiduousness: in 1961, Waugh writes to Ann Fleming, describing a ball he's attended in Somerset at which the stables were floodlit and the horses consequently upset, "One bit an American pornographer who tried to give it vodka." The "pornographer" turned out to be Norman Mailer, who, when consulted by the scrupulous editor, admitted that the horse had bitten him, but that he was not feeding it vodka, just patting its nose.)

It is the exasperated Buck Mulligan who, in the first chapter of James Joyce's *Ulysses,* calls his friend Stephen Dedalus "an impossible person," this impossibleness lying in Stephen's ability to take everything said as personal to himself and thus as an occasion for offense. But Joyce was not "impossible" in his letters; among English contemporaries the best challenger to Waugh in this regard is most certainly Wyndham Lewis, whose own letters (finely edited by W. K. Rose) are relatively unknown. (As far as I can tell, Waugh and Lewis were unaware of each other's existence; at least neither ever referred to the other.) The liberal consensus has it, I should guess, that D. H. Lawrence and Virginia Woolf are the major modern letter writers among English novelists of this century, and Lawrence was, to boot, as impossible a person as one could hope for. But their reputations may suffer from a glut on the market: six large volumes of Woolfian epistles and the prospect of eight Lawrentian tomes. Waugh and Lewis make their concentrated impact on us through a single fat volume of letters each. And both Waugh and Lewis were blessed, or cursed, by a wildness of humor neither Lawrence nor Virginia Woolf possessed.

It is this curse of humor (the phrase is from Lewis's *Tarr*) that turns the impossible person into not just a possible but a desired presence in Waugh's letters. Tired of hearing Berenson's *I Tatti* mentioned in hushed tones by someone who stopped there for a visit? Here is Waugh's *I Tatti:* "We went to see B. Berenson, like Trotsky, in a house which after Harold's [Acton] is a miserable hole." Tired of trying to convince yourself how, really, you love all your children equally, but in different ways? Here is Waugh: "My unhealthy affection for my second daughter has waned. I now dislike them all equally." Tired of expressing your complex ambivalence toward Dickens as a novelist? "I have just read *Dombey and Son.* The worst book in the world." (Nabokov, by comparison to this, is a moderate, judicious critic.) Admittedly, one liners like the above, impossible to answer in any reasonable way, speak to our secret wishes that things could be simpler and more final than they usually seem. But at moments, Waugh's "simplicity," his stubborn refusal to accede to the social and psychological imperatives by which the liberal conscience directs its life, result in strikingly new and valuable perspectives. A prime example of this comes when, after his first wife (Evelyn Gardner, "she-Evelyn") has run away with John Heygate, throwing Waugh into humiliation and bewilderment, he tells Harold Acton that he is going to divorce her because "I cannot live with anyone who is avowedly in love with someone else. Everyone is talking so much nonsense on all sides of me about my affairs that my wits reel. Evelyn's family & mine join in asking me to 'forgive,' her whatever that may mean." Coming up against that "forgive," in the chilly contempt provided by quotation marks, one suddenly entertains a new way of thinking about things. Is it only the impossible person who doesn't know what "forgive" means? Are the rest of us sanely clear about it?

Of course it is easy enough to be impossible about non-Englishmen (with Dickens's Mr. Podsnap as a role model), especially when they are of other races and creeds. But it is not so easy to put them into creative fantasies whose comic energy outshines any moral depravity. So in 1933, upon returning to British Guiana from a trip up the Amazon ("The streets are entirely paved with gold which gives a very pretty effect especially towards sunset. But otherwise it is rather dull"), he writes to his correspondent that "the delight of these simple people at my return is very touching. A public holiday has been declared and all the men & women prostrate themselves in the dust and bring me their children to bless . . . several elderly niggers have already died of excitement." Writing from Jerusalem a couple of years later, he notes that "they have a wall here where the Jews blub, V. sensible idea," an observation made especially memorable by the verb choice and by its "sensible" English approval of the odd custom. Or consider the aggrieved self-righteousness of the following confession, written from California, about how Randolph Churchill has behaved abominably, has been "brutishly" drunk, and has "mocked the Jews." We are invited to consider, by comparison, the innocent Evelyn: "I was not in the least anti-Semitic before I came here. I am now. It is intolerable to see them enjoying themselves." What could the poor fellow have done in the face of such frolicking Californian Jews but embrace anti-Semitism? (He later admitted to Nancy Mitford that he possessed a bit of "anti-Jew feeling" but "not anti-Semite. I rather like Arabs.")

Or there is the impossible anecdote, often involving an animal that has somehow wandered into and disrupted Waugh's civilized routine. Here is the young student at Oxford enjoying a delightful adventure: "I went out for a long and solitary walk, as is my custom, accompanied only with my big stick. In an obscure village miles away I met a white dog and—as is also my custom—addressed it with courtesy." But the promising relationship is shattered when the white dog sees the stick, sets up a howl, causing a "virago of a woman" to appear and accuse Waugh of beating the dog. Crestfallen, he departs. As a journalist in Ethiopia in 1935, enduring much boredom so that a "funny novel" can come out of it, Waugh reveals to his wife Laura the failure of his efforts with a different sort of animal: "I had a baboon but he seemed incapable of affection and he kept me awake in the afternoons so I threw him away." Quite right too; there is only one thing to do with a baboon who has no decent human feelings and is also noisy in the afternoon—throw him away, however one does that. Or there is the witty bawdry and wonderfully bad jokes like this public school one about what wines Princess Mary and her new husband will drink on their wedding night: "She will open her 24 year old port and he will indulge in cider (inside her)." As for proper behavior in the London Library (Lady Mary Lygon has just been elected to membership): "Always go to the closet appointed for the purpose if you wish to make water. Far too many female members have lately taken to squatting behind the Genealogy section. Never write 'balls' with an indelible pencil on the margins of the books provided. Do not solicit the female librarians to acts of unnatural vices." After all, standards must be kept up.

The single most extraordinary letter in the whole collection is one written in 1936 to Laura Herbert, who was to become Waugh's second wife and the mother of his children. A months before, he had revealed to his confidante Mary Lygon that he felt he was cutting a less than glorious figure with Laura, who "came to London with me yesterday but it was not a success for I had a hangover & could only eat 3 oysters and some soda water and I was sick a good deal on the table so perhaps that romance is shattered." Evidently not, but in his letter to Laura asking her to marry him, he takes pains to lay out the assets and liabilities of his character, without aid of romance:

> I can't advise you in my favour because I think it would be beastly for you, but think how nice it would be for me. I am restless & moody & misanthropic & lazy & have no money except what I earn and if I got ill you would starve. In fact its a lousy proposition.

On the other hand,

> you wouldn't find yourself confined to any particular place or group. Also I have practically no living relatives except one brother whom I scarcely know. You would not find yourself involved in a large family & all their rows & you would not be patronized & interfered with by odious sisters in law & aunts as it often happens.

Still, it should be remembered,

> all these are very small advantages compared with the awfulness
> of my character. I have always tried to be nice to you and you
> may have got it into your head that I am nice really, but that is
> all rot.

Who could resist such impossible sincerity? Not Laura Herbert, who married him, bore him one child after another, and stayed home during World War II while Waugh engaged in various odd military enterprises, occasionally taking time out to keep his wife up to the epistolary mark: "I know you lead a dull life now. . . . But that is no reason to make your letters as dull as your life. I simply am not interested in Bridget's children. Do grasp that. A letter should be a form of conversation; write as though you were talking to me." Nor was it simply "Bridget's children" he didn't want to hear about: "No particular interest in your doings [he wrote to Laura from White's, his London club]: to hear that Teresa has sneezed or Bron fallen down does not excite me." He had previously begun a letter to her, also written from White's, with the news that "I have regretfully come to the conclusion that the boy Auberon is not yet a suitable companion for me" —this after a day spent together in London.

It was incredibly lucky for Waugh that he married a woman who was, truly, the Angel in the House. The other stroke of luck was his Catholicism, of which there is of course much in the letters and in respect to which he is at his most serious, most fierce. (There is a particularly striking trio of letters to John Betjeman, trying to argue or bully Betjeman out of his halfway Anglicanism.) Unfortunately, at least for this reviewer (a lapsed Protestant and, worse yet, an American) much of the in-chat among those of the true church is less than gripping, probably because by the standards set in other letters it's not impossible enough. So in 1955, when Edith Sitwell converts, and Alec Guinness has converted, Waugh writes to the former about how "one great sadness in Catholic life is year by year to count the apostasies—seldom from reason, almost always through marrying outside the Church. . . . Then one hears of the Grace of God steadily reinforcing the ranks. It is a great consolation." Left outside this charmed circle, I'm eager to hustle on to the next letter, when suddenly the convert sounds like something more: "I heard a rousing sermon on Sunday against the dangers of immodest bathing-dresses and thought that you and I were innocent of that offence at least." Saved by the comic bell.

Finally, though Waugh will not be remembered for his magnanimity toward other novelists, it's interesting that he treats his equals without condescension, often with affection and admiration. These qualities are to be found in the letters to Henry Yorke (Henry Green) and particularly in the ones to George Orwell) about *Animal Farm* and *1984*, and to Anthony Powell. "I don't quite know how I would define my admiration," he wrote to Powell on the appearance of volume three of *A Dance to the Music of Time*, "I feel each volume of this series is like a great sustaining slice of Melton Pie. [Editor Amory precisely glosses it as 'Elaborate cold meat pie, specialty of Melton Mowbray, Leicestershire.'] I can go on eating it with the recurring seasons until I drop." Alas, he dropped, while the Music of Time played on. The letters from his last years are few and short. "Since we last met," he writes his old pal Nancy Mitford, "I have become an old man, not diseased but enfeebled [he was then in his sixty-first year]." Other letters speak about bereavements, "No work, Feeble health." Still, at moments, something caught his fancy, tickled it into the old style of creating, as in this to Ann Fleming:

> When I saw the doctor he asked about my habits. I said, "I have practically given up drinking—only about 7 bottles of wine & 3 of spirits a week." "A week? Surely you mean a month?" "No, and I smoke 30 cigars a week & take 40 grains of sodium amytal." He looked graver & graver. "Oh, yes, a bottle of paraldehyde a week." He brightened greatly & said: "Now that is an excellent thing. Far too few people use it."

Not even the grave physician could resist, or so it seems, this particularly impossible patient. The reader may be similarly disarmed.

—*American Scholar,* Summer 1981

Talking Piss: Kingsley Amis in his Letters

The Letters of Kingsley Amis, edited by Zachary Leader.
London: HarperCollins, 2000.

THIS BOOK is a handsome physical object, with many appealing illustrations, a chronology of Amis's life, and notes on the major recipients of his letters, followed in some cases by bracketed notations of how the recipient is referred to—thus "Anthony Powell [Tony, A.P., Horse Faced Dwarf, HFD]." There are appendices containing a number of poems, many of them parodies of other poets, sent by Amis to Phillip Larkin. There is Amis's short and telling speech at Larkin's funeral. There are three "Alibi Notes" he wrote to Robert Conquest, cover-ups for extra-marital adventures, and three "Bunny" household notes to his second wife, Elizabeth Jane Howard ("Piney"), with a signature rabbity signoff drawing. All this material, edited within an inch of its life, we owe to the incredibly industrious and imaginatively resourceful Zachary Leader. The old devil himself, if he could read this volume, would, I am convinced, be pleased.

When Larkin's letters were published in 1992, they elicited surprised responses from readers who had admired the poems but were appalled or disgusted by moments of racism and sexism in the correspondence. My guess is there won't be a similar problem with Amis's, since no one familiar with his novels will pick up the letters expecting sweetness and light. Indeed some readers of this volume already suspect that the man who speaks therein may be the great comic writer in English of our just-concluded century. Amis's comedy, increasingly in the later novels but there from the beginning, is instinct with animus, indeed animosity, often more than tinged with a bit of cruelty. Especially notable in this respect is his *Memoirs,* which contains sometimes unsettling remarks about his ene-mies and friends (including Larkin), nastily if humorously directed.

The letters are full of such high-spirited animosity, and I quote one of the best of them in order to establish the usual pitch of things. In one of his last letters to Larkin a couple of months before the latter died, Amis reports on a luncheon at Iris Murdoch's:

> Went to lunch at ole I Murdoch's flat to-day. A Polish Jew held the floor, not up to much but at least pro-Franco, which "shocked" the others. All loved culture and thought everything was marvellous. Isn't Yeats marvellous? Isn't TSE marvellous? Isn't Magritte marv[el]lous? Isn't Flaubert marvellous? One of them "couldn't wait" for some exhibish to open. Another was "very excited" that some mouldering pile had been "saved." And what did I think of Terry K[ilmartin]'s Proust compared with that other fellow's? Ruh-beeble de bobbledy beezle. It is against *that* that we are fighting. And all's to do again. Francophile, a word they used several times unsarcastically, they pronounced Fronko-feel. Starsky and Hutch at 7.40. Oh come on Kingers this plain-man stuff doesn't get yoooghgh

He knows that Larkin is ill and hopes to cheer him up the only way Amis knows how and the way he has been practicing (with Larkin especially) for over four decades: by bringing out the worst in any person or event that falls his way. Larkin's "Vers de Société" opens with the Larkin-figure pondering a social invitation—"My wife and I have asked a crowd of craps / To come and waste their time and ours / Perhaps you'd like to join us?" —to which his first answer is, of course, "in a pig's arse, friend." Amis, having accepted the invite to lunch with a crowd of craps at "Ole Iris M's," couldn't wait to get home so he could write it up, make it live for Philip. "Shocked" by the Polish Jew's defense of Franco, "excited" by an art show about to open or a cultural monument saved, full of enthusiasm for "marvellous" modernist writers and painters, enunciating French matters in an unnatural (that is, un-English) accent rendered perfectly as "Fronko-feel," they are forces against which Amis—like Wordsworth in *The Prelude* but with something other than Wordsworthian fervor—and Larkin have been fighting. What this leaves out however is the TV cop show that "Kingers" looks forward to but allusion to which is also mocked for its plain man, too-easy righteousness. It also leaves out the best moment in the sequence, coming from nowhere: "Ruh-beeble de bobbledy beezle." Is that what the "craps" in their excited chattering sound like? What the silent, registering Amis thinks about their talk? What, in a memorable formulation, "social life" amounts to? Take your pick, but the words were at least as fortifying to me as Amis hoped they would be for Larkin.

I remember some relative or teacher informing me when I was growing up that if you couldn't say something nice about a person you had better not say anything at all. This principle, absolutely inverted, is the driving force of Amis's epistolary performance. For example, talking bad about one's in-laws is undeniably a common way to behave, but nothing quite matches in my experience the creative abuse Amis lavishes on his father-in-law, Leonard Bardwell. As early as 1949, he writes Larkin that "I don't see how I can avoid doing him in fiction if I am to refrain from stabbing him under the fifth rib in fact." Accordingly, "Daddy B." became the inspiration for Professor Welch, who would appear five years later in *Lucky Jim*. Like the professor, Leonard Bardwell was a devotee of folk music— "And the father does folk dancing (polk dancing? pock dancing? fock dancing?)"—so it was to Amis's delight that his father-in-law injured himself while engaging in "some lunatic folk fandango" involving staves. Bardwell reminds Amis of some "imbecile brother of Yeats," who, when asked how he was, "launched into an incoherent account of his recent ailments and protractions." In retaliation, writes Amis, "I now find his sense of smell is defective, so make a point of farting silently in his presence." (He has conveyed this same information to Larkin a few letters previously.)

Meeting him at the train station in Swansea at the beginning of a visit, Amis sings the rondo theme from Beethoven's first concerto (the "Welch theme" in *Lucky Jim*— "You ignorant clod, you stupid old sod") until spotting "his resentful ape's face peering about all round me without seeing me." One of Daddy B's activities while visiting Kingsley and Hilly is recounted thus:

> He's gone out today to see how much he remembers of the geography of Swansea; those are the *ipsissima verba*. Now why, I wonder, does he want to do that? What will he do if he finds he remembers a lot of it? And what will he do if he finds he doesn't remember a lot of it? He goes round in a blue shirt, with his braces in full view, trying to disgrace me.

As the letter to Larkin draws to a close, with a flurry of the signoff word ("bum") he and Larkin use ("Billy go and talk to Daddy; he's in there all on his bum, *bum,* bum bum, bum, *bum*) it becomes necessary for Amis to contrive a postscript:

> You won't believe me, but while I was doing the above, he came and twisted the handle of the study door, behind which I am. He said, Are you in there, Kingsley? Yes, I said, in a cordial, eager tone. All right, he said. What the hell did he want? Did he confuse this room with the shithouse next door? Is it any longer just to speak of him confusing anything with anything? OOoogh, the old . . . the old

The consensus seems to be that Leonard Bardwell was a harmless fellow, but in Amis's practice if you can't turn the fellow into something really dreadful and funny you had better not bother at all. Eliot observed that Ben Jonson's satire was "not by hitting off the object but by creating it; the satire is merely the means which leads to the aesthetic result, the impulse which projects a new world into a new orbit." Something like this happens when Amis goes to work on Daddy Bardwell.

The letters to Larkin, who is far the largest recipient, especially in earlier days of Amis's correspondence, bring out the worst—that is, the best—in him. By trying to amuse his friend, by showing off, by being funnier than (even) Larkin, he adopts a no-holds-barred mode of disparagement fiercer and wilder than either Amis the man or the more reasonable Amis we often see when he's writing to others. (Conquest is second only to Larkin in eliciting "bad" epistolary behavior.) Especially are the letters to Larkin written in the 1940s when Amis is reading for his Oxford degrees, the second of which (B. Litt) he never received, since his thesis was rejected thanks to Lord David Cecil. One knew from remarks how contemptuous he was of Old and Middle English poems, especially long ones, so when he has to write "a bleeding essay all about the sodding old bore Langlad gland I mean," you know *Piers Plowman* may be in for less than full appreciation. Even more hateful because more studied and revered, was "Bare-wolf," that "anonymous, crass, purblind, infantile, *featureless* HEAP OF GANGRENED ELEPHANT'S SPUTUM." Nor is there a letup when Chaucer appears, on whom he is writing an essay referred to as the "levels of C's art as shown in the Cuntherbelly Tails." What he thought of those levels, scatologically described to Larkin, was suppressed in the essay he handed in to tutor, J. B. Leishmann, who "has pronounced himself 'very pleased' with my essay on the levels of Cah warrggh Chaucer's fart. He kept on talking about

Chaucer's humour and I could hardly keep myself from *breaking wind in his face*." But Langland, *Beowulf,* Chaucer, all take a back seat when the writer to be essayed is Dryden:

> I have stopped reading Dryden. He is very like Chaucer, isn't he? I mean, however hard you try, you cannot see *what people mean* who admired them. Now I can see what people *mean* (though I don't *agree* with them) who like DONNE or POPE or WORDSWORTH, or KEATS, or even *MILTON,* but I cannot with Dryden. A second-rate fucking journalist ("OH?"). A SECOND-RATE FUCKING JOURNALIST. ("Oh.").

An irresponsible judgment, but good knockabout fun, of the sort a very clever, very literary young man "getting up" Eng lit. might indulge in. I did something similar with a friend, trading praise and abuse of writers as we studied for our Ph.D. orals. But not to the creative/destructive level Amis takes things, perhaps an expression of his own developing passion to be a great writer—at least better than the likes of Dryden and Chaucer.

Other patches of saying the worst about a writer may speak to the secret hearts of readers who would never themselves admit to harboring such thoughts. About Hopkins, for example (and once again to Larkin):

> I find him a bad poet—all this how to keép is there ány any stuff strikes *me* as a bit unnecessary—and so his defence of his work to Bridges, in spite of Bridges being a bumblock of the first order, seems arrogant to me: You must be wrong when you don't like my stuff, d'you see, because *I know* my stuff's good, d'you *see?* And his silly private language annoys me—"what I am in the habit of calling *inscape" well getoutofthehabitthen*. I had another go at his poetry the other day, and confirmed my previous impressions of it as *going after the wrong thing,* trying to treat words as if they were music. They aren't, are they? If his verse can't be read properly without keysignatures and sharps and flats, *so much the worse for it.* And as for this bitch batch bum come cock cork fork fuck stuff, *what is the point of it?* Eh?

He adds, assuagingly, that he can see why Hopkins appeals—"a sensible man, outside religion and poetry." This paragraph of promising literary criticism gains some of its charm by being sandwiched between thanking Larkin for the "dirty magazine" he sent him and a little slavering over the Italian film star Silvana Mangano ("I bought the Tit bits with Mangano in it and am prepared to believe all you say"). So if readers of these letters aren't prepared to condemn Amis for insensitivity to Hopkins's genius, they can deplore his unblushing, adolescent leer at pornography. In other words, there is something for everyone in this correspondence.

It has been noted how often the scales fall from Amis's eyes; for example, he had thought Keats was merely a bad poet ("I stood tip-toe upon a little hill so I could fart better" was his creative extension of a Keats opening line) but that, as universal opinion had it, a wiser, nicer, more percipient man was to be found in his letters. Not a bit of it:

> I know now that Keats was a self-pitying, self-indulgent, silly little fool (My dear Girl bum) as well as an incompetent, uninteresting, affected, non-visualising, Royal-Academy-picture, salacious, mouthing poet. He's still better than Shelley though.

We are to thank him for the measured putting of his abuse of Keats into perspective by reminding us of Shelley. Sometimes a single sentence is enough to snare and smear one don (David Cecil) and two English poets (Crabbe and Cowper), as in "that POSTURING QUACK Cess-hole thinks Crab's good, doesn't he along with that lunatic stricken-deer bastard who couldn't spell his own name properly." (Yet in *Memoirs,* some years later, Amis would admit that awful as Lord David was, his book on Cowper "really has something to say about Cowper.") On another occasion he does a pretend version of scales-falling-from-eyes, in writing to Larkin about Sylvia Plath (Larkin had treated Plath's work with some sympathy), "You did know she didn't mean to kill herself"? On another occasion, while compiling the *New Oxford Book of Light Verse,* he suggests it would be "fun to include in the anth a poem by Sylvia Plath, one of the really balls-aching ones, and refer in the Intro to her sadly undervalued comic manner."

Some of the best moments occur when Amis engages in teasing Larkin by being impious about Larkin's favorite, Thomas Hardy ("ole Hardy"), whose poems are filled with "all those rotten old words nobody uses and those horrible double-barrelled ones he made up out of his own head, like all-uncared and eve-damps and self-wrapt and fore-folk. . . . Still you use words like that yourself don't you so Iyyyeeeeghghgh . . ." On the eve of one of Larkin's visits to London, Amis contrives the following hellish entertainment:

> We thought we'd lay on a bit of a show for you since you don't come to London all that often. A cocktail party about 5.30 with some of your admirers—George Steiner, Ian Hamilton, Arnold Wesker; Alvarez of course, and I hope A. L. Rowse, though I haven't heard from him yet. Then I've booked seats at *Equus,* which is really the most *exciting* thing to hit the stage for years, and after that a place I know with a marvellous group of young West Indiaaaaeeeeoooghghgh

Or, in response to Larkin's opening an exhibition on D. H. Lawrence at Nottingham in 1980, the following [Amis always refers to Lawrence as DEL]:

> You really are potty about old DEL. How the fuck do you get thru him? Can't you see he's just like Wagner and Pound, a self-solving mystery? Fellows say, "Here's a GRINDING SHIT who never did *Anything* nice to or for *anybody,* and yet he's written all this stuff which is supposed to be frightfully good Funny. But then some of them look closely at the stuff and find that, instead of being frightfully good, it is in fact INSULTINGLY BAD IN EXACTLY THE KIND OF WAY YOU'D EXPECT FROM THE WAY HE BEHAVED. All of a piece. End of problem. Oh well. We all have our little foibles. Wouldn't do if we all thought the same OH YES IT FUCKING WELL WOU

The remarks about contemporaries and recent predecessors in the literary line would make a splendid anthology of what Amis called "horsepissing." Here, without comment, are a few of them: "I don't like Henry Green much, by the way: it takes me too long to understand what he means by the things he says." "The extracts from Mrs. Woolf she gives [Q. D. Leavis in *Fiction and the Reading Public*] show me why I hate her so much. She is guilty *most of the time* of a forcing of sensibility . . . what we get is a kind of intellectual melodrama, the exacerbation of *totally fictitious* states of feeling into a sentimental pipe dream untouched by discipline. . . ." "Reading some of Rilke's letters (You are mad, you know?). He seems on first acquaintance to be one of those Henry James men who are too busy won-dering what a writer is to be one." "Ruskin is a clown but quite a funny one." "I have just come back from my weekly lecture on modern literature, in which I dealt with Ezra Pained and old man T.S.E's *Waste country.* Hon-estly, can you see anything in EP? Buggered if I can." "I've read *The days of the locust* by Nathanael West . . . I feel when reading him as I do with Vir-ginia Wolf: I want to keep saying, 'No he didn't,' 'No, it didn't happen as you describe it,' 'No, that isn't what he thought,' 'No, that's just what she didn't say." "With Prof. Kermode's implied assessment of Robert Lowell as fit to stand alongside Pound I for one have no quarrel." "What do I find in the Observer but a great puff for that John Ashbery whom I excoriated in my last. Greatest living poet in English, the reviewer thought, or possibly so, and 'exciting,' that horrible word—an exciting new film isn't one with lots of car-chases and but a piece of trendy, pretentious stodge."

In concentrating on and quoting extensively from Amis's extravagances in saying and imagining the worst—his refusal or inability to take a mod-erate, "balanced" view of anything—I risk convincing no one not already convinced of the great exhilarations these letters produce. An alternative way to "review" them would be to understand or explain them by invok-ing Amis's psychological limitations, his phobias and fears (of flying, car-driving, being alone), his self-destructive drinking, his sometime cruelty to others. The most egregious example of that latter quality may be found in a chilling letter he wrote his American biographer, Dale Salwak, whom for a number of years Amis had cooperated with, if not encouraged, in var-ious labors. When Salwak sent him the first three chapters of the finished manuscript for comment, Amis replied by saying he considered them "altogether unsatisfactory," that Salwak's "level of performance was so low as not to rate publication." As if that weren't sufficient, there is a capping paragraph:

> Please realise that no imaginable rewriting would rectify the sit-uation. The fact that I have left many passages and pages of your typescript unmarked testifies to my weariness and boredom with them, not to their correctness or adequacy.

Imagine that in the course of a morning. I experienced a very minor ver-sion of what Salwak must have felt, when in 1980 I published a review, in this journal, of Amis's *Collected Poems.* In a letter to Larkin, he mentions the piece ("my first highbrow crit"), then mocks it a bit, then writes in another letter to Larkin a month later, "Yes (re Pritchard) it's a bugger, the people who think you're (one is) good while getting you wrong." I don't know how I got him wrong but, after wincing a bit, decided that trying to "explain" it was not the way to behave—better to relax and enjoy. Wyndham Lewis once said about Joyce's *Ulysses* that no one who ever looked at it would ever want to look behind it. What there is to look *at* in these twelve hundred pages of letters is something like God's plenty, as Amis's hated Dryden remarked about Amis's hated Chaucer. Or is it the Devil's plenty? At any rate there seems to be nothing that remotely approaches it in modern English letters, and for that we're in Amis's—and Zachary Leader's—debt.

—*Essays in Criticism,* October 2001.

R.I.P.

F.R. Leavis (1895-1978)

THE FACTS OF Leavis's life—in the sense of colorful, humanizing events to delight the onlooker—are relatively few. Son of Harry Leavis, proprietor of a Cambridge music store ("Leavis means pianos"), he did service as a stretcher-bearer in World War I where he was mustard-gassed, his digestion permanently affected. He studied with I.A. Richards at Cambridge in the 1920s, then taught in the university as a probationary lecturer but was not offered a permanent position until 1936 (Ronald Hayman says, in his biography, that at one point there was a move on to send him to a job in Tasmania, a move which Leavis resisted). *Scrutiny* was founded in 1932 and survived until 1953, much of its copy written by Leavis and his wife, Queenie; while the books published under his name were largely composed of materials that had appeared in the magazine. Except for the D. H. Lawrence book, there was a relative falling-off, in the 1950s, of his critical productions; then at the end of the decade the notorious attack on Sir Charles Snow and the notion of "Two Cultures." Retirement from Cambridge in 1965; part-time teaching at the University of York; a spate of books of which the last appeared in 1976. Leavis liked to wear open-necked shirts, was a runner back before everybody ran, gave legendary classes in which specimens of literature were "dated," presiding with his wife at comparably legendary tea-parties where visiting Americans—if vouched for—were well entertained.

I have nothing to add to the public account and little to refining the estimate of his critical achievement, but want instead to describe Leavis's impact on a young aspiring academic and, twenty-five years after the original impact, how he remains in my imagination. I never read him as an undergraduate, indeed had barely heard of his name, although I was deeply under the spell of literary criticism; for example, I had learned (from Stanley Hyman's *The Armed Vision*) that Richards, Empson, Blackmur, and

Burke deserved the highest marks as critics, while Wilson, Winters, and Eliot ranked much lower, were flawed and erratic in their practice. Not until I went to graduate school at Harvard did I pick up and read Leavis's work, whereupon I discovered a new hero, a critic who stood at the very head of all the classes. There was a joke going about back then that one could succeed as an English grad student at Harvard if one took pains to be sufficiently dull, and it is true that most, though not all, of my classes were harmless and soporific, relaying information I could have picked up just as well out of standard reference books. Dull or third-rate writers were to be tolerated and appreciated "in their own terms" as the phrase went; for were we not students of literary history preparing ourselves for those moments in our Ph.D. orals when we would be asked about eighteenth-century users of the Spenserian stanza, or challenged to specify the stages of man in "Tintern Abbey," or even to name four picaresque novels and chat about their heroes?

What relation did Leavis have to that sort of thing? His sentences from "Literary Studies" in *Education and the University* made it clear to me why Harvard English was wrong:

> Literary history, as a matter of "facts about" and accepted critical (or quasi-critical) description and commentary, is a worthless acquisition; worthless for the student who cannot as a critic— that is as an intelligent and discerning reader—make a personal approach to the essential data of the literary historian, the works of literature (an approach is personal or it is nothing; you cannot take over the appreciation of a poem, and unappreciated, the poem isn't "there"). The only acquisition of literary history having any education value is that made in the exercise of critical intelligence to the ends of the literary critic. Does this need arguing?

For a rather different reason, it was not about to be argued at Harvard where, except for the example of Reuben Brower (who had studied with Leavis in the 1930s), a very different notion of "English" was current. So we hopeful critics united behind the flag of truth, and I cynically wrote "A" exams discussing Tennyson's view of this and contrasting it with Browning's attitude toward that, saving my real passion for arguments and papers about poems and novels, trying to discriminate between A and B or show that X was better than Y. (Although Harvard English didn't encourage "personal approaches" it was usually tolerant of them so long as you kept your facts straight and handed in a bibliography.)

Anchor paperbacks had just brought out *The Great Tradition* (for ninety-five cents) but Leavis was mostly unavailable in America, and I proudly opened an account at Blackwell's, ordering *New Bearings in English Poetry, Revaluation, Education and the University,* and *The Common Pursuit.* But the great experience was looking up the files of *Scrutiny* in Widener, sitting at a cubicle (the sun was shining outside, other people thought *they* were happy!) and learning the right ways to feel about all sorts of writers: Auden and Joyce and Arnold Bennett; Empson or Santayana or Richards; most of all, D. H. Lawrence. The summer I studied for my orals I remember signing out *Scrutiny* and reading issues during lunch; remember taking over verbatim Leavis's distinctions (in *Revaluation)* among Donne and Jonson and Carew, and his brilliant dispositions of minor eighteenth-century poets. Even if I hadn't read all the poems, I knew my Leavis cold. When the Lawrence book appeared I devoured it with an excitement unmatched since, and once again tried to take over the analyses of *The Rainbow* and *Women in Love*—exactly, of course, the sort of "taking over" that Leavis said one could not, in fact, do.

I don't wish to labor the point, or exult in some piously moral triumph over an earlier self. But though I was all for the unacademic virtues and thought Leavis my standard-bearer, I had precious little of those virtues— "a pioneering spirit; the courage of enormous incompleteness . . . the judgment and intuition to select drastically yet delicately, and make a little go a long way" ("A Sketch for an 'English' School"). I was enormously incomplete all right, but complacent about it too, since I had picked up lines from Leavis about Auden's limitations or Trollope's minorness or Pound's poetic lack of distinction (except for "Hugh Selwyn Mauberley") before I'd even read them, or after superficial acquaintance merely.

What finally turned things around—aside from the human condition of growing up into something more than a graduate student—was my encountering a new writer, Wyndham Lewis, whom Lawrence hadn't liked and for whom Leavis had no respect. Yet Lewis came to figure for me, despite the embarrassments of his political views, as an incomparably richer comic writer than either of them. Whatever *Women in Love* was after three or four readings, it was no longer fun; and hadn't Lawrence himself said that if it isn't any fun, don't do it? And if Leavis could be wrong about

Lewis (the "brutal and boring Wyndham Lewis," he called him in the Rede lecture) maybe there were other writers he was less than right about. By the time I finally got to Cambridge, England, for a brief visit in 1964, I was writing a book about Lewis and felt too nervous to attempt an invitation to tea at the Leavises'. What would I have said when he asked me my subject of concern? At that time Cambridge was filled with anti-Leavis jokes, helped along by Kingsley Amis's recent appearance on the scene. I felt guilty about that too, but contented myself with observing the great man's entry into a lecture by his old *Scrutiny* colleague, L. C. Knights.

No doubt I have followed the common pattern of the deconverted convert, too eager to find the teacher less flexible, open, or humorous than the newly liberated pupil fancies himself to be. But Leavis for all his fine moments of sardonic, dismissive irony (a sarcastic letter about A. L. Rowse speaks of "These flashes of the brilliance of All Souls—further lights on a famed civilization") was essentially a solemn passionately dedicated critic and teacher. One of his epigraphs to *The Common Pursuit*, an indispensable collection of *Scrutiny* essays, quotes a Henry James letter whose following sentence refers to more than James:

> I can't go into it all much—but the rough sense of it is that I believe only in absolutely independent, individual and lonely virtue, and in the serenely unsociable (or if need be at a pinch sulky and sullen) practice of the same: the observation of a lifetime having convinced me that no fruit ripens but under that temporarily graceless rigour.

More so than James, Leavis lived this role to the extent that serious literary people complained about his graceless behavior as a prose writer. It would be a mistake to dismiss such complaints (one of them, I remember, from Anthony Powell) too quickly, as part of that awful modern England of "the Welfare State, the Football Pools, and the literary culture of the *New Statesman* and the Third Programme" (with cinema, bingo, and the telly thrown in) Leavis so often and so predictably inveighed against. He *had* to be the practitioner of "individual and lonely virtue," more than a pinch sulky and sullen: in the words of a friend's brilliant rewriting of Hobbes's man in the State of Nature, Leavis was "solitary, poor, nasty, British and short." Yet every *trouvaille* of that sort brought with it uneasiness about sociable clubbing which produced such good jokes at the expense of absolutely independent virtue.

The many books Leavis published in his seventies, over the last ten years of his life, will not be much loved or long consulted. The endless repetitive rant against technological-Benthamite civilization, the Robbins report on Education, Lord Annan and Lord Snow; the increasing use of a bludgeoning literary jargon (its key terms "constatation," "nisus," and "*ahnung*," each of which causes my mind to go completely blank) —these are boring, even a shade brutal, and he will not be remembered for them. Yet just two years ago (in The *Living Principle)* he published an essay of some 100 pages, for me his last significant piece of literary criticism, in which he comes to terms with Eliot's *Four Quartets,* trying for one last time to express his admiration for and his rejection of the mind, the attitude toward life and poetry—really toward the English language—expressed in that poem. Leavis wants to show why we must finally say *no* to the view of life found there, though as he had said years before in a letter to the *Spectator,* "I have always imagined myself to derive from Mr. Eliot as much as from anybody." He was right, and if in Leavis's hands the early Eliotic strategies of *The Sacred Wood* and the 1921 essays hardened into formulas, they never tried to have things more than unambiguously, nor did they mind (as Eliot came to mind) giving offense.

A few decades ago Leavisian notions of the necessity to read, discriminate, and evaluate were instrumental in saving people from becoming dutiful reporters on the development of the Elizabethan novel or some other crashingly boring phenomenon. Today when literary studies look anthropological, structuralist, linguistical, in a very bad way, and hardly critical, or literary at all, Leavis's example, his books, are more essential than ever.

—New Republic, June 3, 1978.

Criticism on the Record:
B.H. Haggin (1900-1987)

THE DEATH last month of B. H. Haggin, who was a music critic for *The New Republic* for many years, removed from the scene not only a critic of music and musical performance but also a distinguished embodiment—a throwback, one might say—of Matthew Arnold's notion of the function of criticism: "To see the object as in itself it really is." To my knowledge Bernard Haggin never referred to Arnold, but he liked to quote Bernard Shaw, whose brief career writing about musical performances he found exemplary. Shaw gave us his version of the critic's task when he said that some people had pointed out evidences of personal feeling in his reviews "as if they were accusing me of a misdemeanor, not knowing that a criticism written without personal feeling is not worth reading. It is the capacity for making good or bad art a personal matter that makes a man a critic." But this making of art into a "personal matter" is exactly in the spirit of Arnold's praise of disinterestedness: the project of "inflexible honesty," of criticism "resolutely following the law of its own nature." In Arnold's famous though not always admired formulation, the business of criticism is "simply to know the best that is known and thought in the world." Haggin's business was to write about, to further, even to proselytize for, the best that was composed, performed, and danced in the world, and he brought to that business a single-mindedness that makes even Arnold or Shaw look diffuse, though more various, by comparison.

He conducted his critical operations for more than sixty years, beginning with early reviews in the *Brooklyn Eagle*, and coming to maturity in the eighteen years, beginning in 1939, during which he wrote about music and records for the *Nation*. He wrote the Records column for TNR from 1957 to 1966, and served further terms with the *Hudson* and *Yale* reviews. In one of his early books, *Music on Records* (1938), he defended his practice of offering personal judgements that, he admitted, set higher valuations on music by Chopin and Tchaikovsky than did "general opinion," but also set lower valuations on some of Bach and Brahms than did that same opinion. After all, he said, "if I take away with one hand it is to give with the other: if I take away some of Bach's Partitas or Brahms's Intermezzi, it is to give Chopin's Polonaises. . . . If I take away Brahms's Symphony No.1 it is to give Tchaikovsky's Pathétique—to say nothing of Brahms's No.4." And he added, convincingly, that the total of what he gave was more than most readers would be able to acquire for a long time—"before the end of which they will have reached the point where they will have tastes of their own, and will know whether they want to accept my judgment or reject it." In that book, and in the ones to follow—the revised *Music on Records, The New Listener's Companion* in its various editions, *Music and Ballet,* and his collections of reviews—he spelled out his reasons for preferring one composer, one piece of music, one recorded performance to another. Distinguishing among the best, the good, and the not-so-good work of various artists, he gave and took away; but what he gave in my case was indeed more than I was able to acquire for a long time.

The *New York Times* obituary said, rather disapprovingly, that he "worshiped certain artists, notably Arturo Toscanini, at the expense of all others." Certainly Haggin helped me pay attention to (in an often-used phrase of his) the "plastic continuity" of Toscanini's performances of Beethoven, Schubert, and Dvořák, of Haydn, Berlioz, and Verdi. But, as a pianist, I found most useful his writing about Artur Schnabel's playing of Mozart and Beethoven concertos and sonatas, and of Schubert's posthumous sonatas: about the "meditative" character of Schnabel's approach, which operated both with powerful intellect and with powerful emotion; the greatness of the playing, even as it sometimes contained technical flaws and distortions of phrase. But Haggin didn't "worship" Schnabel at the expense of all other pianists, nor did he worship Toscanini at the expense of all other conductors. He championed, though on occasion searchingly criticized, Lipatti and Cliburn and Gould, Ashkenazy and Pollini. By pointing to details in their performance of various works he helped me hear new things in the works themselves—in many cases introduced me to those works. Similar things happened with the Budapest String Quartet, and Balanchine's *Apollo,* and the quality of Bix Beiderbecke's cornet tone.

I began to read Haggin in graduate school, when I was also reading F. R. Leavis's literary criticism. Both Haggin and Leavis insisted on giving and taking away, on ranking artists and their works (in *Music on Records* Haggin divided Sibelius into The Good Works, The Lesser Works, The Poor Works, and The Worst Works). Both were heady, exhilarating fare for someone trying to get his intellectual and aesthetic bearings. Both had eventually to be resisted, and though they insisted that disagreement about a poem or a piece of music was legitimate, even necessary, it was hard to disagree with them. Soon after I met Haggin I tried to argue with his low opinion of Bach's Concerto for Violin and Oboe, but didn't get far. Just two years ago, when I wrote him about enjoying Christopher Hogwood's recordings of Mozart symphonies, he shot back with the strong suggestion that it must have been Mozart, not Hogwood, I was enjoying.

Like Leavis he was notoriously "difficult" as a person, invariably quarreling with the magazines he wrote for and intransigent about his principles. When I invited him, years ago, to lecture at Amherst, the title of his talk was, characteristically, "The Approach to Music" (not "An Approach"). And when after it a student asked whether perhaps musicology might in some cases be of some use as far as listening went, Haggin told him brusquely that no, it was not, ever. Afterward, at a carefully arranged party (once, at another party, a reckless guest had insisted on singing Puccini to him, with disastrous results), one of my colleagues praised a performance of Furtwängler's. On the way back to the inn Haggin said what a nice party it had been, but how very strange it was that this seemingly nice colleague of mine had praised the Furtwängler performance. It was the capacity for making good or bad art a personal matter that made Haggin difficult to deal with and a critic of the highest order. Randall Jarrell, whose friendship with him was one of the pleasing events in recent cultural history, once spoke of Haggin's "clear, troubled, rapturous spirit," and charged him with having "the shameless honesty of the true critic—he couldn't lie to you if he tried." The *Times* obituary stated bluntly that "there are no survivors." True indeed, and that was the way Haggin wanted it.

—*New Republic*, July 6, 1987.

Updike Posthumous

1. His Legacy

REVIEWING A COLLECTION of essays by Vladimir Nabokov, John Updike called him "the only writer . . . whose books, considered as a whole, give the happy impression of an *oeuvre,* of a continuous task carried forward variously, of a solid personality, of a plenitude of gifts exploited knowingly." Never have words of praise for another writer been more fittingly applied to the praiser. In Updike's case, the "continuous task" was that of a writer who for more than half a century performed variously as America's preeminent man of letters. Novels, short stories, poems, essays, reviews of contemporary fiction and art exhibits succeeded one another in a career that opened in the late 1950s on three fronts: *The Carpentered Hen and Other Poems*; *The Same Door* (stories); and *The Poorhouse Fair* (novel). Updike's ceaseless productivity became the object of admiration, envy, and sometimes annoyance on the part of more measured producers. He himself has reflected on his all-purposeness as a literary man, confessing that he could write ads for deodorants or labels for catsup bottles if he had to; in a similar vein he admitted, somewhat ruefully, "Evidently I can read anything in English and muster up an opinion about it. I am not sure, however, the stunt is good for me." The momentary qualm in no way prevented him from getting on with the job.

That job, as he put it in the final sentence of the foreword to his *Collected Early Stories,* was "to give the mundane its beautiful due." In his richly stocked memoir "The Dogwood Tree: A Boyhood," he called himself a transcriber of "middleness with all grits, bumps and anonymities, in its fullness of satisfaction and mystery." Such middleness was to be found, early and late in Updike's fiction, in the experience of a small-town boy who held in his imagination "a Pennsylvania thing" he needed to write about, to "say." He said it most memorably in some of the stories from his first two collections, where, in "The Happiest I've Been," "Flight," "Pigeon Feathers," and others, he gave permanent testimony to the aspirations and confusions, the pleasures and pains of boyhood—of one particular boy under various fictional names, who lives with his parents and grandparents in rural Pennsylvania. American predecessors like Sinclair Lewis and Sherwood Anderson had lamented and mocked the repressive cruelty of small-town life; it was Updike's task, while not denying the repressiveness, to celebrate what was distinctive and valuable about life in the village.

He declared, years after the book appeared, that *Rabbit, Run* convinced him he was not just a writer of short stories and light verse, but a novelist. What most characterized the first Rabbit novel was its rendering of sex. Updike's models included Joyce, D. H. Lawrence, and Edmund Wilson, but the forthrightly detailed sentences, the even intensity of their rhythm and tone, were markedly his own. He wrote *Rabbit, Run* with no thought in mind of the three novels to follow it at ten-year intervals. The expansive invention and humor found especially in the later volumes, *Rabbit Is Rich* and *Rabbit at Rest,* came with the increased confidence and resourcefulness of age. Taken together the novels (published in a single volume, *Rabbit Angstrom,* 1995) constitute a great achievement in American realism, especially the final one, *Rabbit at Rest.* That book, in the words of the English critic Jonathan Raban, is "one of the very few modern novels in English (Bellow's *Herzog* is another) that one can set beside the work of Dickens, Thackeray, George Eliot, Joyce, and not feel the draft."

The Rabbit books are Updike at his peak, but over the decades he produced many other original and surprising novels. Among them, each different from one another, are *The Centaur,* a Joycean treatment of the mundane and its mythological correlatives; the short "Pennsylvania" masterpiece, *Of the Farm; Couples,* his best-selling if not his best book; *The Coup,* a lively experiment in imagining an African country and its dictator leader; and *Roger's Version*—Updike at his densest, most ingenious. The two "Witches" novels, the second of which appeared last fall, show his talents as a comic writer and satirist, not nearly enough appreciated either by hostile or friendly critics. But a mischievous, pervasive humor surfaces in all his writings.

As an essayist, critic, and reviewer of his predecessors and contemporaries, he was sometimes condescended to by more "professional" talents, who may well have been put off by the easy engagement with the common reader he took as his audience. The results of what is inadequately termed "nonfiction" prose are there to be consulted and learned from in thousands of pages collected in six books of criticism (plus two handsome volumes on painters and painting). They lie weighty on the shelf but feel light as air in the reading: essays on Hawthorne and Melville, reviews of Bellow and Philip Roth, repeated efforts to come to terms with Edmund Wilson, Nabokov, and John Cheever; starstruck yet perceptive appreciations of Doris Day, Lana Turner, Gene Kelly. Together they add up to a voluminous and loving record of the last century's high and popular culture. As a critic Updike avoided both bloody-mindedness and arch superiority to his subject. His stated intention was always to enter into what, as he saw it, the artist was attempting to do, and to let the work speak by quoting from it. He bore in mind that, as himself an imaginative writer, he was subject to the judgments of others, not always sympathetic ones.

But whether he wrote fiction or criticism, it was done with a poet's touch. His poetry ranged from the early, delightful specimens of light verse to later poems, often on the subjects of sex and death, that made a deeper mark: as in "Enemies of a House," whose list concludes with "voracious ivy; frost heaves; splintering; / carpenter ants; adultery; drink; death." Perhaps the finest two of his more recent stories, "A Sandstone Farmhouse" and "Journey to the Dead," are moving accounts of endings. The former is about the death of his mother and the end of the Plowville farmhouse where Updike lived with parents and grandparents for five years before going off to Harvard; "Journey to the Dead" concludes with a one-time classics major's visit to a woman, stroke-ridden and dying in a Boston hospital. The man thinks, among other things, of Odysseus' visit to Hades and of Aeneas' descent to Avernus. After attempting to amuse the speechless, unsmiling patient, "He promised, insincerely, to come again, and, like heroes before him, fled."

In an amusing and revealing sketch, "Updike and I," a "man" describes his daily round of breakfasting, reading the newspaper, then heading upstairs to a room "Updike has filled with his books, his papers, his trophies, his projects." The man speculates, "Suppose, one day he failed to show up?" In a related manner, "Perfection Wasted," a poem written at about the same time, muses that "another regrettable thing about death / is the ceasing of your own brand of magic, / which took a whole life to develop and market." The casual, even sardonic contemplation in this unrhymed sonnet culminates with a question, "The whole act / Who will do it again?" and its sadly conclusive answer, "No one." We can only say, in response to the unanswerable, and left with Updike's huge legacy—the brilliant, steady work of decades—that such perfection has not been wasted on the legions of readers who continue to seek it out.

—*Boston Globe,* February 1, 2009.

2. ENDPOINT AND OTHER POEMS: DARKNESS UNDIMMED

Updike was never taken seriously enough as a poet, in part because of his beginnings as a writer of light verse, a phenomenon of the 1940s and '50s. In an interview with Helen Vendler in 1977, he confirmed his modest reputation and allowed that he was writing "less and less of what there seems no demand for" —not just light verse but poems generally. Asked by Vendler to say what he thought lyric poems consisted of, he replied that

> the poem comes with a perception—a breakthrough into nature, which encircles our numbness day and night. And married to the irruption of nature must be something live that surfaces out of language; the language, even when rhyme and metre and sequence and punctuation arc brushed aside, brings a formal element without which nothing happens, nothing is *made.*

When sixteen years later he collected his poems, they were separated into sections for regular verse and its offspring, light verse, which he referred to as "cartooning with words." Even while he had been "working primarily in prose," he wrote, "the idea of verse . . . stood at my elbow, as a standing invitation to the highest kind of verbal exercise—the most satisfying, the most archaic, the most elusive of critical control." It may also be that he has been consistently underrated or ignored as a poet because of his great success as a prose writer. (An unconvinced reader might insist that he *can't* also be that good in verse.) Then there is the poetry racket itself, where the humorless, strange antics of a Jorie Graham arc applauded, and the ceaseless clowning of John Ashbery wins him a place in the Library of America.

Two months after Updike's unanticipated death in late January of 2009 his final book of poems, *Endpoint,* appeared. The movingly apt title is even more so in that forty years previously, he published *Midpoint,* the title poem of which surveyed his life thus far and ended: "Born laughing, I've believed in the Absurd, / Which brought me this far; henceforth, if I can, / I must impersonate a serious man." The impersonation most seriously fulfills itself in the twenty-seven-page "Endpoint," which opens the new volume. This final poem consists of a sequence of unrhymed sonnets, the earlier ones written to mark his birthdays as he aged through his seventies. With its combination of increasingly somber subject and the formal pressures of metrical obligation to line and stanza, there is nothing to rival "Endpoint" in American poetry. Since it overshadows the latter two-thirds of the book, which consist of more traditional Updike ventures, it may be permissible to treat some of the latter poems first, and then confront the poem that precedes them.

"Other Poems," the first of three sections following "Endpoint," contains several examples of Updike's best occasional verse—the occasions being celebrations of remembered popular singers such as Frankie Laine, Doris Day, the doo-wop groups—and the heartbreaking "Bird Caught in My Deer Netting." These poems are about age, death, and loss—the last vividly imagined in "Stolen" when Updike moves into the skin of paintings taken from the Gardner Museum in Boston. In their lonely inactivity, they invite our empathy:

> Think of how bored they get, stacked
> in the warehouse somewhere, say in Mattapan,
> gazing at the back of the butcher paper
> they are wrapped in, instead of at
> the rapt glad faces of those who love art.

Throughout his work, Updike favored what Robert Frost called "loose" as opposed to "strict" iambics, and the looseness shows here in the rough approximations of a decasyllabic line—seven syllables in the first line, eleven in the second and third, eight in the fourth. Prosody takes a back seat to the clever, inventive idea:

> In their captivity, they may dream of rescue
> but cannot cry for help. Their paint
> is inert and crackles, their linen friable.
> They have one stratagem, the same old one:
> to be themselves, on and on.

Like other poets, Updike takes upon himself the task of remembering by re-presenting to our minds vanished things and people we had forgotten

EAR TRAINING: LITERARY ESSAYS

about—as in "Frankie Laine," where a once popular singer from the 1940s and '50s is given his due in twenty lines (one of Laine's hits, "That's My Desire," begins "To spend one night with you, in our old rendezvous").

> The Stephens' Sweet Shop, 1949.
> Bald at work, "butterflying" hot dogs—
> splitting lengthwise for the griddle
> and serving them up in hamburger buns—
> while Boo, his smiling, slightly anxious wife
> (a rigid perm and excess, too-bright lipstick),
> provides to teen-aged guzzlers at the counter
> and in an opium den of wooden booths
> their sugary poisons, milkshakes thick as tar
> and Coca-Cola conjured from syrup and fizz.
>
> A smog of smoke. The jingle at the back
> of pinball being defty played. And through
> the clamorous and hormone-laden haze
> your slick voice, nasal yet operatic, sliced
> and soared, assuring us of our
> desire, at our old rendezvous. Today
> I read you died, at ninety-three. Your voice
> was oil, and we the water it spread on,
> forming a rainbow film—our futures as
> we felt them, dreamily, back there and then.

The atmosphere of the sweet shop along with the "nasal yet operatic" sound of Laine's voice—exactly the right adjectives for it—combine with the poem's other details and resonate with felt life. In Updike's best poems, a living voice can always be detected, especially in this case if one were an American teenager in 1949, loving or being repelled by Frankie Laine. "Her Coy Lover Sings Out," another poem addressed to a '40s icon, Doris Day, confirms what Updike had already written about her in prose:

> Doris, ever since 1945,
> when I was all of thirteen and you a mere twenty-one,
> and "Sentimental Journey" came winging

out of the juke box at the sweet shop,
your voice piercing me like a silver arrow,
I knew you were sexy.

These opening lines initiate the march of time and Updike's love still directed at the singer in 2008.

In a different key from these poems of witty tribute is "Bird Caught in My Deer Netting," although, as in so many of these late poems, death is the presiding genius. Its first third describes the bird's arrival on the fatal scene:

The hedge must have seemed as ever,
seeds and yew berries secreted beneath,
small edible matter only a bird's eye could see,
mixed with the brown of shed needles and earth—
a safe, quiet cave such as nature affords the meek,
entered low, on foot, the feathered head
alert to what it sought, bright eyes darting
everywhere but above, where net had been laid.

Its ensuing struggle is imagined by the speaker:

Then, at some moment mercifully unwitnessed,
an attempt to rise higher, to fly,
met by an all but invisible limit, beating wings
pinioned, ground instinct denied. The panicky
thrashing and flutter, in daylight and air,
their freedom impossibly close, all about!

The poem concludes with a question not to be answered, as the man confesses his helplessness, tinged with remorse at being responsible for the netting:

How many starved hours of struggle resumed
in fits of life's irritation did it take
to seal and sew shut the berry-bright eyes
and untie the tiny wild knot of a heart?

I cannot know, discovering this wad
of junco-fluff, weightless and wordless
in its corner of netting deer cannot chew through
nor gravity-defying bird bones break.

From early on, Updike had been responsive and sympathetic to death in the nonhuman kingdom ("Dog's Death" is a shining example), and this small creature's end is perfectly turned and attuned in the most poignant of these "Other Poems."

There are in addition lighter, more agreeable poems in this section, including one on an unlikely subject. "Colonoscopy" ends with the title procedure completed and the doctor's satisfied announcement: "'Perfect. Not a polyp. See you in / five years.' Five years? The funhouse may have folded." In "Endpoint," the book's sad masterpiece, we observe the folding, gradual in its stages, shockingly sudden in its finality. Its forty-eight unrhymed sonnets combine in the culminating statement of a life: "Birthday, death day—what day is not both?" Updike's *Collected Poems* includes only a few rhymed sonnets; the sonnet for him, as for Robert Lowell in the scores he turned out, was mainly a convenient mold into which thoughts and feelings could be poured—eight- and six-line groupings with a space separating them. There is no reason to regret Updike's decision not to rhyme, since he was not gifted with the brilliant and serious use of the technique as practiced by contemporary masters like James Merrill, Anthony Hecht, and Richard Wilbur.

There is no doubt, however, that writing unrhymed sonnets is a risky operation, since the form is so minimal and an encouragement to garrulity. Lowell's sonnets, for all their occasional success, are more often obscure, disjointed, in willful disregard of discursive clarity. Never one to subordinate clarity to something presumably more important, Updike is less interested in creating resonant lines than in making syntactical sentences that continue over the lines, sometimes even over the white space separating the sonnet's two parts. Here is an example from "Birthday Shopping, 2007":

In the beginning, Culture does beguile us,
but Nature gets us in the end. My skin,
I notice now that I am seventy-five,
hangs loose in ripples like those dunes on Mars

that tell us life may have existed there—
monocellular slime in stagnant pools.
After a Tucson movie, some man in
the men's room mirror lunged toward me

with wild small eyes, white hair, and wattled neck—
who could he be, so hostile and so weird,
so due for disposal, like a popcorn bag
vile with its inner film of stale, used grease?
Where was the freckled boy who used to peek
into the front-hall mirror, off to school?

Where indeed. The opening poem of the sequence, "March Birthday 2002, and After" has the unwilling celebrant enduring

A faint neuralgia, flitting tooth-root to
knee and shoulder-joint, a vacant head,
too many friendly wishes to parry,
too many cakes. Oh, let the years alone!
They pile up if we manage not to die, . . .

The thought of approaching death brings comforting thoughts of boyhood illnesses when he would listen to *The Lone Ranger* from his sickbed and think "that Mother, Father, mailman, and / the wheezy doctor with his wide black bag / exist for him, and so they do, or did."

This is the familiar, recurrent thought of the sequence: adult time running out; the shock of witnessing himself in a mirror now, "so hostile and so weird," from which the only escape is in words re-creating the lost boy, off to school, catching himself in the front-hall mirror. If there is a readerly objection to this move back to childhood, so often repeated in so many of Updike's stories and poems, the poet already knows that "I've written these before, these modest facts, / but their meaning has no bottom in my mind." This is what he called "the Pennsylvania thing," events that weren't always or often felt as happiness as they occurred but now seem nothing less than bliss, caught out of time. Other scenes revisited include his later life as a writer and the selfish, irresistible pleasure of seeing his words into the magic of print and hard covers:

And then to have my spines
line up upon the shelf, one more each year,
however out of kilter ran my life!
I drank up women's tears and spat them out
as 10-point Janson, Roman and ital.

He accords generous recognition to his editors and encouragers at *The New Yorker*, to his publisher, Alfred Knopf, and to the world of comic books and magazine—of print generally, the love of which kindled and continuously animated his writerly life. Behind all this was his mother and the unfulfilled dream of her own never-completed novel, as she sent out pieces of writing and received back rejection slips in "brown envelopes." She "knew non-publication's shame," while "Mine was to be the magic gift instead, / propelled to confidence by mother-love." But he knew that "hers was the purer ambition, hatched / of country childhood in the silences / of crops accruing, her sole companions birds / whose songs and names she taught herself to know." As may be noted from the way I have spliced together various poems in the sequence, it's not the individual line that most counts as a made and finished thing, but rather the cumulative impact of sentences in verse exhibiting what Frost called "the sound of sense," a sound and a sense not essentially different from that in Updike's prose sentences.

The birthday poems up through the year 2007 are a litany of questions; minor complaints; worries about sun damage and bodily decrepitude; thoughts of death, with their corresponding flashbacks into younger life; and unillusioned predictions of how or whether his books will live after he is gone: "A life poured into words—apparent waste / intended to preserve the thing consumed. / For who, in that unthinkable future / when I am dead, will read?" Read not just him but, in the post-Gutenberg era, read anything. So he prays to keep the writing life going for a while: "Be with me, words, a little longer; you / have given me my quitclaim in the sun." A poem from April 14, 2008, "A Lightened Life," presents him in efficient mode, with proofs of his final novel (*The Widows of Eastwick*) FedExed and his taxes mailed off. Even so, he has failed that morning to remember "the computer code / for *accent grave* in *fin-de-siècle*, one / of my favorite words," and the poem ends by asking "What's up? What's left of me?"

The nine pages that follow provide the grim answer, beginning with "Euonymus 11/02/08": "A cold that wouldn't let go / is now a cloud upon my chest X-ray: / pneumonia." This poem about finality ends with another

question: "Is this an end? / I hang, half-healthy, here, and wait to see."
Three weeks later he is in Massachusetts General Hospital, where his diag-
nosis moves from pneumonia to cancer, then its metastasis. Visited by his
family, he asks the appropriate questions of children and grandchildren,
"all the while / suppressing, like an acid reflux, the lack / of prospect black
and bilious for me." As he "uphold[s] the social lie," he thinks of others he
has loved until their deaths and realizes that in his "safe" isolation from the
outside world, his old fear of falling has disappeared, since his destination,
"terra firma," will not be reached by a spectacular fall in a crashing airplane
but "achieved from thirty inches, on a bed."

With a sense of his inglorious "fall" to come, he rises to what for me is
the most moving moment in the sequence. A half century back, he had
written a memoir of growing up in Shillington, "The Dogwood Tree: A
Boyhood" —an early example of his conviction, maintained over the years,
that we were put in the world to praise and to pay attention. The middle
section of "Peggy Lutz, Fred Muth 12/13/08" embodies this conviction:

> Dear friends of childhood, classmates, thank you,
> scant hundred of you, for providing a
> sufficiency of human types: beauty,
> bully, hanger-on, natural,
> twin, and fatso—all a writer needs,
> all there in Shillington, its trolley cars
> and little factories, cornfields and trees,
> leaf fires, snowflakes, pumpkins, valentines.
>
> To think of you brings tears less caustic
> than those the thought of death brings. Perhaps
> we meet our heaven at the start and not
> the end of life. Even then were tears
> and fear and struggle, but the town itself
> draped in plain glory the passing days.

In the culminating affirmation, heaven is redefined as something that
existed back then rather than now—something re-imagined and imaginatively finished, rather than something to come, not yet finished. A week or
so after this poem, "Needle Biopsy" confirms the cancer's metastasis.

After this fact, only two poems remain. The first, undated and titled

"Creeper," is a sonnet, sort of, but now not only unrhymed but unpen-
tametered, consisting of shorter, irregular lines of varying syllables, as if to
suggest the vine as it lets go its leaves:

as if to say, *To live is good*

> *but not to live—to be pulled down*
> *with scarce a ripping sound,*
> *still flourishing, still*
> *stretching toward the sun—*
> *is good also, all photosynthesis*
> *abandoned*, quite quits.

This last look at one of nature's products admires its "stoic delicacy" in
letting go. The final poem, "Fine Point 12/22/08" (its title a last bit of
wordplay) looks to whatever sustenance can be drawn from the Christian
myth:

> Why go to Sunday school, though surlily,
> and not believe a bit of what was taught?
> The desert shepherds in their scratchy robes
> undoubtedly existed, and Israel's defeats—
> the Temple in its sacredness destroyed
> by Babylon and Rome. Yet Jews kept faith
> and passed the prayers, the crabbed rites,
> from table to table as Christians mocked.
>
> We mocked, but took. The timbrel creed of praise
> gives spirit to the daily; blood tinges lips.
> The tongue reposes in papyrus pleas,
> saying, *Surely*—magnificent, that "surely"—
> *goodness and mercy shall follow me all*
> *the days of my life,* my life, forever.

This poem affirms continuity from Sunday school to hospital bed, from
the shepherds' creed of praise to later ones that, like the works of Updike's
lifetime of writing, give "spirit to the daily." The poem's end is a plea, with
words from the Twenty-third Psalm that provoke the poet to interrupt
himself in wonder ("magnificent, that 'surely'") before continuing with

"*all / the days of my life*," where italicized quotation ends and the poet, from his position at the end of things, adds, surpassingly, "my life, forever."

The hospital poems may remind us of a now rather forgotten poet, L. E. Sissman, a friend of Updike's whose work he wrote about admiringly. Sissman's "Dying: An Introduction" and "Homage to Clotho: A Hospital Suite" are sterling examples of confronting one's mortal fate without mawkishness or strident self-pity. Updike wrote of Sissman's last poems, "What other poet has ever given such wry and unblinking witness to his own dying? . . . His poetry gave back more generously than he had received, and carried his beautiful wit into darkness undimmed." Updike's own last poems answer the question by providing one further and unforgettable example of such an art carrying itself into darkness undimmed.

—The John Updike Review, Fall 2011.

3. Reminiscences

John Updike's recent, quite unexpected death last January prompted me to review our correspondence over the past thirty-six years. It was a correspondence initiated by my bothering him with a couple of things I had written, partly about him. I was emboldened to continue bothering him when he responded—and continued to respond, unfailingly—with a brief letter or a packed postcard. So I pretended that he found it salutary to begin his morning by some clearing of the correspondence desk before settling in with the novel, story, poem, or review he was currently at work on. Of the two items I sent him in that first missive, one consisted of paragraphs from a fiction chronicle about his 1972 story collection, *Museums and Women,* paragraphs ending with a rather pompous-sounding prediction that he was "putting together a body of work which in substantial, intelligent creation will eventually be seen as second to none in our time." (For some reason he liked the ring of praise enough to use it on the back of one or another of his books.) I also sent him a talk I'd given on nostalgia that quoted a question he raised in one of his writings: "What is nostalgia but love for that part of ourselves which is in Heaven forever removed from change and corruption?" In his letter back he surprised me by claiming, in himself, a "waning of even the ability to feel nostalgia," which, he said, "maybe is freshest when we are in our twenties and for the first time faced with a great block of subjective time forever set aside."

When I reviewed *Rabbit Is Rich* in 1981, *The New Republic* sent a galley to him, and he made my day with a postcard announcing that I had given "a passable impersonation of that favorite ghost of mine, the Ideal Reader." Meanwhile I had asked him whether, if it were offered, he would accept an honorary degree from Amherst College. He said he would be willing, "providing no speaking (speechifying, I mean to say) is involved," and suggested further that "Just as a nation should conserve its fossil fuel, a writer should try to conserve his face and voice." In 1983 the invitation came through, and although there was no speechifying required, he had to deal with two speech-challenges, both of which were met fully and gracefully. The first occurred as we ascended steps to the president's garden, where drinks would be served. At the top stood a friend, the wife of a faculty colleague, whom I introduced to Updike and his wife, Martha. Without a pause, the friend informed the novelist that her mother had very much disliked his latest, *Rabbit Is Rich* (doubtless for its sex). A smile, a twinkle, and "I trust she won't be here tonight?" asked Updike. A few minutes later as the party began, I introduced him to a rather thick-headed trustee whose business success had left small time for literary matters. He gave his name and number, then asked Updike, "And what do *you* do?" "Oh, I'm a freelance writer," was the mock-modest reply. The trustee appeared satisfied and the evening continued without event. Later that evening we had arranged a small party at our house, among those in attendance two novelists—Alan Lelchuk, then teaching at the college, and Maureen Howard, whose daughter was among the graduates. When Updike wrote to thank me for looking after him, he noted,

> Your post-dinner party was a lot of fun. Maureen Howard had panned *Marry Me*, I had called Lelchuk's *American Mischief* "more trash than truth," and God knows what other slights had been perpetrated, but we sat down cozy as kindergarteners on their first day, determined to be good. A study in craft loyalty.

In anticipation, he had pictured the commencement ceremony itself, held outdoors, as "sun-drenched and laced with chamber music"; alas, the only music consisted of two hymns to Amherst, and soon after things commenced a steady rain began to fall.

It would be wrong to reduce him to the polite, charming, obliging man with only goodwill in his heart. I had a glimpse of a different Updike than the genial host of my solicitations when, overeagerly, I sent him a letter I'd written to the *New York Review of Books,* attempting to rebut some negative aspersions cast on his work by Frederick Crews. In the midst of an otherwise friendly reply, Updike suddenly (I had to look twice before it registered) wrote apropos of the letter, "It's really your friends that hurt you. You credit me with 'a couple of dozen engaging, sometimes moving short stories,' when I've published well more than a hundred that I hoped were rather more than engaging." Never had the word "engaging" looked shabbier to me, but it was too late to substitute a better one. While never again being so reprimanded (as I felt it), he more than once reminded me of the difference between being a writer of fiction and a teacher of, among other things, fiction. When I published a book about my life as a student and teacher, mostly conducted at the same institution, he reminded me that he was not a teacher:

> I found your gracious memoir about all those Amherst years slightly harrowing, in the way that I find colleges anywhere harrowing. Why, I wonder? Everything is so dear—the neo-Gothic buildings, and the intelligent and witty faculty and the shiny-eyed students looking up and being fed.

It was a point to be taken and considered by all celebrants of the golden haze of college days to which our hearts presumably keep turning back. He was careful not to sentimentalize his own not-unhappy years as a Harvard undergraduate.

But he was willing to read, with good grace, so it seemed, the occasional exemplary student paper about his own work. One of them, directed at the Maple stories collected in *Too Far to Go,* received as a comment, "Yes indeed, I could hardly have said it better myself," and he went on to say that he "certainly could not have written a paper so sensitive and free (bringing in her own parents, divorce, etc.) when I was her age." When I taught a seminar divided between his works those of Philip Roth, he professed to be made nervous by the syllabus:

> Just looking at it aroused flutters in my stomach, suspecting that I wouldn't do very well in it—better, perhaps, on the Roth half than the Updike—and thinking of all that reading. I picture you and your 21 students a bit like those people in Gericault's

Raft of the Medusa, gesturing and staring in different anguished directions while the damn thing sinks under you.

He also delivered a question that caused a slight flutter in me: "I keep wondering, if I were an Amherst student would I sign up for your course in Roth and Updike? . . . I would learn a lot, no doubt." No doubt, but just a smidgin of doubt surfaces. What *was* I doing, harrowing him with a course syllabus from one of those "dear" American colleges with shiny-eyed students looking up and being fed? Maybe I should have been giving them Spenser's *Faerie Queene.*

When in the middle 1990s I determined to write a book about him, I asked if he had any objections to the enterprise: no, he said, blessings on me as long as it wasn't a biography. As the book went along (I did not provide him with progress reports or questions), he professed concern for my situation: "The thought of you conscientiously trudging through my oeuvre, making sharp, fair adjudications, haunts me to the point that paralysis has at last afflicted my pen." Had I really done that to this unstoppable producer? Hardly, since the next sentence was "Well, not total, I have cooked up one more book on the misadventures of Henry Bech." So I spared myself any guilt about gumming up the wheels of creativity. His response to the finished book was full and generous. Apropos of his picture on the jacket he began, "Well, there I am, thanks to you—my name 2 ½ inches high and my youthful self posed in hip-high marsh grass." He guessed that perhaps he was more heroic back then, "burdened with sharp angst but sufficiently far from death to give the question an abstract gloss, and making, Norman Podhoretz be damned, some music that hadn't quite been heard before in American letters." Later on, he suspected he might have stayed "too long, and too garrulously, at the party." Five years after my book was published it was reprinted with a brief introduction in which I commented on the books he had written since my first account. Rather pointedly, though as always humorously, he noted that as I "whisked" through the last five years, he "got the reluctant impression that I had become a burden to you, a task that never ends, a kind of hectoring taskmaster like the schoolmaster who awaits Shakespeare's 'school-boy with his satchel / And shining morning face, creeping like snail / Unwillingly to school.'"

We last saw each other in Cincinnati, 2001, at a symposium in his honor. He gave a public interview, two public readings, signed books endlessly, talked to graduate students, and endured twenty-minute talks on his work by me and Donald Greiner—all while giving at least 108 percent effort. I heard from him last in June, 2008, when he was pleased to have delivered a book of stories for publication a year later. Like others who cared, I was stunned at the beginning of this year to learn he was seriously ill. I had recently sent him something I'd written on V. S. Naipaul, and he never acknowledged it—which should have told me something. When a few years ago I had mentioned to him my sadness at the death of the poet Anthony Hecht, he replied that he was sorry to hear of Hecht's death: "At the age of 81, how bad are we supposed to feel. Somewhat bad, I think." About his own death, coming a couple of months before his seventy-seventh birthday, we may be justified in feeling more than somewhat bad. But the books are there.

—*The American Scholar,* Summer 2009.

Terry Southern

TERRY SOUTHERN, whose novel-writing days were behind him, had completed a book about Virgin Records and was on his way to teach a course in screenwriting at Columbia University when he collapsed and subsequently died of respiratory failure. His obituary in the *New York Times* called him a screenwriter and emphasized, as his notable achievements, the scripts of *Dr. Strangelove* and *Easy Rider*. The former of these, as directed by Stanley Kubrick, is truly a marvelous piece of work that may be seen with delight again and again; the latter—except for the scenes in which Jack Nicholson appears—is dismal stuff. But before Southern's Hollywood phase, he produced three short novels, all of which have been unavailable for years. *Flash and Filigree* (1958) and *The Magic Christian* (1959) were published here and in England, under Southern's own name; *Candy*—which for a time enjoyed notoriety—was first brought out in 1958 by Maurice Girodias's Olympia Press, publishers of *Lolita,* and less distinguished "dirty" books. Presumably written by one "Maxwell Kenton," *Candy* was in fact the product of a collaboration between Southern and an Olympia Press hopeful named Mason Hoffenberg. It was eventually published commercially in this country in 1964, the *Lady Chatterley* trial having opened the gates. Southern also produced a collection of short fiction and essays, *Red-Dirt Marijuana and Other Tastes,* a novel about the making of a pornographic film *Blue Movie,* 1970, then after a couple of decades a final novel, *Texas Summer,* an extension of a story he wrote earlier. There are good things in each of these works, but I'll concentrate here on early Southern, the "send-up" novels where his originality is most evident.

Southern was sending up, in these books, the American 1950s, that decade whose most significant icon was The Communist Menace, against which American Good in its varied forms—religion, family, true married love, and good grooming—were massed. In the second half of the decade, true, the Beats had come into their own—Kerouac's *On the Road* and Ginsberg's *Howl* were the principal documents of Beat rebellion against stifling convention—but those writers were "sincere," let it all hang out, and wrote swollen rivers of prose-poetry. By contrast Southern was hip, arch, campy without being inclined toward the homosexual. He had a gift for fixing on midcult media favorites like the popular TV quiz show "What's My Line," watched by all good American families before they went to bed on Sunday night. In this extremely popular entertainment, a panel of celebrities—Bennett Cerf, Dorothy Kilgallen, Arlene Francis, Steve Allen, and other forgotten names—interviewed (blindfolded) a Mystery Guest, who after "signing in" answered the panelists' various questions about his or her identity. In *Flash and Filigree* the show became "What's My Disease," in which the contestant is wheeled in shrouded in a cage and is questioned by the panel on where the disease is located ("Is it—your face?" "Are these manifestations . . . above, or below, the waistline?" "Is it of the limbs?") until eventually one of them asks, triumphantly, "Is it elephantiasis"? Whereupon the following:

> The moderator took up the triumph quickly and with grand good humor. "Yes, it *is* elephantiasis!" and at that moment, as the shroud was dropped and the contestant revealed to them all, the audience took in its breath as one in a great audible gasp of astonished horror, and then burst into applause for the Professor, the contestant, the moderator, and the whole panel. . . .

Nothing in *Flash and Filigree* has much to do with anything else: we move from a dubious character named Treevly, who treats a persistent lesion by packing it with a cancer culture and covering it with a Band-Aid; to Dr. Fred Eichner of the Hauptmann Clinic, who has a major passion for running stoplights at excessive speed; to a protracted seduction scene between "Babs" Mintner, a nurse at the clinic, and her young admirer Ralph. The sex scene (all preliminary of course) runs for pages and has dialogue like this to fuel it:

> "No, Ralph, not any more, please, not now, Ralph, please listen, Ralph, not here, please, let's wait, really, Ralph, darling, please, no really please, oh Ralph I love you please don't, really don't

please Ralph I can't darling I love you please, oh Ralph, please, I can't Ralph . . .

and on and on.

Candy takes the all-American girl—of whom Babs Mintner is a fine specimen—into rather more disastrous experiences for which seduction is scarcely the word. Her "experiences" with, among others, Professor Mephesto, her uncle Jack, and Dr. Irving Krankheit culminate in a quite tasteless scene where she befriends a hunchback, feeds him dinner at her apartment, then can't deny his slobbering importunings: the fellow keeps pointing to his hump and accusing Candy of denying him her favors because of "it," and the poor girl is so embarrassed that she eventually accedes to him. After a quite travestied consummation, the hunchback leaves and wakes Candy from her nap, "cross as a pickle" (an expression occurring more than once in Southern): "'*Darn* it!' she said aloud, and with real feeling for she had forgotten to have them exchange names." Later she decides, with much sentiment, that she will think of him as "Derek."

By the time *Candy* was finally published in this country, Lenny Bruce was fully on the scene, and Southern's outrageousness seemed less eye-opening. But in 1958, after the American public had been entertained with novels like *The Caine Mutiny, Marjorie Morningstar, The Man in the Grey Flannel Suit,* and other corporate enterprises, it was quite something to be introduced to Candy Christian's Aunt Livia whom Candy thinks of as a "lovely and sophisticated" woman. As Uncle Jack Christian picks Livia up to have a drink with him and his niece, Livia notes a pregnant woman on the corner—"She's going to have that baby before the light changes! Good God, did you ever see anything like that? If I look another moment I shalt vomit all over us." She then turns to Candy, asking "You aren't pregnant, I hope?" to which the girl replies. in one of her favorite comebacks, "N-O spells *no.*" After Livia compliments Candy on how lovely she's looking, the girl flushes deeply as Livia proceeds:

> "Have any of the boys gotten into those little white pants of yours yet?" Aunt Livia asked, as though she were speaking about the weather.
> "*Really* Liv," said Uncle Jack, coughing. "This hardly seems the appro—"
> "But, isn't she *lovely?*" his wife persisted, turning to Jack

Christian, "a ripe little piece she's getting to be, I'd say. It seems to me that's the first question that would occur to anyone."

There's a wonderfully "naïve" matter-of-factness to much of Southern's narrative in which the unspeakable is spoken as if, well, anyone in his right mind would say it.

But *Candy* goes on for too long and exhausts its one joke. Southern's most original and permanently rereadable book is *The Magic Christian*, a slim volume of 150 pages about the exploits of billionaire Guy Grand ("Grand Guy Grand"), who spends his life and much of his inexhaustible fortune setting up monstrously embarrassing situations, or—as he puts it—"making it hot for people." In the first of these, from the perch of his day coach stopped at the train station in a small New England town, he calls out the window to the hot-dog vendor for a red-hot, then as the train begins to move and the vendor passes the hot dog to Grand, "Guy Grand leaned out and handed him a five-hundred dollar bill. 'Break this?' he asked tersely." The resulting action may be imagined. Grand's other exploits include constructing an enormous vat, on a street corner in Chicago's Loop, filled with quantities of manure, urine and gallons of blood (purchased from the stockyards) into which he drops 10,000 hundred dollar bills, then stirs them in with a large wooden paddle. Burners are lit, the pot boils and morning finds a "large moronic scrawl" (free $ here) on the vat. Again, he has made it hot for people. In other episodes Grand fixes a prize fight, bribing the champ and the contender to behave in the most effete, mincingly effeminate way until one of them finally lies down in the ring, kicking his heels and weeping in childish pique. He buys a movie theater and proceeds to mess with the clips of famous forties films, like *Mrs. Miniver* and *The Best Years of Our Lives.* In the former, he inserts a few seconds at the point when kindly Walter Pidgeon, thinking idealistic thoughts of Mrs. Miniver (whom he has just met), is idly playing with a paper knife while he sits at his desk. Grand cuts to the knife, holding the camera on it just long enough to be too long, and confusing the audience with the irrelevant thought of violence to come. After the show he stalks about the lobby, muttering "What was that part about the *knife?* . . . I thought he was going to try and *kill* her! Christ, I don't *get* it!" In *The Best Years of Our Lives,* as the World War II amputee courts his small-town sweetheart on the family porch swing one summer evening, Grand inserts a cut to "below the girl's waist where the hooks were seen to hover for an instant and then disappear, grappling urgently beneath her skirt." This is of course supremely tasteless and cruel, but (for some of us) made more than palatable by the perfect diction of "grappling urgently."

Norman Mailer, in *Cannibals and Christians,* said the most interesting thing about *The Magic Christian,* and by extension Terry Southern as well, when he called the book a "classic" in which the aristocratic impulse turns upon itself:

> Never had distaste for the habits of a mass mob reached such precision, never did wit falter in its natural assumption that the idiocies of the mass were attached breath and kiss to the hypocrisies, the weltering grandeurs, and the low stupidities of the rich, the American rich.

For Mailer, *The Magic Christian* marked the end of this aristocratic impulse; it was a classic of Camp. For Southern, it was also, virtually, the end of his run as a novelist: Hollywood, along with plenty of drugs and alcohol, did its work. His "slender, unwholesome talent," as John Simon once put it, may be for an age—the extravagant 1960's—rather than for all time. But he had a thing to say, said it, and never apologized, never explained.

—*Sewanee Review,* Summer 1996.

Music, Musicians

Keyboard Reflections

Piano Roles: Three Hundred Years of Life with the Piano,
by James Parakilas and others. New Haven: Yale University Press, 1999.

THE SURPRISE DELIGHT of last spring for me was the appearance of
a 461-page treasure book containing all I ever didn't know about
the piano. I began piano lessons just before turning age five, continuing
up through high school, and during those years became a performer and
accompanist in countless guises. But I was never interested in the physical
instrument itself, never worried like a fiddle player about strings breaking,
or an oboist whose double reed has suddenly gone bad; nor did I think at
all about the piano as a cultural and historical phenomenon. I was busy
getting the job done, as it were, and while a good sight reader of piano
music, I never learned to "read" the piano. So this book has prompted
some autobiographical reflections.

Although Arthur Loesser's classic of the 1950s, *Men, Women and Pianos,*
is a sizeable compendium of information, mainly historical and cultural,
Piano Roles is richly illustrated as well, with sixty-five color and one hundred forty-two black-and-white examples, cleverly chosen. And although
Loesser's one-man survey provides agreeable continuity of viewpoint, this
James Parakilas-cum-associates volume makes use of various scholarly and
technical expertise in the writings of historians, musicologists, and musical
curators, united by their interest in the instrument whose three hundredth
anniversary is being celebrated. You can read about the piano's invention;
its design and marketing; the difference it made to the great musical period
of 1770-1820; the fierce exertions of its performers—especially Czerny
and Liszt; and its more recent use in Hollywood and in jazz. There are
shorter takes and sidebars on matters such as the piano tuner; silent movies
with piano accompaniment; its significance as a cultural monitor in Jane

Austen's novels; and, apropos of the metronome and piano stool, as occasion for "creative" (certainly breathless) excursions by the Russian writer Marina Tsvetaeva.

The guiding spirit behind the whole enterprise is Mr. Parakilas, a professor of music at Bates College, himself an accomplished pianist as well as a music man with a keen literary sense. (It is he who writes the pages on Jane Austen.) Parakilas is most generous in his acknowledgments of the "group" nature of "Piano 300," the project from which this book resulted. He gives thanks to his fourteen co-contributors and also acknowledges institutions including the Smithsonian, Bates College, and Yale University Press, which have cooperated in making this beautiful and surprisingly affordable volume. Parakilas, however, is the major writer, and he names in his introduction the motive behind *Piano Roles:*

> The theme of this cultural history of the piano is that the piano has always exhibited a unique power to act as a cultural go-between, as a medium through which social spheres that stood in opposition to each other could nonetheless nourish each other.

The piano's "voice," he explains, has a "gift for impersonating other musical natures":

> Although its sound comes from the decaying notes of hammered strings, it impersonates the sustained singing of the human voice. With a single set of strings, it evokes the harmony of a choir, the textural richness of an orchestra, and the rhythmic impetus of a dance band, . . . Played by itself, it puts whole worlds of musical sound at the fingertips of one player. Joining other instruments and voices, it supplies whatever they need to make their illusion complete.

One sees, then, why this introduction begins with reference to a 1915 Irving Berlin musical that featured the song "I Love a Piano" ("I love to stop right / beside an Upright, / Or a high toned Baby Grand"), in which the singer and attendant chorus girls were accompanied by six pianists on six pianos and a giant keyboard that reached across the stage. The show was before my time, nor have I seen the movie *King of Jazz,* in which the Paul Whiteman Orchestra is stationed atop a giant piano, at the massive keyboard of which sit five musicians, in tails, doing whatever they're pretending to do. (A marvelous full-page photograph of this event provides the lead-in to *Piano Roles*.) It's a long way back to Bartolomeo Cristofori, who built the first instrument at the turn of the eighteenth century.

The piano's expressive powers compared to the harpsichord's were greater in that—according to an article of 1711 on the Cristofori piano by its publicist, Scipione Maffei—it could imitate such effects as the orchestra or singers in a chorus while transporting (in Parakilas's words) "the rhetoric and drama of music making in the opera house or church into the private chamber." Such power was what Maffei claimed for the piano, and the harpsichord accordingly lost ground over the century, although it hung on to its position in the orchestra (Haydn switched from harpsichord to piano in 1792). The major press-man and establisher of a piano-centered musical culture was Muzio Clementi, who moved in 1766, at age fourteen, from Rome to England, and was taken up by a rich Englishman, Peter Beckford, at whose Dorset estate Clementi practiced eight hours a day and turned himself into a virtuoso. He went on to perform in European capitals, wrote many sonatas for piano students, and invested in piano manufacturing and music publishing firms. He could play passages—in thirds, sixths, and octaves—at a speed available to no one else, earning the opprobrium of Mozart, who said that Clementi "doesn't have a Kreutzer's worth of feeling or taste—in other words a mere machine." But Clementi's *Introduction to the Art of Playing on the Piano Forte* (1801) was extremely influential and contained original and transcribed music from composers including Bach, Corelli, and Haydn. Music journals sprang up concurrently, and by 1820 there were three of them in England, devoted especially to publicizing Clementi company publications. At age seventy-eight he brought out the first of a series of "keepsake" albums with facsimiles of musical handwriting from the likes of Haydn, Mozart, Beethoven, Weber, and Clementi himself, thus contributing to the "composer worship" that would only increase in intensity over the century.

My impression is that, as with English studies, academic musicologists have become increasingly concerned—as this book's emphasis suggests—with "cultural" matters: such as where the piano was played and by whom (man or woman) and for what sort of audience; or what the particular historical factors were that conspired to produce or further a certain kind of musical style. A recent conference of Haydn scholars, held at my college, gave on the whole much more attention to circumstances of performance than to the aesthetic qualities of the works performed. (Similarly, if you write about Pope's poetry these days you're probably not likely to be analyzing or judging rhetorical effects from one couplet to the next, but talking rather about Pope's relation to The Body or to Gender.) So I was particularly interested in and gratified by what seemed to me the best piece of musical criticism in the book, by Gretchen A. Wheelock (herself a Haydn scholar), "The Classical Repertory Revisited: Instruments, Players and Style." In this essay, while keeping an always sharp eye on the gradual supplanting of harpsichord by piano (coming into its full glory with Beethoven), Wheelock surveys keyboard piano writing by Haydn, Mozart, and Beethoven. An example of her way of combining critical description of the individual piece with situating it in the culture comes as she discusses Haydn's "big" E-flat Major Sonata, Hob. xvi: 52, which she distinguishes from his earlier sonatas—though she notes an earlier "departure" from harpsichord writing in the 1771 C Minor Sonata with its "Sturm und Drang" qualities:

> The markedly different profile [of the E-flat Sonata] is obvious from the grand French-overture-style chords of the opening to the rousing dash of the Presto's final close. This is a fully theatrical work, public in style if not in performance venue, and its fistfuls of notes don't bring delicate hands to mind.

Or she distinguishes among some of Mozart's finest piano concerti:

> Ranging from such works as the C Major Concerto, K. 467, which echoes the pacing and diction of buffo intrigues in *Le Nozze di Figaro,* to the ominous world of *Don Giovanni,* previewed in the opening movement of the D Minor Concerto K. 466, Mozart's handling of both theatrical and intimate gestures is wondrously matched to the versatile persona of the piano and its relation to the varying textures and timbres of orchestral voices. Whereas the opening movement of the A Major Concerto, K. 488, highlights the suave vocal capacity of the piano, that of the C Major Concerto, K. 503, displays the instrument at its most majestic in the confident march of fully "orchestrated" chords and dazzling passagework

She points out, later on, the difference between Beethoven's use of the damper pedal in middle period works like the "Moonlight" and "Waldstein" sonatas, and its presence in the opening bars (illustrated with a full page) of the adagio section to the A-flat Sonata, op. 110. This is criticism that helps us hear more of what we have already sensed in the music.

At the other end of the book (and skipping over completely its nineteenth-century sections on piano virtuosity, especially Liszt's), we have fascinating excursions on the piano in Hollywood film, on different ways of aggressively, even violently making it new (Jerry Lee Lewis grinding it out while standing atop the upright), and on modernist examples of avant-garde exploitations of the instrument in Henry Cowell, Charles Ives, John Cage, George Crumb. Of special interest to me was a deft, brief survey of the piano in jazz conducted by Mark Tucker, a Duke Ellington scholar and himself a fine jazz pianist. With the aid of excellent pictorial shots, Tucker gives us a look at keyboard greats from Jelly Roll Morton to Cecil Taylor, by way of suggesting how pianists in jazz are "middle" men who "can step forward into the spotlight to shine as soloists or stay in the background to join bass and drums in rhythm section chores." He imagines a distinct personality for jazz pianists, "authority figures, sages, intellectuals, teachers, control freaks," sometimes with a "formal, bookish air" and often called "professor," as they assume professor-like roles (Lennie Tristano, Billy Taylor). Tucker even provides a list of "great bespectacled pianists" whose willingness to look vulnerable suggests "an arduous process of acquiring knowledge, of paying dues, but also a certain vulnerability." This is musical portraiture of a high order.

> Softly, in the dusk, a woman is singing to me;
> Taking me back down the vista of years, till I see
> A child, sitting, under the piano, in the boom of the tingling strings
> And pressing the small, poised feet of a mother who smiles as she
>   sings.

I was glad to see that Parakilas honors D. H. Lawrence's poem as giving beautiful voice to, among other things, "the glamour of childish days" for Lawrence and others, stirred up by hearing the instrument so central to the lives of those who studied or listened to it. *Piano Roles* is appropriately and charmingly dedicated jointly, by sixteen of its contributors and associates, to the sixteen piano teachers "who gave us our first piano lessons."

Except for one "Mr. Meyers," they appear to be women, and for most of us I suspect it was our mothers who got us started. My own took me to a Mr. Donald Grey, one of the few male teachers in our area, and he sat me down in September of 1937 in a basement studio room in Binghamton's Arlington Hotel and talked to me about what study of the piano with him would involve. He provided a book, the introductory one in the Mason-Hammond series for piano beginners, then helped me get comfortable around middle C, from which the first easy and soon more difficult pieces to come would receive their bearings. This book's opening challenge, a little excursion featuring middle C and its ascending neighbors D and E, came equipped with unforgettable lyrics: "Loudly brays the donkey / As he goes to hay; / Singing on the wrong key, / In his favorite way." From there it was on to the next, a similarly focused piece about falling leaves: "Red, gold, brown [E, D, C], Flutt'ring down / Leaves are dropping, never stopping, Down, down, down" [E, D, C].

All I remember saying that afternoon was something to the effect of wondering how I would ever be able to play this instrument, which, though only an upright, seemed blackly huge to a four-year-old. At home there was an even larger object, a Steinway studio grand my mother had purchased with $1,500 of her young woman's savings. A capable pianist herself (she supervised music in the public schools of Johnson City, New York), she was much in demand to accompany singing at various events or conduct bits of musical entertainment. She was clear that it would not do for her to become my official teacher, but from the outset she acted as goad to and sustainer of my keyboard efforts, indeed my best critic as—on a daily basis—she would call in from the kitchen, "Play that section again, HANDS ALONE." This is really all the advice any young student needs, and I flourished under it with weekly lessons throughout the year (a couple of vacation weeks off in summer) and progressed from "Loudly Brays the Donkey" to playable bits from Mozart and Haydn.

Don Grey worked on my technique, taught me how to play three notes against two (a valuable skill) and avoided all "cute" pieces that other teachers assigned to lure reluctant or flagging pupils. He stuck to the classical canon and it wasn't too long before I was navigating Chopin's "Raindrop" prelude, refingered for my inadequate reach. Soon I was presumably delighting all sorts of local gatherings from Hadassah to University Women's Club to the Johnson City chapter of Kiwanis, along with seizing the innumerable opportunities for display afforded by school and church. In yearly contests (tournaments, we called them) one presented a program of memorized selections to be judged by some outside authority. There were festivals and recitals and endless ways in which a competent pianist could help out the community, such as, in my case, accompanying the Czech Sokolovna drill team, or doing an intermission number at YM or YWCA dances, the latter an especially dreary chore, even as it held out the remote possibility of meeting there a Young Christian Woman.[1]

World War II summoned my teacher to its service, and I was unmoored until a friend of the family's took me, aged eleven, to play for Ethel Newcomb. Miss Newcomb had been a student of Theodor Leschetizky's, among whose many pupils were numbered, most famously, Artur Schnabel. (Parakilas has a couple of good pages on Leschetizky as master teacher.) Newcomb agreed to take me on for a biweekly or monthly lesson at ten dollars per, an immense sum, so it seemed. These were vivid experiences, consisting mainly of anecdotal reflection (along with servings of shortbread) by Miss Newcomb, a forbidding figure who lived in an old farmhouse in Whitney Point, New York. Sessions would last two hours or more (once stretching to six), and in her piano room with its two enormous Steinways I was introduced to the piano concerto, first Mozart's D Minor K. 466, then Beethoven's Third in C Minor. Miss Newcomb played the orchestral part on the other grand and insisted that I respect the score and its markings: "For ten cents you've got it all down there," she would insist. And she provided stories of the greats—Schnabel, Ossip Gabrilowitch, Vladimir de Pachman—that suggested there was something exciting, even romantic, about a musical career.

But such a professional career was not to be mine. I never practiced with the required intensity or for the length of time she recommended (never exceeded two hours a day, and seldom made that). My parents wanted me to be well rounded, and so did I, this condition more likely to be achieved in a liberal arts college than a conservatory. Perhaps the apex of my piano career came in six weeks spent at a rather broken-down music camp in the Catskills, where I discovered, as if by chance, the wonder of classical orchestral music. It was the overture to *Meistersinger* that did it, along with bits from Tchaikovsky's fourth and fifth symphonies. At one of the regular Sunday afternoon concerts I had the dubious honor of playing Henry Cowell's "Aeolian Harp" (it is touched on in *Piano Roles* as an example of 1923's avant-garde), in which one stood to pluck the piano strings while making awkward use of the damper pedal. A freak piece but doubtless amusing to see the young boy straining to reach the strings while standing on tiptoe in front of the keyboard.

The Parakilas book pays some attention to the piano as site of seduction, and in high school and college I put in a lot of service in dance bands under the illusion that there was something irresistible to the opposite sex in my thoughtful expertise. Nothing turned out to be further from the truth, and although I eventually met my life partner while accompanying Gilbert and Sullivan's *Mikado* (she had the lead role), it was probably my high moral character to which she responded. As for any aspirations to be a performing soloist, I turned into a creditable amateur pianist, devoting myself in graduate school and beyond to learning as much of the repertory—especially the nineteenth-century composers—as I could take in. Here the giving of a recital every few years, attended mainly by loyal and discreet friends, acted as the essential spur. There were enough good moments in these, so I fancy, to justify the time spent practicing and the sickening nervousness that overtook me when the hour approached and it was time to walk out on the stage. Anyone who finds speaking in public an unsettling challenge should hire a hall and give a concert, so as to experience something really unnerving, in a different league.

Is there anything to be gleaned from these reflections, stimulated by Parakilas's enlivening book? One of the characters in John Updike's first novel, *The Poorhouse Fair,* has lived into his nineties and is at times convinced he will persist on the earth forever if he carefully treats "each day of life as the day impossible to die on." I like to think that, occupied at the piano bench, I have felt something like such an intimation of immortality, since like nothing else I have known or am likely to know about, the piano represents—presents—the promise of happiness. Parakilas quotes from an inspiring article that appeared in 1910 in *Musical America,* a magazine my mother subscribed to: "One's piano is a kind of magic mirror which is capable of reflecting to one the whole musical world from classic times to the present, and throughout all lands. It requires only that one put the music on his piano-rack and play it, or, at least play at it." *Only* do that, and things will come out right, even help one resist the temptation to dwell too much on what has been. Perhaps if D. H. Lawrence had been fortunate enough to have learned to *play* the piano, not just listen to his mother singing and playing it, he would have avoided the piercing sensations in the final stanza of his poem:

So now it is vain for the singer to burst into clamour

With the great black piano appassionato. The glamour
Of childish days is upon me, my manhood is cast
Down in the flood of remembrance, I weep like a child for the past.

—*Hudson Review,* Autumn 2000.

Notes

1. Sure-fire applause-getter on these occasions were Debussy's "Clare de Lune" and de Falla's "Fire Ritual Dance." I suppose you could do worse, and it has been done, surely.

Sinatra's Century by David Lehman

IN ONE OF Kingsley Amis's Novels, the protagonist, Garnet Bowen, comes across his wife in the kitchen, helping their child into its coat to the accompaniment of "a song sung very loudly and badly by Frank Sinatra." "You came, you saw, you conquered me," Sinatra sang. "When you did that to me I knew somehow th—" Bowen switches it off: "You tell us how, a part of Bowen's mind recommended. Another part was reflecting that to cut Sinatra off in mid-phoneme was not such uproarious fun as it was with the man who did the religion at five to ten on the wireless, but it was nice all the same. It was only a pity that Sinatra would never know." Loudly and badly is wholly unfair to Sinatra's 1950 treatment of "These Foolish Things," the song from which the lyrics are taken; although it might fairly be said of his signature song "My Way," sung hundreds of times in his later years in what one critic has called "a surly feat of self-congratulation" ("The record shows . . . I did it my way"). But this is the Sinatra centenary, and the commentary on him has been eulogistic rather than disparaging.

A sterling instance of such eulogy—call it over-the-top admiration rather—is this delightful and incisive book by David Lehman. Lehman is a poet, critic, and editor, known for his book on the New York School of poets (Ashbery, etc.) and *Signs of the Times,* a hard-hitting attack on Deconstruction (Derrida, Paul de Man) as a peculiarly toxic form of literary discourse. But who would have predicted this tribute to a singer with whom Lehman has had a lifetime love affair? (Perhaps no fan of Deconstruction could also be one of Sinatra's, but that's hard to prove.) The subtitle to his book, *One Hundred Notes on the Man and His World,* with its crisp pun on "notes," takes the singer from his birth in Hoboken, New Jersey, in 1915, to his death in 1998. The notes vary in length from one to four or five pages, but are always focused on some aspect of his career: his famous performance at New York's Paramount Theater in 1942, when the girls went wild; his rocky marriage and breakup with Ava Gardner; his affiliations with mob types or the infamous Rat Pack (Dean, Sammy, etc.). The 100 notes are pithily, aggressively written, as if to live up to the feisty voice of Lehman's hero, The Voice. He brings out vividly the style of a "generous, dictatorial, sometimes crude . . . powerful man unafraid to use his power," which was what the skinny 130-pounder turned into. More than once, Lehman's sentences consist of direct quotation from a Sinatra song, as in "This is a lovely way to spend an evening" or "This time it would be all or nothing at all."

The latter allusion is to Sinatra's early, great 1939 recording with the Harry James band. Here for the first time the singer, not quite twenty-four years old, has in Lehman's words "caught and embodied the spirit of the words" by way of communicating "that quality of vulnerability mixed with intransigence." As always, in talking about a Sinatra recording, Lehman pays attention to minute but significant pleasures the singer brings out in "All or Nothing at All" by accenting the rhyme words ("appealed to me" with "could yield to me") and softening his voice to an "infinite tenderness" as he imagines the tidal consequence of his passion: "And if I fell, under the spell of your call, I would be caught in the undertow." Of course if you haven't been previously enchanted by the record—which originally sold 8,000 copies in 1939, and a million when it was rereleased in 1942—then you should head to your machine and Google the performance.

We don't need yet another biography of Sinatra, and Lehman has been wise not to try to get too much fact in that can already be sampled elsewhere. His relatively brief book is more like Pete Hamill's *Why Sinatra Matters* (1998), but goes further and deeper than Hamill did into what makes Sinatra's treatment of a song so memorable, inimitable. The crude outline of his career takes him as a band singer briefly with James, then with Tommy Dorsey, then with the launch-out on his own—for example doing nine shows and singing 100 songs on an average day at the Paramount Theater. Then would come the career plunge in the early 1950s after his overtaxed voice gives out for a while and he breaks up with the love of his life, Ava Gardner. He rebounds with his fine playing of the role of Maggio in the film *From Here to Eternity*, then moves into what some consider his greatest period, the 1950s recordings for Capitol Records, with arrangements by Nelson Riddle, among others. The later decades include retirement, unretirement, star performances all over the world, and the ubiquitous "My Way," his defiant personal defense of his life as an artist.

Lehman's informed judgment is that after Sinatra's comeback in the 1950s, his voice on the Capitol recordings was "no longer quite as impressive or as naturally pleasing." But though he has lost some range and ease, and hasn't as great a voice as before, Lehman judges him a greater singer. Records like "I Get a Kick Out of You" or "I've Got You Under My Skin" or "Night and Day" reveal emotions that are shaded: "His joy is edged with irony and sometimes with rue, with melancholy, and sometimes something more, a heartbreak bred in the bone." Yet I was pleased to note that some listeners, including his granddaughter, Nancy Sinatra's daughter, still prefer the timbre of his youthful voice. With those listeners I align myself, feeling that, for all the fine tunes he would record and rerecord, the early eighty-four sides on which he sang with Tommy Dorsey's orchestra are unsurpassed. It may be that, growing up in the 1940s myself and playing in a dance band, those songs have greater force and life for me, partly because I have projected my own satisfactions and disappointments from long ago onto the songs that seemed to embody them.

The recordings with Dorsey begin with a lovely, completely forgotten song of 1940, "The Sky Fell Down," and end in 1942 with "Be Careful, It's My Heart" (Irving Berlin's song in the movie *Holiday Inn*), and "There Are Such Things" ("So have a little faith, and trust in what tomorrow brings, / You'll reach a star, because there are such things"). Along the way we get rollicking jitterbuggy things like "Let's Get Away From It All" and "Snootie Little Cutie," in which the Pied Pipers (Jo Stafford singing) and cute little Connie Haines supplement Frank's performance. And then, how about the How songs, "How About You" and "How Do You Do Without Me," and the absolute charm of forgotten ones like "Polka Dots and Moonbeams," "Dolores," and "In the Blue of the Evening." None of these songs, except for "Be Careful, It's My Heart," make Lehman's list of his twenty favorite Sinatras from the 1940s, and tastes of course vary. After leaving Dorsey in 1942, he did many more fine things with a less interesting orchestra directed by Axel Stordahl.

I am an inadequate guide to the later Sinatra, just because I've never been able to stop playing the early things again and again. But it's fair to say that the last five decades of his singing life are more or less divided into the "swinging" and the soulful. And though there are many good things from the swinging period ("Learning the Blues" perhaps the best), I don't find the finger-snapping, wised-up guy who often substitutes his own words for the right ones—as in intruding "boot" into "I Get a Kick Out of You," which Lehman tells us did not amuse Cole Porter—inevitably irresistible. As for the soulful, there has recently been released a large box of CDs, "Great Songs from Great Britain," in which Sinatra sings beautiful ones like "The Very Thought of You" and "The Gypsy" at a tempo so slow that one's mind or ear occasionally wanders. This is of course a curmudgeon speaking, but the sides with Dorsey combine lyric beauty with enough swingish band background (Buddy Rich on drums; Ziggy Elman, trumpet; Joe Bushkin, piano) to keep me going for the remainder of my days. How could the estimable jazz critic Whitney Balliett have found the recordings with Dorsey mainly "vapid and inert"?

I learned things from Lehman's notes that surely have been noted before, not just Ava Gardner's famous tribute to sex with Sinatra ("He was good in the feathers") but also her scornful response to his later erotic life when he married Mia Farrow ("I always knew Frank would turn up in bed with a boy"). Although his antics with the Rat Pack don't seem terribly amusing, it may be, as Lehman says, that their jokes about black (and Jewish) Sammy Davis, and the white Italian "dagos" (Frank and Dean Martin) may amount to a "critique of racism and bigotry, debunking these things by turning them into jests." But finally it's The Voice that counts, one that Lehman is very good at tracking in its various modes. It was a voice that, whether singing or acting in the movies, "inevitably caught its inflection from the spoken language." The writer of those words, the English poet and critic Clive James, whose own inflected voice is memorable, saluted Sinatra's "sense of the music inherent in speech." Lehman's tribute in *The Sinatra Century* is itself made vivid by its continuous consorting with the spoken language in a fashion his subject might just have been pleased by.

—*Weekly Standard*, December 14, 2015.

Listening to Toscanini

THE CONVERGENCE of two events has shaped my life as a music listener over the past three months. The first was a significant birthday, after which I decided to reacquaint myself with the classical records—many of them long-playing vinyl—that I've lived with over the decades. I resolved to spend less time listening to Dizzy Gillespie and Charlie Parker or the songs Frank Sinatra recorded with Tommy Dorsey in the early 1940s, and celebrate instead Haydn and Brahms and Debussy. As if somebody up there took heed of my resolution, I was made aware that RCA Victor had recently released its archive of Arturo Toscanini recordings, previously available on individual compact discs. Now gathered together were seventeen years of performances with the NBC Symphony, from 1937 until his retirement in 1954, plus a number previously made with the Philadelphia Orchestra and the New York Philharmonic. For seventy-two discs in all, plus a video of Toscanini conducting, the selling price at ArkivMusic was an amazingly low $125. (Purchased as they appeared individually in the early nineties, the price tag would have been more like $1,250.) A day or so after I placed the order, the discs appeared in a large shoebox along with a small handbook—discography, short essays by music critics, photos of the great man at work—in a pocket-sized, elegantly produced handbook. I was in business.

I heard Toscanini conduct just once, when I was fifteen, an NBC Symphony Sunday afternoon program consisting of Beethoven's Ninth Symphony. (What I mainly remember of it was a shameful tendency to doze off after too many activities in a short New York City vacation.) Toscanini had begun to conduct the symphony at the invitation of David Sarnoff, head of Radio Corporation of America, for a series of weekly broadcasts—some were later televised. He would have full authority over the repertory, the soloists (a number of operas were sung), and whether the performance merited a thumbs-up for release on records. Toscanini was then seventy years old, time for a lesser man to have retired, after concluding twelve years with the New York Philharmonic. Previous to that he spent decades as an opera conductor at the Metropolitan Opera in the early years of the last century, as well as with various orchestras in Europe and America. Here was a man who, if it can be believed, conducted Tchaikovsky's "Pathétique" symphony four years after it was written, and had conducted Brahms's "Tragic Overture" in 1896, when the composer was still alive. So to begin a new operation in 1937, and continue with it for seventeen years, retiring when he was eighty-seven, is one of the great heroic stories of artistic achievement.

I began listening to the discs in a serendipitous manner, deferring the operas till later on, letting fancy and impulse take me where they would, and with one performance suggesting another. My point of entry, for no good reason, was Schubert's Fifth Symphony, an early work not much performed and not listened to by me in years, but absolutely delightful to hear under the crisp forcefulness of Toscanini's directing. This was followed by an even more brilliant work, Mendelssohn's incidental music to *Midsummer Night's Dream,* composed when he was sixteen years old. Then came the same composer's Octet, also a teenage work, with a brilliant scherzo, expanded in Toscanini's recording by many added fiddles and articulated with breathtaking intensity. My record player in the living room consists of, among other components, a new, powerful amplifier and two ancient, large KLH speakers, top of the market in their day, now looking a bit like old elephants. One of them has mysteriously died, but the other is sufficient to play the recordings from a time when "stereo" was but a dream on the horizon. The sound, as Toscanini and my equipment deliver it, is on the harsh side, shrill at times but absolutely electric in its tension, detail, and forward impulsion.

Many critics, along with some of the musicians who played under Toscanini, have put words to the propulsive excitement of his performances. A member of the NBC Symphony's bass section, David Walter, spoke of the "large, sweeping movements of the right arm" as one of the means for getting the orchestra "intensely involved." Walter's teacher, Fred Zinneman, onetime member of the Philadelphia Orchestra, said that Toscanini's beat was "very clear and precise, and it was very beautiful; he had the most elegant way of holding and moving that stick . . . so it was almost impossible to make a mistake if one watched him." Another musician, William

Carboni, testified to how much his terrifying demeanor on the stand elicited from the musicians: "That red face—that violence—it could kill anyone. It was like nature—like a raging sea or a thunderstorm: it's bigger than you, and you don't buck it—you have to go along with it." These and other testimonies are from *The Toscanini Musicians Knew,* by B. H. Haggin, who himself had a try at describing the conducting, writing that it exhibited "cohesive tension from one sound to the next . . . changes of sonority and pace that were always in right proportion to what preceded and followed," an effect Haggin called "plastic continuity." The result was an ideal view of the work based on the composer's score and on its performance markings.

One of the listening activities this collection tempts one to engage in is comparing different performances of the same work. For example, we are given three different recordings of Beethoven's "Eroica" symphony, from 1939, 1949, and 1952, and the scrupulous listener may decide which is preferable, which clarifies the most details. One of the liveliest books on the conductor is *The Toscanini Legacy,* by the English music critic Spike Hughes, who is very stern about moments when this or that performance shows Toscanini at less than his best (Toscanini's own attitude toward his performance was one of "relentless self-dissatisfaction"). This comparative activity is probably not essential for a nonprofessional listener intent on refreshing his or her ear, not just in bringing to life relatively unfamiliar pieces like Mozart's early Divertimento, K. 287, but more significantly in taking the measure once more of the nineteenth-century composers—Beethoven, Schubert, Brahms, Berlioz, Wagner, Verdi—whose work the conductor's playing invariably makes new.

During the vinyl era I purchased at modest prices many Toscanini albums, unfortunately often souped up with "stereo sound" that made for unnecessary racket. These LPs have moldered on the shelf, particularly ones that include performances of "lighter" classics, like "The Skater's Waltz" (Waldteufel), "The Moldau" (Smentana), Rossini's overture to *William Tell,* or Sibelius's "Finlandia"—not to speak of triumphant renditions of Sousa's "Stars and Stripes Forever" and "El Capitan." (It has been noted that when Toscanini went on tour with the orchestra in the American South, he played "Dixie," something, however politically incorrect it seems now, I would like to have heard.) One of the musicians interviewed referred to such lighter pieces as "junk stuff," but tags the "Skater's Waltz" as standing out in his memory of great moments. Something like that happened to me on hearing "Finlandia" for the first time in many years.

The piece takes about nine minutes to perform, seven of which are junk indeed, Sibelius at his windiest, most pretentious. Then suddenly a break, and the great, beautiful theme announces itself, as pure and ice-cold as one imagines things to be in Finland. I would expect to be stirred by this or that second subject in a symphonic movement of Beethoven or Brahms, but was unprepared for this burst of noble utterance.

Toscanini can sometimes be heard singing along with the orchestra or singers, especially in rehearsals, none of which, unfortunately, are included in this collection. One of these instances occurred in the third act of *La Bohème*, when, as one of his favorite singers, Jan Peerce, noted, Toscanini sang along with him. Peerce observed that some people said it spoiled the record; for him it *made* the record: "Imagine hearing Toscanini—not planning it, just naturally singing faintly in the background . . . knowing the guy's blood is on that record, and some shmo says, 'That spoils it.' They don't know what inspires people." In "The American Scholar" Emerson says, with students in mind, that great books are for nothing except to inspire. I feel sorry for my own students who, not brought up with classical music, will never hear these performances. For me there is no better word than "inspire" to name the way they can fill someone, perhaps listening from a comfortable chair in the living room, with a sense of heroic possibilities.

—*The Weekly Standard*, November 11, 2013.

Terry Teachout's Ellington

TERRY TEACHOUT is a remarkable man of letters whose interest in the arts is multidirected. Officially he serves as drama critic for the *Wall Street Journal*, and has reported on theater performances all over the country. For *Commentary*, he writes a regular column about music and musicians. His literary and biographical savvy was shown in an excellent biography of H. L. Mencken *(The Skeptic)*, a small book on George Balanchine, and a delightful memoir of growing up in a small town, *City Limits*. More recently he has turned his attention to jazz, with satisfyingly full biographies of Louis Armstrong *(Pops)*, and now Duke Ellington. He has also been a hands-on musician, playing string bass as a young man in a country music group. My acquaintance with his work began when I came across a profile of Woody Herman, who led the great swing band of my youth. Teachout wrote about the last days of the Herman band, with its leader ill, financially strapped, and surrounded by musicians many of whom didn't know the great records of their predecessors from the first and second Herman's Herd of the middle 1940s. Teachout's writing is filled with buoyancy, with deep knowledge of his subjects, a useful wit, and an omnivorous memory—in his ear as well as his mind. It seems inevitable, then, that he would turn to Ellington, the most important jazz composer of the twentieth century and a person of intense aspirations and rich achievement; someone whose life scarcely took second place to the music he wrote and the musicians he led.[1]

There has been an enormous amount of writing about Ellington since his death in 1974, all sorts of testimonials from musicians, more than one biography, and critically focused analyses of his compositional structures. In an afterword, Teachout makes clear what his book is: "Not so much a work of scholarship as an act of synthesis, a narrative biography substantially based on the words of academic scholars and other researchers." If he downplays the book as scholarship, his own source notes, presented in most full detail, come to almost 100 pages. The few extended descriptions of pieces, as with "East St. Louis Toodle-O" and "Ko-Ko," are subordinated to the ongoing narrative, but they show what he is capable of doing if he chooses to do it. He brings to the subject, along with careful delineation of the music and musicians, a stylish verve, as when he refers to an early piece "The Mooche" (1927) as being marked by the muted trumpeter Bubber Miley's "foul growling"; or, when speaking of the great band of 1940-42, he notes, apropos of the alto sax man Johnny Hodges, "In any other band, Hodges would have been the undisputed star of the show, but the entire Ellington band was a murderer's row of soloists, each of whom was determined to rise to the occasion." Hodges's companion in the sax section, the tenor man Ben Webster, is described as "an enthusiastic and inspirational ensemble player" who "hit the bull's-eye whenever he stood up to solo," as in the "damn-the-torpedoes swinger . . . 'Cotton Tail.'" The drummer Sonny Greer ("consistently underrated" says Teachout accurately) supplies a "propulsive rhythmic impetus that turned every up-tempo tune into a stampede." There is a freshness and exuberance about Teachout's language that permeates the book and makes it such a pleasure to read.

The circumstances of Ellington's upbringing and his entrance into the musical world are familiar, and Teachout attends carefully to his middle-class family, one of the light-skinned black bourgeoisie in the U Street/Shaw district of Washington. Ellington's impulse toward becoming, in Teachout's words, an elegant, cultivated gentleman would be importantly furthered by his association with Irving Mills, the canny manager of Ellington's operation from the late 1920s until the Second World War. Mills's marketing idea was to present the Duke as a different kind of black man, "fine-spoken and expensively tailored," someone whom "broad-minded white folk" could accept. Decades later his son, Mercer, wrote that his father thought of music as "a good way to get a girl to sit beside you and admire you as you played the piano." (As a pianist I too had such dreams of glory.) Ellington lost his virginity, so he claimed, at the age of twelve, and throughout his lifetime was a "tireless philanderer," which his marriage to Edna Thompson in 1918 did nothing to hinder. They soon separated, though never divorced, and Teachout speculates that he might have found his nominal marriage useful in fending off girlfriends who hoped to ensnare him maritally. "I started out playing for pussy, not for money," he later remarked, in language that the elegant, cultivated bandleader of earlier days would have avoided, at least in public.

From a six-man group, "The Washingtonians" of 1926, Ellington's orchestra would eventually, at its peak of brilliance, reach fourteen. In his first electrical recording, "East St. Louis Toodle-O," we can hear contributions from three players preeminent in their styles: Bubber Miley, who practiced foul growling with his muted trumpet; Joe "Tricky Sam" Nanton, who did a similar thing with the trombone over a long career with the band (Miley died young); and Otto "Toby" Hardwick, whose playing on the alto and soprano sax provided many identifiable touches of what the jazz historian Gunther Schuller called "his slick, slightly oily tone and lip slurs." Hardwick was seldom a major soloist, although he played with the band on and off for decades, but his touch—not appreciated by all fans of Ellington—is one of the distinct pleasures of listening to the band.

This pleasure in idiosyncrasy, the listener's pleasure in identifying individual soloists ("There's Hodges! . . . Ah, marvelous Harry Carney! . . . Is that Nanton on trombone? No, Lawrence Brown, of course") is one way of accounting for the difference between the Ellington band of whatever era and the bands of his contemporaries. Teachout's way of putting it is to contrast Ellington's operation with the more smoothly blended styles of Benny Goodman, or Artie Shaw, or Jimmy Lunceford. He calls Ellington's sound, by contrast, "a loose festive ensemble sound." Rather than the clean precision of a Goodman piece, Ellington's way was different:

> He preferred to hire musicians with homemade technique that were different to the point of apparent incompatibility, then juxtapose their idiosyncratic sounds as a pointillist painter might place dots of red and green side by side on his canvas, finding inspiration in their technical limitations.

Interestingly, the great jazz trombonist Jack Teagarden didn't like the Ellington band: "He never had a band all in tune, always had a bad tone quality and bad blend." Whether or not the "pointillist" comparison justifies Teachout's claim that Ellington's blend, far from "bad," was, rather, unconventional, it's significant that Teachout reaches out for impressionistic metaphor to get at the specialness of Ellington's sound. My own listening to big band swing in the 1940s was concentrated on three groups:

Stan Kenton, Gene Krupa—above all, Woody Herman. Each of these had a more streamlined feel in its "blend" than did Ellington. And he seldom played as fast or as loud as Kenton, Krupa, or Herman. For me, and perhaps for others, Ellington took some getting used to.

Reviewing Teachout's book in *The New Yorker*, Adam Gopnik posed a large question: "What was it in this dance music, heard in short takes on scratchy 78s, that left its devotees devoted to some larger set of human values?" By way of suggesting the improbability that Ellington's band could inspire such transcendent values, Gopnik feels compelled to play down, even demean, what he thinks are facts about the band and its leader in the late twenties and thirties, producing hundreds of recordings while playing countless gigs all over the United States and Europe. A look at Gopnik's "facts" doesn't inspire assent: "Ellington was a dance-band impresario who played no better than OK piano, got trapped for years playing 'jungle music' in gangster night clubs, and at his height produced mostly tinny, brief recordings." One hardly knows where to start in refuting these claim, but a beginning would be to insist that Ellington's original style at the piano was a lot better than OK. His was not the technical brilliance and flash of a Fats Waller or an Art Tatum, and it's true that occasionally there's not much to be said about one of his solos. But more often his unobvious rhythms and muted tone are essential to the "thicker-textured" (Teachout's phrase) colorings of the orchestral arrangement, again to be distinguished from Goodman's full-speed-ahead procedures on "Don't Be That Way," or "King Porter's Stomp." But the most ludicrous of Gopnik's claims is that all these years produced little more than "tinny, brief recordings." Tinny? "Mood Indigo"? "Solitude"? "Rockin' in Rhythm"? Is there no more to be said for the virtues of three-minute recordings than that they're "brief"? In fact Ellington got into trouble when, time and again, he tried to extend his brief pieces into suites with some sort of thematic content, the best known of which is "Black, Brown and Beige: A Tone Parallel to the History of the American Negro." Contra Gopnik, the great jazz critic Whitney Balliett found those three-minute events to contain "an incredibly rich sound that is one of the delights of Western music." No musician, wrote Balliett, "regardless of his skill could reproduce the timbre, tone, and inflections of Ellington's musicians." Gunther Schuller called it a "perfect balance between composition and improvisation."[2]

What by general consensus represents the Ellington band at its greatest is known as the Blanton-Webster band of 1940-42. Jimmy Blanton was a nineteen-year-old string bass player whose life was cut short, in 1941, by tuberculosis less than two years after joining Ellington, and whose memorable, plucked-bass solos are most vividly heard on a 1940 recording, "Jack the Bear." Ben Webster, already a veteran tenor man and fresh from making a number of sides with Billie Holiday and Teddy Wilson, provided a gutsy, full-throated voice to add to the other saxes—Hardwick, Hodges, and Harry Carney. With Ray Nance having replaced the trumpeter Cootie Williams (he joined Goodman for a spell), the band played a remarkable date in frigid February of 1940 at the Crystal Ballroom in Fargo, North Dakota. This justly named legendary performance was recorded by two young engineers on a portable disc cutter, and features standbys such as "Cotton Tail," "Never No Lament," and "Harlem Airshaft." The result, listened to seventy years later, is as fresh and full as the band would ever sound. After the concert a local fan left a description of the seemingly casual array of the musicians before the concert began, galvanized when Carney, the baritone sax player with a truly noble tone, "began to tap his foot and suddenly the orchestra burst into full cry." The fan, one Daniel Halpern, said, "I felt cheated by the records to which we had been listening for so many months. They were nothing like this." And yet now not only the Fargo concert, but also the concurrent recordings, with the help of today's engineering, sound splendid.

My credentials as an Ellington listener are somewhat suspect, in that I've never listened to very much of what he produced after World War II until his death in 1974. Teachout is obliged to describe the origins and contents of a number of orchestral suites which have not inspired many listeners. More exciting was the Newport Jazz Festival of 1955, in which Webster's replacement on tenor sax, Paul Gonsalvez, took twenty-seven choruses of "Diminuendo and Crescendo in Blue," originally an eight-minute extended piece, electrifying the audience and bringing the band to a renaissance of popular acclaim, short-term though it was. But unless my own case is untypical, I think Ellington will continue to be listened to mainly for the short, three-minute numbers from the years 1927-1942. Teachout says about "Ko-Ko," perhaps the most impressive and most praised recording from this period, that it constituted "a relentless procession of musical events that contained not a wasted gesture." Repeated listenings to its propulsive excitement prompted me—as when reading a poem notable for its diction and rhythmic movement—to look for critical help in unpacking some of its richness. The place where I naturally turned was to Gunther Schuller's pages about it in *The Swing Era*. Much of his commentary is directed at the chord structure of the piece, the way dissonant harmonies are superimposed upon tonality to create the "massive towering chords that arc so satisfying" (he employs the word "bitonality" for the effect). The problem is that Schuller's pages are dense with diagrams that break down the different choruses and show us how (for example) a "G flat ninth chord with a flat five" is superimposed upon "the prevailing E flat minor seventh." What I've left out here are the transcriptions of the chords in the treble and bass clefs, and what happens when I "read" this material is that although I'm a good pianist and good sight-reader, I find it virtually impossible to play those chords on the piano and to hear the effects Schuller directs us to. Of course any attempt to break down and represent technically what the music makes us hear so powerfully is in for difficulty; especially if the chordal structure, the chromatic sequences, are as dense as they are in not just "Ko-Ko" but any number of similarly thickly textured arrangements.

Teachout does very little of such musicological analysis, although his commentary on particular recordings is always shrewd. (In an appendix he presents a list of fifty key recordings.) What he does do, aside from keeping the narrative moving along, is provide telling portraits of Ellington's sidemen as they came, stayed (many), and eventually left. He calls Johnny Hodges Ellington's greatest soloist, with Cootie Williams, "Tricky Sam" Nanton, and Ben Webster not far behind. Although Jimmy Blanton for a sadly brief period was a matchless bass player, he was preceded for many years by Wellman Braud, whose slap-bass technique (as opposed to Blanton's pluckings) helped anchor the rhythm section. Rex Stewart's "half-valve" performances on cornet are but one example of the "idiosyncratic" mix that different styles of playing produced. The long-staying Harry Carney, whom Teachout calls the first great baritone-sax player in jazz, is beyond praise, and there is the curious, rather special contribution by Juan Tizol, the only non-African American in the band (he was from Puerto Rico), who invented attractive solos on the valve trombone. The drummer Sonny Greer was, from the first, one of the band's great drinkers ("all our horn-players were lushes," declared Ellington), but Greer deserves a place especially because he had a tendency to fall off the stand. Ellington finally had to get rid of him, but his array of percussive contributions was admirable. Billy Strayhorn, who did 300 compositions for the band and played occasional piano, has latterly received his due, which he didn't always get for one or another particular piece he invented. And there are others: the earlier-mentioned Otto Hardwick and his serpentine manner of soloing on soprano or alto sax.

But outshining these luminaries is, in this listener's opinion, the trombonist Lawrence Brown, who joined Ellington in 1932 (the same year as his finest singer, Ivie Anderson) and stayed with him on and off for four decades. They never got along, and indeed Brown kept his distance from other band members; since he was the son of an African Episcopal minister, he neither drank nor smoked, earning the name "Deacon," which he disliked, from his compatriots. Brown mapped out his solos in advance, could repeat note-for-note the same solo on future occasions, and was formidably skilled as a technician. (One of the trombonists who later sat next to him said that in five years he never heard Brown make a mistake.) Teachout describes his tone as "chocolate-smooth" and "cello-like," and some of Ellington's more rigorous critics thought he was too smooth to be featured in a jazz band—though Ellington never liked the word jazz. On occasion Brown produced a fast-moving solo, as in "The Sheik of Araby," or "Rose of the Rio Grande," or the final chorus of "Main Stem." But his trademark contribution was slow-paced, somewhat meandering in tone, gorgeously full in its unfolding. He is heard on some of Ellington's most famous hits, like "Sophisticated Lady," "I Let a Song Go Out of My Heart," or "In a Sentimental Mood"; but also on slightly less known gems of songs that are not quite songs and would be very hard to sing. I am thinking of chromatic subtleties like "Prelude to a Kiss," or "Serenade to Sweden," or "A Gypsy Without a Song" from the 1930s band; "Dusk" or "Moon Mist" from the 1940s group. Having loved Brown's playing for years, I was pleased to find that Gunther Schuller, at the end of some dedications from *The Swing Era*, added "In memory of the incomparable Lawrence Brown." Readers of Teachout's pages are invited to go and listen for themselves to hear if Brown was unique. More generally they will surely be stimulated by this fine book to reacquaint themselves with the astonishing achievement that was Ellington's over the years[3].

—*Hudson Review*, Spring 2014.

Notes

1. *Duke: A Life of Duke Ellington.* Teachout's essay on Woody Herman, "Elegy for the Woodchopper," can be found in *The Terry Teachout Reader.*
2. Balliett's comments can be found in his *Collected Works: A Journal of Jazz 1954-2000.* Schuller's comments are from *The Swing Era.* He also wrote about Ellington in *Early Jazz.*
3. President Richard Nixon celebrated that achievement at a seventieth birthday party in the White House in 1969. Upon receiving the medal, Ellington gave "the classic French greeting" of cheek against cheek. Afterward Whitney Balliett's wife said to Ellington that she was glad he had kissed the president, to which the Duke replied, "I always kiss all my friends. So now he belongs." Nixon never had it so good again.

Soap Opera Days, or Days of My Life

WHY SHOULD I, an elderly literary gent who spends much of his time reading, talking, and writing about Shakespeare, say, or W. B. Yeats, spend an hour every weekday watching a soap opera? How odd is it that after a hard-working class teasing out the syntax and ambiguities of Shakespeare's *The Winter's Tale* or some complicated Yeatsian lyric, I come home at noon to plunge wholeheartedly into a world not of language but of characters, of people I like or dislike? After warning students not to "identify" with Prospero or J. Alfred Prufrock, could I be doing that very thing when one of my favorite soap heroes triumphs or suffers? Is it possible to justify the activity of soap-watching not as a momentary fit or frivolous aberration, but as something willingly embraced over four decades? How did this addiction, if that's what it is, take hold, not to let go?

It must have begun where things tend to begin, in childhood, after school, listening on the radio to the adventures of *Jack Armstrong, the All-American Boy,* a serial brought to me by Wheaties late in the afternoon. Sporadic visits to lunchtime soaps like *The Romance of Helen Trent* or *Our Gal Sunday,* or *Ma Perkins* (featuring a lovable fellow named Shuffle) helped things along. But it wasn't until forty years later that as a mature adult I decided to try out a short-lived soap titled *Somerset.* Only a half hour, unlike the other hour-long ones, it didn't seem an excessive amount of time to spend on a diversion. When *Somerset* went under, I moved over to *Search for Tomorrow,* one of the longest-running of the soaps back in 1976. The star of *Search* was an actress named Mary Stuart, who, as Joanne, endured many trials, tribulations, and a number of partners, the most interesting of whom was a southern fellow named Martin Tourner (played, I later realized, by the father of Jennifer Aniston, who hadn't yet swum into my ken).

Perhaps as a result of its half-hour status, *Search* had fallen to the bottom of the ratings, and a local television channel decided to replace it with a mindless talk show. Incensed, I wrote a letter to the powers that be deploring this act of wanton brutality. I also sent the letter to our hometown newspaper, which provoked a column about me that was picked up by the national wire services. Here was a Story: How charmingly incongruous that a (respected) college professor should indulge himself in this way! The whole thing, as we now have been taught to say, went viral: "Prof Lathers in Soaps" was only one of the more inventive headlines the story received. I began to get letters of condolence, all of them from women, who, like me, were fans of *Search*. A lady from Georgia even offered to tape the show as it went along and send me the tapes. My phone began to ring with requests for radio interviews and photo opportunities.

The most exciting of the phone calls was from the producers of the show itself, inviting me to come down to New York City and be king for a day with a tiny walk-on appearance (they eventually paid me seventy-five dollars) and a night's dinner and hotel room at their expense. Accordingly I performed my walk-on task, preceding one of the cast into Bigelow's Bar ("Big's"), where I seated myself on a barstool, spoke not a word, but was given a beer by Big himself. All very satisfying, but this was not the end of the saga. Upon returning home, I got another call from New York, this one from the folks on the CBS show *Good Morning America)* which featured the glamorous interviewer Diane Sawyer. I showed up early in the morning to be made up and primed for my seven-minute talk with Ms. Sawyer; unfortunately the two-hour show had scheduled too many players, one of them the infamous Louis Farrakhan, whose brief career in the news involved his less-than-agreeable attitude toward Jews. Farrakhan preceded me and managed to bewitch the interviewer (not Diane Sawyer) into allowing him extra minutes for his rant, thus cutting into and, it seemed, obliterating my own appearance. Sorry, they exclaimed, including Diane, as I, furiously embarrassed, headed outside for a taxi to the airport and glum trip home.

As I stood on the curb, my makeup still intact, I was followed and hailed by someone from the show announcing that they had squeezed out a seven-minute spot for me after all. Diane Sawyer was charming, alluding to a line from a Yeats poem about how women "eat a crazy salad with their meat," and suggesting that my crazy salad involved soap opera. What did I find absorbing about this low form of art? Groping for a good answer, I said it was a nice change to step down from Milton into the banalities of daily life in a bogus midwestern city. And I claimed that while poems, plays, and novels have their beginnings, middles, and ends, the soap opera plays a different game, its sole aesthetic purpose being to continue the story from week to week without end, until the network decides to kill it. As they would do to *Search* a couple of years after my intervention.

Is there anything in high art that even approaches the soap in its hopefully endless proliferation? I hadn't thought of one until the fiercely outspoken reviewer Marvin Mudrick called a novel from Anthony Powell's twelve-volume sequence, *A Dance to the Music of Time,* "the most interminable soap-opera since Australopithecus," whoever he was. Mudrick's aim was to abuse Powell's novel, but since I love the book he disparaged, it reminded me that I never wanted Powell's *Dance* to end, would have been content to read on and on. In fact the forced ending of any soap after the kill order comes in is extremely painful to watch, in its desperate attempt to make a meaningful and satisfying disposal of the remaining good characters (the bad ones have been gotten out of the way the previous week). When *Search for Tomorrow* breathed its last, Joanne was asked by her longtime pal, Stu, just exactly what she was searching for. "I don't know," said Jo shyly, "tomorrow, I guess."

For the past few years I've been watching a highly rated hour-long soap, *The Young and the Restless.* Young they may not all be, but restless they surely are and should be, worrying about whether they'll still be in business next year or next week. Many of *Y&R*'s characters are rich, running cosmetics firms or other mysterious enterprises. Head honcho is Victor Newman, who has been married to more than one of the current cast members. He is mainly concerned with Family and will stop at nothing to protect his Legacy. Phyllis—once married to Victor's son and now married to Jack Abbott, Victor's hated rival—has just emerged from a year-long coma (very useful staple of soaps) and is out to punish those who have betrayed her in the interim. Michael Baldwin, the suave attorney, is "battling" prostate cancer, fearful it will ruin his husbandly sex life. Neil Winters, another successful businessperson, has recently lost his sight and is as yet unaware that his glamorous young wife, Hilary, is having it on with his son, Devon (a millionaire, by the way). There are many other ongoing plots I will spare mentioning

Because of my encasement in the ivory tower, I've missed all sorts of current expressions that the soap brings to my attention. I now will attempt to "be there" for someone I love, and under no circumstances will I "bail" on that person, but rather "have his or her back" at all times. These cringe-making banalities are really not the fault of the characters, since, in the words of David Slavitt's poem "Soap Opera," "They wade through sorrows scriptwriters devise / in kitchens, hospital rooms, divorce court, jails." The closing lines of this excellent poem may say it all:

Stupid, I used to think and partly still
Do, deploring the style, the mawkishness.
And yet, I watch. I cannot get my fill
Of lives as dumb as mine. Pine Valley' mess
Is comforting. I watch, and I delight in their distress.

—*The Weekly Standard,* March 9, 2015.

Teaching

Teaching Shakespeare

L AST JANUARY a *Washington Post* opinion piece by Jonathan Yardley lamented university and college English departments' lack of requirements, noting that at many prestigious institutions today (he named Amherst College as one) students can graduate without having read a single play of Shakespeare's. The column and a subsequent news story in the *New York Times* produced a number of letters from concerned alumni (say it isn't so, please) and a call to me from the chairman of Amherst's board of trustees requesting information on the subject. I told him that yes, it's possible though highly unlikely for an English major at Amherst to graduate without having read a single play of Shakespeare's—that indeed there had been no required course in Shakespeare, even for majors, for thirty years. I refrained from asking if he thought many alumni spent their evenings perusing *Twelfth Night* or *Troilus and Cressida* or *The Winter's Tale*—even good old reliable *Hamlet* or *Macbeth*. But I did say that, for the first time, I was about to give a lecture course on Shakespeare to fifty or so students and that I would apprise him of the results.

In the catalogue, I had rather tersely described the course by saying that we would read selected plays with attention to their "power and beauty as poetic dramas." A colleague in another department jokingly said that the description sounded like me, by which he meant it was provocative to claim that in studying a great writer we should have in view such old-fashioned, not to mention indefinable, qualities as power and beauty. Of course I had meant to be provocative, at least to remind myself—with a lift from Wordsworth—that poetry was an homage "to the grand elementary principle of pleasure" by which, Wordsworth claimed, we lived and moved—perhaps even when we were reading poetic drama for course credit.

In the opening class I told them it was a dangerous venture we were embarking on, since a recent headline in the *Times* announced "At Colleges, Sun Is Setting on Shakespeare." I quoted the president of Dartmouth College warning that "We mustn't deify Shakespeare," and I asked Why mustn't we do that?, since it had been done by larger spirits than ourselves (Samuel Johnson, Charlotte Bronte, Thomas Carlyle, to name three). More recently T. S. Eliot has adduced Shakespeare as a writer with "the most prodigious memory for words" that ever existed. In this course we would read nine plays, from *A Midsummer Night's Dream* and *Romeo,* to *Coriolanus* and *The Winter's Tale*—the central sequence consisting of *Othello, Lear,* and *Antony and Cleopatra.* I told them the kind of course it wasn't going to be, the sorts of things I wouldn't be inviting them to do with Shakespeare. For example, they would not be invited to provide large-scale "readings" or interpretations of the plays, nor would they be asked to explain or account for the motives of this or that character. "Plot" was a word they would not hear from my lips. The Elizabethan audience and what it would or wouldn't have responded to; matters of stagecraft and dramaturgy in the playhouses of the times; editorial questions of text and emendation—these and other important matters they could read about in our Riverside edition of Shakespeare, but would come up only incidentally in class. Nor was I a proponent of one or another recent "approaches" to Shakespeare, whether new historicist, psychoanalytical, materialist, feminist, or deconstructive: these they could also read about in the Riverside.

By now we were deep in one of those respectful-if-wary silences I unfailingly produce on opening day. Changing pace, I suggested we consider a particular moment in a play they might not yet have read. *Othello,* where near the close of Act 3 the Moor has been persuaded by Iago of Desdemona's guilt. He vows revenge, calls for blood, and in response to Iago's pretense of caution—"Patience, I say, Your mind perhaps may change"—bursts forth with

> Never, Iago. Like to the Pontic sea
> Whose icy current and compulsive course
> Ne'er feels retiring ebb, but keeps due on
> To the Propontic and the Hellespont;
> Even so my bloody thoughts, with violent pace,
> Shall ne'er look back, ne'er ebb to humble love,
> Till that a capable and wide revenge
> Swallow them up.

What were we interested in here? Othello's resolved mind, his fixity of purpose? ventured a student. I didn't say anything, and another student, probably trying to figure out where I was headed, said that it was Othello's language we respond to. But was it Othello's language? Did it believably emanate from his character? Or was it somehow "out of character"? (Alexander Pope, for one, said that the lines should be omitted as an "unnatural excursion.") Yet out of character or not, I said, these lines are thrilling; while not calling out for complex interpretation, they give us the thrill of intense pleasure, even as Othello is signing on for tragic destruction. How does this happen? The answer, we agreed (did "we"? were we a "we"?) was somehow "Shakespeare," and that was our subject this term. In our classes and in the papers they would write, the focus would be unfailingly on what I called the "expressive value" of lines in sequence, how we heard and registered them in our thoughts and feelings.

To talk about expressive value in a passage turned out, not surprisingly, to be a very difficult thing for the majority of the class to do. Largely a group of second-term freshmen and sophomores, their study of literature in secondary school had obviously been conducted in quite different terms. They had been taught, especially with regard to poetry, that the object was to tease out meanings, deep ones if possible, rather than describe how the verse sounded, what it was like to read it. Many of them had been warned against using first person singular, as if that were an inappropriately subjective way to proceed. Now I was asking them to talk in the first person, about what they saw and heard in a sequence of lines. Especially heard: in the early stages of the course I referred more than once to Bernard Shaw's phrase "word music" by way of pointing to Shakespeare's greatness; or to Virginia Woolf declaring, "From the echo of one word is born another word, for which reason, perhaps, the play seems as we read it to tremble perpetually on the brink of music"; or to Robert Frost's insisting that the "ear does it; the ear is the only true writer and the only true reader." But as any teacher knows, it doesn't help much to tell students what you want them to do; only after their not doing it can education perhaps begin.

An example of what I didn't want from them came when a student tried in the first paper to write about expressive value in *Henry IV*, part 1. In that play's opening scene, the king compares Hotspur ("the very spur of honor's tongue") to the wayward Prince Hal, whose brow is stained "with riot and dishonour." The student wrote:

> Every character in the play has a great deal of respect for Hot-
> spur. . . . Even his greatest foe and the source of his deep-rooted
> anger respects his courage. This respect is in direct contrast to
> how the king feels about his son. . . . He wishes that Hal had
> Hotspur's natural noble temperament because they are admira-
> ble and necessary qualities for a prince.

True, and so forth, but not nearly true enough insofar as it gives no sense
of Shakespeare as a writer, a maker of arresting sentence sounds. For that,
the student would need to "sound" Henry's rueful shame, and the place to
begin was with something heard, with tones of voice—a way of addressing
something or someone. Why not point, I suggested, at the poignant exclamation in which the king allows himself to wish that Hotspur, rather than
Harry, were his son:

> O that it could be proved
> That some night-tripping fairy had exchanged
> In cradle clothes our children where they lay,
> And called mine Percy, his Plantagenet!

What are the feelings expressed in such a momentarily indulged wish?
Why is this rueful exclamation both shocking and satisfying, inadmissible
yet beautiful? Since "character" was an inference from such matters, rather
than a given, why not address themselves to Shakespeare's language—to
the play of the play—rather than to Hotspur or Hal or Bolingbroke?

　　After class a student who had had trouble with the paper came to my
office to discuss how she might rewrite it and, in trying to ascertain "what
I was after," said what I would hear more than once over the term—that
she hadn't been asked to do this before: "You mean you want us to write
about the writing"? Well, I replied, everyone says Shakespeare is such a
great writer; yes, maybe we should face up to the writing. Easier said than
done, of course, and her rewritten paper, in its attempt to pay attention
to how the writing sounds, moved from loose paraphrase to the other
extreme, concentrating instead on consonant and vowel repetition—as if
that were what "sound" essentially consisted of. "I can hear it in class when
you read it aloud," said another student, the mysterious "it" being (perhaps) the pace, the swing, the tonal and human feel of a passage. Of course
it is difficult in the extreme to write well about such matters. I had been

trained to practice, nay revere, "close reading," but any professional, interpretive approach to Shakespeare would claim itself as a close reading of the text. My own teaching seemed to be, in its preoccupation with the sound of sense, a different sort of approach, and the student's remark about reading aloud reminded me of how absolutely central that activity was to my classroom procedure. No wonder students who didn't have the ear for it remained, by necessity, mainly eye-readers. A few were dissatisfied, and one young woman, when I asked them on the final exam to write a little about their experience during the term, found that we had insufficiently attended to characters, plots, motifs, "ideas." Indeed we had, but in the interests of what I believed to be even more important than such emphases—the life of the poetry.

Perhaps the most interesting remark on that exam came from a student who had performed at an average level and who now spoke about the nature of what I'd asked them to do. Many teachers at the college, he wrote, "focus on appropriate readings for the purpose of analyzing them in the context of a social movement," the focus being on "an agenda rather than on the works themselves." This course in Shakespeare was something new to him, and, in a formulation that gave me pleasure, he wondered whether he should consider it "a throwback to an older style of teaching, or innovative, since it is now so rare." Thinking of myself as an innovative throwback helped check the impulse toward self-congratulation, but also reinforced me in believing that the only way to keep the sun from setting on Shakespeare is for innovative throwbacks in English classrooms to focus on what really and finally matters: the power of words to raise the spirit and touch the heart.

—Newsletter (Association of Literary Scholars and Teachers),
Autumn 1997.

Amherst English: Theodore Baird

As SOMEONE interviewed in these pages more than once as both student and teacher in the composition course described, I am a less than disinterested commentator on Robin Varnum's account of writing instruction at Amherst College. That won't, however, deter me from singling out the book as a piece of documentation whose appeal should extend beyond local curiosity, even beyond the audience of English professors especially concerned with the teaching of composition. "The Era of Theodore Baird," pompously self-important as it sounds, is not an extravagant rubric to name decades in which flourished a bold and inventive approach to that teaching probably *the* most inventive one ever tried at an American college or university. Over the years, myths of all sorts have proliferated about what was a required course for Amherst freshmen, English 1-2: Composition. *Fencing with Words* provides a reliable and mainly sympathetic history of what went on in this course; it also raises critical questions about what it means to look back on the past, on one's predecessors, on a past "era" in education, without claiming too glibly to "understand" it.

First some facts, as gathered together by the scrupulous researcher. From beginning to end, the heart, soul, and wit of the Amherst composition course was Theodore Baird, who came to teach at the college in 1927. As a graduate student at Harvard he had studied with Irving Babbitt, but Baird was no humanist, nor did he speak from any announced platform of beliefs—religious, social, or moral-ethical. As a young teacher he discovered *The Education of Henry Adams* and at Amherst did the surprising thing of making it the sole text for a semester of freshman composition. This was quite extraordinary, since Adams's book offered a formidable challenge not only to young readers, but to the teacher concerned to "do" something with it in an English class. In fact, and as he admits, the *Education* was one of the books that changed Baird's mind. Varnum quotes a famous pas-

sage from its first chapter that Baird would more than once have recourse
to: "From cradle to grave this problem of running order through chaos,
direction through space, discipline through freedom, unity through mul-
tiplicity, has always been, and must always be, the task of education." Varnum misreads Adams's singular "order" as plural "orders," but she is right
to say that Baird found the notion appealing ("one man's order is another
man's chaos," he liked to say), since the human orders we make are diverse
and conflicting. It was a principle that consistently informed the writing
assignments he would construct for Amherst undergraduates.

Adams exerted a more covert and profound force upon Baird, insofar as
a recurrent pattern in Adams's narrative shows him learning the limitations
of his own language—the "ignorance" he confronts after he has failed to
dispel it by employing one or another "order." Perhaps the most powerful chapter in the *Education* is titled "Chaos," in which, after a slow and
painful illness, Adams's sister dies and his "first serious consciousness of
Nature's gesture" takes the form of "a phantasm, a nightmare, an insanity
of force." The following chapter, "Failure," describes on a more relaxed,
comic note his attempt at instructing undergraduates at Harvard College. One of Baird's homely revisions of this failure-note was to say that
"Education doesn't work," a slogan not popular on college campuses, especially when fundraising is in the air. Indeed Baird seemed to take a wicked
delight in the fact that our attempts to order chaos in one or another way
are prone to failure, though usually in less than tragic ways, and that the
experience of failure may lead to a sharpened, even exhilarated, notion of
what it might be like to succeed. ("Success is counted sweetest / By those
who ne'er succeed," wrote the Belle of Amherst.)

Soon after he arrived at Amherst, Baird put together an anthology of
autobiographical selections titled *The First Years,* "an attempt to provide
materials for a course in the writing of English by directing the student's
attention to his own resources of experience." He knew, he wrote, that in
a general way this was a long-established approach to the teaching of writing; his own idea was to help the individual student attend to his experience by giving him means of comparing "what he has written with the
autobiographical memories of skilled writers." There follows a key assumption: "When the student attacks the problem of writing with subject matter rather than form as the end in view, his interest will be aroused and
matters of form will be subordinated to their proper place. . . . The student
cannot, except by admitting his own deficiencies as a human being, ascribe

his lack of interest in his subjects to his opinion that they are dull and uninspiring."

Although the course Baird would eventually invent and direct, English 1-2, made no use of this textbook or indeed of any texts other than what students wrote, its principle was one Baird never retreated from: that you could make students care about their writing not by teaching them "good English"—the elements of grammar and punctuation—but by asking them to write about their own lives, a subject that presumably only a very few would claim to be devoid of interest.

The First Years (1931, revised 1935) contained selections from Adams, from Edmund Gosse's *Father and Son* and Howells's *A Boy's Town,* and other autobiographical works. But the writer given the most pages, and with whom the anthology concludes, is Marcel Proust, the last volume of whose great work had appeared in English the year Baird came to Amherst. In passages he chose for the anthology, like those having to do with the madeleine, the steeple of St. Hilaire in Combray, or the excitements and disappointments of going to see Berma perform, Baird found what he called in the introduction "the perfection of a kind of writing, occasionally hinted at, occasionally well done, in autobiography, but never before sustained for so long a time nor with such brilliant success." To speak of Proust as an "influence" on the course Baird was inventing would doubtless be crude; yet it is fair to say that *À la recherche* was a supreme effort at running various orders through the chaos of thoughts and feeling of a single mind. On a suitably smaller scale, the effort might be something the Amherst freshman could be invited to try his hand at.

I'm suggesting that the energies Baird would direct into his composition course were continuous with literary experiences he was having of modern masterworks by writers who hadn't yet become objects of academic literary study. The third modern writer whose example—right down to the most intimate matters of tone and temperament—made all the difference to Baird was Robert Frost. As with Adams and Proust, it seems ridiculous to talk about Frost's influence on a composition course that—as Varnum points out, quoting an essay on Baird by Walker Gibson—Frost liked to dismiss as "kid stuff." But pretty much any kind of academic course was kid stuff to Frost, who had spent his time at Amherst and other institutions playing against the system. When Varnum asked Baird if his course owed a debt to Frost in its emphasis on what Frost called "sentence sounds," Baird said he had no interest in talking about any such debt. This seems fair

enough, yet when Frost published his first books of poems and filled letters home from England with his notions of the speaking voice, sentence
sounds, "the sound of sense" and its importance for poetry, he also insisted
on its importance for education. Just before sailing home, he wrote a letter to his fellow teacher at Dartmouth, Sidney Cox, about the difference
between what Frost called "the grammatical sentence" and "the vital sentence," the latter being what he was after and what any teaching of writing
should also be after. In a sentence that has never been commented on, as
far as I know, Frost told Cox, "We will shake the old unity-emphasis-and-
coherence Rhetoric to its foundations." In this gesture of solidarity, which
he was not to act on in any systematic-academic way (such as founding a
new kind of English course), there can nevertheless be heard an animus
against conventional instruction in Good English, at the "correct" grammatical sentence as what could be taught, in grammar school, high school,
and, if need be, once again at college. Baird shared this animus.

"Perhaps you think I am joking. I am never so serious as when I am,"
Frost also wrote to Cox, and the interpenetration of seriousness and joking he shared with Baird, who developed his version independently of
Frost. Both men delighted in playfulness of utterance and were similarly hard to pin down when an interlocutor ventured the equivalent of
"But seriously . . ." Both liked to shock, to discomfit, to put their listeners
momentarily at a loss. Varnum quotes an apt sentence from the introduction to *The First Years,* in which Baird's acerbic yet playful manner may
be glimpsed: he has been attacking rhetoric books that, aiming to teach
students about various kinds of exposition, teach them instead how to
write the deadly dull five-paragraph Perfect Theme (as Baird termed it).
He assumes it is better for students to discover for themselves some of the
difficulties in writing about their own thoughts and emotions; but he also
supposes a certain level of attained literacy:

> I also assume, without undue belief in the natural goodness of
> the human heart, that if at college age a student has not learned
> how to spell *receive,* how to punctuate, how to write sentences of
> greater complexity than those of Arthur Brisbane, he has so suc-
> cessfully resisted the pressure of former teachers that he ought to
> be considered immune and be allowed the precious privilege of
> discovering these intricacies for himself.

In the second edition these sentences (and the now forgotten Arthur Brisbane, a journalist) were cut. Baird, however, remained true to their sentiment throughout his teaching career: the composition classroom was a place where you could talk about ideas, consider interesting questions, look at human experience in various ways. In order to do this, the mechanics of composition were assumed, in a way that they scarcely could be now even at the most "elite" institution of higher learning.

Adams; Proust; Frost: are these the true progenitors of a course in freshman composition that was, so the word went round, really derived from William James's *Pragmatism,* Wittgenstein, Count Alfred Korzybski, or S. S. Hayakawa? In the course's heyday in the 1940s and 1950s, students—I was one of them—tried to look for a magic name at whose door might be laid responsibility for the puzzling assignments set by the English 1 staff. Baird denied that there was any such primal figure behind the inventive questions he made into semester-long sequences of writing exercises. (Varnum, in an appendix, gives the entire thirty-one short papers, final paper, and final exam that constituted the course in the Fall of 1946.) Before assuming that his denial was merely obfuscatory or coy, one might remember that Wittgenstein's *Philosophic Investigations* was not published until 1953 (Baird has said he didn't read Wittgenstein before or afterward); that Korzybski's *General Semantics* was promulgated in a messianic from-on-high manner quite alien to Baird's playfulness; and that James's massively influential *Pragmatism,* which surely Baird *had* read, cannot, except at a level of abstraction so high as to be meaningless, account for the imaginative pedagogy that informed English 1. He did acknowledge the importance of the Harvard physicist Percy Bridgman, whose work on "operational definition" contributed to the insistence that Amherst students define their terms and describe the order of actions they had engaged in. But the books Baird cared most about in his sustained and massive amount of reading were mainly not works of philosophical analysis. Literature, history, biography, travel narrative, scientific accounts (at the nonspecialist level) were his main passions; Shakespeare, Clarendon, Samuel Johnson, Gibbon, Jane Austen, Emerson, Thoreau, Darwin—along with Adams, Proust, and Frost—were the writers he returned to again and again and who informed his sensibility. There was a particular turn to that sensibility, and it provided an essential quality of the composition course. But before addressing this matter, a few remarks about the logistics of English 1-2, drawing upon the facts Varnum has assembled. "The Era of Theodore Baird" takes in years occupied largely by World War II and the postwar Amherst "New Curriculum" that institutionalized, for what turned out to be two decades, a year-long required course in Freshman Composition. During the war years, various Army and Air Force contingents succeeded one another at the college in rapid succession. Among their courses of instruction was one in English, primarily taught by Baird and his two main colleagues in the department, G. Armour Craig and Reuben A. Brower. Brower came to Amherst in 1939; Craig, the next year. Brower would develop a sophomore course in the interpretation of literature, which he later recreated at Harvard as Humanities 6. Craig, who had been Baird's student and who returned to his alma mater to teach for more than forty years, was Baird's main support in the composition course and brought to it an interest in philosophical-analytic discourse, particularly (and recently) as it was conducted in the writings of Kenneth Burke. Burke's "perspectivism," as he expounded it in *Permanence and Change* and *A Grammar of Motives,* was an important validation for the kinds of questions the composition exercises were asking, the kinds of situations they invited students to write about. Varnum quotes some remarks by Craig about how, in a typical assignment, the freshman was directed to

> "do thus and so about X; describe as thoroughly and carefully as you can what you did when you did something about X. . . ." We would always at the end say, "Now, define X. . . ." We frequently had assignments that asked one way or another, "You are in a situation where you're at a loss. What does it feel like? How do you know you're at a loss?" Or in a situation in which you don't understand something that somebody says to you, what is the experience of not understanding? What is the understanding of being at an impasse? How does this differ from the experience in which you were stuck, but you got out of it? How did you get out of it?

For even the best students, who had been congratulated in high school for their literary talents, this was something new, though Proust would have found it old hat. If—as Craig pointed out—students had been brought up to think of "good" English as belletristic, an "effusion," something else seemed to be wanted in this composition course. Puzzled freshmen, he recalled, would ask, "What do you want, sir? Do you want me to talk about metaphor?" The answer, not inevitably helpful, would be something like "tell me what you know, tell me what you did when you did X"—served a tennis ball, found yourself at a loss, used the right or wrong name for something, read a map, drew the skyline of the Holyoke Range.

I don't think it accidental that, as Craig's remarks suggest, the emphasis in the assignments was frequently on being at a loss, an impasse, being stuck, not understanding something. For the challenge in writing was to run some sort of a compositional order through experience, which William James called a blooming, buzzing confusion. In this confusion or chaos one was engaged in doing something other than being a writer: one was getting lost, or playing tennis, or taking out the trash, or being rear-ended by a careless motorist. There is an analogy here with the novelist's problem, insofar as unhappy families prove a better subject than happy ones, and "evil" characters seem more interesting than good ones. As Adams put it: "Chaos is the law of nature; order the dream of man," and nature rather than dream turned out to be the stuff of English 1 assignments.

The expense of energy on the part of both students and teachers in the course was truly prodigious: at each class meeting—three times a week first semester, twice a week in the second—a short paper was submitted, responding to an assignment handed out in the previous class. The instructor took the paper home, read and commented on it (all were ungraded, although teachers kept track of how the individual student was doing), then made it the subject of the following class. A "class" consisted of individual papers, or selected parts of them, being distributed, read aloud, then discussed and argued over. (The authors were not identified.) In the course of the first semester the student wrote thirty-some times; if (as I did) an instructor taught two sections of the course (M, W, F and T, Th, S) he read thirteen hundred or so papers over the semester. The pressure was always there, for better or worse: worse, when the student behaved lazily or cynically or just plain didn't have an idea; worse when the teacher couldn't figure out what to do in a class and ended up juggling or faking while trying to sound in control. But better when a student felt challenged and extended by the difficult questions he was being asked to consider; very much better when the instructor suddenly noted, under his tired eyes, a piece of writing come to life—an individual voice, so it seemed, asserting itself.

As an Amherst freshman in the fall of 1949, I struggled with this strange course, never knowing what "they wanted," and only occasionally writing a sentence or two that elicited praise. In fact it wasn't until a couple of years later, when I read an article Baird had written about English 1 for the alumni magazine, that I saw more clearly the way in which the questions asked had been about words and the wordless. Baird gave an example of a typical assignment that asked the student to write about something he knew how to do, like the good tennis player describing what it is to serve a tennis ball:

> He knows he knows what he is writing about, yet as he begins to address himself to his subject he immediately encounters the inescapable fact that his consciousness of his own action contains a large area of experience quite beyond his powers of expression. The muscular tensions, the rhythm of his body as he shifts his weight, above all the feel of the action by which he knows a stroke is good or bad almost before the ball leaves the racquet, all this and much more lies beyond his command of language, and rendered almost speechless he produces a mess. He knows in the sense that he can perform the action, but he does not know in the sense that he can communicate this action to a reader.

At which point the teacher invites him to distinguish between these two "levels of experience" and to generalize about them.

Varnum devotes a good deal of space in her book to accusations that "mystification" was being practiced; that while the student was being told there were no answers, told it was up to them, the English staff—handing out these daily assignments and handing them back with acid, ironic, or just plain mysterious comments—looked as if *they* knew what things were really about, what the Real Answer was. There's some truth in this, insofar as a section teacher "knew" more about, say, "levels of experience" than the typical freshman did but never handed out such knowledge as something to take notes on. Nor would it have done any good if he had, and it would have foreclosed on the sort of game both teacher and student were engaged in playing. It must be admitted that some students, and even some members of the staff, disliked playing the game and responded with various degrees of hostility or indifference. But why should such divergence come as a surprise? To believe that the course had a doctrine or secret behind it, and that once you'd unmasked that secret (once you knew there were difficulties in writing about how to serve a tennis ball) you could then retire in possession of the truth—that was surely not the point. The point was rather to make your knowledge the occasion for a more subtle, effortful, and interesting use of words, a more artfully composed composition. Baird put it neatly in a communication to Varnum: "The problem is, when you face a class of freshmen, you find they are not used to playing with language. They don't have that sense of play. I would say the purpose of course was to make their lives richer."

From the beginning, Baird attempted to put together a teaching staff that wasn't exclusively "English." The classicist Wendell Clausen once taught the course, as did a physicist, an economist, a historian, a mathematician—perhaps there were others. Thus the "general education" component of the whole enterprise was confirmed. Upwards of fifty different people taught in English 1-2 until its conclusion: aside from Craig, a regular participant (Brower occupied himself with the sophomore course in close reading), there were, preeminently, Walker Gibson, Benjamin DeMott, John F. Butler, Roger Sale, and William E. Coles Jr. (Gibson, Butler, and Coles, subsequent to their term at Amherst, taught composition courses indebted to English 1 at other institutions, as did Jonathan Bishop and Thomas R. Edwards.) But the predominant pattern until the 1960s was for an instructor in English to teach the course for three years—perhaps two sections each term—then move on someplace else. When the pattern changed and more people got tenure, it was difficult to maintain a staff: people wanted to teach their own courses, as why should they not? As Baird moved toward retirement and the college faculty voted to replace the New Curriculum with a watered-down substitute that included required courses neither in English nor in Math-Science, things fell apart—or rather were held together only through the tenacity and stubbornness of Baird's will and commitment. Varnum tells this story well. But rather than dwell on it here, and without forgetting that the staff course was a cooperative enterprise to which numbers of resourceful teachers contributed, I want, by looking a little further at the character of Theodore Baird as it emerges in Varnum's book, to suggest why he *was* English 1 and how, without his intensely individual perspective on life and writing, the course couldn't exist. I'm convinced also that attempts by Varnum, and others quoted in her book, to "contextualize" and understand it as a moment in American education necessarily fall short of a more interesting truth.

In a revealing appendix, Varnum prints an exchange of letters she had six years ago with Baird, who proposed that rather than him telling her more things about the course, she should do an assignment, one involving the Emily Dickinson house in Amherst. Varnum was directed to go look at it, say what she "saw" and then define "looking at a poet's residence." A week later she sent Baird a paper in which she carefully described the house from the outside, also from the inside (a guide showed her around), and concluded with the assertion that "A house . . . can be read much as one reads a poem—as holding secrets of a human heart." To do this, she suggested, something like "empathy" was necessary. Baird responded a few days later, in a letter that Varnum admits disturbed her very much. He first apologized for the phrasing of the assignment and said that, in a class, he would have talked a bit about "seeing." He said her paper was excellent, A+, "very nicely-written, well-organized," and that no one could teach her anything about "this kind of writing." On the other hand, he continued, it was "entirely unsatisfactory." By way of explaining why, he described a visit he had made to his brother-in-law's factory that made X-ray tubes. After touring this operation, Baird said he could have written some "good English" about the factory, even used words like electron, anode, and cathode, but that, nevertheless, he wouldn't have had the faintest idea how the whole thing went together, how it worked. He continued: "I can write and write well about something I know nothing about. In other words the person who saw this building and the things in it on one floor after another did not know what he was looking at or did not know how to see what was there to be seen."

■ ■ ▨ ▧

As a *writer* in that situation, Baird said, he was "just a brother-in-law, ignorant. I would say to him, 'A temple of marvels,' as far as I could go in imagining and expressing that imagining."

Then he turned to Varnum's response to the assignment:

> The Emily Dickinson house as you write about it is a museum.
> Define museum. Here is a cradle, E.D. may have slept in it.
> Here is a table E.D. may have written poems on it. Poems? Was
> she a poet? Where as you look at these objects do you see poetry?
> How do you get from the doorway, a certain style, to a poem?
> What do you *SEE?* You use the word *empathy,* as if that could,
> that word, possibly lead you to the poet.

And he wound up: "The plain fact is the person who looks at a poet's residence is really not able to express much of what he feels. That was (as I see it) the point of the assignment. And the point of many assignments we made, to bring the writer to an awareness of the inexpressible." "Inexpressible" not in the sense of some realm (like Herbert Spencer's "Unknowable") that language can never touch, but rather what words and sentences, however impressive they sound in a particular situation, fail to convey about that situation. If this emphasis encouraged students to be wary about what language could and couldn't do, it also encouraged a more open and imaginative response to the whole matter of expression. In his letter to Varnum, Baird partially recalled a sentence of Frost's: "It has always been a matter of wonder to me that Emily Dickinson—what? lived and wrote poems in Amherst? It is this wonder, the marvel of it that she did, I see when I look if I think at all about it in passing the house. Just as I called the factory a temple of wonders. This is my response to what I do not understand." Varnum tried to roll with the punch, admitting to herself that she didn't know what she meant by "empathy" and that Baird's challenge had made her "reexamine [her] responsibility as a language user and historian." Yet by the end of the paragraph she is also registering her distaste for the way the English staff "undertook to disorient students or trip them up. I would have to confess I was both repelled and attracted by the authoritarian nature of the course." She quotes another remark of Baird's to her about how there is "nothing more interesting for a teacher than making it possible—by setting a trap—for a student to talk himself into something he had not been taught, had not known, could now make an English sentence about." This notion, she says, bothered her: and well it might have, since she had fallen into a trap and failed to write the English sentences that would take her out of it.

In other words, and this is a comment on the overall thrust of her book, Varnum's liberal, enlightened, democratic sensibility really can't take in the mind of a teacher who played the game a very different way and who was, in the words of one of his students quoted here, "a tough guy . . . lively sense of curiosity . . . a very, very interesting man." To her credit, Varnum had enough sense of how "interesting" Baird and his course were to persist in writing her book; but she also feels compelled to draw back at certain points, as if to assure us, and herself, that it's not enough just to be "very interesting." To give herself intellectual support, she brings in the testimony of a member of the college's sociology department who came to

Amherst in 1969, after the composition course was history. In the sociologist's hands, the course is seen not only as authoritarian but as exemplifying
"the locker room mentality or . . . the drill instructor mentality." It is but
a step from saying, as many have, that English 1-2 was *like* "boot camp" to
the claim that it was *in fact* boot camp—a classic instance of not knowing
when you've taken the metaphor too far. Varnum's own nods at sociological contextualization of the course seem to me pious and unconvincing, as
when, speaking of the high standards enforced in English 1, she attributes
it in part to "Cold War militance." This seems to me a dreary and vaporous
way to think about a very "interesting" operation, one similar to taking the
demanding and often frustrating challenge of the course, day by day, and
flattening it out, as does the sociologist, into "terrorizing students." After
all, there are degrees of Terror: English 1 was not run by Marat, Danton,
and Robespierre.

Perhaps it is a question of how much we take it upon ourselves to understand the past and pronounce on its limitations. Varnum has trouble, in
her closing pages especially, when she attempts to say that English 1-2 was
an exciting course . . . but. She begins a paragraph with "It would be too
easy to dismiss English 1-2 as a course designed by white males for white
males." Indeed it would: why lead with that card? She goes on in similar
concessive fashion to say, and rather primly, that "by today's standards"
(What are they? Are they any good?) there were "distasteful" aspects of
the course: it was elitist, authoritarian, and mystified many students. Yet
"despite all this," the course was one in which "teachers and students seem
often to have engaged in real conversation," one that enabled students "to
claim authority over language and their lives." So, current teachers of composition "could learn much that would be of value" from it.

What this cautious balancing leaves out is nothing less than Theodore
Baird, the man who concluded his cover letter to a set of assignments he
handed out to the staff in the summer of 1960 by quoting Thoreau: "Give
me a sentence which no intelligence can understand. . . . There must be
a kind of life and palpitation to it, and under its words a kind of blood
must circulate forever." "These strange words," Baird said, opened up the
possibilities for a writer "in a way that Unity, Coherence, and Emphasis
can never do," by allowing writing to be seen as "somehow the expression
of the imagination, and imagination itself may be mysterious and wild."
Try as she does, Varnum can't rise to the mystery, the passion, the wildness, the mischief and playfulness, that was Baird's and often the course's

trademark. Looking back on his retirement in 1970, he noted, "I always said I could hear the community sigh in relief." As for the burden of the course, "Nobody wants to do the kind of heavy work that we did at reading papers. The minute I got through they dropped it." English 1-2 exists now in the minds of those people who taught it, or tried to; but also in the minds of a great many students who took it. As college alumni, they gather at reunion weekend, in one symposium or another, to talk and argue about the past, particularly this strange, unforgettable composition course. Are they prey to nostalgia merely? When Baird said, echoing Henry Adams, "Education doesn't work," he meant something more interesting than "Education always fails." In remembering English 1-2, students may be remembering perhaps the only intellectual demand ever made on them that they could not meet. Knowing that they couldn't meet it, and still can't, may well be a sign, ironically, of educational success. At any rate, for some of those students, it seems, there was really nothing quite like it before or since, and who is to say they are deceived?

—*Raritan*, Winter 1997.

To the Students

Week 1, Dryden

Dear Class,

Just received word from the Prez that, due to the presence of Covid-19, the campus is going to be off limits beginning this coming week. I'm depending on Bette Kanner to forward my words to you. I'll do this each Friday, describing the following week's material and commenting critically on it. Dryden seems a weird place to begin, since he seems remote (joke) even more than some. But I remember the day after 9/11, I was teaching Ben Jonson's *Volpone* and glad to have something utterly unrelated to what had gone on. So here goes.

Samuel Johnson said that Dryden was "not one of the Gentle Bosoms." The English novelist Kingsley Amis used to exchange letters with his friend the poet Philip Larkin badmouthing the English poets they were studying at Oxford. In one of them Amis says that he can see why people might admire horrible poets like Chaucer, Pope, Wordsworth, Keats, "even Milton." But he cannot see how anyone could admire Dryden: "A second-rate fucking journalist," said Amis. Toward the end of his life Dryden wrote to a young lady and described himself as "still drudging on, always a Poet and never a good one." I, of course, disagree, and we will look briefly at a few examples of his being a poet and being a good one.

So far we've emphasized his astonishing variety but looked briefly at only two examples: the satirist and the elegist. "MacFlecknoe" we called mock-heroic in that the large, elaborate, "heroic" comparisons of a character are replaced by ones that deflate even as they seem to enhance: "Shadwell alone of all my sons is he, / Who stands confirmed in full stupidity." The critic George Saintsbury called it "attacking from above" rather than from below as (we'll see) Pope did. In "Absalom and Achitophel" the mode is generally higher, the heroic comparisons from Latin writing elevating the subject. Read aloud the first thirty lines and see what you hear and see.

And then (the poem is in your Dryden selections, without line numbers), the first twenty-five lines or so about the character of Achitophel. Here Dryden really gets interested in his subject, wonders how and why such a man behaved as he behaved. The "satire" deepens.

In both these poems the sentences state precisely and don't encourage "suggestive" possibilities. Something similar goes on in "To the Memory of Mr Oldham" (also in your selections) where the beauty lies in the exact delineation of what's to be said about the dead poet Oldham (another satirist). Read aloud and think about (listen to) how you want to say the final line: "But fate and gloomy night encompass thee around." This is Dryden the elegist and this genre is continuous with other epistles to this or that man or woman or institution. Johnson said Dryden found it difficult to "exhibit the genuine operations of the heart." I think he exhibits them in the Oldham elegy, beautifully.

Then there is Dryden the translator, of Greek poets, Latin ones, and Chaucer (he sort of attempted to make Chaucer up-to-date in 17th-century language). Our single example is from Lucretius, "On the Nature of Things," where Lucretius considers the subject of the fear of death (example 5 in the handout). Dryden finds it very congenial to argue in verse the way Lucretius argues that the fear of death is not to be feared. Read the lines aloud and see if you can follow the argument and why it is satisfying to follow it. In "Religio Laici" and "The Hind and the Panther," Dryden in his own voice (or an imagined character) performs this argumentative task.

Dryden spoke wryly of what he called "this disease of translation." He had it, all right, and the Lucretius is but one of many that he will not give up. He is eloquent about the character of this poet-philosopher Lucretius, speaks of him as "beforehand with his antagonists, urging for them whatever he imagined they could say." (You should catch this quality in your reading aloud.) He spoke also of "a certain kind of noble pride and positive assertion of his opinions . . . everywhere conscious of his own reason." It fits Lucretius but it also fits Dryden, or one of the many Drydens. A good phrase he uses to characterize Lucretius' manner is "a perpetual dictatorship exercised." He also, speaking of Lucretius but also of the general situation of a translator, says he will avoid both paraphrase and metaphrase; paraphrase in which you are content with a wide approximation of how the poet speaks and means; metaphrase in which each word has a necessary equivalent in English. Dryden's aim, a good one, is to render the translated writer as if he were speaking to a contemporary audience. The important thing is to convince us that this is Lucretius speaking. Enough of me on translation, there are better guides than what can be furnished by my monolingual limitations. But let me mention a great modern poem on the fear of death: Philip Larkin's "Aubade," one of the truly wonderful poems of the last century.

There is a relation between the translator speaking in the downright Lucretian manner and the Dryden who addresses us in the countless prologues and epilogues he wrote for his nearly thirty plays. One example is (example 4) the Prologue to *Aurang Zebe*, one of the more readable of his "heroic" plays (subject of which is always the conflict between love and honor in the hero's mind). Read aloud the first eight lines and see why "downright" is a reasonable word for the manner of address: [the author] "Out of no feigned modesty, this day/Damns his laborious trifle of a play." Before the audience has a chance to make up its mind, you tell them how insignificant your play is. (Of course that might have the effect of allowing the reader to say, well, it's not all THAT bad.) He goes on to complain about "his long-loved mistress, Rhyme" (the play like previous ones is in rhymed verse) and invokes Shakespeare's name as a felt reproach to Dryden's play. After all, Shakespeare is the poet of "Nature" and Nature, Dryden tells us, flies away when you try to express it in rhyme. He also does here what he does elsewhere: looks back at a previous age (the earlier 17th century, the Jacobean dramatists) and finds it, though "less polished, more unskilled," superior to his own productions. Overall I think you can feel and hear the limber liveliness of these couplets. This constant practice helped him immeasurably in his role-to-be of arguer in verse, full of assertions. Mark van Doren, who wrote the best book on Dryden, called him, among other things, "a versifier of propositions" with his "brains in his fingers." So although the plays he wrote are dead as doornails (how dead is that?), the prologues and epilogues are alive with aggressive speech. Of course hardly anybody makes the effort to notice them, and your instructor has read only a relatively small number of them.

Decades after Dryden wrote his prologue to *Aurang Zebe*, he wrote what is my favorite personal epistle, "To My Dear Friend Mr Congreve on his Comedy called 'The Double Dealer'" (example 6 in the handout). Congreve was an up-and-coming young man who had already written one play that was well received (his fourth and last play—a masterpiece, "The Way of the World"—was ahead of him). In this poem to Congreve, Dryden mellows, introduces into things a more rueful, personal note that seems to me beautiful. It opens with reflections about drama in the present age compared to the one just past (the Jacobeans, Shakespeare etc.): "Our age was cultivated thus at length; / But what we gained in skill we lost in strength." Until Congreve came along and exceeded everybody past and present. The praise is absurdly overdone, but beginning with line 41 the personal note is heard: the aged Dryden (he is sixty-two, I believe) passing along the torch to the young aspirant who can be compared to Shakespeare: "Heaven, that but once was prodigal before, / To Shakespeare gave as much, he could not give him more" (63-64) the last line with an extra foot ("alexandrine" they call it) just to emphasize the prodigality. Read aloud the final fourteen lines, noting that poignant "Oh." This poem especially in parts seems to me the perfection of the personal address in poetry. (Maybe I'm overrating it, but what the hell.)

The poem was written in 1694, six years before Dryden's death and the end of the century. One of his last poems is example 8, "An Ode on the Death of Mr. Henry Purcell." An example of Dryden's complicated lyric ability, felt, if you read it aloud (perhaps). It's an overlooked poem, but not by me who is an admirer of the composer, Henry Purcell, one of the very few "great" English composers, Handel being an important other. If you have the chance try to get hold of Purcell's opera, *Dido and Aeneas*, the part of Dido sung by the supremely great soprano, Kirsten Flagstad. Her "When I Am Laid in Earth" the saddest heartbreaker of all arias.

Dryden's final work, a remarkable one indeed, is titled *Fables, Ancient and Modern*. The volume includes a number of longish poems, from Ovid, Bocaccio, Chaucer, the first book of Homer's *Iliad*, and more verse epistles. No need to ask what does or doesn't constitute a Fable. I should have provided a longer excerpt (in #7) from the long allegorical poem "The Hind and the Panther," from which the few lines on the right side of the page are taken. They occur in a sequence from the poem called "Fable of the Swallows," about how a group of religious birds perished unfortunately of the cold. (Incompetent of me not to have done more by way of illustration.) Anyway perhaps the loveliest thing about the late Fables volume is its preface, the first paragraph (example 9) and the beginning explanation of what he's about in the volume. Later he gets very personal, speaking of himself (at almost seventy) as "a cripple in my limbs, but what decays are in my mind the reader must determine." And then, declaring himself "as vigorous as ever in the faculties of soul," he finds no reason to complain:

"What judgment I had increases rather than diminishes; and thoughts, such as they are, come crowding in so fast upon me that my only difficulty is to choose or to reject, to run them into verse or to give them the other harmony of prose." Such as they are: do you remember that line from the Ben Jonson poem "To the World" in which the speaker vows to "make my thoughts, Such as they are / Here in my bosom and at home." Dryden is the legitimate heir of Ben Jonson, never more so than in the preface to these late Fables.

So then I shall imitate his words at the beginning of the poem to Congreve: "Well then, the promised hour is come at last." This is my brief inadequate attempt to introduce you to this great, pretty much unread writer, always "another and the same" as Samuel Johnson speaks of his works. At the end of those few pages from his *Life of Dryden* (in your Johnson book 717-724), Johnson declares, "What was said of Rome, adorned by Augustus may be applied by an easy metaphor to English poetry embellished by Dryden . . . he found it brick and he left it marble." (And I've left out the Latin words.) Now we will proceed to Pope, the shining example of what used to be called, in academic circles, The Augustan Age.

Thus my suggestions for reading Dryden, week of March 23. For Pope beginning week of March 30 : In Oxford World Classics: "An Essay on Criticism"; "Windsor Forest"; "The Rape of the Lock"; "Epistle to Miss Blount . . ."; "Elegy to the Memory of an Unfortunate Lady."

Five poems, "Rape of the Lock" by far the most important and attractive. I will be supplying commentary as I have for Dryden. I would welcome any feedback from any of you about whether you find my commentary useful in your reading/study of the poems. Suggestions welcome. Direct all questions, as well as papers you haven't handed in, to my e-mail, not the English Department's. For those of you who don't have enough to read, you could get started at any time on *Gulliver's Travels*. The Oxford edition has excellent intro and really informative notes, worth taking a look at.

In conclusion, these commentaries resemble the notes I make before a lecture, not designed for immediate publication in periodicals I write for. Just to cover my tracks when you discover an ineptitude or two.

Best wishes in dealing with this enforced "Break." —WHP

Week 2, Pope (1)

I PROPOSE DOING with Pope more or less what I did with Dryden, except here you will have read whole poems, longer poems, with the benefit of pertinent if brief notes in the back of Oxford. I was fortunate in my introduction to Pope. First because it happened toward the end of a great Pope Revival, with the magnificent Twickenam edition of his work. The center of the Pope industry was Yale, with four or five really sharp scholar-critics making him their central focus. One of them, Maynard Mack, would eventually write a mammoth biography of the poet. But there was no danger of approaching him as a remote poet since he seemed to be at the center of the lit crit world. As for the heroic couplet (I learned early to call rhymed pentameter by that name), I had always been partial to rhyme and my only poem I wrote in high school announced that since I was "old fashioned," I liked a poem to rhyme. In Nicholson Baker's terrific novel *The Anthologist,* about poetry, the young Baker remembers being told by a secondary school teacher that they were to write a poem, and it didn't need to rhyme. Baker rightly interpreted that to mean DON'T RHYME, WRITE FREE VERSE. And of course most of what passes for poems nowadays follows that injunction (not to their benefit, often). But the heroic couplet employed as Pope and Dryden steadily employed it offended the senses of serious critics well into the beginning of the last century. Matthew Arnold (in 1871 or so) when he came to those two poets in his great essay "The Study of Poetry" pulled himself up straight and announced that, yes, they were "classic" poets like Chaucer, and Donne and Milton, but that they were "classics of our prose." Real "Poetry" had to be in blank verse or quatrains or the Byronic ottava rima, not in pentameter couplets. In other words, rhyme was OK here and there as long as it didn't assume this used-up form that Dryden and Pope (and Samuel Johnson) had used up.

By the time I came along Arnold was old hat and I was encouraged to accept and admire the heroic couplet as much as any other verse form. And I was lucky enough to study these poets (the heroic coupleteers) under Reuben Brower, who taught Classics and English at Amherst, then at Harvard, and who would eventually write a distinguished book on Pope and heroic tradition (Greek and Latin authors). Brower had opened things up for me (I think I told you this) by reading aloud Dryden's poem about Mr. Oldham. It was natural and easy to go on from there. I took Brower's seminar in Pope at Harvard and by that time I was hooked, getting as much or more pleasure from Pope as from any other English poet.

Pardon this intrusive attempt to tell you where I was/am coming from. I can't say that my excitement about reading Pope has dimmed over the decades, but it's hard to summon up the feeling of freshness that at one point I had. And in the meantime I was learning about and admiring Dryden more and more, even to the point where, like Dr. Johnson, I confessed preferring him to Pope. But that's silly: no need to rank great writers.

To get down to business: we have two weeks and maybe a day or so more to "do" Pope. For the first week I suggest we take as our subjects The Early Pope: "An Essay on Criticism," "Windsor Forest" and "The Rape of the Lock," that last poem a supreme one. I will do no more than point to some places in these poems where I find something especially interesting or memorable going on, and I shall try to show a little bit how Pope makes this happen.

First, and it was Pope's first poem, along with the *Pastorals*, "An Essay on Criticism." There he is, all of twenty-one years old, can't go to Oxford or Cambridge because his family is Roman Catholic; so reads everything, an education by "remote," we might say. As for his health, he is suffering from a complaint not then diagnosed, tuberculosis of the bone. This means, among other things, that he's physically compromised, bent over, will need increasingly to be more or less strapped into clothes. His enemies would triumphantly refer to him as a "hunchback." A recent poet has written of him—alluding to Samuel Johnson's description of him—as "protuberant, behind, before." Vivid, eh? He will later refer in a poem to "this long disease my life." "The Essay on Criticism" employs all the stuff he'd taken in from reading poets and critics, from Homer to Horace and up into contemporary French ones. The best description overall of the writer of the criticism "essay" is Brower's: "a terribly bright young man who has acquired all the right ideas." It's notable that the poem never employs the first person "I," as if there's nothing tentative about the opinions our poet puts forth.

Read the first two parts of the three-part poem, up to line 560. In part one we get handed various truths: that "true taste" is what the critic should aspire to (line 12); that the most important thing is to "follow Nature"(68), "One clear, unchanged, and universal light" (light imagery all over the place); and that you go about following Nature by following the "Rules" (88), "Those RULES of old, discovered, not devised / Are Nature still, but nature methodized." Spend the greater part of your time reading/studying Homer and Virgil (118-129). But don't be pedantic about it; like music, poetry has "nameless graces which no method teach" and it's OK if, genius that you are, you "deviate from the common track" in order to "snatch a grace beyond the reach of art"(155). A fine joke I remember from graduate school talking with a friend: he suggested that the line had to do with a contest between the speaker, enamored of a woman named Grace, and a rival suitor named Art. Thus the speaker's plan "to snatch at Grace beyond the reach of Art." Poor Art. In line 182 to bottom of page and end of Part 1 we have the fervent hymn to the "bards triumphant" who now live in memory. What's notable here is that moments of positive, nay glowing affirmation, will turn in the later Pope to equally fervent but satiric presentations of various examples of bad taste, morals, etc. When the satiric Pope exclaims, it will most often be done ironically. Another way of putting it is to say that, increasingly in his work, the "official," positive, affirmative praise of contemporary England, for which the term "Augustan" has been used, is opposed or undermined by an unofficial voice of disbelief, opposition, satire. We will come to think of this voice as the "real" Pope.

For me the liveliest part of "An Essay on Criticism" is the second one from lines 200 (or so) on for a couple hundred more. In this section Pope devotes his energies not to praising in noble terms how wonderfully the Ancients have done this or that, but in imitating some contemporary examples of how NOT to do it. Maxims handed out emphasize this as in line 215: "A *little learning* is a dangerous thing; Drink deep (etc.)." The line is sometimes quoted with the accent on "learning," as if it were "learning," not "a *little* learning," that's dangerous. This line is one of many in the Essay that have gone into the language as impeccable sentiments, "Fools rush in where angels fear to tread" and many others. My high school yearbook has pictures of us graduating Seniors with a caption underneath, supposedly befitting the person pictured. A favorite one (found in Pope's

"Essay on Man") was "'Tis education forms the common mind; / Just as the twig's bent the tree's inclined" (roughly quoted from memory) as if the guy or girl graduating was an embodiment of such sentiment! Very corny, but it suggests Pope's amazing propensity for making striking couplets and lines that invite themselves to be written on the wall, as it were.

The hundred or so lines beginning "Some to *conceit* alone their taste confine" (l. 289) contain amusing examples of how not to do it in the writing of verse. Pope believes that "the sound must seem an echo of the sense," and he likes to echo different kinds of nonsense. The twenty lines following line 337 contain, for example, a line full of "open vowels" to an absurd length: "Though oft the ear the open vowels tire" or the use of "expletives" (look it up, class) as in "While expletives their feeble aid do join" (that "do" an expletive), or contempt for the monosyllabic as in "And ten low words oft creep in one dull line." Great going! never mind that Shakespeare's plays are full of wonderful monosyllabic lines. Then with line 350 a mockery of boring pastoral poetry (trees and breeze etc.), sounding not so much different from some of the lines in the *Pastorals* Pope wrote as a sixteen-year-old or so. My favorite example of badness is in 356-7: "A needless Alexandrine ends the song / That, like a wounded snake, drags its slow length along."(Alexandrine: an extra foot added to the pentameter, plenty of them in Dryden!) I love how slowly that wounded snake drags itself. So this "negative" section is the liveliest part of the whole poem.

Finally, another example of an "unofficial" attitude rearing its head to contradict the official meaning. After all the praise in different forms of "wit" ("True wit is nature to advantage dressed; / What oft is thought but ne'er so well expressed"), we get a meditation beginning around l. 495 in which the disappointments and vanities of being a witty writer are suggested and lamented ("Unhappy wit . . ." etc.). Another example of how (in hindsight) we can see the young Pope looking ahead to predict how things may not always go smoothly, just as we can't even trust the language to stay firm: "Our sons their father's failing language see; / And such as Chaucer is shall Dryden be." Chaucer already obsolete, Pope thought, and Dryden and maybe Pope himself will suffer a similar fate.

I won't say much about nor ask you to look hard at "Windsor Forest," another early Pope in which his ambitious claims for England and for poetry reach their height. At one point near the poem's end he addresses "my humble muse," but humility is not the main quality one encounters in W.F. Remember he's in his early twenties, convinced, so an older mentor told him that though there have been great poets before him, none has been "correct," and he is in position to be the first of such "correct" poets. Impossible to define the word, but it's an all-purpose way of indicating smoothness and decorum and equableness, all within the heroic couplet. Read the first forty or so lines down to the complacent "And peace and plenty tell a Stuart reigns." How fortunate! The war is over, Treaty of Utrecht signed, and things will only get better. Maybe the best or at least most revealing part of the poem are its opening lines about the vanished "groves of Eden" and how Windsor Forest is replacing them as sung by the young Pope. Particularly notable lines are the ones about how this little world is "harmoniously confused"—"Where order in variety we see / And where, though all things differ, all agree." Soon after I came to teach at Amherst I was asked to supply some sort of verse message to decorate the Christmas card (or maybe it was New Year's) the college sent out to its graduates and current members. I pretended, or maybe convinced myself, that Amherst College was such a favored place, that what we now call "diversity" lived side by side with steady purpose. "Order in variety"? Here was this college of white, male, often privileged students and Pritchard quoting Pope about "variety"! Well, I didn't do permanent harm, but it shows how seductive I found Pope's vision of The Good Place. It's instructive to remember that only forty or so years earlier Milton had published *Paradise Lost*. What a distance is that poem from "The groves of Eden, vanished ere so long" in Pope's rendering.

There is a lot of English history in the poem, hard for us to care about. More appealing are the vignettes about field sports, hunting and fishing, the beautiful death of the "whirring pheasant" in line III or the "mounting larks" as, being killed, "They fall and leave their little lives in air." Ben Jonson's "To Penshurst" is somewhere behind this. But Pope here and elsewhere has a pervasive strain of melancholy as he contemplates the facts of change, time, death as they bear on the little flying things and on things more generally. This melancholy will get into "The Rape of the Lock" in interesting ways. But important to see how that strain contrasts with the "positive," nay boasting tone of the last swatch of a hundred or so lines beginning "Hail sacred peace, hail long-expected days," in which the poet imagines the unbounded Thames river flowing for all mankind, and London visited by "feathered people" (those romantic native Americans!), who muse at how quaintly the Brits are dressed. At the very end of Pope's career he will publish the fourth and final book of his long poem, *The Dunciad*, about the triumph of dullness and extirpation of civilization's light. Nothing could be further from the puffery that ends "Windsor Forest," but both endings are couched in heroic/mock heroic strains.

Now, "The Rape of the Lock" and conclusion of Pope's early career. How can I rise to the challenge of this brilliant piece of writing? It's a poem universally admired, at least I don't know any critic who has disparaged it (maybe some humorless feminists). Samuel Johnson didn't find it said very much about anything but called it "an exquisite example of the ludicrous." "Ludicrous" is the right word for this supremely playful poem. What's difficult is to find words for this exquisiteness without clodhopping all over the couplets. Reading aloud is usually my way out of that.

It was first published in an abbreviated two-book form sans sylphs (the "machinery"), game of Ombre, descent to Cave of Spleen (fourth canto) and the "moral" which Clarissa is given near the end of the poem. In other words, without much of its best stuff. In his introductory letter to Arabella Fermor, Pope says all the incidents in the poem are "fabulous," from the opening dream to the final transformation. Fair enough, and for me that mutes or transforms radically the "social" aspect of the poem, which some would think of as a criticism of contemporary high life. I don't find that persuasive, because of how the fabulous atmosphere turns everything into, well, poetry. Someone once said of Pope that his criticism of life was "simply and solely the heroic couplet." Sounds too simple but maybe not.

Of course we are instructed (by our critics and teachers) to admire the mock-heroic mode, as in the scene that ends part one with Belinda at her dressing table (parody of Juno arming for battle). Fair enough, but hard to keep on admiring the mode once you become aware of how it works ("Puffs, powders, patches, bibles, billet-doux" instead of accoutrements of war). Seems to me that rather than mocking Belinda as inadequate recipient of the heroic mode, Pope manages to make her rather wonderful:

The fair each moment rises in her charms
Repairs her smiles, awakens ev'ry grace
And calls forth all the wonders of her face (140-142).

"Belinda smiled, and all the world was gay": that puts it all in a line. The first 18 lines of Canto 2, beginning the voyage down the Thames, are worth reading aloud as example of the teasing but affectionate play in which she is held by our poet. Some of the most exquisite writing is stimulated by the sylphs, as in the end of Canto 2, 123-136: "Gums and pomatums shall his flight restrain / While clogged he beats his silken wings in vain." I will forever associate that couplet with a moment when, at the President's Garden Party at Commencement time, my aunt remarked about how many people there were in the yard and how could they smoothly get out. A great professor of classics, John Moore, who had a slightly pixieish manner, broke in to declare that there was a trap door which opened from time to time, letting visitors out; although sometimes it got clogged with a macaroon— that sort of thing. Naturally my aunt was speechless. But it's this kind of serious imaginative frivolity that Pope is a master of. Sometimes in a single line: "Or, as Ixion fixed, the wretch shall feel / The giddy motion of the whirling mill." Imagine the play of sound in "as Ixion fixed" and remember the rule from "Essay on Criticism" that "The sound must seem an echo of the sense." I especially like the writing about the sylphs in this poem, can't imagine it without them.

Canto 3 contains the game of Ombre, and here I am a bad guide since I never learned the rules (there have been learned articles on how the game is played, and I didn't read them). So on to Canto 4 and the descent to gnomeland and the Cave of Spleen. Here the good-natured comedy turns a bit dark and Pope for the first time in his works exploits something like the grotesque mode, "Pale spectres, gaping tomb and purple fires," tea pots and goose pies transformed by Spleen into something unpleasant. Pope will return to this mode in his late poem, *The Dunciad;* here we're not exactly horrified, but unsettled rather.

The dramatic climax of the poem is in Cantos 4 and 5 when Belinda laments her sad lot while being reproved by Thalestris for having lost her honor. Belinda, in a rather silly manner, wishes she could have been born in some distant Northern land where existed none of the social, glittering pleasures that have betrayed her. At this point Clarissa takes over the poem and in lines 9-34, Canto 5, gives an eloquent plea in favor of good sense, "since alas frail beauty must decay" and "curled or uncurled, locks will turn to grey" and after all you wouldn't want to die a maid, all forlorn. This we learn from the note is a parody of Sarpedon's speech to Glaucus in the *Iliad.* Pope tells us in a footnote (his own) about this parody. It's important that we don't dismiss (as we may do these days) parody as simply travesty, not to be taken seriously. Serious parody is central to more than one passage in the poem, and even without the heroic allusion Clarissa's speech exhibits worldly good sense. But it's not enough to calm the participants who want and get war. It's not that easy for good sense to control and dismiss the extraordinary happenings we've seen occur in "The Rape of the Lock." Only Pope and the Muse can do that by the closing account of what miraculous thing happens to the lock. I think lines 141 to 150 are quite moving in their summary way, "When those fair suns shall set, as set they must / And all those tresses shall be laid in dust." Seems to me a great ending to this great poem—what do you think?

DEAR CLASS: Here is the reading assignment for the week of April 6. I don't think it's necessary that I break it down in MWF segments.
    "An Epistle to Richard Boyle, Earl of Burlington" (67)
    "Epistle to a Lady" (106)
    "First Satire of the Second Book of Horace" (88)
    "Epistle to Dr Arbuthnot" (93)
    "Epilogue to the Satires, Dialogue One and Two" (114-120)

    For Monday, April 13, *The Dunciad*

I hope you are receiving these notes successfully (haven't yet heard anything from you one way or the other, so I'll assume the best.) Keep up the good work—WHP

Week 3, Pope (2)

D EAR CLASS,
This week is devoted to Pope's epistles and satires, some of them. But first a word about his famous, once notorious long poem, *An Essay on Man*. He came to write this after he had fully established himself as a professional literary person. First came his collected poems (1717), then his translation of the *Iliad* (which set him up comfortably financially, no need of patrons after that), then his edition of Shakespeare, which got attacked for not being scholarly enough, then—with some help from others—a translation of Homer's *Odyssey*. Meanwhile he was consorting with Swift and a couple of other close friends, forming what was called the Scriblerus Club devoted to parodying and mocking contemporaries they didn't admire. He put these contemporaries into a first version of *The Dunciad*, his three-book poem in praise of dullness, pretending to salute it, while mocking fellow poets who were very dull indeed.

Then around 1730, having gotten many things out of the way, he embarked on what would be a four-part poem and a number of ancillary epistles and satires. An unbelievably fertile period, the 1730s. Your Oxford selection omits the *Essay on Man* entirely, as if to suggest it's not as good or important as the accompanying satires and epistles. That may be, and Pope apologizes in a preface for its relative "dryness" compared to the more poetical vividness of satiric portraits. But since, he says, "the science of human nature can be reduced to a few clear points," he will take it upon himself to expound them. This exposition has not worn well, then or now, and Voltaire mocked him for declaring: "Whatever is, is right." In fact at its best the *Essay* is more interesting and complicated than he sometimes makes it sound. I am printing here the opening lines of the second book, maybe the most vivid ones in the whole poem, where he gives us the human situation in brief:

Know then thyself, presume not God to scan;
The proper study of Mankind is Man.
Plac'd on this isthmus of a middle state,
A being darkly wise, and rudely great:
With too much knowledge for the Sceptic side,
With too much weakness for the Stoic's pride,
He hangs between; in doubt to act, or rest,
In doubt to deem himself a God or Beast;
In doubt his Mind or Body to prefer,
Born but to die, and reas'ning but to err;
Alike in ignorance, his reason such,
Whether he thinks too little, or too much:
Chaos of Thought and Passion, all confus'd;
Still by himself abus'd or disabus'd;
Created half to rise, and half to fall;
Great lord of all things, yet a prey to all;
Sole judge of Truth, in endless Error hurl'd:
The glory, jest, and riddle of the world!

Read it aloud and see if you don't think this is pretty fine. ("If this be not poetry, I know not where it can be found," and I quote Samuel Johnson.)

Of course Pope has *Paradise Lost* in mind, but an even more interesting allusion may be to Hamlet's great speech to Rosencrantz and Guildenstern about what a piece of work is man, etc. etc. A line like "Born but to die, and reas'ning but to err" touches the heart. And that final line, Man as "glory, jest and riddle," is about as much as there is to say about The Human Condition. The liveliest parts of the *Essay* are those in which man is treated not just as glory or jest, but as riddle. (Remember Dryden's question about why Achitophel would "punish a body that he could not please.") The best thing said about the *Essay* was by Samuel Johnson (it's in your selection from the life of Pope in your Johnson text): "This Essay affords an egregious instance of the predominance of genius, the dazzling splendour of imagery, and the seductive power of eloquence. Never were penury of knowledge and vulgarity of sentiment so happily disguised. The reader feels his mind full though he learns nothing. . . ." Johnson in the course of dispraising the poem begins to praise it! The "disguise" of poetry is that it makes your mind feel "full."

Your Oxford selection is only part of Pope's output in the 1730s, and I'm further cutting by not assigning all of it. It's divided into epistles and satires, but the division isn't absolute (the epistles contain satirical portraits, and there are epistolary sequences in the satires.) Pope conceived of a group of four poems titled "Epistles to Several Persons," the earliest of them, "To Burlington," eventually conceived as the climactic one of the four. It's notable for containing the first full-length portrait of a "character," Timon the prodigal aristocrat who is the living embodiment of bad taste—in architecture, landscape design, entertainment (food and drink), etc. But before he is introduced there are 100 or so lines staking out the aesthetic and moral issues to be considered (the Epistles were also known as Moral Essays for a time). I propose to slight these issues, some of which are pretty hard for us to care about. Reuben Brower, who wrote about the poem at length, was among other things a bit of a landscape gardener himself, and I also felt clumsy when confronted with his confident sentences about Roman art, 18th century architectural principles and suchlike. What came and comes alive for me is the brilliance of the Timon portrait: "Who but must laugh the master when he sees / A puny insect shivering at a breeze" (ll. 107-8). Read aloud the extended portrait from 99 through 168, first the misconceived grandeur of the place on the outside, then inside at the dinner table where "gaping Tritons spew to wash your face," and where what should be a "genial room" has been turned into a "temple, and a hecatomb." True religion is perverted and softened by the ecclesiastical inappropriate: "To rest the cushion and soft dean invite / Who never mentions hell to ears polite." That "soft dean" is masterly! Pope introduces himself at the end of the portrait ("I curse such lavish cost and little skill"), then proceeds with four lines that say, well this aristocrat keeps people employed and confers financial benefit to his servants. Then four more lines beginning at 173 and ending with a far-sighted prediction: "Deep harvests bury all his pride had planned / And laughing Ceres reassume the land." But this consolation, if that's what it is, finds little further employment in the epistles and satires. Again the doing of How Not To Do It, in Timon and his works, elicits Pope's most imaginative play.

The epistle I like best, and surely the most substantial one, is "To a Lady" also known as "The Characters of Women." I discovered it in grad school, memorized huge chunks of it and went around quoting it to a girl I had hopes for, but she didn't like the poem, which set me back a bit. It has provoked, as you can imagine, commentary by members of both sexes. The "lady" in question is Martha Blount, with whom Pope was very friendly. She comes into her own at the very end of the poem. But much of it is taken up, in no particular order, with various "follies" Pope attributes to the female persuasion. They range from harmless, even attractive, to deathly and desperate. (By the way, the notes at the bottom of the page for this and other poems are Pope's own.) The forming conceit of the poem is one of painting women in various aspects of behavior in order to show how "Ladies, like variegated tulips show; / Tis to their changes half their charms we owe." But many of the changes are disagreeable ones, at least to the sharp-eyed speaker. (Remember, Pope is four feet six, not liable to sweep any woman off her feet. His portraits are often not without petulance.) What keeps the poem moving and, for me, obviates any serious criticism of these women, is the heroic couplet (surprise!). "You purchase pain with all that joy can give / And die of nothing but a rage to live." Chloe is censured because she's heartless and Pope kills her with a great couplet: "Virtue she finds too painful an endeavor; / Content to dwell in decencies forever." At times things almost get out of control, as when he warms to the task of dissecting Atossa (passage beginning line 115, read aloud to end of the portrait). He manages to make me feel that his exclamation about her—"Strange! by the means defeated of the end"—is a real expression of wonder at how this could happen (again, as with Dryden asking about what makes Achitophel tick).

The poem is maybe crammed with too many instances of what looks like at times a put-up job. But when at last it settles into a concerted joint portrait of women (and remember, these are aristocrat ones, high life, as in "Rape of the Lock"), something very powerful and moving transpires. The extended sequence begins in line 219, "Yet mark the fate of a whole sex of queens! / Power all their end, but beauty all their means." It continues down through "Beauties, like tyrants, old and friendless grown / Yet hate repose and dread to be alone," and we begin to realize this state may cover states of life different from the whole "sex of queens" bunch. "See how the world its veterans rewards": if you look you may find many sorts of old people whose reward isn't what it might be or what they foolishly thought it would be. But even the luckless beauties grown old are transformed by Pope into something strangely beautiful:

> As hags hold sabbaths, less for joy than spite
> So these their merry miserable night ;

> Still round and round the ghosts of beauty glide
> And haunt the places where their honor died (139-142)

Their "merry, miserable night": isn't that scarily unforgettable? (Obviously I haven't forgotten it.)

The last forty or so lines gives us the Lady to be praised, full of charm, good humor, and a subtle power over her man ("And if she rules him never shows she rules") and sounding like someone who has heeded Clarissa's advice in the Lock poem. Sort of feels as if Pope doesn't want to end, or doesn't quite know how best to end—but surely the final compliment to her and to himself is perfect: "To you gave sense, good humour, and a poet." During resurgent feminist days in the 1970s or so, there was more than one article or argument about the poem. What are we to think about this picture of women as drawn by the male? I don't find such controversy very interesting because it's not "the male" but Alexander Pope who is writing rather than acting, if that's a fair distinction to make. For those who wish to investigate further there are some lively stories about his once admired then not admired Lady Mary Wortley Montague, no mean poet herself. She gave at least as good as she got. Anyway it doesn't take one far to talk about "satire" in this epistle; or at least should be admitted that any satire is pretty skin deep only and that the real imaginative energies of the poem lie elsewhere and in more "positive" directions, whether by way of deploring the "whole sex of queens" or rising warmly to give the Lady her final due.

Pope becomes more directly satirical in the imitation of Horace (pp. 88-92) where the poem's voice becomes more improvisatory and casual (such is the pretense) than in the past, even more so than the "moral" epistles he was writing currently. The poem—call it "To Mr Fortescue"—is significant in that for the first time Pope creates a second speaker who questions, agrees or disagrees with, the main one. So you get "F" and "P," "F" for friend of P. He is mainly a straight man, relatively innocent in worldly ways and worried that P will get himself in trouble by speaking ill of someone. His counsel throughout is moderation, exactly the quality which P is more and more calling into question. But part of P conceives himself as a moderate, not to be bound by any strict principle of what should or shouldn't be done and said. Thus lines 51-69 (read aloud) that end "In moderation placing all my glory / While Tories call me Whig and Whigs a Tory." It's as neat as that, except when it isn't, and by line 105 a different P emerges, exclaiming his commitment to virtue, hatred of vice: "What, armed for virtue when I point the pen / Brand the bold front of shameless, guilty men." No two ways about this as F becomes increasingly an excuse for P to proclaim his irrefutable position. This technique will reach its apex in "Epilogue to the Satires," assigned for next week.

The central satire, Pope at his greatest, is the "Epistle to Dr. Arbuthnot" (a physician-pal of Pope, Swift and John Gay). It's a poem cobbled together from different occasional parts, and it goes on for rather too long in the course of making memorable portraits of self and others, friends and enemies. The Arbuthnot epistle begins with the poet's self-portrait as now, a famous writer, besieged by various aspiring would-be poets he disdains: ("Poor Cornus sees his frantic wife elope / And curses wit, and poetry, and Pope"). Then we move into some autobiography as the poet asks (line 125) "Why did I write?" Could be a real question, or just an opportunity for more clearing of the decks. He couldn't help himself ("I lisped in numbers, for the numbers came") More and more in later Pope you'll find yourself besieged often by names of people you have no idea about except that they're virtuous or vicious. That's maybe enough. You plough through lines and sequences that you can barely follow in order to reach one of the three extended portraits in the poem, the first of which is the portrait of Atticus (193-214), in real life the suave literary critic and poet Joseph Addison, now forgotten except by devotees of 18th century Eng. Lit. Read aloud, admiring the precision and snap of the couplets ("Damn with faint praise, assent with civil leer") that reveal Atticus as a temporizing, unsatisfactory person whose inadequacies are almost occasion for lament ("Who would not laugh if such a man there be? / Who would not weep if Atticus were he?"). Quite wonderful, and it will contrast with and set off the more unpleasant portrait of Sporus to come. "Unpleasant" is of course too prissy a word for the brilliant mixture of contempt, disgust, and thrilling invention lavished on this figure.

The Sporus portrait runs from lines 305-35. Great to read aloud. But in what spirit exactly? Surely we can't be outraged like Pope by the way Lord Hervey looks, speaks, acts—all without qualification, awful. By comparison Dryden is cool and urbane in taking apart Flecknoe or Achitophel, attacking from above whereas Pope comes from below, wherever that is. I've read this aloud in class more than once with much satisfaction. Responding to what at the end of the last paragraph I called Pope's "thrilling invention," Wyndham Lewis comes to mind: "The Greatest Satire is

Non-Moral," he declared, and I think Sporus is an example of that kind of greatness. In defending Pope from accusations of being something like a fiendish monkey pouring burning oil on his victims, the critic F.R. Leavis found instead something richer, deeper, more complicated, and he abused Lytton Strachey for crudely simplifying Pope into the fiendish monkey. I have to say no to Leavis, yes to Strachey, at least with respect to this probably most brilliant of all P's satiric portraits. In reading the Sporus passage I think we feel quite free of any moral, "human" questions of fairness, responsibility, understanding—all these we throw overboard, as did, I think, Pope, who believed that (in the language of the Horace satire) he was lashing the front of "shameless, guilty men." "His criticism of life was simply and solely the heroic couplet": more and more I see the truth in what looks like an unjust reducing of Pope the humanist/moralist.

What about the ending of the poem—the last eighty or so lines after Sporus? I get the feeling of Pope finding himself with a few further things he needs to say and saying them straight out, more or less. He mourns his father, he defends his mother, and he honors the family of the Popes: "Hear this, and spare his family, James Moore!" That outburst is about as far from the urbanity of Dryden as you could get and suggests that Pope wasn't kidding himself when he described the life of a wit as "a warfare upon earth."

Dear Class: For the week of April 13 we will finish (off) Pope with the two dialogues of 1738 ("Epilogue to the Satires") and *The Dunciad*. This will make three weeks on Pope, equivalent to what we accorded Milton. It means that Swift and Johnson unjustly get crammed into the final two weeks. Apologies, doing the best I, we, can. I don't need to say that you are in my thoughts for reasons not just academic. There will be a final paper, on Dryden and Pope, with directions/suggestions to be handed out. I am concerned however that not all the Milton papers have yet arrived—I believe there are five outstanding—and I would be grateful for any explanations and reassurances the not-yet-handed-in-ones could give me. Possible that something got lost in what we may call the "shuffle." At any rate I hope you're getting some satisfying reading down along with everything less satisfying. Best wishes from here—WHP

Week 4, Pope (3)

IHAVE BEEN TRYING to imagine your feelings, your responses to these final poems of Pope's career, and I was surprised to discover that, having read them many times over the years, my situation as a reader was not all that different from what I imagine yours to be: overwhelmed by names and events you have no comprehension of and which the (inadequate) notes in your edition scarcely explain. What I'm saying is—and especially with regard to *The Dunciad*—my difficulties are similar to yours: that familiarity has in the main not made things much easier for me to navigate this writing. One of Pope's most influential critics from the last century, F.R. Leavis, declared that the names both in *Dunciad* and "Epilogue to the Satires" were unimportant; that you should just disregard them and pay attention to "the poetry." Would this were as easy to do as Leavis claims! For me, the "poetry" is so implicated with names and historical events that if you discount them you have a lot less left to work on. And "work" is what you have to do in reading these poems. It's not like struggling with Milton until you begin to feel familiar with the way the verse moves, the way Milton's syntax eventually reveals itself to disclose meaning. Pope's couplets often seem pretty self-enclosed, and you feel that if you miss the joke, the insult, you can't "get it" by paying attention to rhythm, the movement of verse—to the "poetry."

Something else that distinguishes these last poems from those of other English poets, Wordsworth, or Keats, or Thomas Hardy, is that when you encounter them after studying (or whatever you do) "Essay on Criticism," "Rape of the Lock," "Epistle to a Lady" and "Epistle to Arbuthnot," you find yourself being asked to care about, to like and admire even, a poet whose self-display is often hard to admire. Everyone is ready to shed sympathetic tears when reading Keats's odes, written so close to his death and with such fine sentiments displayed in them; but how do you "relate to" this fiercely self-righteous, put-upon, totally virtuous figure we're asked to care about in late Pope? What happened to the charm of "Rape of the Lock" or the fine character studies in the Epistles? Often it seems we're being asked to do the work of admiration or contempt merely on the basis of a name, delivered in a scornful or admiring tone. An exaggerated way to put it is to say that we're invited to care about Pope the man, the poet, rather than—or not just—in the poems the man produces. Further, we're invited to see this man, these poems, as the summit (a tragic one, perhaps) of a career. Whereas with late Wordsworth you just have many more poems, many of them dreary enough, with Pope there's no letup of the fireworks that sometimes threaten to blow us out of the water.

With respect to "Epilogue to the Satires," the two dialogues are indeed dialogues, between Pope and another (P and F). He has done this to some extent in other satires, but not as a poem's overall technique. Disagreements, interruptions between the two speakers are central to the poems' art. It's a long way from the beautiful continuities of Clarissa in "Rape of the Lock," or of the Pope who speaks out in that excerpt from the "Essay on Man" ("Sole judge of truth, in endless error hurled / The glory, jest and riddle of the world). In fact I'm not aware of anything like it in any other English poet. Nobody is likely to say, when asked about their favorite poem, Oh I just LOVE Pope's "Epilogue to the Satires!" That's the extent to which the dialogues are rather special instances of poetic art.

But in fact, I'm someone who deeply admired these dialogues, especially the second one. Why? I think it has something to do with the form itself. There was a time when I found it amusing to write dialogues, though not in verse, between someone who sounded the way I thought I sounded, believed what I thought I believed and another voice, a challenger in opposition. In these dialogues I, the real Me, would always triumph, usually to the extent that my opponent ended up sounding foolish and wrongheaded. (If my old notebooks weren't locked up in Johnson Chapel I'd take a look at them, and also take a look at a paper I wrote for a Pope seminar about Dialogue 2.) In Pope's dialogues F always has P's interests at heart, tries to persuade him to moderate his scorn for one reason or another. Or says, rather sagely, that the reason P is so upset is that his friends are out of government power rather than in (that was the case in the 1730s and 40s when the Whigs took over.) Or says it's OK to "lash the greatest" of the pols as long as they're in disgrace. In other words he advocates the "sly, polite, insinuating style" found in Horace's odes and satires. Of course

Pope loved Horace, but isn't going to let him be used to damp down his ever-increasing ardor. In the first dialogue that "ardor" comes out beginning in line 113 when P pretends to make the case for Vice: "Virtue, I grant you is an empty boast / But shall the dignity of Vice be lost?" No way! P takes over the poem in a long peroration we can call The Triumph of Vice. The thirty lines, 140-170, are devoted to this mock-salute--or rather what begins as a mock-salute to vice, then turns into an impassioned rant about how "Old England's genius" is being dragged in the dirt as Virtue shows itself powerless to fend off wickedness in various forms. There's very little subtlety in this rant, but as rant it's a pretty lively one, good to read aloud as I trust you will. (You can also compare its disillusion to the optimism at the conclusion of the early "Windsor Forest." Pope has come a long way since then.) The poem ends abruptly, nothing resolved, with P having nothing stronger to say than that he holds the whole scene "in disdain." This sets the stage for "Dialogue Two."

The second dialogue is really the end of something, as far as Pope as satirist and moralist can go. His back is to the wall and it gets there through a most inventive use of the two voices, interrupting each other (look at the first 65 lines for example), quarreling, self-justifying, weighing the virtues of prudence as against letting it all hang out. I think this poem is unquestionably the most interesting use of dialogue in English poetry, although it's never had (seems to me) fully proper appreciation. I won't attempt that here but rely upon your imaginative sense as lively readers to bring out its life. As we move toward the poem's climax there's a good deal of P praising various good men, overwhelmed now in the tide of bad ones. A really fine moment is around line 120 when F responds to P's question in the middle of a line: "Faith the thought's no sin / I think your friends are out and would be in." Just what we've been wondering: is this whole business any more than a party-line sour grapes rant, and it's a good stroke that Pope includes this possibility in the dialogue. Then Pope lets F put another telling question in 157 ("Hold sir! For God's sake what's the affront to you?"). P answers with a telling sequence of scatological abuse, and if we virtuous readers are disgusted, so is F at "this filthy simile, this beastly line," setting up P to get down to ultimates most directly in 198-9: "Ask you what provocation I have had? / The strong antipathy of good to bad," ending in the claim that he "feels for all mankind." At this point, line 205, comes the great moment in the poem, again in the middle of a line when F remarks "You're strangely proud." It's that word "strangely" that turns the whole thing up a notch, introducing a note of wonder in the now rather impressed F and allowing P the eloquent explanation of what it is to be "touched and shamed by ridicule alone." For me one of the great moments in English poetry and an underappreciated one. See if you agree as you read P's great last words as a satirist/ridiculer who is ready to hang it up. F is (maybe) overcome, and provides a fatuous conclusion by suggesting that P write more Essays on Man. Whatever that means—be philosophical and weighty instead of nasty and personal—it's a wonderful anticlimax to what precedes it. Then as final conclusion, there is P's (now Pope in no disguise at all) unashamed prose note in the face of "bad men," justifying what he has done. If you were looking for comparable moments of heroic assertion in Eng lit, you could go to William Blake, speaking out prophetically, or maybe Yeats at the end of his career ("The Circus Animals' Desertion"). Or you could go backwards and listen to Hamlet praising the world he no longer delights in. Anyway, that's my pitch for Dialogue 2.

And now "The Dunciad." It's hard enough for me to "teach" this monster of a poem in class and even worse by mail. I'm never satisfied that I've been halfway adequate in introducing it. Why? Partly because of the overwhelming junk with which it's cluttered. In the one-volume shortened edition of the great Twickenham edition of Pope, it occupies 100 pages, pages replete with all the notes Pope wrote to the poem, plus what the modern editor contributes. Hard to see the forest, etc. etc. And of course these notes and the poem itself (whatever "itself" means here) are full of names we care nothing about. Doesn't sound promising.

Remember (I remind myself) that the original "Dunciad" was published seventeen years before its final four-book version. It was the main poem Pope wrote between his translations of Homer and the epistles/satires of the 1730s. Its major antecedent was "Rape of the Lock," its mode that of mock heroic, now mock heroic oriented toward the grotesque. You get a bit of grotesque in the Cave of Spleen passage from Canto 4 of "Rape"; now it is the prevailing mode. The earlier "Dunciad" was in three books, with Theobald, the Shakespearean editor who had criticized Pope's Shakespeare, as the head dunce. Then the notes began to mount up and Pope engages with his enemies directly and morally in the satires and epistles. What is left to do after "Epilogue to the Satires"? Well, turns out he had one more trick up his sleeve. He wrote a final book to the poem, longer and more ambitious, and more extreme than anything he'd ever done before. One of his commentators called it nothing less than "the undoing of God's creation"; a slightly more modest claim would see it as the end of Renaissance Humanism, the Christian version of life and letters that had been adhered to for centuries. The dunces are no longer just boring, merely a threat to literature; their reign means the end of "light" ("Light dies before thy uncreating word") as universal darkness buries all. Pope had never gone quite this far before. You could say he left it for the English Romantic poets—Blake, Wordsworth, Coleridge, Shelley—to unearth and reconstitute it.

I haven't mentioned Milton (remember him?), who is all over the poem as one more "light" to be put out. He's there locally: the beginning of *Paradise Lost*, Book 2:

> High on a throne of royal state, which far
> Outshone the wealth of ORMUS and of IND. . . .
> Satan exalted sat, by merit raised
> To that bad eminence . . .

In "MacFlecknoe" Dryden converts him downward into the father of Shadwell ("The hoary prince in majesty appeared, / High on the throne of his own labour reared") leaving the way open for Pope to salute the king of Dunces:

> High on a gorgeous seat, that far outshone
> Henley's gilt tub, or Flecknoe's Irish throne . . .
> Great Cibber sate, the proud Parnassian sneer,
> The conscious simper, and the jealous leer,
> Mix on his look . . . (Book 2, 1-6)

Colley Cibber (great name!), a harmless playwright and critic, has now been installed as head of the Dunces and will preside over the heroic games that make up Book 2 of the poem. In my doubtless crudity, I find amusing things like the pissing contest (who can reach the highest) and the race through excrementitious circumstances. You might try reading aloud one of these "events" and see if you find it worthy—if the run of Pope's couplets at times even make for beauty in the sordid. To describe urinating by a venereal challenged dunce as "The rapid waters in their passage burn" almost turns shameful physical effort into something noble.

One of the best early sequences in the poem occurs in Book 1 lines 115-

135 describing Cibber at poetic composition; "Swearing and supperless the hero sate," etc. This is the purely literary satire on a writing dunce (evidently Cibber was pretty lively but I've never read him) that marks the earlier three-book version of the poem. Pope and his friends in the Scriblerus Club (Swift, Gay) collaborated on an enterprise titled *Peri Bathos* or "The Art of Sinking in Poetry" that made much play with bad writing as tending downwards to darkness and oblivion. Got the idea from Dryden it seems. Anyway "Sinking from thought to thought, a vast profound!" is the idea. I like particularly (please read aloud)

Round him much embryo, much abortion lay,

Much future ode, and abdicated play;
Nonsense precipitate, like running lead,
That slipped through cracks and zigzags of the head.

ZIGZAGS! How did he come up with that one? If you get more or less stuck in Book 1, drop it and pick up at Book 2 with the aforementioned heroic games. You may just skip Book 3 entirely—I always get lost there. But read the fourth book in its entirety, especially the final lines under the asterisk on p.173. There are a number of superb sequences earlier in Book 4, and I would single out lines 282-335 (or thereabouts), the account of the young fop's grand tour of the continent ("Europe he saw, and Europe saw him too"). If you by any chance remember the poem or have your Ben Jonson handy think of the early "To William Roe" that I made something of in class—farewell and welcome home again to the friend about to set out for Europe, ending "This is that good Aeneas . . . this man hath travailled well." A reference in Pope's parody of the grand tour ("Safe and unseen the young Aeneas past") enforces the parallel, this second Aeneas (Pope's) being adept at sinking in poetry and other pursuits.

Who can be adequate to the end of "The Dunciad"? Not me, folks, and my way of dealing, as usual, but more so is to read aloud and marvel. This is no longer a purely literary "sinking" but the "all-composing hour" in which even the "Muse obeys the power." Art after art goes out along with public and private virtue, religion, philosophy, science, everything succumbs to the "dread empire, Chaos" restored. Really there has been nothing like this before or since in English poetry, and it's especially moving if you've been hanging around with Pope for awhile and remember how he started out to be a "correct" poet and talked in "Windsor Forest" about the world "harmoniously confused / Where order in variety we see ,/ And where, though all things differ, all agree." Now, thanks to the god of Dullness (goddess, I mean) "Light dies before thy uncreating word" and "Universal darkness buries all." What a way to go out!

So I urge you to make an effort with "Dunciad," and don't feel incompetent if you keep getting lost, banging your head against this or that impenetrable reference. Take away what you can take away; try to imagine how, for all the painful follies it exhibits, laughs at, excoriates, the result to the discerning reader like you or me may be pleasure. If you can't find any pleasure in it, give yourself some time and read a book like . . . like *Gulliver's Travels*.

In the not too distant future I will send you suggestions for the remainder of this fraught term. No final exam, an event that for me only works if we're here physically. Suggestions for a third paper, on Dryden and/or Pope. And if you have the time an invitation to write something optional about your experience of this course. In hopes that the Larger Situation will improve if ever so slightly—fare forward. —WHP

Week 5, Swift

I MAY HAVE BEEN some help in reading Dryden and Pope—at least so I presume after hearing from a couple of you. With Swift, I have my doubts, mainly because he's such a strange character whose relation to his reader is almost never straight and who delights in destabilizing any stable procedures. He writes to Pope at one point that while Pope and his friends want to reform things, make the world better, he wants to "vex" it. Perfect word for his delight in unsettling things. The other more practical difficulty in presenting him to you is that I had planned to do some serious photocopying of different aspects of this writer. Given the fact of two weeks left and altered circumstances I won't attempt it. More than once I've regretted my decision NOT to use the Norton anthology, which prints a variety of Swiftian performances.

Enough whining. In the best of pedagogical situations, no one really knows what to say about Swift. A critic I much admire, Marvin Mudrick, called him a "crook," a colorful way of emphasizing how he's always getting away with this or that, never playing it straight, always delighting in upsetting expectations. In the extraordinary work of his early years, *A Tale of a Tub*, he puts readers in a position of not knowing where they are from sentence to sentence; in setting up expectation only to contradict it and move in another direction. *Tale of a Tub* has a completely undependable, unreliable narrator—in that aspect it has affinities with recent post-modernist hijinks. The chapter that's excerpted in Norton is titled "A Digression on Madness," and if you expect a digression to cast light on the question being pondered, nothing could be further from the truth. Perhaps the most infamous sentence occurs when our friendly narrator is pretending to investigate the philosophical question of how to understand a phenomenon. Should one stay on the surface, reporting what's there to be seen, or should one go deeper, penetrate to where the truth may be hid. He pretends to be concerned with suggesting how the insides of things are at odds with their outsides. As one of his proofs he tells us: "Last Week I saw a woman flay'd, and you will hardly believe how much it altered her Person for the worse." WHAT?? This is one sentence from a bewildering variety that seems to have no intention beyond putting the reader in one untenable position after another. We are "vexed" and thus conclude that vexation is the whole point, and we are to be entertained by continually missing it.

A narrative without an authoritative voice, then, with no clear distinction between the foolish, pointless, verbal ingenuities, and a solid Author standing behind them who knows what's pointless and what's not. I spend this much time on a book you haven't read, *Tale of a Tub*, because to a somewhat lesser degree a similar situation prevails in *Gulliver's Travels*. I would suggest you read GT by moving through the first two books fairly rapidly, noting the different kinds of "discoveries" Gulliver makes, first as big man among the little, then the other way around. Samuel Johnson didn't like Swift much (didn't like his playing around with religion, Dean of St. Patrick's Cathedral in Dublin though he was) and didn't like his fascination (not too strong a word) with matters scatological, a mild example of which is Gulliver putting out the fire in the Queen's palace by urinating on it (this in Lilliput). In Boswell's *Life of Johnson* he has Johnson saying scornfully about GT that once you think of the big men and the little men the rest is easy. (Your Johnson text includes nothing from his life of Swift.)

The first thing we register about GT is the sheer playfulness of much of it, especially in the first two books. I saw a movie of it when I was seven years old or so and still remember the image of Gulliver tied down (in Lilliput) with hundreds of minute little threads. George Orwell, who has written well about the book, says he read it just before his eighth birthday (it was to be given him as a present) and has returned to it innumerable times. So have I, but I'm afraid with not all that much of Orwell's delighted fascination. And I've never been very good at "teaching" it, partly because reading aloud (my "thing") doesn't produce similar satisfactions to reading aloud Milton or Pope. Its dry, minute style (as someone called it) is pretty relentless: I did this, then I did that, and then I did something else. We're invited to think of it as a parody of travel books, but that doesn't make it come alive for me. The main argument among readers is whether to take Gulliver the character as object of satire, often convicting himself by the pompous things he says (about England, about human beings), or to see him as, in the final book, an increasingly frustrated idealist whose disappointment in mankind elicits our sympathy or pity. As far as I can see, both these viewpoints are true ones and a function of Swift's irresponsible fooling around with his protagonist, now decent and thoughtful, now arrogant and stubborn, now—and most importantly—what Orwell called a "stooge" for Swiftian ironies. There has been an argument about whether or how much we are supposed to admire the Houhynms (I can't never spell it) and sympathize with our hero's failure to become (as it were) one of them. Or do we see his final alienation from wife and family, normal life, to be another tough joke on Swift's part—another instance of "vexing" human nature?

Orwell called GT a great book written by a man who was diseased, permanently depressed; but that this aspect of Swift's character is a partial truth about human beings generally, endowed with inner selves aghast at the horrors of existence. Swift told Pope that life was a "ridiculous tragedy," but unlike tragedy there's no patient development of a tragic vision of things. For Swift things are foreclosed; it's just a matter of time before he pulls the plug. What after some years of reading it I find most memorable are the wonderful new perspectives that the big/little trope provides: Gulliver's watch, for example, or bits of whiskers that he makes into a comb. At times there's real shock, as when the monkey gets loose and torments him. I remember a vivid movie, maybe from the 1950s, called "The Incredible Shrinking Man," about a guy exposed to nuclear rays who proceeds to get smaller and smaller, ending up in a cage (still dressed in his suit and tie) where he's pestered by a cat. Wouldn't mind seeing that one again.

I realize that GT is enough to take up three classes' worth of reading. You might well skip Book 3, or part of it. I find it less than "fun" going, but its chapters 5 and 10 should be read, 5 for its examples of outlandish "utopian" behavior; 10 for its memorable portrait of the Struldbrugs, people who live forever. Usually I hand out a sheaf of six or seven poems by Swift, but I'm going to cut that down to a mere two out of the very large body of poetry Swift wrote. Most of his poems are in octosyllabic couplets (rhymed tetrameter), many of them jingle a bit; Dr. Johnson dismissed them by saying there simply wasn't much to say about them. Swift, when young, wrote a number of unreadable Pindaric odes in the "high" manner. Very boring. Also a couple of not-boring fables, one of them, *Cadenus and Vanessa*, portraying himself as Dean and the young woman whose education he "oversaw" for a time. There were two younger women, the first of whom, Stella, was the recipient of a number of birthday poems of which I'm providing one. But he is most notorious for his anti-feminist, misogynist (?) poems, of which "The Lady's Dressing Room" is the strongest. Strong enough supposedly to make the mother of Laetitia Pilkington, a literary lady, throw up her dinner. (So legend has it.) In the 19th century the novelist Thackeray, writing about Swift, deplored these poems, as well as the fourth book of GT, as obscene creations testifying to the fact that Swift was going, had gone mad. (He died of what we now call Menière's Syndrome, a disease of the ear causing vertigo.) D.H. Lawrence, following Thackeray decades later, decided "The Lady's Dressing Room" and other of Swift's female satires indicated a sick inability to accept the physical facts of women's bodies. So the discovery by Strephon, in "The Lady's Dressing Room," "Repeating in his amorous Fits / Oh Celia, Celia, Celia, shits!" (I suspect that in many printings the final word was not spelled out) indicated Swift's deranged horror at the event. Whereas for Lawrence, self-righteous Lawrence, it was just part of the facts of life. I think (and if you've read Lawrence you won't be surprised) that his own humorlessness ran up against Swift's scabrous, irresponsible temperament. Anything for a little more vexation, and calling the disgusted male lover by that Pastoral name Strephon adds to the travesty. But as in so much else of Swift, the energy is in the negative—an inadequate word, granted.

The other poem is a very different matter, the last of his many birthday poems to Stella, "Stella's Birth-Day" that begins "This Day whate'er the Fates decree, / Shall still be kept with Joy by me." This is I think a beautiful, a moving poem, and at least serves to alleviate the bad taste left in one's mouth by some of Swift's writings. I plan to read this aloud for you but also apologize for this pell-mell treatment of a great writer. A great prose writer whose famous definition of good style was "Proper words in proper places." That so much of his energy went into setting up improper words in proper places is part of his fascination.

Week 6, Samuel Johnson

HERE WE ARE at an end, with not time or place enough to do more than gesture at this great writer. There is a way of talking about Johnson that says, it's not that his writings are so wonderful but that he is the fortunate recipient of the most entertaining book ever written, *The Life of Johnson*, as James Boswell wrote it. The Norton anthology, absence of which I keep regretting, has fifteen or so pages with some of the best bits of this enormous book. It was responsible for my discovery of Johnson when I was just your age, a junior, and an extraordinary member of the senior class, a true Johnsonian character, recommended it. He seemed to have committed large swatches of it to memory, and I was taken by the performance. I asked him what edition of Boswell's *Life* I should purchase and he said by all means the Oxford University Press one because, among other virtues, it had a magnificent index that would include such an item as "reindeer." Was he kidding? When I acquired the 1500-page book as a graduation present I sure enough looked up "reindeer" in the index. There it was, p. 476, a single reference to one of Johnson's pronouncements that goes as follows: "Were I a rich man, I would propagate all kinds of trees that will grow in the open air. A greenhouse is childish. I would introduce foreign animals into the country; for instance the reindeer." (An editorial footnote told me that "the project was realized when a visitor to Lapland brought two specimens back to England for his Northumberland estate, where they bred; but the race has unfortunately perished.") I doubt that anyone but myself has been introduced to Samuel Johnson in quite this offhand, forgettable way. But not forgettable, since I just turned to p. 476 in Boswell's Life and "reindeer" was still there.

I urge you to familiarize yourself with this remarkable book, which I am in the process of rereading with undiminished pleasure (am I beginning to sound like Johnson? Not really.) I can't think of any book with comparable powers of attraction on the fifth or fiftieth reading. Maybe Jane Austen's novels (and she was an admirer of Johnson). But what about you first-time, some of you, readers of SJ without benefit of Boswell? Try an experiment involving aloud-reading: on p. 419 of your edition of Johnson's major works, the first paragraph of his preface to his edition of Shakespeare's plays. This is the kind of Johnsonian sentence it's easy not to follow, or get something wrong in the enunciation of: a single sentence called (officially) the Periodic Sentence. The Norton anthology has a go at characterizing J's style here and elsewhere: extended sentences; phrases and clauses moving to carefully controlled rhythms; language that is general, often Latinate, frequently polysyllabic. Since you've put in time with Milton's verse in *Paradise Lost* you may be equipped to navigate successfully a Johnsonian sentence/paragraph. There are those who find this style cumbersome, pretentious, a travesty of how "English" should be written. Some find the charge to be true also of a sequence in Milton. Matthew Arnold asked us to admire what he called "the grand style" with respect to *Paradise Lost*. I think the epithet does for Johnson as well.

It's an easy transition from the Johnsonian sentence above to the prevailing style of his poems, of which he wrote relatively few. The best-known and admired one is "The Vanity of Human Wishes," an imitation of one of the Roman satirist Juvenal's poems. Read the first twenty lines aloud and note how strong is its prose sense; it could stand right up there with the paragraph from the Shakespeare preface. Even readers who have more or less come to terms with Pope's satires may find Johnson's a harder sell; after all, poetry should "show," not "tell," and should be "concrete," with abundant images doing their work. As in an ode by Keats: "Forlorn; the very word is like a bell / To toll me back from thee to my sole self" (penultimate stanza of "Ode to a Nightingale"). Compare the final two lines of Johnson's opening twenty: "Impeachment stops the speaker's powerful breath, / And restless fire precipitates on death." The note tells me that "precipitate" derives from its use in alchemy, but I don't "see" anything as "restless fire precipitates on death." It certainly sounds authoritative, final, satisfying. But to build a poem of 350 or so lines on such "abstract," "general" terms is risky. Try another sequence, lines 73-90, about the uncertainty of reputation, be it literary or political. Before you know it the personage whose portrait hung on the wall is out of favor and taken down: result— "The form distorted justifies the fall; / And detestation rids th'indignant wall." Again, nothing to visualize, hang on to sensuously: detestation and indignant do the work. Johnson's phrase "The grandeur of generality" is a good one to characterize how his poetry works in "Vanity" and elsewhere. By contrast Pope's lines are full of vivid, strikingly named instances of "life" ("Yet let me flap this bug with gilded wings / This painted child of dirt that stinks and stings"—Sporus in the Arbuthnot epistle). Johnson as poet has rightly been called a reactionary; he had little sympathy with various poetic styles that superseded ones he admired like Pope's: pastoral reflection (he disliked "Lycidas"), descriptions of nature written in blank verse (James Thomson's very popular "The Seasons"), topographical or "georgic" accounts of places. One of my favorite moments in Boswell's *Life* occurs when somebody recommends an 18th century poem "The Fleece," about the care of sheep: Johnson: "The subject, Sir, cannot be made poetical. How can a man write poetically of serges and druggets?" There is mention of a recent poem by a clergyman, Dr. Grainger, "The Sugar-Cane":

> Johnson said, that Dr. Grainger was an agreeable man . . . but "The Sugar-Cane" did not please him, for, he exclaimed, "What could he make of a sugar-cane? One might as well write the 'Parsley-bed, a Poem'; or 'The Cabbage-garden, a Poem.'"

Warming up, Johnson pretends to see possibilities in the subject:

> "I think one could say a great deal about cabbage. The poem might begin with the advantages of civilised society over a rude state, exemplified by the Scotch [Boswell was a Scot] who had no cabbages till Oliver Cromwell's soldiers introduced them, and one might thus shew how arts are propagated by conquest . . ." He seemed to be much diverted with the fertility of his own fancy.

Stepping away from the grandeur of generality to write poems about how to tend sheep or cultivate sugar-cane he found ludicrous, and I think we agree he had a point. But "The Vanity of Human Wishes," in its commitment to generality rather than particular, colorful subjects, makes for hard reading—it's as hard as Greek, said Johnson's friend, the actor David Garrick.

Even though you haven't read much or any 18th-century English poetry beyond Dryden (d.1700), Pope and Johnson, I want to point you toward a great moment (for me) in the criticism of poetry. It occurs in T.S. Eliot's essay, "Johnson as Critic and Poet" when Eliot takes up the question of why Johnson was so certain that his own style and that of fellow poets he admired was the Best Style—a refinement of earlier roughnesses and crudities, even of Shakespeare who frequently (for Johnson) in his plays wrote obscurely, his thought unable to find proper communicative form (think especially Shakespeare's late plays). Eliot agrees that this provinciality showed a lack of the historical sense, whereas you and I, possessing such a sense, can admire Johnson *and* Milton *and* Shakespeare. Eliot suggests that we who have the historical sense may develop it by understanding a critic, like Johnson, in whom it's not apparent. Yet, "If the eighteenth century had admired the poetry of earlier times in the way in which we can admire it, the result would have been chaos: there would have been no eighteenth century as we know it. That age would not have had the conviction necessary for perfecting the kinds of poetry it did perfect." This seems to me profound.

About a hundred pages of our selections are devoted to Johnson's tale, *Rasselas*, written quickly, so legend has it, to pay the expenses of his mother's funeral. I used to find this cautionary tale much fun, but that has waned (I always know what's coming next, etc.), and if you don't have time to read it all, here is an excerpted version consisting of chapters 1, 8, 10, 18, 26, 29, 31-2, 40-1, 44-5, 49. *Rasselas* enforces the moral issues raised in "The Vanity of Human Wishes" and the many essays Johnson wrote as a coming literary man, a large selection from *The Rambler* here included. We can unjustly reduce the moral issues of this tale by considering chapter 32, in which Rasselas and his friends visit the pyramids and Imlac the sage comments on how in his view (the true view) they "have been erected only in compliance with that hunger of imagination which preys incessantly on life and must be always appeased by some employment. . . . I consider this mighty structure as a monument of the insufficiency of human enjoyments." Looking back on my reading of this tale I realize how as a young man I liked to be entertained with sonorous meditations, in those stately sentences, that told me how everything will fall short of any expectations of life I may hold. That (in the line from an old joke) "all the toys will break" and we're getting older and more fragile by the minute. I no longer find it exhilarating to contemplate such truths. But give *Rasselas* a try and see how it strikes you. Reading aloud various sonorous passages may help bring it to life.

If there were time, instead of a week left, I would suggest you read John-son's travel narrative, *A Journey to the Western Islands of Scotland,* which has some solid satisfactions conveyed in a prose not so formal as he made use of in "Vanity" and *Rasselas.* Instead we'll dip very lightly into his prefaces to the dictionary he compiled and the plays of Shakespeare he edited. The pages on the dictionary run from 307 to 335 and contain a few examples from that book. Swift had written a proposal for "correcting, improving, and ascertaining the English tongue," a prescriptive enterprise that John-son found himself unable and unwilling to follow. Crudely, his edition is "descriptive" and proceeds by way of breaking down each word into (it may be) several distinct senses, with illustrative quotations from English writers in literature, philosophy, and science from the 17th and 18th cen-turies, the dictionary would have as its assumption the hope to improve readers in matters of religion and morality, so the illustrative examples were themselves chosen with regard to their appropriateness for such a task. Read aloud the concluding paragraph (pp. 327-8) with its great heart-piercing but also boastful claim that the book "was written with little assis-tance of the learned, and without any patronage of the great; not in the soft obscurities of retirement, or under the shelter of academic bowers, but amidst inconvenience and distraction, in sickness and in sorrow." If he has failed, he writes, "I have only failed in an attempt which no human powers have hitherto completed." Isn't that something? If you find it so you are on your way of becoming an admiring reader of Samuel Johnson.

A couple of further remarks about the dictionary: in preparation for it, Johnson read (reread?) the collected works of Shakespeare, Bacon, others, and put vertical lines around passages to be included (as illustrative of the word) while underlining the word to be illustrated. Among the examples in your selection, you might consult the amount of commentary the word "fall" incurs. Johnson says about it, "This is one of those general words of which it is very difficult to ascertain or detail the full signification. It retains in most of its senses some part of its primitive meaning, and implies either literally or figuratively descent, violence, or suddenness." So you can see how instructive a single item can be. This unbelievable achievement took him seven years to complete: 40,000 words, 114,000 quotations to find which he read through . . . everything. And just now I realized your selection contains his famous letter to Lord Chesterfield apropos of the dictionary (pp. 782-3, a real killer).

For the other preface, to his edition of Shakespeare, I suggest you read pp. 419-433 in which, "not dogmatically but deliberatively written," he hoped to "recall the principles of the drama to a new examination." There are a number of interesting deliberations in the preface, but I'm singling out one in which (p. 428) he notes that Shakespeare now and then gets "entangled with an unwieldy sentiment which he cannot well express, and will not reject; he struggles with it for a while, and if it continues stubborn, comprises it in words such as occur, and leaves it to be disentangled and evolved by those who have more leisure to bestow on it." In other words, Shakespeare is sometimes obscure and that that happens when language gets the better of him. In our days, we have learned to call this "entanglement" "complex," rather than obscure, and take it as exemplifying what F.R. Leavis called Shakespeare's "exploratory-creative use of words." Johnson wouldn't have understood such talk; as editor, part of his task was to clear up verbal confusions (so he took them to be) or instances of Shakespeare being unable to deliver the sense of what, in current jargon, he was "trying to say." When he comes to Hamlet's famous "To be or not to be" soliloquy he says that its sense exists in the mind of the speaker but doesn't get fully transmitted into the words he speaks. So Johnson proceeds to provide an elaborate paraphrase that complicatedly (as I see it) mistakes the sense of the passage. He sees himself as helping out Shakespeare by disentangling the speech and bringing out more clearly its meaning. This is very different from you and me revelling in the brilliance of Shakespearean utterance.

Another useful perception I take away from the preface has to do with the comedy/tragedy distinction. Johnson was doubtful that the distinction was a real or useful one: "Shakespeare's plays are not in the rigorous and critical sense either tragedies or comedies, but compositions of a distinct kind; exhibiting the real state of sublunary nature, which partakes of good and evil, joy and sorrow, mingled with endless variety of proportion and innumerable modes of combination." This perception, "not dogmatically but deliberately written," backs up the claim Johnson makes about "recalling the principles of the drama to a new examination." Let me call your attention as well to pp. 457-46l, an example of Johnson's annotation of a famous speech from *Measure for Measure*. He quotes some lines from the Duke's speech to Claudio who is condemned to death— Thou hast nor youth, nor age; / But as it were an after-dinner's sleep, / Dreaming on both . . ." and proceeds to gloss "dreaming," beginning with "This is exquisitely imagined." The result is, well, exquisite.

Johnson's final piece of important criticism was his "biographical and critical prefaces to the works of the English poets." I'll say of them only that they're endlessly rereadable. The ones that concern you particularly are the pages your editor excerpts from the lives of Milton, Dryden, and Pope. (I believe in my suggestions for a final paper I directed you to the comparison on p.737 of the last two poets.) This is, of course, a great tour de force, and I mention it only to bring out, in its final paragraph, the lovely (and sly) wit with which Johnson closes the matter: "If the reader should suspect me, as I suspect myself of some partial fondness for the memory of Dryden, let him not too hastily condemn me; for meditation and enquiry may, perhaps, show him the reasonableness of my determination." Perhaps, and in my (craven?) admiration of Johnson I have become convinced that the personal note is reasonable indeed.

A pronouncement from one of Johnson's periodical essays in *The Rambler* goes as follows: "The secret horror of the last is inseparable from a thinking being, whose life is limited and to whom death is dreadful." I fell for this pronouncement decades ago and it has surely not become any less than a resonant truth about life and about reading. T.S. Eliot, whom you've heard me quote numerous times this term, once declared in one of his most influential essays, "Tradition and the Individual Talent": "Someone said: 'The dead writers are remote from us because we *know* so much more than they did.' Precisely, and they are that which we know." As English studies shrinks in popularity, relevance, etc., that "we" is becoming an ever smaller cohort. As your instructor in "Great English Writers," I welcome you to that cohort in the belief that if you have been touched by some writer, some piece of prose or verse, enough so that you're moved to find out more, to reread and read on, I consider it mission accomplished. And to give some finality to this course in which the dead writers suddenly became, alas, "remote" from us, I suggest you read aloud a late poem of Johnson's, "On the Death of Dr. Robert Levet," whose final stanza goes thus:

Then with no throbbing fiery pain,
No cold gradations of decay,
Death broke at once the vital chain,
And freed his soul the nearest way.

FINAL PAPER DUE MAY 15. Send to me please. And if you choose to write on Swift or Johnson, please propose a question that you proceed to explore. With best regards—WHP

■ ■ ■ ■

Selection from Boswell's *Life of Johnson*

He spoke slightingly of Dyer's Fleece.— 'The subject, Sir, cannot be made poetical. How can a man write poetically of serges and druggets? Yet you will hear many people talk to you gravely of that excellent poem, The Fleece.' Having talked of Grainger's Sugar-Cane, I mentioned to him Mr. Langton's having told me, that this poem, when read in manuscript at Sir Joshua Reynolds's, had made all the assembled wits burst into a laugh, when, after much blank-verse pomp, the poet began a new paragraph thus:—

'Now, Muse, let's sing of rats.'

And what increased the ridicule was, that one of the company, who slily overlooked the reader, perceived that the word had been originally MICE, and had been altered to RATS, as more dignified.

Johnson said, that Dr. Grainger was an agreeable man; a man who would do any good that was in his power. His translation of Tibullus, he thought, was very well done; but The Sugar-Cane, a poem, did not please him; for, he exclaimed, 'What could he make of a sugar-cane? One might as well write the "Parsley-bed, a Poem;" or "The Cabbage-garden, a Poem."' BOSWELL. 'You must then pickle your cabbage with the sal atticum.' JOHNSON. 'You know there is already The Hop-Garden, a Poem: and, I think, one could say a great deal about cabbage. The poem might begin with the advantages of civilized society over a rude state, exemplified by the Scotch, who had no cabbages till Oliver Cromwell's soldiers introduced them; and one might thus shew how arts are propagated by conquest, as they were by the Roman arms.' He seemed to be much diverted with the fertility of his own fancy.

CREDO: Confessions of an Impenitent Reviewer

MY SUBJECT, the trials and pleasures of a lifetime book reviewer, will be illustrated by some, I hope, amusing and occasionally disturbing things that have happened to me over the decades. Remember first that reviewing is a species of criticism and that the classic statement about it was made by Matthew Arnold in "The Function of Criticism at the Present Time" (1864). At the beginning of that great essay, Arnold clears the ground for his defense of criticism by weighing the merits of the critical versus the creative power. Although traditionally the critical power has been judged to be lower than the creative one, Arnold questions whether it is true that "all time given to writing critiques on the work of others would be much better employed if it were given to original composition." Would we prefer that Samuel Johnson, for example, had produced more plays like his single, ill-fated *Irene,* instead of writing *Lives of the Poets*? Wouldn't we rather have heard something of Wordsworth's criticism of his contemporaries or his reflections on the art of poetry, than to be presented with ten more Ecclesiastical Sonnets, of which he turned out so many, so dutifully and dully, in his later years?

Descending the scale of writers, I reach myself, someone woefully uncreative to the extent of never having given birth to a novel, a short story, a lyric poem, not even an epic; the occasional satiric or humorous verse turned out for some family occasion is my sole claim to creative fame. But I have written a lot of criticism, and much of it not in the academically respectable mode of the scholarly book or essay, but in the reviewing mode rather. Reviewing books has not always and is perhaps still not always considered an activity worthy of academic credit. "But that's just a review" is a way of suggesting that the piece of writing in question didn't originate in or for itself, didn't develop an argument or set forth an interpretation or theory, but was dependent on someone else who had committed something original— new poems, a collection of short fiction. A colleague of mine once informed me that it was a waste of time to spend it reviewing other people's books rather than getting on with your own. Evidently I didn't believe him and now, many years later, my assumption is that the lowly review need not be lowly; that it can contain as valuable criticism as is to be found in more highly regarded venues like the article or essay, or (to put academic class in it) the monograph. Some autobiography may clarify the assumption.

How did it happen, I ask myself, since back in graduate school my friends and I had no notion of ourselves turning into professional *writers*. We wanted to teach English, maybe at a college like Amherst, read books and student papers, and carry on a lively intellectual life with our colleagues. To that end it was necessary to produce a Ph.D. dissertation, but after that not much, if anything, else. Dr. Johnson declared famously that no one but a blockhead wrote anything except for money. We were blockheads, doubtless, but who would pay us? Anyway we were scared, or at least I was scared, when a fellow graduate student told me that an English professor of his at Harvard wrote on his paper "Conceivably publishable," and suggested *The Arizona Quarterly* as a possibility. Was *that* the way things were headed? Well, it didn't turn me on. When I was fortunate enough to land a job at Amherst, no one who hired me, bless them, cared to look at anything I had written up to that point; nor, with the exception of urging me to finish my dissertation, did any member of the English department or administration push me in the direction of publication. The villain, or hero in this case, was the editor of the *Amherst Alumni News*, who one day called up and said he had a new book on Henry James by an Amherst graduate and would I like to write a brief review of it for the magazine? Why, yes I would indeed, especially since the book was Richard Poirier's *The Comic Sense of Henry James.* Poirier was one of my mentors, and I was excited to read, admire, and write about his book. Amherst College didn't pay me anything but I got to keep the book, still an excellent one for its insights into *Washington Square* and *The Portrait of a Lady.* At any rate, that began things.

I got tenure at Amherst with no one in the department having looked at my now completed dissertation. One was judged rather on how one had contributed to the departmental staff courses (this involved writing for colleagues) and how adequate one's teaching was guessed to be. Tenure achieved, I tried to publish my dissertation on Robert Frost without success, and I produced a couple of articles about individual writers. But sending out essays to magazines and waiting for their response was a slow business: too long a space between typing out the piece and its substantiation in print—what Frost called "the trial by market everything must come to." I needed something more than the *Alumni News* as a venue, and the break came in the spring of 1967 when a note from Frederick Morgan, editor of *The Hudson Review,* invited me to write something called an omnibus review of recent volumes of poetry. *Hudson* was at that time and still is a distinguished "little magazine," a quarterly subscribed to by at most a few thousand readers, presenting in its front pages new poetry, essays, and fiction—back then such writers as Pound, Wallace Stevens, Thomas Mann, and others appeared there—and in its back pages quarterly reports on the state of things in the arts, music, ballet, theater, movies, plus reviews of what the editor judged to be important recent books, mainly, though not exclusively, literary ones. My assignment was to peruse thirty-some books of recent verse from which I would select ten or so that I wanted to comment on, stringing the comments together artfully for about 5,000 words. The books arrived, one slim volume after another, were dutifully stacked on the mantelpiece or piano, and I felt like a professional. Here was work to be done by April 25, and for which I would be paid! The notion was to select from the thirty-five or so volumes a reasonable number (ten, say) around which could be built a more or less coherent essay. The fun was partly in making the transitions from one book to the next, and the order I hit upon—one I'd seen present in other such omnibus reviews—was roughly from undistinguished or boring efforts to what struck me as the real thing, verse that could be read with pleasure, even admiration.

Once I decided which books I wanted to write about, the work felt almost like play. It all comes back in a rush of sentiment: a warm night in April, working unaccustomedly in my office, the windows open, student stereos blasting out the Beatles' *Sergeant Pepper,* while I listened on the radio to basketball playoffs between the Celtics and Philadelphia, meanwhile composing sentences like the following about May Swenson's book *Half Sun Half Sleep:*

> May Swenson begins and ends in mannerism. She is forever
> tinkering, taking apart a cat, a watch, a poem. Without evident
> embarrassment she can tell us (in "The Watch") that the watch-

maker ". . . leaned like an ogre over my / naked watch. With critical pincers he / poked and stirred. He / lifted out little private things with a magnet too tiny for me / to watch almost. 'Watch out!' I / almost said. . ." I'm just not sure what kind of good fun this is. She is endlessly feeling things and relentlessly fashionable about what there is to grab: "On Handling Some Small Shells from the Windward Islands" —the pretentious-unpretentious title tells the story, as does the chic disposition of words on the page, not just in old-fashioned pentameter but like this:

Their click as of crystal,
wood, carapace and bone.

> *A tintinnabular fusion.*
> *Their friction spinal and chill*

as of ivory embryo
fragments of horn. . . .

And there are many flashier topographical effects to be observed, if not delighted in, elsewhere. For May Swenson things exist so that poems can be written about them, and if most have been discovered there's always "A Basin of Eggs"; "Their cheeks touching, / their cheeks being / their bellies, their / bellies being undimpled, / dimples of dark being." I suppose so, but why couldn't they have been left alone just to lie there as old eggs, instead of taking their place, in a hyped-up poetic universe? May Swenson has nothing to say, and her many ways of saying it drove me to exasperation.

Where did all this animus come from? With a sense of exhilaration, I, the non-poet, skewered a number of, as I thought, pretenders to poetical talent, expressed mixed praised and blame for others, then at the end declared myself heartily in favor of Louis MacNeice's *Collected Poems.* It was easy to find words to bash May Swenson or Lawrence Durrell, but with MacNeice I found myself straining for terms of approval that couldn't be confused with an enthusiastic advertising blurb. At which point, or soon afterwards, a fundamental truth about book reviewing dawned on me: it is easier to find fault than to praise convincingly. The inanity or pretentiousness of a writer, of a poem, are temptingly easy targets for the critic's clever tongue;

but the subtlety or refinement of a poem, a writer, are harder to put words to.

But I was a man on the make, in search of a new career and not above showing off in the process; after all, others had done it before me, in the pages of *Hudson* and elsewhere. At any rate Fred Morgan liked what I wrote and immediately invited me to review something else. Not so welcoming was the senior man in the Amherst English department to whom I showed my review. He professed fear for my physical safety as he conjured up a vision of outraged poets descending on my office, intent on rendering physical harm for what I had doled out. "I cannot see why you do this," he went on:

> You are so modest, so un-self-seeking. Are you going to pursue this course and sacrifice every poet's (except for a dead Limey) goodwill for a witticism? . . . There you are I say, dancing around the flames occasionally throwing in another slim volume. . . . Well, I read and laughed and then as always felt guilty. . . . But I am finally on the side of the bad novelists, the bad poets, when they are made fun of. Perhaps I have no idea of good clean fun. Certainly your imbecile examples are imbecile. . . . But, you will say patiently, holding your head in your hands, Somebody has to do this. And I reply like lightning, Why? And more personally, why you? I do not believe that this single omnibus performance will ruin life for you. But I cannot see any future in it. The attention finally turns from the personalities of the poets . . . to the personality of the Reviewer. It is much better than here expressed I think.

After picking myself up off the floor, I somehow proceeded not to heed Theodore Baird's counsel—did not turn in my new badge as a reviewer but persisted in the folly, beginning to write two or three times a year for *Hudson,* sometimes omnibus reviews of poetry or fiction, more often recent biographies, books of criticism, selections of essays or letters. Of course reviewing for *Hudson* or any quarterly meant that by the time the piece appeared, the book would probably be old news, and if an editor lets things pile up it can become really embarrassing. I reviewed a bit for other quarterlies, like *Partisan* and *Kenyon,* but was more than excited, almost four years after that first appearance in *Hudson,* to receive the *New York*

Times Book Review's seal of approval, to the extent of being asked to review a book of poetry for them. (That seal has subsequently, with the advent of Sam Tanenhaus as editor, been withdrawn.)

As you might suspect, there are many varieties of editorial behavior in relation to the review one has submitted and what actually gets or doesn't get printed. Model editorial behavior in this regard was displayed by John Gross, who first at *The New Statesman,* then at the *Times Literary Supplement,* would commission a piece, read it promptly when it arrived, then phone up mentioning specific suggestions for changes to be made or at least contemplated (there wasn't any e-mail in 1973), or asking me to reconsider this or that sentence. It's more likely that an editor will cut, and without getting permission, when the review is too long to fit that week's space or when he or she deems this or that sentence superfluous or unnecessary. Sometimes your editor reads the review in your presence. Ian Hamilton, editor for a time of an English monthly, *The New Review,* silently surveyed my lengthy attack on Stephen Spender while we drank bitter at a pub in Soho, The Pillars of Hercules. O.K., he grunted, no changes. Morgan at *Hudson* scarcely ever changed a thing, sometimes, surely, when the piece might have been the better for some changes. It is a hard fact for reviewers to admit that anything they hand in might really be improved with another run through the typewriter. Yet sometimes running it through again changes the emphasis for the worse. This happened when I reviewed John Fowles's novel *Daniel Martin* for the *Times* and was told it would appear on the front page of the book review (my first time!) but—therefore?—the beginning was wrong. First I'd quoted some improper language that mustn't appear in a Family Newspaper (I think the word "bastard" may have been in question). But also I'd started off by expressing reservations about the book overall. Couldn't I lead off in a more . . . *positive* way? I complied, but with the effect of turning the review into a firmer endorsement—something that the *Times* would like to have on their front page—than in my heart of hearts I meant. But I didn't see that at the time.

Along the way I have had editors improve my prose by removing its nuance, spoiling its tone, even splitting an infinitive or two. (Editorial assistants feel they have to earn their keep.) Occasionally one is almost pleased by the candidness of an editor's statement of what he does or doesn't want. Daryl Hine, who used to edit *Poetry,* once accepted an omnibus review of mine with the exception of a concluding paragraph about John Ashbery full of adverse comment: "I'm tired of printing remarks with which I don't agree," wrote Hine unabashedly; "and anyway I think yours are somewhat bitchy." I may have stepped into some sexual politics there, but instead of raising a stink and taking back the whole review, I simply took out the paragraph on Ashbery and soon after planted it in another context. Isn't necessity the mother of invention? At another time my review of a book on Auden was rejected as "too cerebral for our readers," as the editor said I would well understand. I did not understand it at all, nor did I understand the $40 kill fee I received instead of the originally promised $200. But I cashed the check and never wrote for *Inquiry* again (I was pleased when it soon folded).

It is hard though to find adequate words for the frustration that comes when a pretty good sentence or paragraph one submits comes back mangled beyond recognition. An egregious example of such mangling is the following paragraph as I submitted it, which began a review of a biography of the novelist Henry Miller:

> There was a time not too long ago, at the college where I teach, when a rebellious student, in hopes of disconcerting the English department, would propose to write his honors thesis on Henry Miller. At that time (the middle 1950s) *Tropic of Cancer* and *Tropic of Capricorn* were kept securely locked up in a part of the library designated Cage, and could only be consulted on the most deeply sworn of intellectual vows. By 1990, the year Miller died, all that had changed. Kate Milett had attacked him in *Sexual Politics* (along with D. H. Lawrence and Norman Mailer) as an apologist for woman-hating, and Mailer's 1976 counterattack in his selection from Miller's writings *(Genius and Lust)* was largely ignored. More important in Miller's loss of appeal for younger readers was the very availability of books once difficult to acquire. The magic was diminished to the point where, at least within my hearing, Miller has ceased to be a subject for literary argument; nor does he have a place in current anthologies of American literature.

When the proof arrived (filled with botches by the *TLS)* some helpful underling had decided that what I thought to be a lively opening (the rebellious student, the Cage, the magic of those unavailable titles) wouldn't do at all. So the review now began rather more prosaically: "By

1980, the year that Henry Miller died, his writing was no longer considered particularly subversive or shocking." I figured I could just lay it to anti-Americanism. But very dismaying.

From the behavior of editors, let us turn to the behavior of readers after the review has appeared. Usually one doesn't receive letters from those whom one has reviewed unfavorably—but occasionally they fire back a reply. The novelist Jerzy Kosinski, after I had termed his novel *Cockpit* to be in the running for the most obscene novel of the year, wrote me a letter on PEN club stationery that simply said, "I am sorry you did not like my novel." Was he kidding, or just practicing old world Polish courtesy? A rather more vigorous protest came, I thought, from the novelist John Irving, whose *The Hotel New Hampshire*—successor to his best-selling *The World According to Garp*—featured such characters as a bear named State O'Maine and a dog named Sorrow who has halitosis and is highly flatulent. The dog is eventually put out of its misery, stuffed and stuck in a closet, but one day the stuffed dog falls out of the closet, causing the narrator's grandfather, a football coach named Iowa Bob, to have a fatal heart attack. I called *The Hotel New Hampshire* "a teenage monstrosity," one of the worst books ever, and noted that although I knew its author, John Irving, was a serious wrestler, I would not be wrestled into submission. A few weeks later in the mail came a cleverly drawn, bawdy cartoon of a scrawny figure named The Critic (male) doing something unpleasant to the Work of Art (female). Under it was the message "Noted your comments in *Hudson Review* on my novel," signed J.I. Did this mean he was headed for Amherst for purposes of subduing me in a headlock, or whatever wrestlers do? But Irving never showed. A couple of years later, at a college class reunion, an old student of mine asked me slyly, "Been getting any mail from Irving recently?" It became suddenly clear that it was the student, not John Irving, who had sent me the cartoon.

Meanwhile some of the poets my mentor had warned me about after that first omnibus review seemed to be gathering their forces to do me harm—after all, even paranoid reviewers have enemies. The poet Donald Justice was said to be smarting over some words of mine about his poems, to the extent that on one occasion when the English department at Amherst wrote Mr. Justice asking whether he'd be interested in serving as a visiting writer, he replied that he couldn't be associated with any institution in which a person named William Pritchard was to be found. Twenty years afterwards, when I met him at Bread Loaf, it was clear he hadn't forgotten.

Mark Strand, later to be poet laureate, was quoted as threatening to punch me in the lip if he ever caught up with me. When we did finally meet, it was over a drink and he seemed to have forgotten any threatened unpleasantness. Closer to home, James Tate, a member of the University of Massachusetts creative writing program, was said to have characterized my critical sensibility with a one-syllable unprintable epithet. I kept spying Tate about town, lurking in the bank or checkout counter at the supermarket, and we studiously avoided each other. Until one evening, when as my wife and I entered the front hall of some people who had invited us to dinner, I caught sight of—in the adjoining living room—none other than Tate seated among the guests. I must have blanched or winced or done something notably notable, since our hostess said in a concerned tone, "Are you all right?" But I needn't have worried. Tate and I were introduced and behaved toward one another as if the furthest thing from our minds was anything to do with poet and reviewer. Such are the virtues of insincerity by way of making a social evening endurable.

Sometimes in the mail it really *is* awful, the single worst letter I've ever received, anonymous, after I'd reviewed Roth's *Sabbath's Theater* in the *New York Times Book Review* (people do read this). Avert your eyes as I quote the first sentence: "Only a cheap little ass-kissing two-bit fucking English professor would have stooped to calling this Jew bastard's latest pile of dogshit his richest and most rewarding." From that point on it's a question whom he hates more, me or Roth: the "slimy kike," or "Fags" like your reviewer who "should be destroyed with concentrated AK-47 fire." Pretty much of a standoff, I'd say. Anyway I decided to let Philip Roth know about the note and he did not take it lightly, instructing me to send it to him (without getting my fingerprints on it) and he would be in touch with the FBI. He did not that fall show up in person to accept the National Book Award for *Sabbath's Theater*—his speech was read by someone else.

An equally disgusted, if less threatening and obscene, response came from a Boston woman who picked up on a slighting remark I made about Amy Lowell, whom Adrienne Rich had called by far the most interesting of the three Lowells (the others being James Russell and Robert) treated in a biography I had reviewed. I called Rich's judgment absurd, though not surprising coming from an ardent feminist, and went on to make an unkind judgment about Amy Lowell's poetry. The Boston woman addressed her letter:

Sir:

The footnote in your NYTBR review of *American Aristocracy,* implies that you teach literature.

The tone of your comments about Amy Lowell and Adrienne Rich reminds me of cracks made by the beer filled young lads of Kenmore Square after a Red Sox loss to the Yankees.

[Then, warming to the task] You degrade yourself and your calling by taking such cheap shots. Of course, you live in a world so small, provincial, narrow that no one you know is capable of finding the efforts of Amy Lowell, successful or not, of human or historical interest.

Your cheap shots only reveal your self-chosen limitation.

After a little more abuse she concluded: "I know I've seen enough of your sensibility and bigotry and narrowness in this one review, I would not care to endure reading any more of your sentences. Shame on you, shame." I remember it being the single missive in that day's office mail, and it took me a few minutes of heavy breathing before I returned to my tasks. I decided not to answer her.

On the other hand, sometimes you are accused of being arrogant and provincial in a way that's downright fun and in which you end up admiring the wit of your assailant. This happened to me when, in a review of a very long John Barth novel, I referred to an earlier, very long one of his, *The Sot-Weed Factor,* as a book few would willingly reread and that many failed to read through even once. A woman from John Barth country in Maryland wrote a letter to the *Times* in which she said that, during the first three days of July, she had asked people who called her on the phone how many times they had read *The Sot-Weed Factor.* Every single person had replied, "well, only a couple of times *straight* through—now I kind of tend to skip around." She revealed that her respondents included "a printer, several former students, two poets, three so-called housewives, an old high school buddy, two university colleagues, an optometrist and an editor." Admittedly, she said, it wasn't a very sophisticated survey, "But at least I looked beyond myself to verify my sweeping generalization, which is a lot more than I can say for Mr. Pritchard." Right on, Ms. Clarinda Lott.

Sometimes a review brings on letters inviting one to assist the letter writer in the completion of a manuscript he or she is working on, or perhaps requesting the name of an agent who would be interested in the project. These letters must be politely but summarily dealt with. Then there was Mr. Louis Longo from Brooklyn, who sent me a copy of his novel for my reading pleasure; Mr. Longo said that he did this for anyone on a first appearance in the *Times Book Review* (hard to believe, isn't it?). Sometimes all you get is a brutally efficient postcard, like the one that commended my review of John Fowles's novel but added that I'd called by the name "Nell" a character who was actually "Beth" (or was it the other way around?) and concluded the accusatory sentence with "You Ninny." Most frustrating and puzzling of all came an unsigned postcard with a Buzzards Bay postmark (now, who did I know on the Cape?) in response to an essay I had published on the poet Philip Larkin. It read: "Your article 'Philip Larkin' is absolute gibberish. You can't *write!* Absolute *rubbish!*" Another student hoax? I checked and confirmed it was not the person who sent me the fake John Irving cartoon. This mystery will never be unraveled, I'm afraid.

On occasion, a response from the person reviewed is sufficient to convince the reviewer he's made a mistake. It happened to me when a poet named Gary Gildner wrote me a courteous but firm note telling me that in my haste to generalize about his book of poems I'd overlooked certain ones that proved my generalization too simple. On looking at his book again I decided he was right, and wrote to make awkward amends—amends that were partially delivered when a later book of his fell my way and I bent over backwards (doubtless compromising my objectivity) to praise it. Most bizarrely, some years back when I had thoroughly expunged from my mind a brief, dismissive paragraph I'd once written in an omnibus fiction review about a very short, forgettable it seemed, novel curiously titled *Olt*, by one Kenneth Gangemi, I had made some clever remark about how the jacket copy, in which Mr. Gangemi revealed that he'd grown up in Scarsdale and attended RPI, was as interesting as anything in the novel itself. Imagine my surprise, indeed consternation, when, browsing a clever little book titled *Rotten Reviews*, ed. by Bill Henderson, I discovered my own name under a comment taken from the review of Gangemi years before. The introduction of the volume thanked him as one of the novelists and poets who had sent in the "meanest" notices of their work. So I wrote Mr. Gangemi, who had treasured up my rotten review all those years and finally got to use it, conveying my good wishes and apologies—to which he very pleasantly responded by sending me a recent book of his.

Looking back over the hundreds of reviews I've turned out, I detect

not so much a "development" of sensibility as what looks like a softening, or is it a ripening (possibly a mellowing or rotting?) of critical judgement. That is, I don't seem to be much on display anymore as the fierce
guardian of standards, chewing up and spitting out some novelist or poet
who doesn't come up to snuff. Partly this has to do with age: whereas it
once seemed perfectly appropriate to poke at some fairly established figure who was older than me, it now seems less than dignified to take one
at a young man or woman who's just produced a first novel or book of
poems that will immediately fall into obscurity anyway. Henry James, in
"The Art of Fiction," reminds us of the difference between a bad novel and
a good one: "The bad is swept with all the daubed canvases and spoiled
marble into some unvisited limbo, or rubbish-yard beneath back-windows
of the world, and the good subsists and emits its light and stimulates our
desire for perfection." Do we need the reviewer to make this happen? Then
there's another explanation for mellowed sympathies which has to do with
the fact that I can now more or less command the books I want to write
about. Over a recent, representative year, I published fifteen reviews of
varying length that break down as follows: novels by Sue Miller and John
Updike; an omnibus fiction chronicle surveying ten novels; a critical book
by Helen Vendler on Yeats; James Wood's *How Fiction Works;* a collection
of poems by Mary Jo Salter; biographies of V. S. Naipaul, Ezra Pound, the
James family, Emily Dickinson and Thomas Higginson; Library of America volumes of Edmund Wilson's essays and of Elizabeth Bishop's work;
Robert Frost's collected prose; the correspondence between Bishop and
Robert Lowell. Some of these I requested; some were suggested to me and
I accepted. I note that except for the Salter there are no reviews, as there
once were many, of books by contemporary poets. This may have something to do with my disinclination, in the face of so much contemporary
verse, to spend time with it—a suspicion that the Poetry Game is a club
from which this reviewer is excluded. In all these pieces just mentioned,
ranging from 1,000 to 3,500 words, I find but a single rotten review (Paul
Fisher's book about the James family), and richly deserved it was.

   The question still remains, as posed by my old teacher: "Why does anyone need to do this, and more specifically, why you?" I continue to review
because it helps give a shape to my life, day by day, week by week. The
long-term disease of writing a book has eventually its cure and attendant
gratifications, but you may never finish it, whereas it's a good bet you'll
survive to read your 1,200 words about X or Y. Then there is the executive

pleasure in planning and revising your reviewing strategy. I begin by subscribing, at the outrageous price of $189 a year, to *Publishers Weekly*, a magazine of no interest except for its lists of upcoming books at the end of each issue. I see that a novel or biography is due to appear three months or so from the date of the current issue, and I check ones I might be interested in dealing with. Then, since it won't do to wait for them to call you, I drop a line with a proposal; with e-mail you usually hear back quickly. My main loyalties and promise of reviewing space are to *The Hudson Review*, where I try to appear, more or less, in each quarterly issue. In *Hudson* space is not a problem. For shorter flights, there is the *Boston Globe*, and now—much less dependable, due to the newspaper crisis—the *Chicago Tribune*. The *Washington Times*, a standby for years, has gone by the board. Other possibilities are, from time to time, the liberal Catholic biweekly, *Commonweal*, and *The American Scholar*. I hang on by my fingernails, if that, with the *Times Literary Supplement*.

As a potential reviewer I care not about the magazine's politics, so if William Kristol's Bomb Tehran *Weekly Standard* asks me, for some reason, to write about Robert Frost's *Notebooks*, I accept. For years in the right-wing *Washington Times* I shared space with the famous Oliver North, who has a weekly column setting things straight. Then there are those magazines that have forgotten me, most prominently the *New York Times Book Review*. The *New Republic* under Leon Wieseltier is no more hospitable, though when I wrote Wieseltier for permission to reprint something I'd published there years ago, he replied warmly, thanking me for all the good pieces I'd done for them, as if I were totally embalmed, unable any longer to lift a pen. It's also unlikely that I will ever again grace the pages of *TV Guide*, which once solicited a piece about my adventures as watcher of, and briefly participant in, the soap opera *Search for Tomorrow*.

At the risk of comparing oneself to one's betters, I note that along with being a great poet, T. S. Eliot was a great reviewer. It's now common knowledge that his brilliant appreciations of Ben Jonson, Dryden, the Metaphysical poets—just to name three of his best—were prompted by the invitation to review a book. Unlike the scholarly essay, which must justify itself by bringing out some new aspect of a writer's work or correcting the inadequate interpretation of earlier critics, the reviewer is bound by no such rules, although he may indeed bring out a new aspect of his writer or correct misapprehensions. The reviewer is not only free but expected to take the book at hand as a chance to speak to large matters of a writer's achievement, comparing him with contemporaries and predecessors in an effort to explore the achievement. Under the confines of a thousand-word limit—or in more spacious situations double or treble that length—the reviewer can embrace limits as a provocation to speak out—sometimes, doubtless, recklessly—in order to elicit something essential about his subject. Another great reviewer, Randall Jarrell, put it most extravagantly in "The Age of Criticism" when he declared that "taking the chance of making a complete fool of himself—and, sometimes, doing so—is the first demand that is made upon any real critic: he must stick his neck out just as the artist does, if he is to be of any real use to art."

By becoming a reviewer over the years I have grown apart from much in the academic profession of English studies, although with age it might have happened anyway. But why on earth should I attend the Modern Language Association convention to hear papers titled "Canonicity and Theory: Toward a Poststructuralist Pedagogy," or "S(e)izing Power: Gender, Representation, and Body Scale"? These titles are from a few years back; I know one should not indulge in such easy game, and perhaps things have gotten a bit less grim. But I prefer to spend my time in attempting to come, however briefly, to some new valuation of a writer I love or know insufficiently well. (As an example from the second category, I've recently published a piece on Elizabeth Taylor, the novelist; upcoming is one on T. B. Macaulay; beyond that, W. D. Howells.) There is also the fact that, as a teacher, reviewing feeds into my classroom procedure, and vice versa. Trying something out in a class sometimes leads to the idea getting developed into print; certainly I find myself trying out in a review remarks I may later refine and complicate, I hope, in the room with those eager young minds.

I claimed that reviewing gives a sort of shape to one's day-to-day life. Or is this just a clever way to justify what is in fact, like soap opera or drink, an addiction? Could I really stop doing it, even if at some level I "wanted" to? The English reviewer Geoffrey Grigson, one of the most savage to practice in this century, said that the only reason for continuing to review was to acquire books for one's library that are otherwise too expensive to buy. I thought of him awhile back when I received Oxford University Press's magnificent four-volume boxed set of Samuel Johnson's *Lives of the English Poets* ($500) and again when the same press parted with A. E. Housman's letters, in another boxed two-volume set ($330). On the other hand, I failed to snare Peter Davison's twenty-volume edition of George Orwell; nor did the collected works of Bernard Shaw fall as a freebie into my hand. Grigson also wrote, "One shouldn't review books. Not unless they are books one ardently wishes to promote. I should like to check in myself an ardent wish to demote, now and then." Yet he never checked this wish, that I could see, and continued to review widely until the end of a long life. V. S. Pritchett, his much more benign countryman, finally put down his pen at an age somewhere over ninety. I should be so lucky.

Perhaps we may end by listening to Orwell, who in his cruelly shortened life, dying at forty-seven, produced among other writings a ton of reviews. (I put him with T. S. Eliot as one of the finest twentieth-century review-ers.) In "Why I Write" Orwell found that there were four great motives for writing prose that any human being will share, to one or another degree. Here I'm concerned with only the first motive for writing, which Orwell defines as "sheer egotism" and comments on as follows:

> Desire to seem clever, to be talked about, to be remembered after death, to get your own back on grownups who snubbed you in childhood. It is humbug to pretend this is not a motive, and a strong one. . . . The great mass of human beings are not acutely selfish. After the age of about thirty they abandon indi-vidual ambitions . . . and live chiefly for others, or are simply smothered under drudgery. But there is also the minority of gifted, wilful people who are determined to live their own lives to the end, and writers belong to that class.

One may not necessarily want to employ the word "gifted" to all writers, especially to oneself; but "wilful" and even better, "selfish," self-centered—I think this an important insight into why *I* write. It remains to be decided whether the particular genre of writing I've dealt with here is any more or less benign than other kinds. Grigson, to quote him once more, pro-nounced flatly that reviewing was a disease. If so we may end by slightly adapting some lines from Pope's "Epistle to Dr. Arbuthnot" in which he is talking about the writing life and which I take the liberty of personalizing:

> I left no calling for this idle trade,
> No duty broke, no father disobey'd.
> The muse but serv'd, as if she were a wife
> To ease me through this long disease, my life.

— *Yale Review,* October 2010.

Acknowledgments:

WITH THE EXCEPTION of the Preface, all essays in this volume have previously appeared in the following publications: *Amherst, Boston Globe, Essays in Criticism, Hudson Review, Literary Imagination, New Republic, Newsletter (Association of Literary Scholars and Teachers), Raritan: A Quarterly Review, Sewanee Review, Teaching What We Do: Essays by Amherst College Faculty, The American Scholar, The John Updike Review, The Weekly Standard,* and *Yale Review.*

The essays have also appeared in William H. Pritchard's previous books of criticism including:

Dinosaur Reflections: Literary Essays and Reviews (Northhampton, MA: The Impress Group, 2021)
In Search of Humor: Literary Essays and Reviews (Northhampton, MA: The Impress Group, 2018)
On Poets and Poetry (Athens, OH: Swallow Press, 2009)
Playing It by Ear: Literary Essays and Reviews (Amherst, MA: University of Massachusetts Press, 1994)
Shelf Life: Literary Essays and Reviews (Amherst, MA: University of Massachusetts Press, 2003)
Talking Back to Emily Dickinson and Other Essays (Amherst, MA: University of Massachusetts Press, 1998)
Updike: America's Man of Letters (Amherst, MA: University of Massachusetts Press, 2000)
What's Been Happening to Jane Austen? (Northhampton, MA: The Impress Group, 2011)
Writing to Live (Northhampton, MA: The Impress Group, 2015)

Credits

About the author

WILLIAM H. PRITCHARD is the author of several essay collections and literary biographies including *Randall Jarrell: A Literary Life* and *Updike: America's Man of Letters*. He is professor of English emeritus at Amherst College where he taught for sixty years. He lives in western Massachusetts.